Ethnographies of Movement, Sociality and Space

Material Mediations: People and Things in a World of Movement

Edited by **Birgit Meyer**, Department of Philosophy and Religious Studies, Utrecht University, and **Maruška Svašek**, School of History, Anthropology, Philosophy and Politics, Queen's University, Belfast.

During the last few years, a lively, interdisciplinary debate has taken place between anthropologists, art historians and scholars of material culture, religion, visual culture and media studies about the dynamics of material production and cultural mediation in an era of intensifying globalization and transnational connectivity. Understanding 'mediation' as a fundamentally material process, this series provides a stimulating platform for ethnographically grounded theoretical debates about the many aspects that constitute relationships between people and things, including political, economic, technological, aesthetic, sensorial and emotional processes.

Volume 1
Moving Subjects, Moving Objects
Transnationalism, Cultural Production and Emotions
Edited by Maruška Svašek

Volume 2
Growing Artefacts, Displaying Relationships
Yams, Art and Technology amongst the Nyamikum Abelam of Papua New Guinea
Ludovic Coupaye

Volume 3
Object and Imagination
Perspectives on Materialization and Meaning
Edited by Øivind Fuglerud and Leon Wainwright

Volume 4
The Great Reimagining
Public Art, Urban Space and the Symbolic Landscapes of a 'New' Northern Ireland
Bree T. Hocking

Volume 5
Having and Belonging
Homes and Museums in Israel
Judy Jaffe-Schagen

Volume 6
Creativity in Transition
Politics and Aesthetics of Cultural Production Across the Globe
Edited by Maruška Svašek and Birgit Meyer

Volume 7
Death, Materiality and Mediation
An Ethnography of Remembrance in Ireland
Barbara Graham

Volume 8
Ethnographies of Movement, Sociality and Space
Place-Making in the New Northern Ireland
Edited by Milena Komarova and Maruška Svašek

Ethnographies of Movement, Sociality and Space

Place-Making in the New Northern Ireland

Edited by

Milena Komarova and Maruška Svašek

berghahn
NEW YORK • OXFORD
www.berghahnbooks.com

First published in 2018 by
Berghahn Books
www.berghahnbooks.com

Library of Congress Cataloging-in-Publication Data

Names: Komarova, Milena, editor. | Svašek, Maruška, editor.

Title: Ethnographies of movement, sociality and space : place-making in the new Northern Ireland / edited by Milena Komarova and Maruška Svašek.

Description: New York, NY : Berghahn Books, 2018. | Series: Material mediations : people and things in a world of movement ; Volume 8 | Includes bibliographical references and index.

Identifiers: LCCN 2018001777 (print) | LCCN 2018017012 (ebook) | ISBN 9781785339387 (ebook) | ISBN 9781785339370 (hardback : alk. paper)

Subjects: LCSH: Northern Ireland--Social conditions--21st century. | Place (Philosophy)--Social aspects--Northern Ireland. | Group identity--Northern Ireland. | Social conflict--Northern Ireland.

Classification: LCC HN398.N6 (ebook) | LCC HN398.N6 E75 2018 (print) | DDC 306.09416--dc23

LC record available at https://lccn.loc.gov/2018001777

British Library Cataloguing in Publication Data

A catalogue record for this book is available from the British Library

ISBN 978-1-78533-937-0 hardback
ISBN 978-1-78533-938-7 ebook

Contents

Figures

Acknowledgements

Intellectual work is never a stand-alone exercise. It is always and without exception collaborative: *what* we write and *how* we write it is always born in dialogue with the ideas of others; *whether* we write depends on the encouragement and the support of others. You are holding this book because we, the authors and editors, have each and together been generously helped along the way to writing and publishing it. We extend our warmest thanks to all who, knowingly or not, have walked this way with and beside us. Above all, there is one group of collaborators, without whom any kind of social research is doomed to fail, we would like to mention at the very start. These are the people that we study, and whose voices we represent and draw upon in our analyses. We are grateful to them all.

The initial thoughts for this book first arose in 2013 when, fulfilling the role of postgraduate coordinator in anthropology at the then School of History and Anthropology at Queen's University Belfast, Maruška facilitated the weekly anthropology postgraduate seminar. Partly student led, the seminar offers a platform for students in anthropology, ethnomusicology, Irish studies and other disciplines to present and discuss their research at different stages of completion. It is characterized by lively discussions about theories, methods and ethical issues around fieldwork, often ending in a visit to the pub. Maruška would like to take the opportunity to thank all the postgraduate students who have attended the anthropology postgraduate seminar in the past decade for their creative input and dedication. The work presented by MA and PhD students in 2013 was of such a high standard that the idea for a possible publication arose.

Due to the location of Queen's University Belfast, the MA and PhD programmes in anthropology and ethnomusicology tend to attract students interested in aspects of Northern Irish politics, in particular 'the Troubles' and their legacy. Until a few years ago, research-based dissertations focused, for example, on victimhood and commemoration, political murals, marching bands, and processes of peace building. As this book demonstrates, more recently students have also chosen alternative topics, partly in reaction to the changing social and political landscape of the region. This sparked the idea for a book that would challenge the image of Northern Ireland as a conflict-ridden society.

In fact, the idea tied in with Maruška's own research at the time that examined creativity, improvisation and the use of artefacts and spatial surroundings by Hindu migrants from India and their offspring in Belfast. The fieldwork, conducted together with research fellow Amit Desai, was part of the collaborative research project Creativity and Innovation in a World of Movement (CIM). Funded by HERA, CIM brought together researchers from universities and research institutions in Austria, Norway, the United Kingdom and the Netherlands who worked at field sites across the globe. Maruška would like to express her sincere thanks to the HERA Joint Research Programme Cultural Dynamics, which was co-funded by AHRC, AKA, DASTI, ETF, FNR, FWF, HAZU, IRCHSS, MHEST, NWO, RANNIS, RCN, VR and the European Community FP7 2007–2013 under the Socio-economic Sciences and Humanities programme. She is particularly grateful to the scholars who were part of CIM (Stine Bruland, Amit Desai, Øivind Fuglerud, Barbara Graham, Tereza Kuldova, Fiona Magowan, Birgit Meyer, Maria Øien, João Rickli, Arnd Schneider, Kala Shreen, Barbara Plankensteiner, Leon Wainwright and Rhoda Woets), as the discussions within the consortium often touched on issues around spatial practices, materiality and movement, and thus fed into the ideas developed in this book.

Looking for a co-editor, Maruška turned to the sociologist Milena Komarova, a long-time friend and colleague at Queen's University Belfast and, at the time, a research fellow at the Institute for the Study of Conflict Transformation and Social Justice (now the Senator George J. Mitchell Institute for Global Peace, Security and Justice). Milena had long worked on understanding how cities such as Belfast, often referred to as 'divided', serve as stages both of ethnic and national conflicts, and of 'ordinary' everyday life. Her research on the relationship between urban space, place, everyday life practices and conflict, began while working as a postdoc on a large interdisciplinary research project entitled 'Conflict in Cities and the Contested State' (CinC) and funded by the ESRC (2007–2013). She owes an enormous debt of gratitude to all of the CinC crew at the three universities of Cambridge, Exeter and Queen's Belfast who led her to develop her research for the project beyond the sociological tradition, and across the fields of architecture, anthropology and geography. Her work with her CinC colleagues and friends at Queen's University Belfast has directly enabled her contribution to this volume. Milena is especially indebted to Liam O'Dowd, Madeleine Leonard, Katy Hayward and Martina McKnight, who have all long nurtured her work with extraordinary generosity, intellectual vigour and friendship. Both Martina and Katy have worked with Milena on the particular themes that her chapter explores, while Martina was directly involved in the initial stages of the associated fieldwork. Thanks are also due to other colleagues with whom Milena has worked over the years on the issues related to making and transforming space and place in Northern Ireland – from sociology, the Institute of Irish Studies, planning and architecture, the cross-disciplinary Contested Space reading group, and the Mitchell Institute (all at Queen's University Belfast), as well as from CityReparo.

Most of our contributors were existing MA and PhD students at the time we first approached them to participate in the book (Elisabeth de Young, Erin Hinson, Angela Mazzetti, Kayla Rush and Augusto Soares), and we asked a number of recent PhD graduates to write additional chapters (Nick McCafferty, Naoko Maehara and Malcolm Franklin). We would like to thank all of them immensely for their hard work and, not unimportantly, for their patience. Due to our academic duties, it has taken far too long to finally publish this work. After the first drafts were written in 2014 and 2015, we organized the conference 'Space, Movement, Conflict' in October 2015 to give all contributors the opportunity to meet and present their work in a wider interdisciplinary context at Queen's University Belfast. We are grateful to those presenters whose work has not been included in this edited volume for their input and feedback to the theme of the conference: Alexei Gavriel, Conor McCafferty, Panagiotis Loukinas, Rachel O'Grady and Andrew Woollock. We would also like to express our gratitude to Hastings Donnan, director of the Senator George J. Mitchell Institute for Global Peace, Security and Justice, for the institute's financial support of the conference.

Furthermore, we would like to thank our much-respected colleague Dominic Bryan, who has supported this project from the start, and who has generously agreed to write the Afterword. To the two anonymous reviewers, who wrote highly encouraging reports, we also express our gratitude. Marion Berghahn and the production team at Berghahn Books deserve equal thanks for their competent help and efficient guidance. Last but not least, we express our appreciation to Gordon Ramsey for his excellent work on the index.

Maruška Svašek and Milena Komarova
Belfast, September 2017

INTRODUCTION

Spatiality, Movement and Place-Making

Maruška Svašek and Milena Komarova

Vignette 1

As a young child, I had always loved visiting the city. A chance to wonder at the huge fanciful department stores filled with treasures. A chance to get a special treat of fish and chips or tea and cake. But one day that changed. The city was under attack. In the chaos we were forced into the path of the explosion. My senses were overwhelmed: the dull thud; the shattering glass propelling through the air before crashing to the ground; the screaming and shouting; and the sight of helpless policemen and shoppers trying to figure out what to do in all this chaos. I was uninjured but the encounter left its mark. My visits became less frequent and eventually stopped. (Reflection on 'the Troubles', Angela Mazzetti, 2016)

Vignette 2

During my fieldwork in Belfast, one of the members of the women's group told me how they bonded over everyday problems and supported each other. 'When my daughter Kate was 19,' she said, 'the fella who she was with was an absolute dick. I remember speaking about her with the girls, in WLP. "Yes, yes, that's terrible," I said, "let me tell you what happened to my girl."' Talking about such things, Catholic and Protestant women found out that they had a lot in common. 'You have the same problems,' she explained; 'There is just this underlying thing of Catholics and Protestants, but it's not of our making, and it's not of their making'. (Reflection on fieldwork, Andrea García González, 2016)

Vignette 3

MS: Remember where we first met?
MK: We met through the children's crèche of course! I think I had seen you coming and going, with Tristan in the pram, up and down the Rugby Road. I could tell that, like me, you were not a native to Belfast but I have always been shy in making new acquaintances so I didn't approach you. I can't remember exactly the first time that we spoke but you probably spoke to me first.
MS: I also can't remember exactly when that was, but I do remember being really happy to meet another migrant mother, and the fact that our children got on well. I also remember the contrast of the atmosphere in the crèche and, only five minutes away, the dynamics of the university environment; having to switch all the time to a different mode of being. I liked making friends outside the professional sphere. (Conversation between Maruška Svašek and Milena Komarova, 2016)

Vignette 4

Sitting in front of my computer in the peaceful atmosphere of my home in rural Ireland, I follow online discussions about Northern Irish politics and evolving conflicts. My engagement with social media links me to other people and places in and beyond the region, and the research process is often a surprisingly intense experience. The pages and timelines, simultaneously open on my machine, reveal past and emerging threads of emotional interventions, tongue-in-cheek conversations, hurtful insults, and playful remixes. Digital research requires continuous decision making about whether or not to click on a given link. Concentration and discipline are key in the face of the multiple tracks. (Reflections on online research, Augusto Soares, 2016)

This book challenges widespread images of Northern Ireland as either a 'conflict-ridden' or a 'post-conflict' society – images that have dominated both academic writing and media reportage. The contributions to this volume seek to enrich these politics-laden approaches with more varied perspectives on life in the region. While we do not deny that decades of both violence and peace making have strongly shaped Northern Irish society, we argue that an overarching focus on political conflict and reconciliation severely limits insights into the histories and spatial practices of individuals and groups in the region, and into the nature of conflict as such. In our view, an approach that foregrounds the analysis of sectarian and territorial tensions between unionist (or loyalist) Protestants and nationalist (or republican) Catholics, overlooks the more diverse processes of place-making that individual members of these groups are involved in, and sidelines the voices of other inhabitants in the region, including non-sectarian 'locals', migrants, refugees, and people of different religious and ideological persuasions, and sexual orientations.

The four vignettes at the start of this introduction demonstrate that people born in, or migrated to, Northern Ireland have been caught up in a diversity of spatial experiences that cannot be understood through the prism of political agency alone. Their authors, all contributors to this book, reflect on personal and fieldwork experiences that emphasize specific aspects of spatiality. In the first vignette, Angela Mazzetti, born and raised in Northern Ireland, remembers a bomb exploding at the time of 'the Troubles'. In this example, there is no denial that her concrete, multi-sensorial experience of 'the conflict' had a strong impact on her everyday movements at the time. In fact, the situation of ongoing violence continued to influence her life choices as she decided as a young adult to move to England in the 1980s. More recently, she has returned to explore the effects of 'the Troubles' on her peer group in an attempt to make sense of her past.

In the second vignette, Andrea García González, who grew up in Madrid and came to Belfast to conduct MA research in 2014, writes about the friendships between Catholic and Protestant women in Belfast. The text shows that their shared experiences as mothers created mutual understanding and conviviality within the group. Here, it is clear that an analytical focus on past conflicts and ongoing ethno-religious tensions does not suffice to explore the women's social and emotional interactions, even though they constitute a reality that also marks their predicaments.

The third vignette throws light on our own experiences as working mothers and migrants, and reminds us that Northern Ireland is not only populated by 'autochthonous' citizens, but increasingly by people of diverse national backgrounds. Our conversation – Milena is Bulgarian, and Maruška was born in the Netherlands as the daughter of a Dutch mother and a Czech father – alludes to our mutual identification as new arrivals in Northern Ireland in the late 1990s, when we were trying to create a sense of home. The dialogue also refers to the quick adaptations needed when moving from one socio-spatial context to another, in this case the crèche and the university environment. The necessity to adjust rapidly to different and changing surroundings is a more general feature of the human condition and, in situations of conflict, this need can manifest itself through flight or fight responses, as illustrated by Mazzetti's words. In García González's vignette, women travelled from majority Catholic and majority Protestant neighbourhoods to meet up in agreed upon spaces where they reoriented themselves emotionally as female friends, downplaying other identities and loyalties. Our own verbal exchange illustrates that life in Northern Ireland (both past and present) also includes adjustments between settings unrelated to sectarian tensions or political conflict.

In the last vignette, the Brazilian journalist and PhD student Augusto Soares addresses movement in another spatial realm, namely that of the digital world. His reflections remind us that in the Internet age, much social interaction, including social science research, takes place in a digital arena that connects distant places and people. Highly relevant to this book, the Internet allows individuals who refuse to meet face-to-face to interact in the online sphere. In the case he describes, the digital space creates the potential for humorous interaction and ironic comments on politicians and paramilitary groups. The interactions also potentially reinforce territorial claims, mutual animosity and conflict.

As the examples indicate, this book provides a critical perspective on territoriality, political conflict and conflict transformation. While avoiding a narrow focus on 'ethno-national' territoriality, it investigates a wide variety of spatial discourses, practices and embodied experiences. In our view, this broader approach is not only relevant to research in Northern Ireland, but can also be productive in other regions. As such, our findings aim to contribute to the wider scholarship on post-conflict societies.

Space, Place and Territoriality

This is a book about place-making – from the smallest scale of individual intimate sensorial experience to the large scale of political geographies of nation and state. At all of these levels, as Cresswell (1996, 2010) reminds us, spatial processes inform the ways in which people live their lives. For over two decades, academic theories of 'place' and 'space' have proliferated across the social sciences and humanities, reflecting its axiomatic centrality to both the ontology of human life and our attempts to make sense of it. In the words of Low and Lawrence-Zúñiga (2003: 1), 'all behaviour is located in and constructed of space', and the theorization of spatial perspectives has become 'an essential component of sociocultural theory'.

Being migrants, our own histories of mobility and our changing understanding of life in the region have strongly motivated us to produce this book. Growing up in Bulgaria and the Netherlands at a time when the only news in the international media about Northern Ireland reported stories of violence, our initial image of Northern Irish society had been strongly tainted when we arrived in Belfast almost two decades ago. Perceiving Northern Ireland through the lens of conflict, we were overly wary of being caught up in territorial clashes, especially during the marching season. We also both consciously chose not to live in streets marked with flags or coloured pavements, which are indicators of territorial identity (see Figures 0.1, 0.2 and 0.3).

Tellingly, some of our worries about violence were based on hypersensitivity and silly misunderstandings. When, for example, a few weeks after her arrival in 1999, Maruška told one of the secretaries at the then School of Anthropological Studies that she was scared because she had heard

Figure 0.1 Loyalist mural and painted kerbstones in North Belfast. Photo by Milena Komarova.

Figure 0.2 Peacewall in West Belfast. Photo by Milena Komarova.

Figure 0.3 Orange Order parade in West Belfast. Photo by Milena Komarova.

shooting during the weekend, the secretary laughed and explained that it was almost Halloween, and that, for the first time in many years, people had been allowed again to set off fireworks. To her, the sound (and sight) of firecrackers marked a return to 'normality'. The reference to 'normality' reminds us that Northern Ireland is not only a place of conflict and conscious peace building, but also a setting of 'ordinary' activities – a place, to paraphrase Therborn (2011), where people live, work, raise children, make friends, and enjoy themselves; an environment in which people visit relatives, do their shopping, and talk about mundane things (see Figures 0.4 and 0.5); an educational hub where internationally mobile individuals study, teach and conduct research, thus linking the region to locations elsewhere in the world. This book in fact illustrates the latter point, as eight of the eleven contributors are not British citizens, but Japanese (Maehara), American (DeYoung, Hinson and Rush), Brazilian (Soares), Bulgarian (Komarova), Spanish (García González) and Dutch (Svašek). Of the three British contributors, two were born in England and settled in Northern Ireland (Franklin and McCafferty) and one moved in the opposite direction (Mazzetti).

As scholars, we find ourselves in an intellectual landscape which has, by necessity, been overwhelmingly focused on aspects of conflict, sectarianism and reconciliation. The resulting studies have depicted Northern Ireland as a deeply divided society, a 'territorialist' place where bordered spaces

Figure 0.4 Jogging in South Belfast. Photo by Milena Komarova.

Figure 0.5 Shoppers near Victoria Square. Photo by Maruška Svašek.

inform practices of social control, classification, communication and political symbolism (Sack 1986). There are of course good reasons for this kind of scholarship. As Ó Dochartaigh (2007: 475) has argued, when internal sectarian boundaries are produced and intensified by disputes over international borders, '[t]erritory as both stake and strategy [is] at the heart of violent conflict'. In Northern Ireland, territorial conflict is ultimately generated and experienced at the intersection of ethno-national identities and place; it is engendered through 'the content of space [and] how it is imbued with forms of meaning' (Nagle and Clancy 2010: 79). Both during and after the end of the Troubles, political meaning has been inscribed in the Northern Irish landscape through rituals and material and symbolic practices that have marked specific neighbourhoods as 'loyalist' or 'republican' territories. Numerous scholars[1] have explored such practices, providing detailed studies of murals, flag displays, parades and commemoration ceremonies. Their work has convincingly shown that highly visible territorial divisions reflect 'broader social struggles over deeply held collective myths [that] concretize . . . fundamental and recurring . . . ideological and social frameworks' (Low and Lawrence-Zúñiga 2003: 18).

Geographers, sociologists, anthropologists and even planners tend to distinguish between 'place' and 'territory'. While 'place' is a malleable, habitable space to which people have varied emotional attachments (Gieryn 2000), 'territory' is often understood as a process of claiming and bordering areas by particular groups (Brighenti 2010). Gaffikin and Morrissey (2011), for instance, note that in cities marked by territorial conflict, the fight for control strongly influences the spatial experience of the inhabitants. As the map of Belfast in Figure 0.6 outlines, spatial division is still a reality for many inhabitants. Majority Protestant and majority Catholic groups continue to dominate specific areas, and numerous urban spaces are divided by 'peace walls'. In the Afterword to this book, Dominic Bryan reflects on the spatial proximity of people living on the opposite sides of these walls. The map of Belfast also shows that various parts of the city, such as the university area and the city centre, are non-sectarian or culturally diverse locations, due to mixed student populations and the influx of migrants.

It must also be noted that, since the summer of 2016, territoriality has gained new meanings in Northern Ireland in the light of the Brexit referendum. While a majority of Northern Irish voters, fearful that Brexit would reinstate hard borders between Northern Ireland and the Republic of Ireland, expressed the wish to remain in the European Union, the UK-wide referendum resulted in a vote for separation. The continuing (and indeed again increasing) relevance of territorial discourses and practices in Northern Ireland, Europe, and beyond, means that questions of ethno-national conflict remain highly topical. Yet, to borrow a phrase from O'Dowd and McCall (2008), this perspective can also act as a 'cage', as a limiting interpretative framework that can only explain certain aspects of social, political and cultural life in the region.

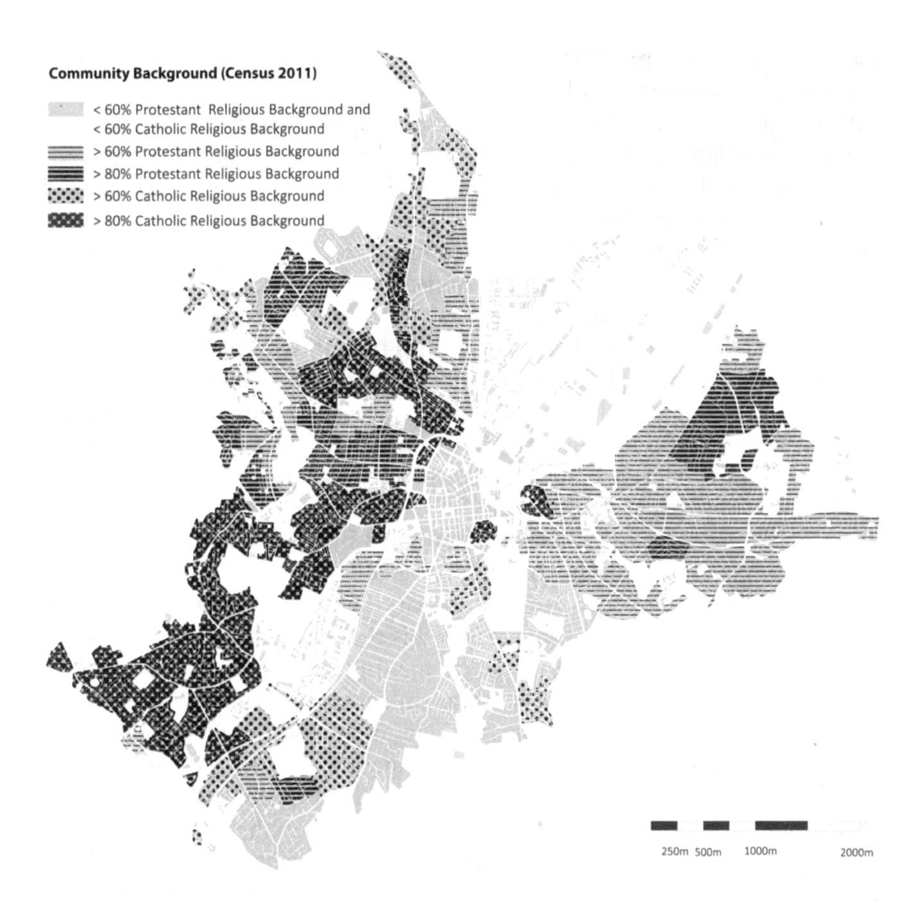

Figure 0.6 Map of Belfast by Community Background. The map is based on pre-2014 council boundaries and does not reflect the current Belfast council area. Reproduced courtesy of Chris Karelse.

Conflict: A Multifaceted, Processual Perspective

So how can we escape this cage? One of the ways out, we argue, is to take a multifaceted and processual approach to the study of conflict, not just focusing on large-scale political oppositions but also taking smaller-scale tensions into account. Such an approach is based on the view that everyday strains are innate to human existence and that, to understand political conflict and the occurrence of large-scale violence, it is necessary to explore how small-scale tensions may (or may not) lead to violent confrontations (Ashmore, Jussim and Wilder 2001).

Three arguments are crucial. Firstly, mundane conflicts between people are common, and while they often have no wider societal relevance, they are spatially significant. Minor stressful encounters are usually local and may last only minutes – for example, when a baby cries as her mother drops her off at the crèche, or when grandparents get annoyed when their teenage grandson is constantly texting on his mobile phone, giving his sole attention to geographically distant friends. In these cases, familial obligations and daily movements are enacted or ignored, and what is at stake is the socio-spatial performance of kin identity. In the latter example, there is a clear mismatch of experience and expectation between the locally oriented grandparents and the trans-local attention of their grandson, causing momentary irritation. Irritations can also simmer or intensify over long periods. But even then, they do not necessarily turn into factional oppositions that are played out beyond the sphere of the family. Disagreements between siblings over their parents' inheritance, for example, can strongly shape the interactions of later generations of kin, dispersed across distant locations, but often they remain within the family sphere. Yet while family disagreements may be irrelevant when measured against full-blown intergroup violence, they are still an important element in the spatially lived lives of individuals.

Secondly, even when societies are troubled by violent conflict, or when people attempt to tackle histories of violence in post-conflict situations, we need to bring into focus the complexity and diversity of struggles for power in other socio-spatial spheres. In this respect, social science analyses have often overlooked types of place-making in Northern Ireland that emanate from the daily lives of women, children, young people, the elderly, non-heterosexual individuals, the disabled, migrants, refugees, or even ex-political prisoners. Conflicts linked to competing claims over uses of space among such social groups, and played out in relationships of subjugation, oppression or cooperation, have remained rather peripheral to the bulk of social science of Northern Ireland, or have been subsumed under the logic of competing national or sectarian claims.[2] This volume aims to throw light on the complexities of these tensions.

Thirdly, a processual perspective is needed to explore how intergroup interactions within particular locations are shaped by concrete spatio-temporal dynamics. Local clashes between individuals and groups that become intensified and gain political significance can result in serious intra- and inter-group battles. Non-political conflicts, in other words, can transform into sectarian wars. To explore these processes, we can draw on findings in various disciplines. Social psychologists, for example, have developed theories of social identity (Tajfel and Turner 1979) and self-categorization (Tuner and Oakes 1986) to explore the minimal conditions of intergroup conflict (Tajfel 1978 Oakes and Turner 1980; Brewer 1979; Wetherell 1982). Evolutionary psychologists have argued that increasing population density has led to a human inclination to categorize large numbers of people into 'friends' and 'enemies', enabling the management of socio-spatial relationships (Kurzban and Neuburg 2015; Kurzban and Leary 2001). According to Paladino and Castelli (2008), one of the strategies to evade conflict is to avoid approaching members of perceived out-groups and remain in one's own territory, and, using a coalitional index model, Boyer, Firat and Leeuwen (2015) have recently found that perceived threat tends to increase commitment to in-groups and the preferential treatment of in-group members, even at the expense of individual gain.

Increased group identification can lead to prejudices towards, and the discrimination of, those perceived as outsiders, and intergroup conflicts can build up over time (Brewer 1979, 1999, 2001; Taylor and Doria 1981). A disagreement between neighbours, for example, can slowly escalate into an enduring fight between neighbourhood factions whose public spatial performances of mutual resentment reinforce perceptions of 'us' and 'them'. What needs to be acknowledged, however, is that the people embedded in antagonistic situations are only in extreme cases fully defined by them. After all, people are normally engaged in multiple identification processes that are informed by all sorts of experiences, desires and frustrations. Daughters and sons become lovers, partners and parents, and take up different professions and hobbies, have unique, idiosyncratic life trajectories, and are engaged in multiple processes of place-making.

Four contributions in this book explore the significance of the spatial legacy of 'the Troubles' to place-making activities in Northern Ireland, but do so through the eyes and experiences of individuals or groups considered only sporadically in most publications. Many of the contributors zoom in on alternative place-making processes, for example among migrants, refugees, social circus performers and entertainment seekers. The overall approach in this volume thus aims for 'fertile complication' (Dovey 2008), throwing light on the interweaving processes of place-making in and beyond a narrow focus on political conflict. It poses questions such as: How are power relations exercised in the making of place in different social spheres? How do practices of place-making enable or question particular expressions of social identity in terms of gender, age, ethnicity, religious affiliation, and political alliance? And how do spatial processes inform and afford individual life trajectories?

Place and Place-Making: Analytical Dimensions

To address these and other questions, it is necessary to sketch the outlines of relevant theories of space, place and movement. Appadurai (1996) has contended that all social phenomena are emplaced and are constituted through location, materiality and meaning. In line with this argument, Gieryn (2000: 471) has identified three 'necessary and sufficient features' of place. Firstly, place refers to geographic location, a unique spot in the universe which, although finite, has elastic boundaries. Secondly, places have physical or material forms through which social differences, inequalities and collective actions are shaped and manifested. Thirdly, all places are invested with meaning and value through processes of identification, naming and representation. Places, in other words, are 'endlessly made, not just when the powerful pursue their ambition through brick and mortar, not just when design professional [*sic*] give form to function, but also when ordinary people extract from continuous and abstract space a bounded, identified, meaningful, named and significant place' (ibid.).

The individual chapters in this volume show a wide variety of (often conflicting) ways in which individuals and groups in Northern Ireland understand and use specific locations, thus reproducing or challenging particular relations of inequality through spatial actions. Various contributors zoom in on emotional attachment to certain locations and investigate related issues of belonging and non-belonging. This theme resonates with work by the political geographer John Agnew (1989), whose analytical definition of place comprises three dimensions: *location*, a point in space with specific relations to other points in space; *locale*, the broader context of social relations for individual locations; and a *sense of place*, the subjective feelings associated with a particular location. This third dimension has been addressed by numerous anthropologists exploring emotional learning processes in human ecologies (Milton 2005), feelings of belonging and displacement among migrants and refugees (Brun 2001; Valentine, Sporton and Nielsen 2009), and memory, materiality and emotions (Heatherington 2005; Lysaght 2005; Svašek 2005, 2012; Milič 2012).

The idea of 'place-making' echoes the Lefebvrian understanding that space is socially produced, that it is simultaneously 'conceived', 'perceived' and 'lived'. What distinguishes the notion is its emphasis on 'making' and potential transformation. Place, as Gieryn (2000: 467) affirms, is an 'interpretative frame through which people measure their lives, evaluate others, take political positions, and just make sense'. Tim Cresswell concurs:

> Because we live in place, as part of place, and yet simultaneously view place as something external, place can be thought of as a centre of meaning and an external context for action – as ideal and material. ... Place, as a phenomenological-experiential entity combines elements of nature (elemental forces), social relations (class, gender, and so on), and meaning (the mind, ideas, symbols). Experience of place, from a phenomenological perspective, is always an experience of all three realms, each of which affects our actions in place. (Cresswell 1996: 156–57)

Through his succinct investigation of the relationship between place and socio-cultural power Cresswell (1996: 161) helps us to delve further into this line of argument. Because place is an immediate and material context of our actions, he suggests, it acts as a 'fundamental form of classification', helping us to order the world into 'us' and 'them', 'here' and 'there', and to 'make interpretations and act accordingly'. Place, in other words, contributes to the creation and reproduction of action-oriented beliefs and ideologies that naturalize place identifications. In Belfast, for example, the Falls Road has been produced as a street that cannot be but 'Catholic' and 'nationalist'. By contrast, the Shankill is regarded as an inherently 'Protestant' and 'loyalist' area. Such fixed territorial place-identity reifications often rest on underlying moral claims that have political significance.

Figure 0.7 Cross-carrying procession. Photo by Milena Komarova.

Here '[t]he "nature" of place [is] offered as justification for particular views of what is good, just and appropriate' (ibid.), making it a terrain of ideological struggle between ideas, symbols, representations and meaning.

Clearly thus, place is not only the multilayered context of our everyday lives but it also intrinsically connects with ontological questions, urging us to wonder 'who we are', to employ specific categories and markers of self, and to make particular identity claims to 'community', 'ethnicity' and 'nation' (Dixon and Durrheim 2000). As some of the chapters in this book demonstrate, people often have unequal powers to fix and spatialize social identities, to claim rights to access and control the use of specific locations. Ideas of neighbourhood ownership can, for example, challenge the presence of non-residents in the area, ideas that in Northern Ireland have been spatially performed through demonstrations against Loyal Order parades. By contrast, organized walks and processions across socio-spatial lines of division, such as Belfast's 'peace walls', can question specific notions of difference (see Figure 0.7). This again shows that '[p]laces are not inert containers. They are politicized, culturally relative, historically specific, local and multiple constructions' that reflect multiple 'voices' (Rodman 2003: 205). Consequently, we have to explore 'the contests and tensions between different actors and interests in the construction of space' (ibid: 209).

This argument directly reflects in the aim of this book to break free of preconceptions of Northern Ireland as a conflict-ridden place by examining both the multiplicity of voices in the making of place, as well as its multi-locality. Multi-locality also refers to relations between geographic locations through bodily movement and to changes of specific locations over time. This is apparent, for example, when new people settle in a particular neighbourhood and, as a result, the spatial experiences of both existing and new populations change. To newcomers, memories of past and distant settings profoundly shape the understanding and experience of new sites, and existing populations often compare new socio-spatial developments to earlier experiences. In Northern Ireland, such processes occurred on a larger scale when Catholics and Protestants had to relocate due to 'Troubles'-related territorial tensions, and when migrants started moving to the region in larger groups in the late twentieth century. People's different socio-economic, ethnic, religious and other backgrounds also influence their attitudes to spatial change. To explore this diversity, we suggest a framework that focuses on three interrelated dimensions of spatiality and place-making, namely discourse, practice and embodied experience. The remainder of the introduction elaborates this perspective.

Place, Identity and Place-Making: Discursive Constructions

Dixon and Durrheim (2000) emphasize that rhetoric or discourse is a fundamental tool through which places and associated identities are imbued with meanings. Symbolic constructions that link identity to place are, for example, deployed within everyday familial discourses, justifying specific spatial actions in the home. A father, regarding himself as 'head of a household', may claim the most comfortable chair in the living room as 'his', without much thought, assuming that it is his right to sit in it. Influenced by dominant gender discourses, his wife and children may take this small act of place-making for granted, accepting it as a 'natural' state of affairs. Yet as Cresswell (1996: 8) argues, 'value and meaning are not inherent in any space or place' but 'must be created, reproduced and defended' through discursive representations that structure social practices. While such practices can cement taken-for-granted meanings vis-à-vis place, individuals can also contest or resist specific place-identity constructions. Place is thus an ongoing discursive production, a multi-vocal act of imagining.

Reviewing a tradition of writing in social psychology that highlights the relationship between language, self-narration and place,[3] Dixon and Durrheim (2000) argue for a discursive approach to place-making and identity formation that goes far beyond the realm of individual mental engagement. Instead, the focus is on 'collective' constructions of place, a social and political process whereby people perform place identities through site-specific forms of verbal and non-verbal communication. An example is the temporary transformation of a football pitch into a place of collective and competing nationhood when the crowd, dressed in the nation's colours, sing the national anthem and shout national slogans. Another example is when a war memorial, not really noticed on an everyday basis, annually transitions into a place of national heroism and victimhood through ritual speeches and embellishment. Such discursively produced links between self and place, Dixon and Durrheim argue, can have crucial social and political dimensions and effects. In the first case, the enthusiastic support for opposing teams, and in the second, feelings of shared suffering and pride, reflect and reinforce deeper animosities or a sense of solidarity. The two occasions can also be connected when the ritual warfare of sport (a Polish–German football match; an Irish–English rugby game) is experienced as an extension of the bloody histories of war between 'us' and 'them'. In the Northern Irish case, dominant discourses of 'Irishness', 'Britishness' and 'Northern Irishness' have long shaped people's place identities (Graham 1997; Reid 2004). Yet as this book will show, other discourses have also influenced people's site-specific feelings, for example through the lens of images of 'gender', 'diaspora' and 'cross-community'. Distinct identity discourses also intersect, for example when migrant groups are framed (or frame themselves) as new 'communities' that need to secure a peaceful place in society through interaction with existing, formerly antagonistic 'communities'. In this case, an overall 'cross-community' discourse connects the politics of reconciliation to anti-racist policies.

The Social Practices of Place-Making

The discursive dimension of space must be combined with an analytical focus on spatial practice. Cresswell (1996: 16) pays extensive attention to the importance and centrality of practice, particularly since place-specific social practices have ideological effects that may be used to affirm or contest a status quo. He also suggests that place-making processes can be explored as concurrent production and consumption: 'Practice is simultaneously a form of consumption (insofar as the actor acts according to assumed norms, he or she "buys" them) and a form of production (as the actor, by acting in accordance with assumed norms, contributes further to the continuation of accepted "commonsense" place meanings)'. (Ibid.: 17).

We would like to emphasize here the relevance of Bourdieu's (1977) theory of practice, which understands everyday life and social action as the outcome of an 'often non-conscious sense of 'fitting in'/ being at ease, or not' (Smyth and McKnight 2010: 7). In Cresswell's interpretation, both conscious and unselfconscious modes of acting can lead to a multitude of spatial actions that sustain and reproduce specific place-encoded hierarchies and identities. A revealing Northern Irish example is how Orange Order lodges' members of different generations have continued to meet and organize activities in their buildings, regarding Orangeism as a crucial part of their family history and cultural heritage. By entering these structures and engaging in a variety of activities that also spill out into the public realm, lodge members perform unionist or loyalist identities in very visible ways. Through routinized practices such as marching that are highly exclusive, their practices of place-making clearly sustain discourses of difference. Some of the contributors to this volume demonstrate how persistent practices of division and contestation within unionist or loyalist and nationalist or republican spheres, as well as in the often tense 'interface' areas, have continued to reproduce generations-old predispositions.

In Bourdieu's analytical framework, feelings of belonging and non-belonging to place are informed by symbolic and material forms of capital that have distinct value in certain social fields, but are worthless in others (Bourdieu 1977; Leach 2005). The knowledge of how to perform *puja* (an act of worship in Hinduism), for example, can be highly valuable to Hindus in Northern Ireland who worship their deities on a regular basis, both at home shrines and in various temples in the region (Svašek 2016). Their ability to perform the right rituals and celebrate festivals that are central to Hindu practices is most likely irrelevant in other Northern Irish localities. Such practices are, however, occasionally 'normalized' in public spaces, which happened in October 2015 when ArtsEkta, a non-profit organization, organized 'a thrilling celebration of a classic Indian tale' in front of the Belfast City Hall. The show, funded by the Northern Irish Arts Council, had been inspired by various Hindu festivals (see www.ninenights.co.uk).

Numerous authors have used theatrical metaphors to explore socio-spatial practices that produce or contest place-specific identities. Rose (2002) has used the term 'enactment' to describe strategic practices that link specific discourses to social space. 'Enactment', he suggests, 'is comprised of the material acts and gestures that make texts a recognizable feature of social life' (ibid.: 393). In a similar vein, Anderson and Jones (2009), have employed performance theory to argue that place-making practices are integral to people's lived experience of identity. De Certeau (1984) has stressed the significance of mundane performances of subversion by individuals who use acts of walking, naming, narrating and remembering to challenge dominant voices in society. Such small-scale acts, he argued, often serve as means by which individuals reappropriate the landscape. In the words of Low and Lawrence-Zúñiga (2003: 22), different levels and scales of enactment, from 'public festivities, parades, performances, and spontaneous demonstrations' to the minutiae of touch and bodily comportment have also been used to 'temporarily invert dominant power relations to contest political and social issues'.

When exploring spatial practice, a longer-term perspective on the construction, use and transformation of particular buildings and structures is also needed. An obvious example from Northern Ireland is the 'peace walls' of Belfast and Derry (Londonderry). Perhaps ironically, these structures have become more numerous and have, in individual cases, been enlarged or extended, rather than reduced or dismantled, during the last decade of peace building (Jarman 2012). Other changes in architecture reflect the growth and spatial presence of migrant populations. The Indian Community Centre in Belfast, for example, was established in a former Methodist church in North Belfast, bought by Indian migrants in the 1980s. More often than not, appearances of new or transformed architectural structures and cityscapes trigger different responses in different groups and individuals.

Embodied Experience: Being in, Attaching to, and Moving through Place

This brings us to the third dimension of our analytical framework: that of embodied experience. This perspective emphasizes that people, as inherently mobile beings, are engaged in dynamic processes of sensorial and affective interaction as they constitute, and move through, changing spatial settings (Jensen 2009, 2010; Jiron 2010). Drawing on phenomenology and cognitive theories of perception, scholars like Csordas (1990, 1994) and Milton (2002) have argued that emotional experiences in specific spatial settings are shaped by memories and expectations. For Milton (2005: 37), to be in the world means to be engaged in a constant learning process whereby 'emotional reactions, feelings and expressions arise and develop out of a complex interaction between an individual human being and their environment'.

As Karen Lysaght has shown in a study of fear and the use of space in Belfast, expectations of danger amongst certain groups of Protestants and Catholics at the time of her research were informed by a 'tacit agreement . . . on the nature of violence and on the relative threat posed by various situations', which lead to the use of a 'variety of spatial strategies . . . to offset potential danger'. These strategies involved 'complex mapping processes', whereby space is carved into safe and unsafe zones, where both macro- and micro-territorial considerations exist, involving respectively the 'other side of town' or the 'other side of the street' (Lysaght 2005: 140). Clearly, when understanding spatial practices, affective processes need to be taken into account. For Csordas, 'embodiment' is a constant process whereby multi-sensorial experiences are objectified and inscribed in the body. Of interest here is the link between perception and the different senses, often selectively hypercognized in different contexts. As made clear in the first chapter by Angela Mazzetti, violent conflict can be smelled, heard, seen, tasted and touched. Both perpetrators and victims of violence may hear gunshots, smell the smoke of explosions, see people running for safety, taste blood when wounded, and carry the bodies of those killed. Our broader focus in this book acknowledges that, in politically tense situations, people also feel sensations and sentiments that are not directly related to concerns about safety. In the relative security of their domestic settings, for example, people experience affective relatedness through sensuous interaction, touching each other, sharing meals, listening to music, and so on. Such activities can instil a positive sense of kinship and define the home as a place of intimate belonging. Engagements related to work, hobbies and friendships can also help people to positively attune and attach to specific environments. Milligan (1998: 6) has used the term 'place-attachment' to describe the process that occurs when recurrent and memorable experiences transform a location into a place of bonding and emotional investment.

The perspective of physical movement is essential when exploring embodied experiences of spatiality and place-attachment (Edensor 2010). Importantly, people move between locations in different manners, which influences not only their perception of the environment but also the ways in which they experience their own bodies and construct a sense of self. Walking, cycling and driving are each associated with characteristic rhythms and social interactions (Jensen 2009). Running the Belfast Marathon, for example, informs a sense of movement and identity that differs from doing the school run, or taking a bus to the airport. What is clear is that mobility, as a fundamental socio-spatial practice and experience, is an essential means of constituting place, and that sensorial perceptions and experiences through movement do not occur in social or political vacuums.

Movements through the environment are, of course, to a great degree limited by architectural infrastructures. The physical presence of streets, shops, houses and traffic affects how bodies sense and move through the urban landscape. Dovey (2005, 2008) has argued that buildings are 'inherently coercive [as] they enforce limits to action and enable social practice to take place' (2005: 291). The built environment as a whole, he contends, mediates and materializes forms of power over users of space, for example through coercion, manipulation, seduction or authority.[4] In Belfast, specific architectural strategies were meant to manage the use of public space in an attempt to gain control over paramilitary action during 'the Troubles'. Since the start of the peace process, developers and government agencies have built numerous impressive structures to attract locals and tourists to Belfast, including state-of-the-art shopping malls, the Titanic museum, the Waterfront Hall and major works of public art (Hocking 2015). In different working-class neighbourhoods, reimaging projects have replaced the more aggressive loyalist and republican murals with toned-down symbolic messages. In addition, in several locations in the city, migrants have opened specialized shops and supermarkets, and some migrant organizations have moved into highly visible community buildings.[5] All these changes account for new ways in which the city is experienced in the twenty-first century.

Movement, Method and Knowledge

This brings us to questions about methodology. Which methods can be used best to explore the politics and poetics of movement and place-making in Northern Ireland to provide an understanding of 'a world of incessant movement and becoming, one that is never complete but continually under construction, woven from the countless lifelines of its manifold human and non-human constituents as they thread their ways through the tangle of relationships in which they are comprehensively enmeshed' (Ingold 2011: 141).

While an in-depth discussion of methodological issues is far beyond the scope of this introduction, it is crucial to address the issue in this book. Over a decade ago, Law and Urry (2004: 403–4) argued that existing methods of research in the social sciences and humanities did not deal well 'with the fleeting – that which is here today and gone tomorrow'; 'with the distributed – . . . that which slips and slides between one place and another'; and 'with the multiple – that which takes different shapes in different places'.

One of the more pressing matters, in our view, is to acknowledge that our own research activities are as spatially embedded as the activities of our research participants. We agree with Tim Ingold who has argued against models of scientific knowledge production that oppose an assumed 'objective space' of science to the 'subjective places' of the inhabitants of research sites. His dynamic perspective on habitation and movement[6] emphasizes that scientific knowledge

> grows in a field of practices constituted by the movements of practitioners, devices, measures and results from one laboratory to another. Thus, contrary to the official view, what goes for inhabitant knowledge also goes for science. In both cases, knowledge is integrated not through fitting local particulars into global abstractions, but in the movement from place to place, in wayfaring. Scientific practices have the same place-binding (but not place-bound) character as the practices of inhabitants. (Ingold 2011: 154)

Earlier, we proposed an analytical framework that distinguishes three interconnected dimensions of spatiality and place-making, namely discourse, practice and embodied experience. The remainder of this section will examine how this perspective can help us to think critically and reflectively about the production of knowledge through various methods.

Starting with the first dimension, the purpose of discourse analysis in spatial research is to identify knowledge formations that reflect, and make assumptions about, specific notions of emplaced subjectivity, and to examine how different individuals and groups of people reproduce, reinforce or challenge ideas around identity and territoriality through both habitual and conscious discursive constructions. Researchers have explored these processes employing various methodologies, for example recording relevant speech events during council meetings. They have also learnt to recognize recurrent and competing discursive constructions of spatial subjectivity while spending time with relevant research participants, holding informal chats, conducting interviews and producing biographical narratives. Discourses of spatiality and spatial subjectivity have also been explored through the investigation of letters, archival records, newspaper articles, and digital media posts. Importantly, these research materials have to be analysed against the background of wider social and political structures that legitimize territorial claims.[7] Photography and film have added an important visual aspect to spatial research, demonstrating, for example, how related verbal and visual discourses naturalize specific claims to spatial ownership. The question is how academics' own spatial histories and movements influence their research, and how their positionalities and spatial presence influences communication with their research participants. How, for example, does the particular phrasing of an interview question, posed at a specific location, build on and trigger particular discursive constructions?

To continue with the second dimension of our analytical approach, discourses are produced and reproduced through spatially embedded practices. As noted earlier, our understanding of practice is mainly based on Bourdieu's practice theory, which highlights that people operate in dynamic social fields that are often hierarchical. To gain access and power in these fields, they need to acquire specific forms of social, symbolic and cultural capital. From a methodological point of view, the exploration of socio-spatial practice calls for longer-term research engagement with research participants who occupy different and changing positions in concrete social fields. The resulting comparative perspective provides insights into the spatial activities through which individuals, in interaction with others, shape and negotiate spatial interaction. For researchers interested in practices of place-making, this means that questions should be asked about the specific kinds of knowledge and social networks that enable individuals to enter and appropriate specific spaces, and to literally follow their research participants to locations that may be far apart (Hannerz 2003; D'Andrea, Ciolfi and Gray 2011). To gain a good sense of such activities, and to be able to distinguish between 'what people do and what they say they do', researchers need to get to know their research protagonists over longer periods. Sharing time and space, in other words, is a crucial dimension of successful fieldwork (Hammersley and Atkinson [1983] 1995). The method of participant observation, a process of deep hanging out with research participants, can take many forms, from participation in political meetings to attending funerals or helping out with the washing-up. It may also require a willingness to learn new skills, such as playing the flute to enable research into marching bands (Ramsey 2011). Again, a critical awareness of our own movements into and out of the fieldwork setting, and into our own changing habitual conduct, is crucial. For example, increasing familiarity with the spatial movements of our research informants must be discussed in our interpretations.

Finally, the spatial movements of research participants and researchers generate specific embodied experiences. As has been pointed out by researchers who have used the 'walking method', moving at a slow pace through a relevant environment can help to revive memories that trigger rich narrative accounts (Kusenbach 2003; Mitchell and Kelly 2011; Buscher, Urry and Witchger 2011; Hodgson 2011; Shortell 2015). The specific sounds, sights, smells and tastes of a particular location can have strong emotional associations that are less easily recalled in more conventional interview situations. Importantly, it is not just the lived experiences of research participants that shape academic knowledge. Emplaced in 'ethnographic contexts' (Pink 2008a: 179), in interaction with their research participants researchers themselves produce memorable encounters through a 'range of "shared" multi-sensorial experiences and collaborative productions' (Pink 2008b: 2). Consequently, as fieldworkers we need to be aware of our own movements in the field.

Interim: A Short Reflective Exercise

While writing this introduction, we reserved one day to consider this issue through an activity that was both ethnographic and autoethnographic – ethnographic, because we exchanged ideas and tried to understand each other's spatial experiences; and autoethnographic, because we actively reflected on our own perceptions and feelings. On a cloudy day in June 2016, we walked through Belfast and explored how we each mapped and interpreted the city as a result of our previous experiences. Our first task was to choose a starting point and roughly decide how we would progress during the day. After some thought, we decided to set off from University Square, on the main Queen's University campus. In the light of our personal histories, this was an unsurprising choice as our offices were situated there and we had frequently met in one or the other for work. Aiming to move through a variety of areas in the city, some visibly marked by sectarianism but others less clearly influenced by territorial politics, we planned to walk first to the Royal Victoria Hospital (RVH) in West Belfast where Milena's children had been born, and to end up at the Ulster Hospital where Maruška had given birth to her son. The choice to include the two hospitals corresponded to the logics of our own family histories in Northern Ireland. Our planned route also reflected our interest in territorial divisions in the city. Walking away from the university area, we would first pass through a Protestant/loyalist neighbourhood, then cross over a motorway footbridge to reach the RVH, return to the university area through a Catholic/nationalist neighbourhood, and finally drive by car through East Belfast to the Ulster Hospital in Dundonald. The chosen route showed our awareness of symbolic markers of political identity and conflict, and demonstrated familiarity with different urban planning and infrastructural projects. As will become clear, throughout the walk our professional knowledge constantly conversed with our private memories and experiences of people and spaces, both in and beyond Northern Ireland.

Walking down the Donegall Road, the north boundary of the loyalist area known as 'The Village', leading to the Royal Victoria Hospital, we

Figure 0.8 Unionist marker: Poppies. Photo by Maruška Svašek.

were reminded of recent official attempts to reimage the city. This policy of reimagination has aimed to remove aggressive sectarian symbols and replace them with alternative visual imagery. Along the road, we saw an eclectic concoction of symbols of loyalism and unionism that were now purposely interspersed with the imagery of the neighbourhood's 'forgotten' class and gender history (see Figures 0.8 and 0.9).

These recent attempts at reimaging jarred with some of our earlier experiences as researchers and residents of Belfast. Milena explained to Maruška that she had walked down the Donegall Road on numerous occasions, particularly during her first years in Belfast. At that time her encounters and interactions with local residents had influenced her early impressions of the city. While most of her journeys had been smooth and unremarkable, on one occasion, en route to the RVH for a maternity appointment, she had a frightening experience when entering the footbridge over the M1/Westlink motorway that links the neighbourhood to the hospital grounds (see Figure 0.10). Already on it, she realised belatedly that a raucous group of boys of the age of about eleven had gathered on the bridge and were banging on its metal caging with wooden bats. The group's rowdy behaviour, her vulnerability as an expectant mother and the caged, narrow structure of the bridge, made Milena feel threatened (see Figure 0.11). She thought of retreating but reasoned that such an attempt would be all too obvious, and likely to attract unwanted attention. Instead, her glance lowered as she proceeded forward, hoping to pass by the group unremarked. As she levelled with them, however, one of the children fixed his eyes on her and,

Figure 0.9 Reimagining: Suffragettes. Photo by Maruška Svašek.

Figures 0.10 Footbridge. Photo by Milena Komarova.

Figure 0.11 Metal cage. Photo by Milena Komarova.

swinging his bat back and forth, hissed in her face 'you f–ing fenian!'[8] Barely managing to keep her wits about her, she briskly walked on. The physical attack that she expected never happened and, leaving the bridge on softened feet, she vowed never to take that route again.

This incident, vividly remembered while we walked across the bridge, had changed Milena's awareness of, and sensitivity to, how she was perceived as an 'outsider' in Northern Ireland. Experiencing first-hand the way in which local communal divisions often serve as a lens through which 'otherness' in general and new migrants in particular are perceived, made her question the very possibility and meaning of 'neutrality'. Her research in and on Northern Ireland since has often confronted her with how 'others' are ascribed affiliations (or 'sides'), depending on perceived cultural, national or racial background. The scary experience has directly influenced how she manages her professional identity 'in the field', and even how she teaches research methodology.

However, since that time, Milena has often been back to the area for research purposes. Standing once again on the footbridge on the day of our urban tour, her private experiences of the location were also strongly tinted by later research and by communication with Maruška. We saw it as a noisy and polluted space of poor quality, and commented that the road (the Westlink) beneath us clearly reinforced exclusion from the city. We spoke of the 'doughnut' of roads (Sterrett at al. 2012) around the city centre that

Figure 0.12 Roads as barriers. Photo by Milena Komarova.

has destroyed pedestrian connections, creating a barrier effect for deprived inner-city communities who depend on walking (Figure 0.12). Research on Belfast rarely investigates how such barriers result in spatial patterns of communal division and forms of social deprivation.

Having passed through the RVH grounds and exited from its west end, we now found ourselves on the edge of the nationalist Falls Road area. The sight of republican graffiti and symbols of nationalist identity that were immediately visible evoked for Milena powerful memories of walking here for the first time on the day of arriving at the hospital to give birth to her daughter (Figures 0.13 and 0.14). She remembered feeling particularly intimidated by a sign on an external hospital wall in support of the IRA. It had now faded away, although another republican sign could be discerned on almost the same spot.

At that time, having only recently moved to Northern Ireland, the abbreviation IRA encapsulated the entirety of Milena's knowledge about this place. This was knowledge that had been gleaned from listening to news bulletins since childhood and that evoked only images of violence. She explained to Maruška that she had felt fearful, unsettled and worried about the safety of delivering her child in this hospital. This made Maruška think of her own encounters with, and imaginations of, 'sectarian' perspectives. Being Dutch, she had once attended a celebration of Queen's Day organized by the Dutch society in Belfast when her son was about three years old.

Figure 0.13 'Broadway Defenders' sign. Photo by Milena Komarova.

Figure 0.14 'Brits Out' sign. Photo by Milena Komarova.

Figure 0.15 Exhibition space. Photo by Milena Komarova.

Following Dutch traditions, she had dressed him in orange clothes. When, travelling by train to Belfast where the celebration was to take place, she had become aware of staring passengers, she suddenly realized that the orange colour might mark her out as a 'Protestant' family and she began to feel ill at ease. This feeling emerged again when, during a flight from Belfast to Amsterdam a year later, a drunken passenger asked her where she lived, and she responded 'Northern Ireland'. With a rather aggressive tone of voice, the obviously nationalist man shouted that she should have answered 'Ireland!'

Our own memories of sectarianism were evoked in direct response to the urban environment. Yet, we also had many other experiences that undermined territorial readings of the landscape. Taking a break in the cafe of the Cultúrlann centre on the 'nationalist' Falls Road, we were reminded of the numerous times we had been in this place before: Milena had sung and shared Christmas dinners with her choir in the building. Maruška was drawn to an exhibition of Rita Duffy's artwork in the adjoining gallery, an artist she had got to know during earlier research on creative production (Figure 0.15). Again, our perception of our surroundings clearly intertwined with memories of a variety of past experiences, only some related to politics. Interestingly, some memories were also evoked by our belongings. The jotting pad that Milena was using for her field notes, for instance, was an old unused school notebook from her 'communist' childhood, its plain appearance and Cyrillic script apparently at odds with the place, time and

Figure 0.16 The old notebook. Photo by Milena Komarova.

purpose for which it was now used (Figure 0.16). For her, however, the notebook signified connectedness with earlier phases in her life in a different spatial and political realm. As Milena began to recall her memories, Maruška vividly remembered the social and economic conditions in state-socialist Czechoslovakia, a country that she had visited many times during the Cold War. In deep conversation, we were transported back to other times and places, and no longer noticed the cafe around us.

Our day ended with a journey by car to the Ulster Hospital. The relative swiftness of our movement in the car made us aware of the way different modes of transportation affect how much, and what, can be seen in the landscape. On the way, Maruška told Milena about the difficulties her son had faced after birth and the support she had received from the nurses in intensive care. We ended agreeing that motherhood had made us identify with Northern Irish and other mothers, and had given us access to new socio-spatial contexts in our current place of residence, such as nurseries, schools and the homes of our children's friends.

The above shows that the route we chose to take, the stories we told each other, and our changing and contradictory sense of place as we moved through the landscape, were all linked to our personal histories as researchers, mothers, migrants, artists, and once-upon-a-time children in faraway places. Our experience of Belfast on that day clearly drew on overlapping aspects of the 'personal' and the 'professional', the 'past' and the 'present', and places 'here' and 'there'. To produce the reflective textual outcome of our urban walk – the very words you are reading right now – we had to select and translate a complex reality of movement and multi-sensoriality into an argument relevant to this book. We hope that the resulting 'interim' has shed some light on our own histories of mobility and place-making, and on their momentary resonance with the place-making activities of others.

The Chapters in the Book

Spatial issues related to histories and memories of the Troubles are most centrally addressed in the first three chapters of this book. In Chapter 1, Angela Mazzetti explores her own experiences of growing up in Northern Ireland in the 1970s and 1980s in an autoethnographic analysis. Her self-reflective narrative considers the importance of first-hand experiences, visual cues, and media reports to her perception and use of public space at the time, exploring how they shaped her anticipation that certain sites were 'dangerous', and others 'safe'. Her account confronts the reader with a world of saturated senses and emotions. She describes, for example, walking by a shop after an explosion, a place in which her senses were 'flooded with the destruction: the black charred remains of what were once colourful toys and trinkets; the sound of water cascading down through the walls and ceiling'. Exploring how she coped with the embodied memories of such experiences, she investigates how concrete temporal, seasonal and situational factors during childhood and early adulthood contributed to a changing sense of (social) self.

The theme of self in transformation also weaves though Chapter 2, in which Erin Hinson investigates how, between 1972 and 1988, former Ulster Volunteer Force and Red Hand Commando prisoners formed positive place attachments to the compounds of the Maze/Long Kesh prison through the production and use of artefacts. Hinson builds upon Milligan's concept of locational socialization, and shows how the prisoners, as they developed their skills, were not only engaged in the crafting of a variety of objects, but simultaneously crafted the social and material prison environment. Learning to work with leather, paint and other materials also helped them to pass time and gain a sense of agency within the confined setting, producing a mental space in which they could 'escape' from this reality. Craft production also facilitated communications with the outside world, as artefacts were sent to family and friends as gifts and commodities, connecting the local to the extra-local. In addition, Hinson shows how in the twenty-first century, the artefacts have been newly framed in an exhibition space established by the ex-prisoners. Their aim was to challenge the one-dimensional perception of themselves as loyalists and murderers, supplanting these perceptions with a multi-dimensional view that includes their past as skilled craftsmen and artists.

In Chapter 3, Elizabeth DeYoung uses walking as a methodology for uncovering how the physical environment of Belfast reflects broader narratives of remembrance through plaques that commemorate people who died during 'the Troubles'. Regarding the streets as 'repositories of stories', she explores how she encounters the memorial plaques in highly segregated working-class areas. As in Chapter 2, material production and display are regarded as an important process in which place is being made and place identities are being claimed. The walking method that DeYoung uses also opens questions of memory, forgetting and victimhood, and reminds the reader that the materiality and practice of commemoration has the power to render people, things and events invisible, just as much as to bring them into the limelight. The analysis emphasizes spatial dimensions in Halbwachs' theory of collective memory, demonstrating that place-making and mobility are crucial aspects in the reconstruction and reshaping of past events within present-day frameworks.

Andrea García González turns the focus in Chapter 4 to processes of multiple identification that are only partly territorial, zooming in on relations of friendship and gender. Based on twelve months of ethnographic fieldwork with a women's group in Belfast that included members of both Protestant and Catholic backgrounds, she questions the more pervasive static notions of place characteristic of communal divisions and ethnonational conflict. Based on de Certeau's understanding of 'speaking' as an opportunity to challenge dominant spatial discourses and practices, she explores the alternative 'space of female friendship' that is created by the women through regular face-to-face verbal exchange. The analysis demonstrates that the group members practise cross-community female friendship in newly appropriated spatial settings, including a Protestant community centre and a gym. Their 'mutation' of dominant territorial discourse thus problematizes divisions between and within their communities, not only in terms of rigid communal identifications, but also of established gender relations as they share a critical view on male dominance. Ultimately, González demonstrates that the discursive space of female friendship is a space of political possibility.

By contrast, in Chapter 5, Milena Komarova examines how in urban environments characterized by political conflict material change resonates and intersects with everyday movements and commemorative practices, with varied spatial and temporal effects. Building on Brighenti's (2010) work on visibility, Komarova investigates how a transformation of a physical barrier (a security gate in one of Belfast's longest and oldest 'peace walls') is affecting nationalist–unionist territorial divisions in the area. The analysis focuses particularly on the temporary opening of the gate to allow the annual Orange Order Whiterock Parade to pass through, a moment when territorial tensions rise as nationalist demonstrators gather to protest. Komarova compares the specific spatial and affective dynamics at this contentious moment with less contentious, everyday uses of the gate, and contrasts the case with more peaceful parades in other parts of the city. The chapter specifically discusses the impact of the replacement of the once-solid iron gate by a see-through structure, a change reflecting the longer-term goal of completely demolishing the dividing wall. On a positive note, she argues that the new visibility produced through such changes 'can serve to transform territoriality and to support and extend the public nature of urban space'. Yet, as she also suggests, the way visibility and movement are used strategically as part of both mundane embodied practices and organized events, modifies and occasionally subverts the effects of this spatial change. Finally, Komarova also addresses the effect of mediatization and the appearance of the resulting film fragments in digital space on the permeability of the new security structure at the study site.

A peace wall is also traversed in Chapter 6, but here with the aim to challenge ethno-national division and offer a way out of territorial conflict. Kayla Rush explores the Lift the Cross (LTC) initiative, organized by River of Hope Pentecostal Fellowship (RHPF) in West Belfast in a well-known interface area of the city. Presented as a spiritual solution for the divided inhabitants, the initiative involves street-level interactions with local geographies through daily 'cross walks' and 'cross vigils' through Catholic and Protestant neighbourhoods. Like Komarova, Rush is interested in questions around visuality and spatiality. Based on six months of fieldwork with the group, she examines urban walking as a way of knowing and enskillment, and as an opportunity for visual manipulation of the environment. In their acts of carrying or standing with the crosses, LTC participants quite literally inscribe or 'etch' the image of the cross over places in West Belfast on a daily basis – both in literal embodied ways and in highly visual virtual spaces. While the embodied inscription of this 'crucicentric' vision is performed in situ, its online representation engages what Rush calls the 'Facebook gaze', and produces new, religion-themed forms of urban *flânerie*. In both cases, the aim is a symbolic rearrangement of perceptions and discourses of West Belfast, foregrounding the Pentecostal view. Rush argues that, notwithstanding their limited success in changing the image and experience of West Belfast for urban residents whom they physically encountered on their daily walks, the participants in the initiative successfully engaged online spectators.

In Chapter 7, Augusto Soares is also interested in digital practices and explores the spatial interplay between offline events and movements on the Internet. He investigates how, through processes of intertextuality, administrators, users and followers of the political and satirical commentators' blog LAD ('Loyalists Against Democracy') generate and multiply meaning in a process of constant (re)production and inversion as they criticize, mock, or full-heartedly support aspects of local social and political life. The posts by LAD afford trans-local communication in ways rarely realizable in the offline world, particularly in a region with sharp spatial divisions. Yet, this is not to suggest that the variety of reconfigurations ignited by discursive online place-making are straightforward or unproblematic when it comes to addressing social and political conflict. While on the one hand acting as a space for dialogue and for developing ties beyond one's own social background and political affiliations, it is recognized, on the other hand, that the online can lead to diversifying and heightening hostile contacts and attitudes, and brings new modes of conducting and experiencing these. Either way, Soares demonstrates how the online provides a platform and a potentiality, a discursive space for particular political expression and exchange that is often not possible in the physical spaces of Northern Ireland.

In Chapter 8, in his analysis of the annual Belfast's Festival of Fools, Nick McCaffrey demonstrates, however, that the region *does* provide opportunities for joyful intermingling when the city centre is temporarily transformed into a place of laughter. In contrast to the small-scale meetings of the women's group discussed in Chapter 4, the festival links Belfast to places outside Northern Ireland, bringing artists from around the world to the streets of Belfast. As with similar festivals across locations in different countries, the festival is aimed at local audiences who look for family-oriented entertainment and travel from different locations to take part. Consequently, it provides the opportunity for interactive spatial sociality that transcends practices of Protestant/unionist and Catholic/nationalist ethno-political place-making. McCafferty investigates to what extent the festival organizers, performers and audiences are engaged with the reconciliatory aims of official policies of 'shared space', a concept that reflects an intention to change spatial perceptions and practices, leading to a more inclusive society. Interested in affective and sensorial dimensions of sociality, he also explores the influence of the festival's specific bodily experiences on the perceptions of interacting performers and audience members.

Emotions are also central in Chapter 9, in which Maruška Svašek examines an event organized by senior members of the Indian Community Centre (ICC) in Belfast, a former Methodist Memorial Church Hall. During the event, several groups of elderly people were invited to celebrate Diwali and participate in a documentary about ageing. Exploring discourses of 'community' and 'cross-community' typical to Northern Ireland, the chapter investigates the transformation of the ICC into a cross-community place. The shared aim of the participants was to draw attention to the plight of Northern Irish elderly people and find support for the different organizations they were part of. As the chapter shows, there was, however, a limit to the ways in which specific people and things could be reframed for new purposes. The case demonstrates that people do not have unlimited power when shaping social situations through spatial or material engagement. Imbued with meaning and agency, some sacred artefacts demanded specific behaviour, as they played a central role in the lives of Hindu worshippers.

In Chapter 10, Naoko Maehara sheds light on the spatial experiences and practices of the growing number of migrants in Northern Ireland. More specifically, she explores the processes of emplacement among Japanese women (one of the smaller migrant populations) living in different parts of the region. The women are all married to 'local' husbands. Born and raised in Japan, leaving behind familiar spaces and places back home, they have encountered and interacted with their new physical and social environment in myriad ways. Unfamiliar surroundings – new sights, sounds, smells, weather, language, food, and ways of doing things – have caused the women to experience an occasional sense of loss. Hoping for integration in their husbands' society, the women have also shaped, or tried to shape, positive representations of their surroundings. Expectations of life in 'the West' and Ireland have influenced their experiences of cross-cultural marriage and motherhood. Informed by particular concerns, social and affective goals, desires, and future prospects, Northern Ireland has become a different space for each of them. The analysis of emplacement, whereby the women transform an unfamiliar physical space into a personalized place, shows how their experiences, are also infused with conscious reflections and interpretations.

In the final chapter, Chapter 11, Malcolm Franklin investigates the myriad ways in which asylum seekers and refugees have sought to find a semblance of belonging in Northern Ireland through socio-spatial practice. The majority of those who arrived in Northern Ireland during the time of the research in 2010–11 relied on agents operating within people-smuggling networks, which were decisive in determining their destination country. In other words, the people central in the analysis did not choose to end up in Belfast. In their subjective life narratives, the physical setting of the urban environment of Belfast contrasted with memories of rural life in distant countries. The chapter builds on the perspective of 'home' developed by Rapport and Dawson (1998) that contends that lives are lived in movement and that identity is formed and adjusted in processes of transit and transformation. This dynamic notion of home and (non-)belonging helps to emphasize the fact that the lives of asylum seekers and refugees are not only shaped by experiences of uncertainty and apprehension, but also by the creation and use of social networks in the new environment. The inquiry demonstrates that 'home' is a processual and mutable product of social activity, and that the analysis of displacement and loss of home must be related to a critical investigation of refugee policies and local political dynamics in the places of arrival.

As Dominic Bryan argues in the Afterword, the book as a whole provides valuable insights into small and large conflicts arising in specific socio-spatial settings in twenty-first century Northern Ireland. Each chapter highlights different aspects of movement, sociality and place-making, exploring questions that are relevant to research far beyond the region.

Maruška Svašek is reader in anthropology at the School of History, Anthropology, Philosophy and Politics at Queen's University Belfast, and fellow at the Senator George J. Mitchell Institute for Global Peace, Security and Justice. Her major publications include Anthropology, Art and Cultural Production (2007), Emotions and Human Mobility: Ethnographies of Movement (2012), Moving Subjects, Moving Objects: Transnationalism, Cultural Production and Emotions (2012), and (with Birgit Meyer) Creativity in Transition: Politics and Aesthetics of Cultural Production across the Globe (2016). She is co-editor (with Birgit Meyer) of the Berghahn Books series Material Mediations.

Milena Komarova is a research officer at the Centre for Cross Border Studies, Armagh, and a visiting research fellow at the Senator George J. Mitchell Institute for Global Peace, Security and Justice, Queen's University Belfast. Her work spans the fields of conflict transformation, urban sociology and border studies, exploring the intersections between public space, place, identity and bordering practices, within and without ethno-nationally 'divided' cities. Milena has published on the spatial aspects of conflict transformation in Belfast, such as urban regeneration, the development of 'shared space', the management of contentious parades and protests, and on the role of visuality and movement in 'post-conflict' and 'post-socialist' cities. Her publications include 'Imagining a "Shared Future": Post-Conflict Discourses on Peace-Building', in K. Hayward and C. O'Donnell (eds), Political Discourse and Conflict Resolution: Debating Peace in Northern Ireland (2010); and (with Liam O'Dowd) 'Belfast, the "Shared City"? Spatial Stories of Conflict Transformation', in A. Björkdahl and S. Buckley-Zistel (eds), Spatializing Peace and Conflict: Mapping the Production of Places, Sites and Scales of Violence (2016).

Notes

1. See, for example, Brown and MacGinty 2003; Bryan 2000, 2007; Bryan and Gillespie 2005; Bryan and McIntosh 2007; Bryan and Stevenson 2009; Bryson and McCartney 1994; Buckley 1985; Cashman 2008; Donnan 2005, 2006, 2014; Feldman 1991; Harrison 1995; Jarman 1993, 1997; Jarman and Bryan 1998; Lisle 2006; Loftus 1990, 1994; McCormick and Jarman 2005; McIntosh 1999; Nic Craith 2002; Ramsey 2011; Rolston 1991, 1992, 1995, 2003; Ross 2007; and Santino 2001.
2. Aspects of place-making in Northern Ireland that do not overtly address, explain or suggest a way out of political conflict have attracted relatively little attention from anthropologists, political scientists or sociologists. O'Dowd and Komarova (2013) comment on the power of influential 'spatial narratives', most prominently those of the 'conflict' and of the 'new post-conflict capitalist' city, to shape the ways in which physical changes, particularly in Northern Irish urban landscapes, have been envisioned and imagined by policymakers and academics.
3. See, for example, Proshansky et al. 1983; Burkitt 1991; and Bonauito et al. 1996.

4. All this also speaks to the relationship between movement, visuality and visibility in lived environments. It is through the visual, Hodgson (2011: 55) suggests, that we 'read' the urban landscape, and make decisions 'about the paths we want to make'. Murray (2014) discusses how readings of visual cues and street semiotics impact on our perception and use of space – for example, to determine whether one is in the 'right' part of the city. Scollon and Scollon (2003, as referred to by Murray 2014) have called this a process of 'geosemiotics'.
5. After their completion, 'buildings hide the many possibilities that did not get built, as they bury the interests, politics and power that shaped the one design that did' (Gieryn 2002: 38–39).
6. Partly based on work by the sociologist David Turnbull (1991), Ingold argued that those who use comparative observational data tend to make brief visits to local settings with the aim to 'collect' research material. Analysing these materials elsewhere, in their office or lab, they tend to regard their own movements into and out of these locations as irrelevant. This, Ingold argues, is how 'the researched', framed as 'data', come to be associated with subjective place, and the researchers get the status of objective outsiders who conduct scientific work (do their comparisons, make conclusions) in an abstract space of scientific rationality. Ingold criticized approaches that assume that 'places exist *in space*' (Ingold 2011: 146, italics in original), and introduced the concept of the 'pathway' to explore how, as individual people inhabit the world through movement, their horizons constantly change. In his terminology, emerging and interweaving individual trajectories create dynamic 'meshworks', conceptualized as interlinking trails and knots of intertwining lifelines. He preferred the idea of the evolving meshwork to what he saw as the restrictive perspective of network theorists who regard connections between individuals as lines between static dots.
7. See Wetherell and Potter 1988; and Hall 1992.
8. Derogative for Catholic.

References

Agnew, J. 1989. 'The Devaluation of Place in Social Science', in J. Agnew and J. Duncan (eds), *The Power of Place: Bringing Together Geographical and Sociological Imaginations*. London: Unwin Hyman, pp.9–29.

Anderson, J., and K. Jones. 2009. 'The Difference that Place Makes to Methodology: Uncovering the "Lived Space" of Young People's Spatial Practices', *Children's Geographies* 7(3): 291–303.

Appadurai. A. 1996. *Modernity at Large: Cultural Dimensions of Globalization*. Minneapolis, MN: University of Minnesota Press.

Ashmore, R.D., L.J. Jussim and D. Wilder. 2001. *Social Identity, Intergroup Conflict and Conflict Reduction*. Oxford: Oxford University Press.

Bourdieu, P. 1977. *Outline of a Theory of Practice*. Cambridge: Cambridge University Press.

Boyer, P., R. Firat and F.V. Leeuwen. 2015. 'Safety, Threat, and Stress in Intergroup Relations: A Coalitional Index Model', *Perspectives on Psychological Science* 10(4): 434–50.

Brewer, M.D. 1979. 'In-group Bias in the Minimal Intergroup Situation: A Cognitive-Motivational Analysis', *Psychological Bulletin* 86(2): 307–24.

———. 1999. 'The Psychology of Prejudice: Ingroup Love and Outgroup Hate?', *Journal of Social Issues* 55(3): 429–44.

———. 2001. 'Ingroup Identification and Intergroup Conflict: When Does Ingroup Love Become Outgroup Hate?', in R.D. Ashmore, L.J. Jussim and D. Wilder (eds), *Social Identity, Intergroup Conflict and Conflict Reduction*. Oxford: Oxford University Press, pp.17–41.

Brighenti, A. 2010. 'On Territorology: Towards a General Science of Territory', *Culture and Society* 27(1): 52–72.

Brown, K., and R. MacGinty. 2003. 'Public Attitudes towards Partisan and Neutral Symbols in Post-agreement Northern Ireland', *Identities: Global Structures in Culture and Power* 10: 83–108.

Brun, C. 2001. 'Reterritorializing the Relationship between People and Places in Refugee Studies', *Geografiska Annaler* 83(1): 15–25.

Bryan, D. 2000. *Orange Parades: The Politics of Ritual, Tradition, and Control*. London: Pluto Press.

———. 2007. 'New Colours for the Orange State: Finding Symbolic Space in a Newly Developed Northern Ireland', in J. Wilson and K. Stapleton (eds), *Devolution and Identity*. Aldershot, Hampshire: Ashgate, pp.95–110.

Bryan, D., and G. Gillespie. 2005. *Transforming Conflict: Flags and Emblems*. Belfast: IIS.

Bryan, D., and G. McIntosh. 2007. 'Symbols and Identity in the "New" Northern Ireland', in P. Carmichael, C. Knox and R. Osborn (eds), *Devolution and Constitutional Change in Northern Ireland*. Manchester: Manchester University Press, pp.125–137.

Bryan, D., and C. Stevenson. 2009. 'Flagging Peace: Struggles over Symbolic Landscape in the New Northern Ireland', in M.H. Ross (ed.), *Culture and Belonging in Divided Societies: Contestation and Symbolic Landscapes*. Philadelphia, PA: University of Pennsylvania Press, pp.68–84.

Bryson, L., and C. McCartney. 1994. *Clashing Symbols: A Report on the Use of Flags, Anthems and Other National Symbols in Northern Ireland*. Belfast: Institute of Irish Studies.

Buckley, A. 1985. 'The Chosen Few: Biblical Texts in the Regalia of an Ulster Secret Society', *Folklife* 24: 5–24.

Bonautio, M., G.M. Breakwell and I. Cano. 1996. 'Identity Processes and Environmental Threat: The Effects of Nationalism and Local Identity upon Perception of Beach Pollution', *Journal of Community and Applied Social Psychology* 6(3): 157–75.

Burkitt, I. 1991. *Social Selves*. London: Sage.

Buscher, K., J. Urry and K. Witchger. 2011. 'Introduction: Mobile Methods', in K. Buscher, J. Urry and K. Witchger (eds), *Mobile Methods*. New York: Routledge, pp.1–20.

Cashman, R. 2008. 'Visions of Irish Nationalism', *Journal of Folklore Research* 45(3): 361–81.

Certeau, M. de 1984. *The Practice of Everyday Life*. London: University of California Press.

Cresswell, T. 1996. *In Place, Out of Place: Geography, Ideology and Transgression*. Minneapolis, MN and London: University of Minnesota Press.
———. 2010. 'Towards a Politics of Mobility', *Environment and Planning D: Society and Space* 28(1): 17–31.
Csordas, T.J. 1990. 'Embodiment as a Paradigm for Anthropology', *Ethos* 18(1): 5–47.
——— (ed.). 1994. *Embodiment and Experience: The Existential Ground of Culture and Self*. Cambridge: Cambridge University Press.
D'Andrea, A., L. Ciolfi and B. Gray 2011. 'Methodological Challenges and Innovations in Mobilities Research', *Mobilities*, 6(2): 149–160.
Dixon, J., and K. Durrheim. 2000. 'Displacing Place-Identity: A Discursive Approach to Locating Self and Other', *British Journal of Social Psychology* 39(1): 27–44.
Donnan, H. 2005. 'Material Identities: Fixing Ethnicity in the Irish Borderlands', *Identities: Global Studies in Culture and Power* 12(1): 69–105.
———. 2006. 'Changing Relationships in the Irish Borderlands', *Anthropology in Action* 13(1): 69–77.
———. 2014. 'Commemoration City', in E. Viggiani (ed.), *Talking Stones: The Politics of Memorialization in Post-conflict Northern Ireland*. New York: Berghahn Books, pp. xi–xv.
Dovey, K. 2005. 'The Silent Complicity of Architecture', in J. Hillier and E. Rooksby (eds), *Habitus: A Sense of Place*. Aldershot: Ashgate, pp. 283–96.
———. 2008. *Framing Places: Mediating Power in Built Form*. London and New York: Routledge, 2nd edition.
Edensor, T. 2010. 'Walking in Rhythms: Place, Regulation, Style and the Flow of Experience', *Visual Studies* 25(1): 69–79.
Feldman, A. 1991. *Formations of Violence: The Narrative of the Body and Political Terror in Northern Ireland*. Chicago, IL: University of Chicago Press.
Gaffikin, F. and M. Morrissey. 2011. *Planning in Divided Cities: Collaborative Shaping of Contested Space*. Chichester: Wiley-Blackwell.
Gieryn, T. 2000. 'A Space for Place in Sociology', *Annual Review of Sociology* 26: 463–96.
———. 2002. 'What Buildings Do', *Theory and Society* 31: 35–74.
Graham, B. 1997. 'The Imagining of Place: Representation and Identity in Contemporary Ireland', in B. Graham (ed), *In Search Of Ireland: A Cultural Geography*. London: Routledge, pp. 192–212.
Hannerz, U. 2003. 'Being There . . . and There . . . and There! Reflections on Multi-site Ethnography', *Ethnography* 4(2): 201–16.
Hammersley, M., and P. Atkinson. 1983 (1995). *Ethnography: Principles in Practice*. London: Routledge.
Harrison, S. 1995. 'Four Types of Symbolic Conflict', *Journal of the Royal Anthropological Institute* 1: 255–72.

Heatherington, T. 2005. '"As if Someone Dear to me had Died": Intimate Landscapes, Political Subjectivity and the Problem of a Park in Sardinia', in K. Milton and M. Svašek (eds), *Mixed Emotions: Anthropological Studies of Feeling*. Oxford: Berg, pp.127–44.

Hocking, B.T. 2015. *The Great Reimagining: Public Art, Urban Space, and the Symbolic Landscape of a 'New' Northern Ireland*. New York: Berghahn Books.

Hodgson, F. 2011. 'Structures of Encounterability: Space, Place, Paths and Identities', in M. Grieco and J. Urry (eds), *Mobilities: New Perspectives on Transport and Society*. Farnham: Ashgate, pp.41–64.

Ingold, T. 2011. *Being Alive: Essays on Movement, Knowledge and Description*. London: Routledge.

Jarman, N. 1993. 'Intersecting Belfast', in B. Bender (ed.), *Landscape: Politics and Perspectives*. Oxford: Berg, pp.107–38.

———. 1997. *Material Conflicts: Parades and Visual Displays in Northern Ireland*. Oxford: Berg.

Jarman, N., and D. Bryan. 1998. *From Riots to Rights: Nationalist Parades in the North of Ireland*. Coleraine: Centre for the Study of Conflict.

Jensen, O. 2009. 'Flows of Meaning, Cultures of Movements: Urban Mobility as Meaningful Everyday Life Practice', *Mobilities* 4(1): 139–58.

———. 2010. 'Negotiation in Motion: Unpacking a Geography of Mobility', *Space and Culture* 13(4): 389–402.

Jiron, P. 2010. 'Mobile Borders in Urban Daily Mobility: Practices in Santiago de Chile', *International Political Sociology* 4(1): 66–79.

Kurzban, R., and M. Leary. 2001. 'Evolutionary Origins of Stigmatization: The Functions of Social Exclusion', *Psychological Bulletin* 127: 187–208.

Kurzban, R., and S. Neuberg. 2015. 'Managing Ingroup and Outgroup Relations', in D.M. Buss (ed.), *The Handbook of Evolutionary Psychology*. Hoboken, NJ: Wiley and Sons, pp.653–75.

Kusenbach, M. 2003. 'Street Phenomenology: The Go-Along as Ethnographic Research Tool', *Ethnography*, 4(3): 455–85.

Law, J., and J. Urry. 2004. 'Enacting the Social', *Economy and Society* 33(3): 390–410.

Leach, N. 2005. 'Belonging: Towards a Theory of Identification with Space', in J. Hillier and E. Rooksby (eds), *Habitus: A Sense of Place*. Aldershot: Ashgate, pp.297–314.

Lisle, D. 2006. 'Local Symbols, Global Networks: Rereading the Murals of Belfast', *Alternatives: Global, Local, Political* 31(1): 27–52.

Loftus, B. 1990. *Mirrors: William III and Mother Ireland*. Dundrum: Picture Press.

———. 1994. *Mirrors: Orange and Green*. Dundrum: Picture Press.

Low, S., and D. Lawrence-Zúñiga. 2003. 'Locating Culture', in S. Low and D. Lawrence-Zúñiga (eds), *The Anthropology of Space and Place: Locating Culture*. Oxford: Blackwell Publishing, pp.1–48.

Lysaght, K.D. 2005. 'Catholics, Protestants and Office Workers from the Town: The Experience and Negotiation of Fear in Northern Ireland', in K. Milton and M. Svašek (eds), *Mixed Emotions: Anthropological Studies of Feeling*. Oxford: Berg, pp. 127–44.

McCormick, J., and N. Jarman. 2005. 'Death of a Mural', *Journal of Material Culture* 10(1): 49–71.

McIntosh, G. 1999. *The Force of Culture: Unionist Identities in Twentieth-Century Ireland*. Cork: Cork Univeristy Press.

Milič, E.M. 2012. 'Artefacts as Mediators through Time and Space: The Reproduction of Roots in the Diaspora of Lussignani', in M. Svašek (ed.), *Moving Subjects, Moving Objects: Transnationalism, Cultural Production and Emotions*. New York: Berghahn Books, pp. 159–74.

Milligan, M.J. 1998. 'Interactional Past and Potential: The Social Construction of Place Attachment', *Symbolic Interaction*, 21: 1–33.

Milton, K. 2002. *Loving Nature: Towards an Ecology of Emotion*. London and New York: Routledge.

———. 2005. 'Meanings, Feelings and Human Ecology', in K. Milton and M. Svašek (eds), *Mixed Emotions: Anthropological Studies of Feeling*. Oxford: Berg, pp. 25–42.

Mitchell, A., and L. Kelly. 2011. 'Peaceful Spaces? "Walking" through the New Liminal Spaces of Peacebuilding and Development in North Belfast', *Alternatives: Global, Local, Political* 36: 307–25.

Murray, L. 2014. 'Reading the Mobile City through Street Art: Belfast's Murals', in L. Murray and S. Upstone (eds), *Researching and Representing Mobilities: Transdisciplinary Encounters*. Basingstoke: Palgrave Macmillan, pp. 99–128.

Nagle, J., and M. Clancy. 2010. *Shared Society or Benign Apartheid: Understanding Peace-Building in Divided Societies*. Basingstoke: Palgrave Macmillan.

Nic Craith, M. 2002. *Plural Identities – Singular Narratives: The Case of Northern Ireland*. New York: Berghahn Books.

Oakes, P.J. and J.C. Turner. 1980. 'Social Categorization and Intergroup Behaviour: Does Minimal Intergroup Discrimination Make Social Identity More Positive?', *European Journal of Social Psychology* 10(3): 295–301.

Ó Dochartaigh, N. 2007. 'Conflict, Territory and New Technologies: Online Interaction at a Belfast Interface', *Political Geography* 26(4): 474–91.

O'Dowd, L. and C. McCall. 2008. 'Escaping the Cage of Ethno-National Conflict in Northern Ireland? The Importance of Transnational Networks', *Ethnopolitics* 7(1): 81–99.

O'Dowd, L., and M. Komarova. 2013. 'Three Narratives in Search of a City', *City: Analysis of Urban Trends, Culture, Theory, Policy, Action* 17(4): 526–46.

Paladino, M.P. and L. Castelli. 2008. 'On the Immediate Consequences of Intergroup Categorization: Activation of Approach and Avoidance

Motor Behavior Toward Ingroup and Outgroup Members'. *Personality and Social Psychology Bulletin* 34(6): 755–768.
Pink, S. 2008a. 'An Urban Tour: The Sensory Sociality of Ethnographic Place-Making', *Ethnography* 9(2): 175–96.
Pink, S. 2008b. 'Mobilising Visual Ethnography: Making Routes, Making Place and Making Images', *Forum: Qualitative Social Research*, 9(3). Retrieved 12 March 2018 from http://nbn-resolving.de/urn:nbn:de:0114-fqs0803362.
Proshansky, H., A.K. Fabian and R. Kaminoff. 1983. 'Place-Identity: Physical World Socialization of the Self', *Journal of Environmental Psychology*, 3(1): 57–83.
Ramsey, G. 2011. *Music, Emotion and Identity in Ulster Marching Bands: Flutes, Drums and Loyal Sons*. New York: Peter Lang.
Rapport, N., and A. Dawson. 1998. *Migrants of Identity: Perceptions of Home in a World of Movement*. Oxford: Berg.
Reid, B. 2004. 'Labouring Towards the Space to Belong: Place and Identity in Northern Ireland', *Irish Geography* 37(1): 103–13.
Rodman, M. 2003. 'Empowering Place: Multilocaloty and Multivocality', in S. Low and D. Lawrence- Zúñiga (eds), *The Anthropology of Space and Place: Locating Culture*. Malden, MA: Blackwell Publishing, pp. 204–23.
Rolston, B. 1991. *Politics and Painting: Murals and Conflict in Northern Ireland*. London: Associated Universities Press.
———. 1992. *Drawing Support 1: Murals in the North of Ireland*. Belfast: Beyond the Pale Publications.
———. 1995. *Drawing Support 2: Murals of War and Peace*. Belfast: Beyond the Pale Publications.
———. 2003. *Drawing Support 3: Murals of War and Peace in the North of Ireland*. Belfast: Beyond the Pale Publications.
Rose, M. 2002. 'The Seductions of Resistance: Power, Politics and a Performative Style of Systems', *Environment and Planning D: Society and Space* 20(4): 383–400.
Ross, M.H. 2007. *Cultural Contestation in Ethnic Conflict*. Cambridge: Cambridge University Press.
Sack, R. 1986. *Human Territoriality: Its Theory and History*. Cambridge: Cambridge University Press.
Santino, J. 2001. *Signs of War and Peace: Social Conflict and the Use of Public Symbols in Northern Ireland*. Basingstoke, Hampshire: Palgrave.
Shortell, T. 2015. 'Introduction: Walking as Urban Practice and Research Method', in E. Brown and T. Shortell (eds), *Walking in Cities: Quotidian Mobility as Urban Theory, Method, and Practice*. Philadelphia, PA: Temple University Press, pp. 1–22.
Smyth, L., and M. McKnight. 2010. 'The Everyday Dynamics of Belfast's "Neutral" City Centre: Maternal Perspectives', Conflict in Cities Working Paper 15. Retrieved 17 November 2015 from http://www.urbanconflicts.arct.cam.ac.uk/publications/working-papers.

Svašek, M. 2005. 'The Politics of Chosen Trauma', in K. Milton and M. Svašek (eds), *Mixed Emotions: Anthropological Studies of Feeling*. Oxford: Berg, pp.195–214.

——— (ed.). 2012. *Moving Subjects, Moving Objects: Transnationalism, Cultural Production and Emotions*. New York: Berghahn Books.

——— 2016. 'Undoing Absence through Things: Creative Appropriation and Affective Engagement in an Indian Transnational Setting', in M. Svašek and B. Meyer (eds), *Politics and Aesthetics of Cultural Production Across the Globe*. New York: Berghahn, pp 218–44.

Sterrett, K., M. Hackett and D. Hill. 2012. 'The Social Consequences of Broken Urban Structures: A Case Study of Belfast', *Journal of Transport Geography* 21: 49–61.

Tajfel, H. 1978. *Differentiation between Social Groups: Studies in the Social Psychology of Intergroup Relations*. London: Academic Press.

Tajfel, H., and J. Turner. 1979. 'An Integrative Theory of Intergroup Conflict', in W.G. Austin and S. Worchel (eds), *The Social Psychology of Intergroup Relations*. Saint Paul, MN: Brooks/Cole.

Taylor, D.M., and J.R. Doria. 1981. 'Self-serving and Group-serving Bias in Attribution', *Journal of Social Psychology* 113(2): 201–11.

Therborn, G. 2011. 'End of a Paradigm: The Current Crisis and the Idea of Stateless Cities', *Environment and Planning A* 43(2): 272–85.

Turnbull, D. 1991. 'Inside the Gothic Laboratory: "Local" Knowledge and the Construction of Chartres Cathedral', *Thesis Eleven* 30(1): 161–74.

Turner, J.C., and P. Oakes. 1986. 'The Significance of the Social Identity Concept for Social Psychology with Reference to Individualism, Interactionism and Social Influence', *British Journal of Social Psychology* 25: 237–52.

Valentine, G., D. Sporton and K.B. Nielsen. 2009. 'Identities and Belonging: A Study of Somali Refugees and Asylum Seekers Living in the UK and Denmark', *Environment and Planning D* 27(2): 234–50.

Wetherell, M. 1982. 'Cross-cultural Studies of Minimal Groups: Implications for the Social Identity Theory of Intergroup Relations.' In H. Tajfel (ed.), *Social Identity and Intergroup Relations*. Cambridge: Cambridge University Press, pp.207–240.

Wetherell, M., and J. Potter 1988. 'Discourse Analysis and the Identification of Interpretative Repertoires', in C. Antaki (ed.), *Analysing Everyday Explanation: A Casebook of Methods*. Thousand Oaks, CA: Sage Publications, pp.168–83.

1

Growing Up with the Troubles
Reading and Negotiating Space

Angela Stephanie Mazzetti

> Given the vicissitudes of the human drama, it is a wonder that anyone is left physically or psychologically healthy
>
> —S.E. Hobfoll, 'Alone Together'

Introduction

It was the mid-seventies and I was about eight years old. We were setting out on our annual summer holiday adventure and on this occasion circumstances dictated that we travel through Derry. As this was our first visit, our only knowledge of the city was based on the regular radio and television news reports, which portrayed a place of violence and danger, of sectarian attacks, paramilitary shootings and bombings, and a heavy military presence. If my mother had considered our neighbouring city, Belfast, a dangerous war-torn disaster zone, Derry was by comparison akin to her view of Armageddon. As such she was anxious and had instructed us not to attract any unnecessary attention to our car. This included instructions not to 'mess about' or make any abrupt movements (which could be misinterpreted by either the security forces or paramilitaries as someone pulling a gun on them), and if we were stopped by either the security forces or paramilitaries we were not to say anything, not to smile and not to stare. Overwhelmed by trying to absorb this array of instructions and with concerns for our certain impending death, I decided to hide in the back footwell of the car. As we entered the city we were stopped at an army checkpoint. My father wound down his window. A soldier enquired as to the nature of our journey, as normal procedure required. At this point I had to come out of hiding so that he (the soldier) could check the passengers to validate our story – again normal procedure. I remember looking around at this strange landscape: large concrete blocks, corrugated iron and barbed wire; buildings and walls scrawled with graffiti; soldiers in padded, mottled uniforms crouched down as far as my eyes could see with their rifles pointed at our car. For the first time (that I can remember) in my life, I felt fear, a feeling deep down in my stomach. I didn't know what to do. As we left the checkpoint, I resumed my hiding place until we had safely reached our holiday destination.

I would consider myself to have lived a normal childhood albeit under the rather abnormal circumstances of the Troubles.[1] Although there have been many studies on the impact of the Troubles on children and young people,[2] the majority of these studies have focused on the psychological and behavioural consequences of the conflict.[3] Few studies have focused on the process, and therefore on how children experienced the Troubles, how they made sense of their world, the emotions they felt, and how they learned to cope with the mundane and the not-so-mundane aspects of growing up in the shadow of violence. In the opening vignette I presented a rather mundane aspect of everyday life, a car journey. However, in the context of a region engulfed in an intra-state conflict, even the ordinary can suddenly become the unexpected. Road blocks preventing access through planned routes were a common feature of car journeys and often led to unanticipated diversions through unknown spaces. On this occasion we found ourselves travelling through this notorious and yet unfamiliar city.

Much of the research in Northern Ireland focuses on dangerous spaces based on objective quantifiable data (such as the number of incidents), with less on subjective assessments based on perceptions of fear (Lysaght 2005). Space in Northern Ireland is highly politicized, rooted in centuries of historical events that have shaped and reshaped the religious, historical and cultural schisms that underpinned the conflict (Darby 1995). Space elicits emotional reactions and has the potential to be simultaneously appraised as safe or dangerous, depending on who[4] controls and who is negotiating the space (Feldman 1991; Lysaght and Basten 2003; Lysaght 2005). Based on objective measures of danger, we were travelling through a dangerous space. However, as a young child I was not aware of 'fatal incident' or 'number of death' statistics, and based on these same statistics objectively I had travelled through a more dangerous space as I regularly enjoyed shopping trips to Belfast.[5] My fear was not the result of my understanding of such objective information but rather the result of my subjective appraisal[6] founded on what I already knew about Derry and my evolving lived experience of the city.

My appraisal of danger was in part influenced by my parents' anxiety.[7] Derry (Londonderry)[8] was renowned for being a deeply segregated city.[9] In these segregated urban spaces, communities developed highly localized mental topographies[10] of safe and dangerous spaces, and a range of spatial codifying practices[11] and spatial norms[12] of behaviours to enable their 'daily flows' (Lysaght 2005) and movement through them (Feldman 1991; Lysaght and Basten 2003). As we had never visited Derry, we had no knowledge of the local topography and therefore did not know which areas were safe and which were not.[13] Additionally, Derry was portrayed by the media as a dangerous place, and I had observed many reports of shootings, bombings, riots, rubber bullets and violence.[14] Certain events, specifically those involving multiple deaths, had a significant impact throughout the region and became 'grievous punctuations in the collective memory of the Troubles' (Smyth and Hamilton 2003: 15). The city bore the legacy of Bloody Sunday[15] and was therefore 'tagged' (Lysaght and Basten 2003) as a 'dangerous place'. Yet I was a frequent visitor to my local city, Belfast, which was equally portrayed by the media as a 'warzone' and also bore the legacy of significant incidents such as Bloody Friday.[16] Yet I considered Belfast to be an exciting and safe place rather than a dangerous place, as I had experienced Belfast, and I knew how it felt. Belfast was familiar and had fanciful shops, pretty colours and special treats. I had no such prior lived experience of Derry and, therefore, no happy memories of shopping trips or treats – only my anxious anticipation as to what I might encounter.[17]

My assessment of 'danger' was also influenced by my emerging feel for this city, based primarily on the negative visual images I was absorbing. Visual codifying practices such as kerbstone painting, murals, parades and graffiti have become part of the demarcation of space, and which serve as explicit identity cues as to which group controls that space (Lysaght and Basten 2003; Zurawski 2005; Goeke-Morey et al. 2009). I had encountered graffiti and barricades before, but in familiar surrounding where I knew what they represented. In these new and unfamiliar surroundings, I was unsure how to interpret their significance. Although some codifying practices were universal in their message (for example, red-white-and-blue painted kerbstones or the red hand of Ulster flags), their interpretation was highly influenced by where, when and how they were used. Visual displays therefore simultaneously serve as a salutation to those of the same group, as a warning to those of the other group (Zurawski 2005), or as a means of antagonizing the other group through reinforcing difference and distinctiveness (Jarman 1999; Trew 2004). All I knew was that Derry felt wrong, and so I distanced myself from it by hiding.[18]

Lysaght (2005) notes that knowing what to fear is crucial to experiencing fear, and as such, fear is not an irrational or uncontrollable emotion but rather a learned response to information cues. As a young child I learned to 'read space', an embodied and multi-sensory appraisal of information cues, in order to assess my situation as normal or abnormal, as safe or dangerous. This process involved drawing on a myriad of information sources including visual cues, media sources, and parental guidance. In the opening vignette I provided a snapshot of this process – a process I will further explore in this chapter. I discuss how I learned to 'read space', how appraisal influenced my coping behaviours and routines in my daily negotiation of space, and how my appraisals and behaviours changed with context and developed over time.

Much research on the Troubles has relied on traditional methods, and there is value to adopting a wider range of conceptual perspectives, research methods and methods of data analyses (Muldoon 2004). In this chapter, I present my autoethnographic account of growing up during the Troubles. Autoethnography uses personal experiences to purposefully reflect on the self within a sociocultural context (Coffey 1999) and is therefore an effective approach for gaining a deep insight into sociocultural phenomena through reflection and analysis of one's personal experiences of those phenomena (Reed-Danahay 1997).[19] In reflecting on past experiences, it is important not to equate memory with history and fact (Cappelletto 2003; Kirmayer 1996). Autoethnography seeks to 'extract meaning from experience rather than to depict experience exactly as it was lived' (Bochner 2000: 270). In painting a picture of one's life, there is no one true picture but rather multiple images and traces of events (Denzin 2014). This chapter is not an event history of the Troubles. I make no claim that what I present is a historically accurate recall of events; but neither is this an act of fiction embellished with fictional characters and dramatized emotions. None of the details have been purposely changed for dramatic effect. However, they are presented from my perspective and I acknowledge that my recall may be hazy and also contested.[20] Simply, these are my memories of selected events,[21] as I remember them.

My Narrative

My Childhood (circa 1966–1977)

I was baptized and raised a Catholic, and the church faith was embedded within our family beliefs and rituals. We did not, however, consider ourselves to be either Irish or nationalist; my parents demonstrated no allegiance to the Republic of Ireland or to any of the nationalist political parties or republican paramilitary organizations, and they instilled tolerance and moderation as core values of our beliefs. I was born and grew up in the town of Lisburn,[22] on the outskirts of Belfast. Lisburn was a predominantly Protestant town but, unlike Belfast or Derry, it had few segregated residential districts, and as such, both communities had to coexist on a daily basis in order for normal life to function. Visual symbols and rituals were prominent throughout the town and they reflected the town's unionist affiliation. In the town centre, union flags and the red hand of Ulster flags flew from lampposts and shop and bar facades. In the more loyalist residential areas, the kerbstones and lampposts were painted red, white and blue, and union flags and the red hand of Ulster flags flew from lampposts and houses. In the mixed residential areas, the displays were less prominent, with the odd flag dotted in the landscape. We lived in such an area. However, as marching season approached, the visual displays increased, and union flag bunting decorated the town centre, flags adorned all of the lampposts in and out of the town, and the residential landscape became more decorated with flags. These visual symbols were a vital cue as they provided a very blatant indicator of the community membership, and its affiliation to that space. As we were part of the minority community in the town, we avoided the predominantly loyalist housing estates and stuck to the integrated residential and communal areas. Like most children in Northern Ireland, I attended a segregated school. This segregation made us easy targets for sectarian attacks. On a number of occasions, we arrived to broken windows, petrol-bombed classrooms or sectarian graffiti. On one occasion one of our classmates arrived at school and we were informed that his family had been burned out of their home the previous evening. He stood before us in the only clothes he had left, and we were asked to gather whatever spare clothes we had at home so that they could be passed onto his family.

In addition to the local community spaces, our town garrisoned the British army headquarters in Northern Ireland during the Troubles. The barracks was heavily fortified with corrugated-iron fencing and barbed wire, and access into and movement around the barracks was monitored and restricted, with security cameras, armed observation posts and vehicular ramps. The sky was filled by a seemingly constant clack of all manner of helicopters, which flew in and out of the army camp. They hovered and circled low in the sky and the sound was deafening. As a child they terrified me, and on hearing them I wanted to run and hide, although I knew that this was not an appropriate course of action as it would arouse their suspicion and could lead to me being shot at. The security forces were highly visible in the town and it was common to see them patrolling either on foot or in armoured vehicles. Once when I was in the car with my mother and father, we ended up driving behind an army patrol vehicle. It was usual for the soldiers to sit in the back, looking out with their guns visible. As we bumped over each pothole in the road, my mother became more agitated, eventually asking my father to pull over. As he did so rather reluctantly, she explained that she had feared that one of the guns would go off and therefore she could not rest until they were out of sight. Therefore, although I was taught no hatred of the armed forces, I came to associate their presence with danger. Although they routinely patrolled the town, I knew not to go too close to them, but I also knew not to run from them or hide from them. Over time I came to recognize what was considered to be a 'normal' or 'abnormal' level of security presence in the town, and therefore what signified routine monitoring and surveillance as opposed to the increased security routines associated with imminent security threats. I learned to differentiate the different sounds associated with the different styles of helicopter and armoured vehicle, which provided a clue to the purpose of their presence and as such the climate of the town.

After a number of bomb attacks in the early 1970s, much of the town centre became a controlled zone with restricted vehicular access. As such, although it was normal to see parked cars in the residential areas, the sight of a parked car in the town centre, near the police station or other public building, was sinister and foreboding. The larger shops conducted security searches on entering, to protect their stores from incendiary attacks and it was normal practice to have both bag and body searches on a routine shopping trip. I remember seeing one of the major stores after an attack. My senses were flooded with the destruction: the black charred remains of what were once colourful toys and trinkets; the sound of water cascading through the ceiling and down the walls; and I can still recall the rancid stench that saturated the air.

I also went on regular shopping trips to Belfast and I looked forward to visiting the large department stores with their fanciful window dressings and the Aladdin's cave of all manner of glittering treasures. I often had tea and cake or fish and chips as an additional treat. However, the city centre was often a target for bombers, and no latitude was granted for Saturday afternoon shoppers. Often a series of scares about devices would be announced or even detonated at the same time to maximize chaos and panic. One afternoon we encountered this, for as we were evacuated from one area we were moved in the direction of an explosion. My senses were overwhelmed: the dull thud; the shattering glass propelling through the air then crashing to the ground; the screaming and shouting; and the sight of helpless policemen and shoppers trying to figure out what to do in all this chaos. For a moment my world stopped before I was jolted back to reality. I was uninjured, but the encounter left its mark, and Belfast excursions became less frequent and eventually stopped.

We also experienced the aftermath of such attacks closer to home as we lived opposite the main hotel in the town, which became a target for bombers. Often a flurry of activity would suddenly ensue in the street outside, followed by a stern knock on the front door, which signalled the order to evacuate our home, or, alternatively to open the windows, close the curtains, and hide out until the 'all clear' was given. As a small child this was all strangely sinister and strangely fascinating at the same time, and I remember frequently peeking from behind the curtains to watch the commotion outside. On one occasion, I could not resist the temptation to watch the little 'robot' defuse the bomb. However, my intrigue was met with castigation from the soldiers to get away from the window and back to safety. Many evacuations turned out to be hoaxes, but the events, hoax or real, left their mark on our home. Our house was damaged a number of times. The front window in our 'good room' (the room kept tidy from the clutter of family life to be enjoyed only by visitors) faced out onto the front of the hotel, and it was in this room that my mother displayed her finest ornaments including a large figurine of a shepherd boy, which sat in the window. As a child it became a fascination that despite our windows rarely surviving a bomb, miraculously, this figurine did. One early evening while cooking dinner, we got the knock to evacuate. It turned out to be a hoax, but we returned home to a rather smoke-damaged kitchen realizing that, in our hurry to leave, we had forgotten to turn off the stove. Over time this surge of pre-evacuation activity and that stern knock became recognizable, and we instantaneously knew the routine.

Even when not physically close to the conflict, radio and television news reports brought us regular updates from around the province. In an age before mass electronic communications and mobile phones, this was our only source of timely information. The radio was switched on first thing in the morning and the television news was the last programme before bedtime. The political climate could change quite rapidly, and the news provided practical information on road blocks, diversions, and temporary 'no-go' areas. In addition, we had daily and weekly local newspapers which brought us more detailed stories and images from around the region. As a child I was surrounded by news and images of the Troubles, and as the conflict intensified I came to understand the violence as part of everyday life. I remember one time as I played with my Cindy dolls, my mother queried why I had pulled off their arms and legs. My response was that they had been in a bomb. My mother was appalled, and I was duly chastised, but I could not understand what I had done wrong.

Once a year, we would depart our home town and head for the Republic of Ireland on holiday. Although my father had a good knowledge of the routes and roads in Northern Ireland, this annual event inevitably meant we had to travel through 'bandit country' (the colloquial term given to the border between Northern Ireland and the Republic of Ireland). Our trips to the Republic highlighted that although we should be experiencing a sense of Catholic solidarity and therefore 'in-group' status, this was not the case. Speaking with a Northern Irish accent and driving a car with a Northern Irish registration plate, we were often victims of suspicion and discrimination. There seemed to be little empathy in the Republic for the situation in the North, and an overwhelming assumption that everyone from the North was a terrorist, paramilitary, thug, or all of the above.

As a child, I was mainly accompanied on my journeys by my parents or my siblings, and as such I relied on them to keep me safe and tell me what to do. The only journey I was allowed to undertake alone was the one to and from school. I knew I had to stick to the prescribed route and follow my mother's warnings: 'don't go near any parked cars' (they had a tendency to blow up); 'don't get too close to the soldiers' (they might shoot you); 'don't get too close to the police' (you might get caught in the crossfire); 'don't pick anything up' (it might explode); 'don't talk to anyone' (information can be used to hurt you). The purpose of this 'rule book' was to ensure that I could travel unnoticed through the shared routes and, de facto, without harm. I not only knew that I had to follow the rules, but also the importance of following them. I was aware, even from a very young age, that this was not a game. Following the rules was not optional. It was the difference between life and death.

My Adolescence (circa 1978–1985)

In 1978 my small world expanded as I started grammar school. The school was about five miles away from our home in the direction of Belfast, and so rather than walking to school, I now had to catch a bus. As our school had a large catchment area I was now part of a wider Catholic community that existed outside of Lisburn. As a child I had been quietly navigating through space unnoticed, however I now travelled as part of a pack and there was less emphasis on being invisible as our identity was overtly displayed by our school uniform. Our school was sandwiched between other Protestant schools and there were regular skirmishes as the pupils all collided at lunchtime and home time at the small series of shops and cafes that serviced the area. These encounters were generally verbal rather than physical, consisting of sectarian name calling or chanting. However, after a number of more serious incidents, the school changed the start and finish times and restricted movements at lunchtime. Similar changes had to be implemented whenever the violence escalated in the region or there was a major event. I remember during the hunger strike when tensions were extremely bitter. We were advised by our headteacher to take an alternative route to school through more neutral areas, and to come to school in 'civvies'. I remember a bus journey characterized by that terrible feeling deep down in my gut that I had not experienced for a long time – fear. However, once inside the school gates, these feelings disappeared. I was safe, and we debated our fashion choices for that day without actually discussing the reason why we were all wearing our ordinary clothes. Ironically however, in an attempt to make us 'invisible' (through not wearing our uniform) and protect us from attack, we simultaneously became 'visible' as the only young people in the area not wearing a school uniform.

Once safely inside the school gates we were generally protected from any events taking place outside. Sometimes it felt like school provided a 'stopwatch' to the Troubles, where every day I learned new and interesting things, where I could laugh and play, act the fool, and be a teenager. However, one day while sitting in class there was the recognizable dull thud and the windows shook. We knew that the bomb was either very close, or a very large bomb somewhere further afield. When the school day ended, I caught my usual bus home. As I travelled closer to my home I recognized the signs that something was not right. As I walked to my home the full extent of the earlier bomb blast became apparent. I felt sick. The hotel stood in ruins and our house had been badly damaged. Shattered glass and displaced roof tiles lay scattered across the front garden. My mother sat in our 'good room', accompanied by an official who was completing compensation forms. My mother was visibly shaken as she sat in this normally pristine room now littered with shattered glass and broken ornaments, including her prized shepherd boy.

As a teenager I was becoming more aware of the violence and of the deep divisions that permeated my society. I also started to develop an awareness of intra-group differences. Grammar school was my first encounter with wealthy Catholics whose parents had professional jobs and who lived in the affluent areas that were generally devoid of the union bunting and painted kerbstones I was accustomed to in my town. This was also the first time I had encountered people from the segregated Catholic areas. One time I arranged to meet a friend who lived in West Belfast. This visit highlighted that being Catholic was only one dimension of identity, and to fit into this environment I would also have to be a republican, and therefore I felt anxious and intimidated by this space.

In my teens, my world was expanding as family holidays were no longer 'at home' but abroad, and school trips also took us to exciting European cities. This gave me an insight into how outsiders viewed Northern Ireland. During a Christmas shopping trip to London, I had purchased a lovely gift for my mother from a well-known department store, which they had expertly wrapped as an added charm. At the airport we were herded from one security check to the next, and I watched resentfully as the security staff unwrapped my present so that they could look inside. The media portrayal of the Troubles was farreaching, and we were constantly reminded – regardless of which European city we were visiting – that we were from a warzone. There was an implicit (and at times more explicit) view that those from Northern Ireland were aggressive warmongers and terrorists. I wanted to shout out 'we are just normal people', but inside I quietly started to wish that I lived in a more 'normal' society.

My Early Adulthood (circa 1985–1989)

In 1985, I went to Queen's University in Belfast to study social anthropology. I now had the opportunity to widen my pool of friends and develop friendships with exciting and interesting new people, not only from across Northern Ireland but from all over the world. However, this was an aspect of my environment that I was finding increasingly difficult to master. One relationship with a Protestant boy who came from a segregated area in Belfast resulted in break up after he was threatened by 'sanctuary' protectors from his local community.[23] A second relationship also hit rough ground as my Protestant partner struggled to differentiate between being a Catholic and being an IRA sympathizer. I was the former but certainly not the latter. However, any time there was a major event he would blur these identities into one. Throughout the Troubles there were periods of fraught violence and anxiety and periods of relative calm, and the political climate had a knock-on impact on interactions with others.

During this period, my family moved house to a location on the security perimeter of the army headquarters. There was a heavy army presence in this area and it was not uncommon to find myself confronted by a camouflaged soldier hiding out in the garden. As a child I had never thought of the security forces as ordinary people; however, as a young woman coming face-to-face with them in such close proximity, it led to a number of awkward encounters. Should I say hello? Should I pretend I had not noticed them? Our new location had resulted in us being sandwiched between loyalist and nationalist families. One night I was woken by that recognizable flurry of activity. The nationalist family had been petrol bombed and they suspected their loyalist neighbours, which led to a period of fraught relationships. This event left me feeling very anxious. What if it had been our loyalist neighbours? Would we be their next targets? This led to a period of intense night-time 'cat napping' and eventually to insomnia. I would sleep when I came home from university and sit up at night, watching and listening, just in case. After a while, I started to stay with friends at Queen's rather than come home.

Whilst studying at university, I secured a summer job at the army headquarters. I now had the opportunity to negotiate this restricted space behind the barricades. This experience brought me into regular contact with soldiers and I came to realize that underneath the weaponry, the uniform and the 'cam cream', they were not that intimidating. They were just people and I began to appreciate that fear was not one dimensional. It was not just the civilians who experienced fear, but also the security forces. I also came to realize that many of these young men had not joined the armed forces because of their ideological values and beliefs but rather because they came from deprived areas and they needed a job. At a department party I met someone special. Having experienced the bitterness and frustration of inter-group romantic relationships between Protestant and Catholic, I found his attitude refreshing. As he was stationed near the border, our contact was intermittent. My commute to visit him involved three bus journeys, with the landscape changing from red-white-and-blue to green-white-and-orange a number of times along the way. His commute to visit me involved using the army bus, which made regular exchanges between the various army camps. Often our visits were cancelled when the journey was considered too dangerous. After a short period, he decided to leave the army and we decided to get married. The week after he made his final journey on the army bus to start his new life as a civilian in Lisburn, the army bus was bombed resulting in multiple deaths. I started to realize that living in Northern Ireland was akin to a cat having nine lives – and I reflected on how many I had used and how many I had left.

As I started to think about the future, about raising a family, about pursuing a career, I became more and more despondent. I was tired of the politics, of the daily spatial manoeuvres and rituals, of the obscene graffiti, and of the hatred. One day we were shopping in a local supermarket when the coin mechanism from our trolley broke and flew into the air, resembling an impressive 'whirring' sound. We both instantly dropped to the floor much to the amusement of the other shoppers. This seemingly insignificant incident dramatically brought my vulnerability into focus, a vulnerability to which I had been exposed every day of my life up to this point, but I was now aware that my appraisal of everyday life was starting to change. As time went by, I could no longer imagine living a 'normal' life in Northern Ireland as the very real abnormality of that life was coming sharply into focus. I felt that I could no longer cope with the stress of living in such a volatile and hostile environment – my coping reserves were empty. Within a few weeks of the supermarket incident, we had secured jobs in England and relocated.

Conclusions

In this chapter, I have presented my own personal experience of growing up during the Troubles. In particular I have explored the factors that influence the appraisal of situations as safe or dangerous, and the resulting coping responses adopted to carry on with a 'normal' life amidst the conflict. Lazarus (1991:151) posits that 'much in life is a restatement of past struggles'. Consequently, throughout our lives we will encounter similar situations and we develop a generalized approach to appraising the significance and meaning of these encounters. As such, we only require the appropriate cue to trigger this meaning. As a child, I quickly learned to recognize the surge of activity that accompanied a threatening event; when a parked car symbolized a threat and when it was just a parked car; when a noise outside was just a noise and when it was more sinister. This multi-sensory appraisal enabled a quick and decisive reaction, and minimized the potential for harm. To enable day-to-day life to function, a series of spatial practices were observed (Lysaght 2005). This unwritten 'rulebook' (Lysaght and Basten 2003) provided guidance on how to navigate safely through shared or unfamiliar places. This rule book was initially informed by my parents, and through their guidance I learned to use a variety of spatial tactics to maintain my day-to-day well-being. These included travelling quietly through shared spaces to limit unnecessary attention, sticking to known 'safe' routes and staying clear of 'no-go' areas, avoiding contact with the security forces in case I got caught in the crossfire, and not engaging in conversations with strangers.

While emphasizing the everyday activities of life, 'it is important not to create a false sense of normality' (Lysaght 2005:128). The political climate in Northern Ireland provided 'an all-embracing atmosphere' (Lysaght and

Basten 2003:238), which influenced spatial tactics. As such, the 'rule book' was not fixed, and during times of political tension – such as marching season or the aftermath of an incident – tactics had to be changed. These rules were not irrational, and I knew this was not a game. The rules were there to keep me safe. My childhood was set in the context of the most intensely violent period of the Troubles (Smyth and Hamilton 2003), and the threats were very 'real', with civilians accounting for the largest share of recorded injuries and deaths as a result of the Troubles (ibid.). It is only now as an adult with my own child that I can reflect on how my mother must have felt waving her husband and children off each morning and hoping that they would all return home again unharmed.

The Troubles provided many 'traumatic punctuations' (Smyth 1998:13) to my 'normal' life. In particular, attacks on my 'sanctuaries' (my home, my school, my family) and 'lucky escapes' were poignant reminders of the volatility of my situation. At times I felt overwhelmed, and I engaged in a range of coping strategies to keep going. Cairns (1996: 55) emphasizes that coping is not the same as 'mastery over the environment' – as in the context of political violence, there is much that cannot be mastered. At times I normalized my environment (my game with my Cindy dolls) and at times I distanced myself from my surroundings (by hiding in the footwell of the car or engaging in frivolous conversations at school). As I developed into a young adult my assessment of my environment changed and I increasingly started to 'misread' encounters as dangerous when they were routine. Lazarus (1991) warns that generalized patterns of appraisal can transcend the specifics of an encounter and therefore trigger inappropriate or exaggerated emotional reactions. Cairns (1996) too, speculated that being predisposed to specific events in childhood could have long-term impacts if these events are encountered again in adulthood. After twenty-two years of living with the 'constant drip of the Troubles' (Cairns nd, cited in Roe et al. 2014), I had had enough. Lazarus (1999) highlights that appraisal involves an assessment of what can be done to improve a situation and whether or not things are likely to change. As a young adult, I started to realize that things would not change. The cumulative emotional and physical impact of living with conflict had depleted my coping resources, and so I joined the many young people of Northern Ireland who contributed to the brain drain of the region as a result of the Troubles (Dunn 1995).

Due to the longevity of the conflict, the Troubles permeated my entire childhood and early adulthood, and residues of this experience still impact my life today. Like a motion picture, emotional experiences proceed continuously over time (Lazarus 1999) and therefore it may be many years before impact becomes apparent (Cairns 1996; Smyth 1998). Lazarus (1991) highlights that although personal narratives provide an interesting insight into how individuals appraise and cope with life's struggles, we also need to make comparisons with others. Smyth (1998: 13) highlights that few adults in Northern Ireland have lived in relative peace, as 'for those of us who grew up here, and who are in [our]forties [or]younger, the Troubles [have]provided the societal context – and often traumatic punctuation and turning points – to our lives as children and adults'. Moving forward there is a need to capture the experiences of other 'ordinary people' who, like me, grew up in the shadow of the Troubles. We know little of the long-term impact of the Troubles (Cairns 1996; Smyth 1998), and yet understanding this impact is an important area for social research so that we can better understand conflict and build more peaceful societies (Muldoon 2004; Cummings et al. 2013).

Angela Mazzetti is part-time PhD student at the School of History and Anthropology, Queen's University, Belfast. She is currently researching the long-term impact of growing up during 'the Troubles' on stress and coping. Relevant publications include 'Using a Visual Timeline Method in Stress Research' (*SAGE Research Methods*, 2014) and 'Occupational Stress Research: Considering the Emotional Impact for the Qualitative Researcher', in P.L. Perrewé, C.C. Rosen and J.R.B. Halbesleben (eds), *The Role of Emotion and Emotion Regulation in Job Stress and Well Being*, Emerald, 2013).

Notes

1. 'The Troubles' are generally considered to have lasted from 1969 with civil unrest and the subsequent mobilization of troops to Northern Ireland to restore order (Dunn 1995) until the signing of the Good Friday Agreement in 1998 (Muldoon 2004). During this period, over 3,700 people were killed (Hargie, Dickson and Nelson 2003) and over 40, 000 were injured (Smyth and Hamilton 2003). Smyth (1998) highlights that although the term 'the Troubles' may seem to understate the scale and severity of the conflict, it has nonetheless become the accepted term for the conflict.
2. For reviews, see Cairns 1987; Cairns and Cairns 1995; Cairns 1996; Smyth 1998; Hargie, Dickson and Nelson 2003; the 2004 special issues of the *Journal of Social Issues*; and the 2014 special issue of the journal *Peace and Conflict: Journal of Peace Psychology*on the life and work of Ed Cairns.
3. These studies have revealed rather conflicting views, which researchers suggest may be due to a variety of conceptual, methodological and ethical issues inherent in the studies that were undertaken. See Mazzetti (2015) for a review of these issues.
4. Hargie, Dickson and Nelson (2003:11) note that the two protagonists of the conflict are generally referred to as the 'Nationalist/Catholic community, which seeks unity with the Republic of Ireland and separation from the United Kingdom' and the 'Unionist/Protestant community, which has the diametrically opposite perspective of supporting the link with the rest of the United Kingdom and opposing unity with the Republic of Ireland'. Despite the complexity of factors influencing the conflict, Murray (1983: 216) suggests that the terms 'Catholic' and 'Protestant' provide convenient, although often misleading, 'labels under which the conflict can be compartmentalised.'
5. See Smyth and Hamilton (2003) for a review of incident statistics by geographical location.

6. Cairns (1996) suggests that we know little about the information sources used by children in their appraisal of events, but he suggests possible sources may include parents (particularly the mother) and the media.
7. Fraser (1973), a child psychiatrist working in Belfast during the Troubles, highlights that the fears expressed by the children referred to him reflected the fears expressed by the children's parents at home. Smyth (1998) suggests that the culture of secrecy that permeated the region resulted in families not openly discussing their experiences or fears. She posits therefore that parents often failed to provide children with the information they needed to understand what was happening in their environment. She suggests that this led to children filling the gaps in their understanding with fantasies that were often worse than reality. Although conducted post-Troubles, in their research of mother–child dyads, Merrilees et al. (2014) found that mothers who are more affected by violence tend to have lower levels of psychological well-being, which in turn is associated with maladjustments in their children.
8. Hereafter referred to as Derry.
9. Although residential segregation predates the Troubles, the escalation of sectarian violence in the early 1970s resulted in large-scale population displacement and relocation, particularly in the cities of Belfast and Derry (Darby 1995; Smyth 1998; Lysaght and Basten 2003).
10. Feldman (1991) posits that a physical and ideological continuum of space evolved in these segregated urban spaces as 'mental maps' to enable the local communities to cope with their spatial interactions. He suggests that this continuum comprised the inner 'sanctuary' which was made up of one homogenous group, an area of 'barricades' to physically protect the sanctuary from attack by the other side, and a series of contested and adversarial 'interfaces' in the spaces that existed between the two community groups.
11. Jarman (1999) highlights how rituals and practices are used in Northern Ireland to symbolize the deeply embedded beliefs and assumptions of the distinct identities.
12. Lysaght and Basten (2003) note that communities developed localized 'unwritten rule books' that prescribed the appropriate behaviour for moving through space. This included staying clear of hostile 'no-go' areas and therefore avoiding conflict; varying the route taken to reduce predictability of movement and therefore reduce the risk of attack; removing or covering any visible symbols of identity such as school uniform to avoid being recognized as a member of the other group; and limiting the disclosure of personal information, such as names, which could disclose community identity. As religious identity was embedded into every aspect of life, it was possible through the process of telling to determine someone's group affiliation by using a series of institutionalized cues learned in childhood – for example, asking someone their forename or surname, which school they last attended, where they lived, which sports they played, etc. (Gallagher 2004; Trew 2004).
13. Smyth (1998) notes that although residential segregation made communities feel safe (because they were living amongst their own), paradoxically it also made the groups more vulnerable as they became marginalized into community enclaves and therefore easily identifiable as 'sitting targets' by the other community. As the number of 'tit-for-tat' attacks escalated, a culture of 'conspiracy consciousness' and suspicion of the 'other side' developed (Boal and Douglas 1982), and Feldman (1991) notes that access to the 'sanctuary' became vehemently protected and restricted. Zurawski (2005) suggests that the communities engaged in active surveillance, with people watching to monitor who travelled through their space, as it became increasingly important to know who everyone was and to which group they belonged.
14. Cairns (1996) highlights that even children who lived in relatively peaceful areas and therefore were not directly exposed to violence had nonetheless acquired detailed information about the conflict from media sources.

15. Bloody Sunday: 30 January 1972. During a civil rights march in Derry, 14 were shot dead by the British Parachute Regiment (Dixon and O'Kane 2011).
16. Bloody Friday: 21 July 1972. The Provisional IRA set off twenty-six bombs in Belfast, killing 11 and injuring 130 (Dixon and O'Kane 2011).
17. Cairns (1996:51) highlights that children may suffer from 'anticipation neurosis'; consequently, children do not have to directly encounter violence to be affected by it.
18. Studies of coping have highlighted that children adopt a variety of strategies such as denial, distancing and an avoidance of thinking about the situation (Cairns 1996; Smyth 1998), and ideologically based active engagement with the political violence (Cairns 1996; Gallagher 2004).
19. This biographical nature of investigation has led to criticisms that autoethnography can be too focused on the self, rendering the technique narcissistic, self-indulgent and 'non-scientific' (Denzin 2014). However self-exposure without an analysis of the broader sociocultural context results in a memoire, a journal entry, but not ethnography (Ellis 2004; Chang 2008). In order to make a scholarly contribution, it is not enough simply to tell an evocative story; we need to reflect on the personal experiences within the context of broader theoretical concepts (Denshire 2014).
20. In writing about myself I bring the lives of others into my narrative (Wall 2008), but their actions are presented from my perspective and I must acknowledge that they may tell a very different story (Chang 2008). Personal experiences are 'shaped by a politics of representation' and hence personal experience is 'neither self-evident nor straightforward: it is always contested and always therefore political' (Denzin 2014: 36).
21. The examples chosen reflect the aims of the volume, namely to develop a spatial approach to social and political interactions in Northern Ireland.
22. Although Lisburn is now categorized as a city, it was a categorized as a town during the Troubles. As such I refer to it throughout this narrative as a town.
23. Boal and Douglas (1982) highlight that surveillance and violence were not always outwardly directed to the 'other' community but often inwardly directed within the group in order to maintain group conformity and norms, a form of what Zurawski (2005) termed 'community policing'. As examples, Boal and Douglas highlight that 'tarring and feathering' and 'kneecapping' were regular punishments for those who deviated from the prescribed community norms of behaviour, such as fraternizing with the 'enemy'.

References

Boal, F.W., and J.N. Douglas. 1982. *Integration and Division: Geographical Perspectives on the Northern Ireland Problem*. London: Academic Press.

Bochner, A.P. 2000. 'Criteria against Ourselves', *Qualitative Inquiry* 5:266–72.

Cairns, E. 1987. *Caught in the Crossfire: Children and the Northern Ireland Conflict*. New York: Syracuse University Press.

———. 1996. *Children and Political Violence*. Oxford: Blackwell.

Cairns, E., and T. Cairns. 1995. 'Children and Conflict: A Psychological Perspective', in S. Dunn (ed.),*Facets of the Conflict in Northern Ireland*. Hampshire, UK: Macmillan Press, pp.97–113.

Cappelletto, F. 2003. 'Long-Term Memory of Extreme Events: From Autobiography to History', *Journal of the Royal Anthropological Institute* 9: 241–60.

Chang, H. 2008. *Autoethnography as Method*. Walnut Creek, CA: Left Coast Press.

Coffey, P. 1999. *The Ethnographic Self*. London: Sage.

Cummings, E.M., et al. 2013. 'Longitudinal Relations between Sectarian and Non-Sectarian Community Violence and Child Adjustment in Northern Ireland', *Development and Psychopathology* 25: 615–27.

Darby, J. 1995. 'Conflict in Northern Ireland: A Background Essay', in S. Dunn (ed.),*Facets of the Conflict in Northern Ireland*. Hampshire, UK: Macmillan, pp. 15–26.

Denshire, S. 2014. 'On Auto-ethnography', *Current Sociology Review* 62: 831–50.

Denzin, N. 2014. *Interpretive Autoethnography*. Thousand Oaks, CA: Sage.

Dixon, P., and E. O'Kane. 2011. *Northern Ireland since 1969*.Harlow: Pearson Education.

Dunn, S. 1995. *Facets of the Conflict in Northern Ireland*. Hampshire, UK: Macmillan.

Ellis, C. 2004. *The Ethnographic I: A Methodological Novel about Autoethnography*. Walnut Creek, CA: AltaMira Press.

Feldman, A. 1991. *Formations of Violence: The Narrative of the Body and Political Terror in Northern Ireland*. Chicago, IL: University of Chicago Press.

Fraser, M. 1973. *Children in Conflict*. Trowbridge: Redwood Press.

Gallagher, T. 2004. 'After the War Comes Peace? An Examination of the Impact of the Northern Ireland Conflict on Young People', *Journal of Social Issues* 60: 629–42.

Goeke-Morey, M.C., et al. 2009. 'The Differential Impact on Children of Inter- and Intra-Community Violence in Northern Ireland', *Peace and Conflict: Journal of Peace Psychology* 15: 367–83.

Hargie, O., D. Dickson and S. Nelson. 2003. 'A Lesson Too Late for the Learning? Cross-community Contact and Communication among University Students', in O. Hargie and D. Dickson (eds), *Researching the Troubles: Social Science Perspectives on the Northern Ireland Conflict*. Edinburgh: Mainstream, pp. 85–106.

Hobfoll, S.E. 2002. 'Alone Together: Comparing Communal versus Individualistic Resiliency', in E. Frydenberg (ed.), *Beyond Coping: Meeting Goals, Visions and Challenges*. Oxford: Oxford University Press, pp. 63–81.

Jarman, N. 1999. 'Commemorating 1916, Celebrating Difference: Parading and Painting in Belfast', in A. Forty and S. Küchler (eds), *The Art of Forgetting*.Oxford: Berg, pp. 171–95.

Kirmayer, L.J. 1996. 'Landscapes of Memory', in P. Antze and M. Lambek (eds), *Tense Past: Cultural Essays in Trauma and Memory*. London: Routledge, pp. 173–98.

Lazarus, R.S. 1991. *Emotion and Adaptation*.New York: Oxford University Press.

———. 1999. *Stress and Emotion*. New York: Springer.
Lysaght, K.D. 2005. 'Catholics, Protestants and Office Workers from the Town: The Experience and Negotiation of Fear in Northern Ireland', in K. Milton and M. Svašek (eds), *Mixed Emotions: Anthropological Studies of Feeling*. Oxford: Berg, pp.127–43.
Lysaght, K., and A. Basten. 2003. 'Violence, Fear and 'the Everyday': Negotiating Spatial Practice in the City of Belfast', in E.A. Stanko (ed.), *The Meanings of Violence*. London: Routledge, pp.224–44.
Mazzetti, A.S. 2015. 'Children of the Troubles: The Need to Explore the Long-Term Impact on Appraisal and Coping', *Explorations of Northern Irishness Special Edition, Queen's Political Review* 3: 54–64.
Merrilees, C.E., et al. 2014. 'Youth in Contexts of Political Violence: A Developmental Approach to the Study of Youth Identity and Emotional Security in their Communities', *Peace and Conflict: Journal of Peace Psychology* 20: 26–38.
Muldoon, O.T. 2004. 'Children of the Troubles: The Impact of Political Violence in Northern Ireland', *Journal of Social Issues* 60: 453–68.
Murray, D. 1983. 'Schools and Conflict', in J. Darby (ed.), *Northern Ireland: The Background to the Conflict*. Belfast: Appletree Press, pp.136–50.
Reed-Danahay, D. 1997. *Auto/ethnography: Rewriting the Self and the Social*. Oxford: Berg.
Roe, M.D., et al. 2014. 'Professor Ed Cairns: A Personal and Professional Biography', *Peace and Conflict: Journal of Peace Psychology* 20: 3–12.
Smyth, M. 1998. *Half the Battle: Understanding the Effects of the 'Troubles' on Children and Young People in Northern Ireland*. Belfast: Litho Printers.
Smyth, M., and J. Hamilton. 2003. 'The Human Costs of the Troubles', in O. Hargie and D. Dickson (eds), *Researching the Troubles: Social Science Perspectives on the Northern Ireland Conflict*. Edinburgh: Mainstream, pp.15–36.
Trew, K. 2004. 'Children and Socio-cultural Divisions in Northern Ireland', *Journal of Social Issues* 60: 507–22.
Wall, S. 2008. 'Easier Said than Done: Writing an Autoethnography', *International Journal of Qualitative Methods* 7: 38–53.
Zurawski, N. 2005. 'I Know Where You Live!': Aspects of Watching, Surveillance and Social Control in a Conflict Zone (Northern Ireland)', *Surveillance and Society* 2: 498–512.

2

Crafting Identities

Prison Artefacts and Place-Making in Pre- and Post-ceasefire Northern Ireland

Erin Hinson

> The prison is probably some of the darkest hours I've ever had, but there was rays of sunshine, and the artwork was one of the means of escaping, one of the means of maybe reasserting myself as a person, as an individual – I am not a number. And the artwork represents memories of that time, what I was thinking and where I was at, and I suppose they are a double-edged reminder, in terms of the time when I had to stand strong and I could study and I could train and I could paint. But it's also a reminder of the place that I was in, which afforded me so much time to do that. But no one can get away from the fact that spending twelve to fifteen years in that prison affects you and your development and the course of your life. And I had made that choice and I suppose I was fortunate being able to paint and draw and make things. That was one of the ways I filled my time.
>
> —'Dave Smith', former UVF prisoner

Contemporary academic accounts of prison experiences have often utilized the memories of former prisoners in order to recall the physical and social space of the prison (Garland 2001; Sinnerton 2002; Novosel 2013; McAtackney 2014; Smith 2014). In light of this, some scholarship has advocated for explorations into the role of material culture as an elemental part of this dialectic relationship (Saunders 2004, 2009; Carr and Mytum 2012). Aiming to draw connections between materiality and space within the compounds of the Maze/Long Kesh prison,[1] which operated during the conflict in Northern Ireland from 1972 to 1988, this chapter will address the memories of Ulster Volunteer Force and Red Hand Commando (UVF/RHC) prisoners concerning their engagement with craft production. As

UVF/RHC organizational leadership intentionally introduced material production to the fabric of prison life, reinforcing it as a method of socialization for incoming prisoners, the production of artefacts by these prisoners provides a nuanced lens through which to examine the interaction of space, place and materiality within this specific prison environment.

While these artefacts were produced within a specific time and context, they now exist today within the context of a post-ceasefire Northern Ireland. These remnants survive in various contemporary settings, from storage containers or home displays to archival collections across the province. Consequently, this opening vignette demonstrates how the artefacts function now as repositories for memories and identities that are being renegotiated and reinterpreted through current discourses of materiality, spatial and identity politics. As many of these objects are being displayed in a new exhibition space, creating a place where memories of past experiences are reimagined in the present for a future political project, this chapter will begin by introducing this exhibition through a discussion of former prisoners' engagement in conflict transformation. This will provide contextualization for the memories recalled and the experiences described.

Following from this contextualization, the chapter will provide a brief discussion of imprisonment as spatial politics. As evidenced by the epigraph at the start of the chapter, prisoners made direct connections between their engagement with the production of handicrafts and the maintenance of their individual and group identities. Though constantly faced with the stark reality of imprisonment, where the prisoners were physically and emotionally removed from society, community and family, it demonstrates how material culture functioned to maintain a sense of individuality. Through exploring the effects of this interrelationship, this chapter will uncover the significance of artefact production to the personal and political experiences of the compound prison environment. The chapter will conclude by arguing how the artefacts constitute evidence of the former prisoners' desire to challenge the one-dimensional perspective of their identities as political agents and killers, instead humanizing their prison experience and substantiating their identities as craftsmen.

Contemporary Political and Spatial Context

After surviving over twenty-five years of sustained intercommunal violent conflict[2], the declaration of the Combined Loyalist Military Command (CLMC)[3] ceasefire in August 1994 put many former loyalist combatants and prisoners on the path towards redefining themselves and their experiences during the conflict. Although for some the origins of this work began well before the ceasefires, the CLMC announcement ushered in a new political and spatial arena for former combatants. The many processes and projects with which former UVF/RHC members have sought to redefine their role in a peaceful, post-ceasefire Northern Ireland has been the subject of much academic discussion (McEvoy 1998; Ervine and McCauley 2001; Rolston 2007; Shirlow and McEvoy 2008; McCauley, Tonge and Shirlow 2010). However, this chapter marks the one of the first publications directly addressing the materiality and spatial politics of these processes of conflict transformation. The narratives analysed throughout this chapter represent memories of past engagement with the production of material culture within the compound system. These memories are being recalled within a specific and significant spatial context that exists within and has been influenced by the UVF and RHC's engagement in the internationally acclaimed process of Decommissioning, Demobilization and Reintegration (DDR) (Rolston 2007). As such, I will first need to briefly outline how these processes led to the creation of the site-specific spatial and emotional context for my research.

Shortly after the announcement of the CLMC ceasefire a group of former UVF/RHC prisoners founded the organization EPIC (Ex-Prisoners Interpretive Centre), whose primary objective was 'to address the problems surrounding the reintegration of politically motivated prisoners into the community' (EPIC 2015). The founding of EPIC and the involvement of many former prisoners in a wide range of community work allowed these men to engage with their communities in a different spatial and political context than they had in their pre-prison lives. As these community-driven projects continued to grow throughout the 1990s, former prisoners also began to address the legacy of their imprisonment, and they developed new methods for encouraging different understandings of loyalist prison experiences.[4]

These efforts continued as the peace process advanced into the 2000s; however, in order to contextualize the current engagement with UVF/RHC prison material culture, I will need to introduce the narrative of one former UVF prisoner whose work since his release has been instrumental in furthering this development. Almost all of my interviews with ex-prisoners, including the opening excerpt from 'Dave', took place at an exhibition space in North Belfast, which displays handicrafts and artworks produced by UVF and RHC compound, H-block, and current prisoners. The space is the project of Action for Community Transformation (ACT), a non-profit organization that helps former UVF members to transition from paramilitary to community membership through engaging with the processes of DDR. The exhibition space was created by former YCV prisoner William Mitchell, ACT's project coordinator.[5] In our interview, William explained that the idea for this space derived from his experiences working on an ACT Initiative cross-community project a few years previously. He recalled that he had been facilitating a group visit by young Israeli and Palestinian people, and after the group had been hosted by republican ex-prisoners in their museum space the day before.

> I met them in the car park of the Shankill Leisure Centre because we didn't have an office at the time. We didn't have a space, and when they wanted to see what they'd seen in comparison to the day before, they were taken on a walking tour of the murals of the Shankill. We had nothing to take them to. That was the eye opener for me at the time. I was thinking, we tell this story that's almost virtual because we had nothing physical that firms it up – we need to create a physical space that helps support the telling of the story.

Therefore, in creating this space, which first opened in June 2014, William and the ACT staff and volunteers have developed a new physical space and an emotional place to engage with contemporary processes of conflict transformation.[6] As such, though the artefacts were produced pre-ceasefire, during the height of the conflict, they are now being re-contextualized post-ceasefire in a project that aims to use the artefacts as a method for discussing conflict transformation.

For William the political machinations of contemporary loyalism originated in the prison experience, and the prison handicrafts are an integral part of that narrative:

> It can all be traced back to special category prison, prison-ship, and we don't shy away from that. It was significantly influenced at the time, as you know, by Gusty Spence. So the reason for showing it in the form that it's shown in, mostly through handicrafts and art, is because it's the one physical remainder from that time that demonstrates that. So it's the one thing that people have kept hold of, that they're willing to share; there are other personal things there, there are letters on exhibition and so on and so forth, but that's the main physical part of what's left of that era.

For most of my participants, their motivations for engaging with my research are connected to similar ideas of demonstrating a different perspective of the UVF/RHC prison experience (DS 2015; JC 2015; RW 2015; JW 2015; AJ 2015).[7] In this sense, their memories about past experiences with materiality become part of this contemporary political project. Several of my participants have donated objects for display at the ACT space because they feel strongly that the handicrafts demonstrate an undervalued aspect of the prison experience (DS 2015; JW 2015; RW 2015). As a result, their contemporary narratives about the production and meaning of the handicrafts are a part of their post-prison identities – identities that seek to challenge the dominant perception of them as political agents who went outside the law in order to commit crimes against society. Moreover, as the objects are given new meaning through placement in a new spatial context, those identities and meanings combine to illustrate the potency of memory and materiality in creating a sense of place for former prisoners outside the original place of their imprisonment. Therefore, having contextualized the narratives used in their contemporary political and spatial meanings, this chapter will now analyse the production of prison handicrafts through the theoretical lens provided by Milligan's concept of place attachment.

Prison Background, Spatial Politics, and the Compound System

In order to understand the prison experiences of the Ulster Volunteer Force (UVF) and Red Hand Commando (RHC), we will first briefly explore the spatial and psychological politics of imprisonment in pre-ceasefire Northern Ireland.[8] Following a formal alliance in 1972, the UVF and RHC agreed that all prisoners in the Maze/Long Kesh prison would be subject to UVF leadership. As a result, the structure and routine of the UVF prison leadership worked to enforce similar methods of socialization, constructions of prison identities and place attachments, and engagement with material culture for all affected prisoners.[9]

The British government created the compound system of institutional confinement when they sent the newly created special category paramilitary prisoners to the Maze/Long Kesh site in December 1972.[10] The placing of special category prisoners within the compounds led to an unconventional method for containing sentenced prisoners.[11] The primary goal of conventional prison systems was 'the deprivation of liberty with a limited reformatory role' (von Tangen Page 1998: 25). Within twentieth-century penology, the primary goal of imprisonment was the removal of the criminal offender from the physical space of everyday society and community. Therefore, the prisoners were immediately placed in a spatial environment that exists outside the bounds of ordinary life.[12] As a result, the spatial politics of the prison were represented by the dominant power structure in place. In a conventional prison the structures gave the prison authorities the power to exercise control over both subjects and society (Foucault 1977). Prior to the construction of the compound system, prisons in Northern Ireland exemplified these characteristics of conventional containment.

In contrast to conventional prisons, the compound system structure completely altered the normal patterns of prison power relations, as it transferred a significant portion of the operational power from the prison authorities to the paramilitary leadership.[13] The effects of this unconventional method can be further understood by examining how the prisoner's self-perceptions changed with their transition to imprisonment. Crawford argues that the most noteworthy shift in prisoner identity within conventional confinement occurs in what he termed 'the translation from normal to discredited' (Crawford 1979: 16), or what Goffman classed as the 'process where the self is systematically mortified' (Goffman 2006: 174). As I will argue in this chapter, the unconventional structure of the compound prison arrested the processes of translation and mortification by providing a physical space and a communal social place, which in-turn encouraged individuality and self-determination amongst the prisoners (Crawford 1979, 1982; Garland 2001; McEvoy 2001).

One of the first actions carried out by the prison authorities within a traditional system is the removal of personal possessions – an act that represents the transition of the inmate from 'individual person' to 'deindividualized prisoner', and demonstrates the dominant power groups control over the prisoner's personal space (Goffman 2006).[14] As a result, the structure of institutional life is characterized by a 'loss of autonomy, material possessions, individual expression, community, and family life, and even basic personal security' (Casella 2007: 2). However, having arrested the normal processes of translation from person to criminal, the compound system and special category status left the UVF/RHC leadership with a confined space devoid of that traditional institutional structure. What resulted was the implementation of a UVF command structure that created both time and physical space for prisoners to engage with material culture. As UVF leadership further developed this structure, they intentionally included modes of artefact production – handicrafts and mural painting – into the structure of everyday life.

Prison Experiences and Material Culture

Elementally, my contribution to this edited collection is concerned with how the prisoners formed place attachments to the prison's physical and emotional spaces through making and using objects. Milligan (1998: 2) defined place attachment as the 'emotional link formed by an individual to a physical site that has been given meaning through interaction'. She explained the two-step process of place attachment, arguing that a site first becomes known, thus transitioning from a space to a place, and then 'to the extent that a known site becomes an object to which an individual is emotionally bonded, as opposed to one that is simply known about, the site becomes one to which a place attachment has been formed' (ibid.: 7). Hence, when a person forms an emotional bond to a site, be it positive or negative, they have also formed a place attachment.

An integral element to forming a place attachment is the creation of a place identity. Milligan employed Hummon's concept of the term, which he defined as an interpretation of the self that uses place to signify a specific identity (Hummon 1986: 34). He maintained that these place identities emerge 'as the individual, drawing on experiences and cultural imagery, defines his or her relation to the environment' (ibid.: 34). Consequently, investigating ex-prisoner narratives regarding their involvement in artefact production will reveal how they used these experiences and the cultural imagery around them to define their individual and collective relationship to the space and place of the prison.

Milligan's concept of 'locational socialization', in which people learn about the meaning of certain locations and how to behave socially within those locations, is a critical element to analysing the role of artefact production within the social environment of the compounds (Milligan 1998: 16). She utilized Lofland's definition, whereby one 'continually learns about the meaning of different locations, about what is expected to go on where, and who is expected to be doing it' (Lofland 1985: 69, in Milligan 1998: 16). Combining the Milligan and Hummon approaches, allows us to examine whether the production of artefacts facilitated the creation of prison place identities and attachments.

Although these prisoner narratives will be used to better understand the formation of place attachments in the past, the recollections are occurring contemporaneously. Both Svašek (2008) and Belk (1990) recognized the emotive power of nostalgia when recalling past experiences and discourses. Nostalgic responses, which occur when recalling past events and experiences, strengthen any emotional bond to the place of that recollection, in both a material and an imagined sense. Therefore, the nostalgic recollections of the prison experience found in the selected ex-prisoner narratives are emblematic of Belk's concept of 'rich textural memories', and are produced through discussions of prisoner engagement with material culture. Critical to understanding the evocation of these nostalgic memories is the contemporary context in which they were produced. As such, this chapter concludes with analysing how the narratives of past experience and present re-experience are reinterpreted and redefined through a contemporary exhibition of prison-made artefacts.

Production of Handicrafts

Without question, the most significant form of material culture was the production of what the prisoners termed 'handicrafts'. Handicrafts ranged from a diverse production of leatherworks to glass painting, pin boards, canvas painting, woodworking, decorative handkerchiefs and pillow cases, and objects used in parading, such as flags, banners and collerettes. Political identities and symbols associated with the UVF/RHC were common themes, but many artefacts also displayed aspects of other personal or cultural identities. Handicraft production occurred in two distinct phases and locations. A comparison of these locations will further illuminate how handicrafts enabled the production of various place attachments and identities throughout the UVF/RHC prison experience.

Crumlin Road Prison Production

For many prisoners, their introduction to handicrafts occurred while held on remand within the Crumlin Road prison (MT 2015; JC 2014; RW 2014; AJ 2015). The conventional format of the Crumlin Road and the transitory nature of prisoners on remand[15] limited their ability to produce a variety of handicrafts, and most former prisoners stated that painting or drawing on cloth handkerchiefs was the prominent form of handicraft (MT 2015; JC 2014; RW 2014; DS 2014). Place attachments are not inherently positive in their construction or maintenance (Milligan 1998). Although most ex-prisoners described the production of handicrafts as a fundamentally positive experience, that positive experience must always be considered within an individual prisoner's overall experience in and attachment to their place of imprisonment. However, for many former prisoners, handicraft production did represent a positive element of the otherwise predominantly negative experience of being imprisoned. This complex formation of place attachments is easily identifiable in Dave Smith's statement in the opening vignette. For Dave, a former UVF prisoner who served twelve years, the handicrafts he produced are a reminder of the experience of making them, but they are also a reminder of 'the place that I was in, which afforded me so much time to do that'. This and other multifaceted attachments will be further examined through other ex-prisoner narratives. Additionally, as the Crumlin Road represented a traditionally formatted prison, one which embodied Casella's (2007) characteristics of institutional life (outlined above), the narratives uncovered by my research reflect a more ambivalent and negative place attachment than similar compound narratives.

John Craig, a former UVF prisoner, maintained that his identity as a 'political prisoner' was initially formed and supported by collective actions in the Crumlin Road, such as making handicrafts and military-style drilling, and reinforced with feelings of comradeship (JC 2014). Through John's memories about his early experiences in prison, Milligan's notion of the transition from space to place (outlined above) can be utilized to explore how his narratives demonstrate the formation of site specific identities and place attachments. Exemplifying the intrinsic multivocality of identities, he claimed the politicized identity, as a UVF political prisoner, became more prevalent during imprisonment because 'in the prison you weren't necessarily the brother or the son, you were the UVF prisoner, and that was the trumping identity'. During my first interview with John we were talking about various forms of handicrafts when he made a direct connection between the 'trumping identity' of the UVF prisoner and craft production. Reflecting on the meaning of that production, he stated: 'We were transferring that identity and the various symbols into the leather, and sending them out'. In this sense, the handicrafts represented the physical transference of that political symbolism from inside the space of the prison to the outside world. Therefore, the interrelated social actions of creating the object and sending it out to family and supporters re-established and maintained the presence of the outside world in the combined processes of prison place-making and material culture.

These processes manifested differently in the environment of the Crumlin Road prison. The conventional design of the prison utilized wings and cells in order to separate and isolate the prisoners, resulting in a confining spatial environment, which limited their mobility. John recalled that decorating handkerchiefs took his mind off the predicaments of his life as a prisoner, having to live in a highly controlled environment: 'It was like a pastime, and while it was a pastime it was also a distraction, a distraction from the reality of the prison and the prison walls and the prison cell, and being in the cell with three people, and three people having to share that small space in some way'.

This sentiment was echoed by Richard Warren, another former UVF prisoner, whose perception of the handkerchiefs implied a correlation between the social action of making the object and the strength (or lack thereof) of the place attachment to the Crumlin Road. When I asked Richard what his first experience of handicrafts was, it led to a discussion about the challenges of the volatile environment of the Crumlin Road prison. As he explained, the nature of remand, where prisoners are constantly moving between prison cell and courtroom, leads to an unstable environment:

> On remand it wasn't about doing it for trying to make any kind of money, it was maybe just passing time. But on remand the place was just completely unsettled; you had different people coming through all the time. There was trouble in the jail near enough every week. So you never really got much, you never settled in to doing anything, you never felt settled.

He also contended that this unstable environment limited prisoner access to implements, thus limiting the scope of production and the variety of design. Further elaborating on these difficulties, he stated: 'Because you were on remand it was pretty unstable, so you wouldn't have had a great deal; there wouldn't have been a great deal of implements in it – most of the handicrafts and the hankies would have been UVF badges, YCV badges'.[16]

Through this exploration of personal narratives from John and Richard, I have found that the handkerchiefs (Figure 2.1) became an ephemeral

Figure 2.1 Handkerchief made in Maze/Long Kesh prison. Photograph courtesy of ACT.

signification of the prison experience in the Crumlin Road, with the unsettled environment of the prison having directly impacted the production of artefacts. The cloth material used was thin and cheap, and the writing implements were basic, easily accessible and replaceable, reflecting the instability and uncertainty of life on remand, and revealing the construction of tenuous place attachments. Milligan (1998) argued that a key element of place attachment is its inevitable disruption, a process which takes place when a group or an individual is displaced from a physical site. Milligan further elaborated this contention by explaining that 'any physical relocation results in a change in experience, and in the possibility of linking a new experience to past experiences' (ibid.: 9). As such, UVF/RHC prisoners' attachments to the Crumlin Road became disrupted with their transfer to the compound system at the Maze/Long Kesh site. Without the direct physical link to the prison, the emotional bond established through the place attachments weakened with time and distance. However, John and Richard's recollections demonstrate that an element of these place attachments exists in their memories of the handicraft production. Nonetheless, the disruption of their place attachments to the Crumlin Road allowed them to form new attachments to the Maze/Long Kesh as they adjusted to the drastically different spatial and social environment of the compounds.

Compound Prison Production

Milligan's concept of 'locational socialization' will now be applied in order to analyse how the prisoners learned to perform specific identities within the compound system, according to their engagement with material production and other social actions. The compound's military-style regime functioned to socialize the incoming prisoners into the distinct prison structure and daily life. When I asked John to describe how much of his day was spent on handicrafts, he outlined the daily routine as follows:

> Everybody had to be out of their bed by nine o'clock, they had to be ready for ten o'clock to do the general duties. Everybody had a role to play with regards to the cleaning and upkeep of the cages [loyalist and republican prisoner terminology for the compounds], whether that was picking up the buts from around the yard, scrubbing the ablutions, or cleaning out the actual hut itself. Everybody had a role to play. So that would have lasted for half an hour to an hour; after that then you could do what you wanted. But you know, when I said you had to be out of your bed by nine o'clock, we also had to make our own bed packs, so it was quite a military type of regime that was there at that particular time. So normally from eleven o'clock to maybe four o'clock would have been the period when people could do whatever they wanted – so that's when most of the handicrafts would have been done in that particular period.[17]

As evidenced in that extract, the making of handicrafts became an integral element of the compound regime and was therefore a significant method of locational socialization as a sub-process of place attachment formation.

Several former prisoners spoke to me about the significant change between the handicraft production in the Crumlin Road and that in the compounds, both in terms of availability of materials and in the time and space available to produce objects (MT 2015; JC 2014; RW 2014; DS 2014). The unconventional structure of the compounds represented a different physical and political space for place- and object-making. Consequently, I have found that ex-prisoner narratives affirm that these processes of locational socialization occurred in part through the enskillment of handicraft production. This is most evidently shown through the narrative descriptions of the compound cooperative system.

With minimal access to various handicrafts while held on remand in the Crumlin Road, for many prisoners the compounds represented their first interaction with wide-scale production. When he spoke about his personal transition from the Crumlin Road to the compounds, John emphatically stated:

> Going down to Long Kesh prison camp and into the cages, it was almost like a cottage industry. The handicrafts, there was various handicrafts, the leathercraft – and the leathercraft varied between the wallets, the handbags, the plaques even – and you had the soft toys, where a few people done the soft toys, and then you had the glass making and some people for short periods of time were doing work with matchsticks and lollipop sticks, building windmills.

As mentioned earlier, although the prisoners were kept to a strict routine, their free time in the afternoon allowed for the development of this so-called 'cottage industry'. Initially this industry, which in effect became an assembly line of handicraft production, supported efforts to raise funds for prisoner welfare. During our second interview when I asked Andrew Jones, a former UVF prisoner, if he had made a lot of items for the cooperative, he immediate responded, 'At the start yeah, everyone did'. Andrew's response demonstrates how the mandatory participation in cooperative handicrafts facilitated individual prisoners' adaptation to the communal social environment of the compounds. As he continued to speak about the cooperative system he explained that, at least at the start, 'there was a real emphasis, not just on handicrafts, there was an emphasis on this, socialism, or maybe it was a form of communism, and that everybody sort of was treated equal and if something came in from the outside it had to be divided equally'. This illustrates how the cooperative system was utilized, particularly in the early years of the compounds, when conditions were difficult and provisions limited (Green 1998), in order to sustain a standard of living within the UVF/RHC compounds. It also shows cooperative production as integral to the communal environment of the compounds, where handicraft supplies and the benefits of their commoditization were shared equally amongst prisoners (MT 2015). This communality illustrates the politicization of the productive process through its framing as an equalizing, 'communist' activity.

Another essential element to the cooperative system was the distribution of these communally produced items through the work of prisoner welfare organizations. This distribution created tenuous links between the prisoners' material production and their supporters and family members outside the prison. Through this link the family members functioned as active agents, often bringing or sending materials and supplies into the prisoners. Additionally, within this process the artefacts functioned as material mediators of identifications and long-distance support. During our final interview, Richard and I were discussing how handicrafts were bought and sold on the outside when he relayed a personal anecdote about his family's interaction with the cooperative. He explained that a lot of items made for the cooperative would have been balloted, or auctioned, in local clubs in order to raise funds for the two main prisoner welfare organizations, the Orange Cross and the Loyalist Prison Welfare Association, who were then responsible for allocating the profits from the sale of these items. Given the 'communistic' approach of UVF/RHC leadership at the time, this meant that the proceeds would be distributed equally amongst all prisoners.

Although it was understood that these ballots were only to be used for items produced through the cooperative, several industrious family members attempted to ballot individual items as well, and as a result faced consequences from paramilitary leadership. Richard explained: 'Some people did that and my aunt done it a few times and got her knuckles rapped for doing it. So it would have got people coming along to you and saying you're not allowed to ballot, that's the cooperative ballot and you're not allowed to do it as an individual'. As such, balloting items to raise money for an individual prisoner, as opposed to for the collective benefit of the group, was viewed as subverting the purpose of the welfare organization for personal gain. Richard's memory about his aunt receiving punishment for this very action speaks to the role of material culture in the power and control established by paramilitary organizations, both inside and outside the prison. This particular narrative demonstrates how, through the complex processes of the collective production and sale of handicrafts, the prisoners remained connected to their organization, supporters and family. Furthermore, in order to benefit all prisoners, the UVF/RHC prison leadership emphasized the collective group place identity of 'political prisoner' over any personal identities through the politicization of the production process and the enforced participation in the cooperative system.

Another significant process developed through the prison material culture was the enskillment of prisoners into a wide range of media and techniques. All incoming prisoners were expected to participate in the cooperative system, and were enskilled into various techniques through this experience. For Richard, the co-op marked his introduction into leatherworking, having previously encountered pinboard making on his first stay in the compounds while awaiting trial. Upon arrival at the compounds, he remembered that a new prisoner would be allocated an 'easy element of the

Figure 2.2 Leather chequebook case made in Maze/Long Kesh prison. Photograph courtesy of ACT.

leather end of things' that would have indicated their role within the co-op and their work in support of the organization. This communal element to artefact production represents the UVF's emphasis on the maintenance of a group identity, linked to the political ideology of the UVF/RHC. Richard recalled that 'the co-op element of it [handicrafts] would have been for the organization. Your role within the co-op, you either did the modelling end of the things, or you were inside [working on the inside of the leather], or you were a dyer, or you were a thonger'. His narrative also outlined the various skills – modelling, dying or thonging (hand stitching the leather) – imparted to incoming prisoners as a part of their participation in the cooperative system (for example, see Figure 2.2).

Essentially, these ex-prisoner accounts substantiate how the handicraft production enabled locational socialization on a site-specific level. Thus, as the prisoners were introduced to handicraft production in the form of the cooperative system and taught certain skills in order to fulfil their assigned role, they were also taught what to expect and how to behave within the social structure of the compounds. Through involvement with this aspect of prison material culture, the prisoners created a sense of place within the compounds, as the physical space was given meaning through interaction (Milligan 1998: 2). The physical spaces of the compound huts were also transformed through these processes of enskillment. When

I asked Andrew to speak about his involvement in the cooperative, he recalled:

> I can remember, one of my memories of Compound 11 was each hut had a handicraft table – in fact the hut I was in had two, they'd one at the top of the hut and one down near the bottom. They were huge tables, they were like a basic sort of banquet table; it was just a tubular steel frame with a probably 12 x 6 top on it. And you get a dozen, maybe fifteen people around it. Now most of it was used for cards, playing cards, but on occasion, you know and at the very start we did have some handicraft classes.

As prisoners sat around these large tables, placed in the middle of the shared spaces of the huts, they also transformed the social space of the hut into a place where the outside world was debated and discussed. Many former prisoners have told me that the fabric of their daily lives was established in these places. Men would share personal stories, newly acquired literature or music, as well as anything discovered from local or world news events, while being enskilled into handicraft production, or during other social activities, such as card playing, all of which took place in these communal living spaces (DS 2014; RW 2014; JC 2014; JW 2015, AJ 2015). As a result, the outside world, imagined through personal stories of pre-prison life, remained an integral part of their prison place identities and attachments.

As I have demonstrated, the narratives relating to the cooperative production uncover the development of prisoner place attachments through their enskillment into artefact production. Stokowski argued that the 'power of place is not only in its aesthetic or behavioural possibilities, or its iconic status, but in its ability to connect people in society, encourage development of personal and social identities, and reinforce sociocultural meanings' (Stokowski 2002: 373). Thus, the innate performativity of social identities within the cooperative system elucidates how UVF/RHC compound prisoners formed powerful place attachments through the construction of prison place identities. The prisoners were encouraged to develop connections with each other through this collective production of object, identity and culture. The handicrafts produced did facilitate the creation of group place attachments through locational socialization. However, the production also held personal meaning for prisoners, which varied in strength and significance according to individual experiences, and demonstrated varied levels of enskillment as well as personal place identities and attachments.

For most compound prisoners, artefact production represented one of many activities with which they chose to fill their days. Motivations for this engagement in personal production represent themes of personal development, psychological and emotional survival, increased self-autonomy, enskillment, and economic gain. Several former prisoners recalled a predisposition towards creativity, and admitted having an interest in art prior to joining a paramilitary organization (JW 2015; MT 2015; DS 2014). On average these men were more likely to continue steady production throughout their sentence, while other men benefited more from the combination of a physical fitness regime, informal reading or formal education (RW 2014; JC 2014; AJ 2014).[18] Not every UVF/RHC prisoner participated in personal handicraft production, but for those who did the primary benefit was the physical and mental engagement in an activity that temporarily removed them from the reality of imprisonment. Andrew compared long-term imprisonment to 'groundhog days' in the sense that there was little or no variance either in the daily routine or in the appearance of the physical environment of the prison. Although the UVF's instituted regime created a level of structure to the daily lives of prisoners, for large portions of each day the prisoners were responsible for their own time.

Thus, narratives of artefact production tend to represent highly individualized prison experiences, demonstrating the diversity of attachments and identities formed in the compounds. When I first met Michael Thompson, a former RHC prisoner, he told me how he had been changed by his prison experience through the act of painting. He recalled that he first became interested in painting while watching another prisoner produce oil paintings. He approached the man about learning how to paint, and after acquiring the necessary skills he spent a large portion of his twelve-year sentence painting for himself and others (Figure 2.3). While telling me

Figure 2.3 Painting by MT from Maze/Long Kesh prison. Photographed by the author with consent during interview on 20 January 2015.

some anecdotal stories about his overall prison experience, he looked at me, laughed quietly, and said, 'People ask me how I did twelve years in jail, says I, "Half the time, I wasn't in jail. When I was sleeping I wasn't in jail, and when I was painting I wasn't in jail". It was a way to shut out the world around you'. Michael's narrative is very similar to John's earlier memory about the effect of handicraft production on his experience in the Crumlin Road prison, and illustrates how the process of enskillment moved his immediate focus away from his space of confinement towards learning a new technique or type of handicraft.

Dave, who spent the majority of his sentence painting murals, glass images, drawing, and making leatherworks, echoed Michael's notion of escapism through material production. He told me that for him, the ability, and at times necessity, to improvise materials and means appealed to his creative inclinations. Dave arrived several years into the operation of the compound's 'cottage industry'. As he described the wide-ranging handicrafts he encountered upon his arrival, he contended that 'whatever art form was there, we were always looking to improve it but certainly the main thing for me about the art was escape. That for hours you could be doing something that was creative and that you could improve on'. Dave's narrative illustrates how the structure of the compounds allowed for and encouraged processes of improvisation and creativity through engagement with material culture, all while demonstrating how those processes are linked to the broader social and cultural life of the prison.

Nonetheless, for some prisoners, personal handicraft production was significant because it gave them the ability to ease the burden that imprisonment placed on their families. When I spoke to William Mitchell about his own personal production during his thirteen-year sentence, he told me that he did not make handicrafts merely to pass the time. He expressed his more personal motivations for production:

> I had loads of other ways of passing the time but you know at the start that became a good source of removing the hardship from your parents, which at the time, myself, I was quite young as you know, so it just fell to my mother and father, the burden of making sure I was clothed and so on and so forth. So any way of alleviating that, I was up for doing it, and so that was what we did.

William's narrative about his own motivations illuminates how these processes of enskillment not only taught prisoners self-discipline, creativity and improvisation but also had tangible implications for improving their life, both inside and outside the wire fences of the compounds. For William, Richard and John, although they could not make enough money to relieve the burden for their family entirely, the act of being able to contribute to their own livelihood in prison had a significant psychological impact on them. This, in turn, impacted the formation of their overall place attachment to the compounds, because it allowed for the development of a positive emotional bond to the production of handicrafts by giving prisoners 'a sense of importance and a bit about their own self, and having some way of contributing to themselves and then contributing to maybe a dependent family member or else being less dependent on their family through the production of some of these handicrafts' (JC 2014). Therefore, although the objects symbolized the politicized place identities of compound prisoners, both to the prisoners and to those who purchased the objects outside the prison walls, they also symbolized the maintenance of their own sense of self as well as a connection to their family and community outside the prison.

Another method by which personal production maintained connections to the outside world was mural painting. Much like aspects of the cooperative, mural production was a way in which the prisoners transformed the space of their imprisonment, asserting individual and group agency over the decoration of the space. Although the limitations of this chapter prevent me from producing an in-depth analysis of the mural painting, a narrative from one of the mural painters will most effectively demonstrate how material culture and events outside the prison intersected on a daily basis.[19] During my second interview with Dave, who had been one of the two main mural painters in the compounds, we flipped through photographs of various murals together and talked through his recollections as he saw each image. When we reached an image of a mural commemorating the motorized division of the 1914 UVF, he immediately remembered the day he painted the image and interjected (my responses are in italics to contextualize his narrative):

> Okay, Lord Mountbatten [*Lord Mountbatten, tell me about him*], 1979, August 24th [*Yes*] Blew up, Silver Shadow [*On the boat*] on the boat [*With his nephews*] nephews, on the same day as the 18 Paras died down in Warrenpoint. I was painting that. [*Seventy-nine*] Absolutely, because this is the, this is Messines [hut], it's a definite, up here's the TV and all that and the radio would have been virtually on that far side. I'm getting it all out [the materials to paint] and the next thing is there's breaking news coming through, there's been this and been that, and there was other stuff on that day too, because they were the two headline acts and I remember people saying did you hear that? What was that? And then the news just went into a frenzy, like, they knew it was someone down in Donegal, or Sligo, but then once it came as Lord Mountbatten, it was like whoa, the TV didn't know do you cover all these British soldiers getting wiped out in Warrenpoint or do you do Mountbatten – and there was other stuff that day. So through my whole time doing that [painting the mural], that's the context of that.

Dave's frenetic narrative demonstrates Belk's distinction that objects of nostalgia produce richer narratives, because rather than serving as 'simple cues to propositional memories involving knowledge *that* something occurred, these objects provoke rich textural memories involving knowledge *of* the experience recalled' (Belk 1990: 671). Therefore, when prompted with the image of the mural painting, Dave was able to remember the experience of painting the mural, more so than the knowledge that he painted it. Although the prisoners were removed from the spaces, places and events of everyday society, these locations and experiences interjected into the processes of place identity and place attachment formations constantly occurring through engagement with material culture. As Dave was painting a mural image of a historical narrative from a broader UVF cultural identity that solidified aspects of a prison place identity, he also experienced the real-life events of the violent conflict continuing outside the bounds of the prison space. Hence, the material culture of the compounds functioned to solidify those multivocal place identities and attachments, while also transforming the sociopolitical spaces of the prison environment.

Past Experiences, Contemporary Motivations

The prison narratives analysed in this chapter have demonstrated how memories of pre-ceasefire experiences with material culture are still significant to how many ex-prisoners view themselves within a post-ceasefire political and spatial context. As mentioned at the start of the chapter, most of the men interviewed for this research speak positively about their experiences with prison handicrafts because they feel that highlighting that element of the prison experience can help to create a new and certainly more empathetic view of former prisoners and their experiences. Consequently, the final segment of this chapter will introduce some of these narratives in order to demonstrate how, for many men, these artefacts represent the opportunity to challenge preconceived notions and societal stereotypes about their membership in paramilitary organizations, their prison experiences, and their post-prison efforts to redefine themselves and these stereotypes.

All of my final interviews with Dave, John, Richard and Michael, took place in the ACT exhibition. As such, towards the end of each interview I asked each of them why the handicrafts are important to them now and what they hoped visitors would gain from seeing them on display. Dave's excerpt at the beginning of the chapter comprised part of his answer about the importance of the handicrafts, but he further elaborated that for him the 'artwork challenges the stereotypes, that we were all monsters, illiterate morons, that actually there were some real craftsmen in that prison, republican and loyalist, that produced magnificent stuff, which are there for better or worse to remind people of the days that we were in'. For Richard, the variety of handicrafts on display represented the progression of the styles and techniques developed, which is important to him: 'Because that reflects, I think how most of the people matured as well, and how they developed, so it wasn't just in the handicraft that developed but that's just a physical method, physical representation of that development'. He further elaborated on this concept of growth, and stated: 'For me, the whole peace process began in Long Kesh through Gusty's Camp Council, and I think the growth and development of that needs to be reflected and I think that [the handicrafts] can be used with that to display it'. John's narrative about the exhibition space more directly resonates with William's motivations for creating the exhibition. He contended that the handicrafts were a contributing factor to 'the story that needs to be told'. When I asked him to elaborate on whether that story was the broader story of the prison experience, he answered:

> I think it's a broader story in relation to the conflict itself, with regards to people's motivation, you know, what was happening at the time, what motivated people to do what they done, and that journey through to Long Kesh. And then what they experienced going into Long Kesh, while in Long Kesh, and since coming out of Long Kesh. And what they've been doing since – you know, have they been contributing to promoting the use of violence or have they been contributing to some other peace-building stuff?

As these final narrative excerpts have demonstrated, for many former UVF/RHC compound prisoners, the physical specimens of the handicrafts symbolize the personal and political transformations that took place within the prison walls. Most of these men have continued those processes after release within the spatial and political contexts of conflict transformation projects, further signifying the dynamic connection between object and place that was created through the development of prisoner place attachments and identities, while simultaneously demonstrating the relevance of these identities and attachments to their post-prison lives.

Conclusion

How former UVF/RHC compound prisoners perceive the meaning and value of the handicrafts produced during their time of imprisonment is intrinsic to complex processes of both political and personal place-making at the Maze/Long Kesh prison, and is linked to post-ceasefire discourses of conflict transformation. The prisoners formed site-specific place identities by defining their relation to the compounds through participating in a wide range of enforced and voluntary social actions. These actions, which for many included the production of handicrafts, socialized the prisoners into the particular structure of the compound environment. Through the implementation of the UVF's structure, the handicraft production became integrated into the fabric of sociality within the spatial environment of the compounds. The compound prisoners therefore learned how to participate positively in this structural system through the making of objects.

When considering the artefacts within a contemporary context, they become symbols of the prisoners' place attachment and associated identities when reimagined or re-experienced through the creation of nostalgic recollections. Within the context of my research, many of these recollections took place in a new political and cultural space, which helps to re-contextualize the memories and artefacts within contemporary discourses of conflict transformation. Milligan argued that all place attachments are inevitably disrupted – which in this instance occurred when prisoners were released from the compounds and the prison itself was closed. Today, the artefacts signify the prisoners' emotional and material attachment to the compound environment, and following the disruption of that attachment they have re-established or reconstructed that place attachment through remembering the artefacts within the context of the research interview.

As the artefacts act as repositories for memories and meanings attached to the compound prison experience, the former prisoners' perceptions of the artefacts in the present contributes to more cohesive understandings about the role of artefacts in creating a sense of place and the past (Belk 1990: 669). The ex-prisoner narratives analysed in this chapter elucidate the inclusion of handicraft production in the prisoners' ability to comprehend and adjust to the spatial and social reality of the compounds. Personal narratives regarding handicraft production, both for collective and personal gain, demonstrate the multivocality of the objects and identities created, while also highlighting the intersection of materiality and place-making within the specific space of the compounds. A primary implication of this investigation is the production of narratives rich with nostalgic content that interrogate cultural conceptions regarding connections between material culture, place-making and identity construction, both in past and present experiences of distinct political spaces.

This chapter makes a definitively new and inventive contribution to the application of anthropology towards material culture studies, because it marks the first publication to adapt Milligan's place attachment theory to a discussion of narratives about the making, using and displaying of prison-made artefacts. Although several recent publications have addressed the connection between appropriation of space and place within modes of confinement through the production of artworks and crafts, this particular approach has never before been applied to the prison systems operational during the conflict in Northern Ireland (Saunders 2004, 2009; Carr and Mytum 2012). By discussing the diverse and evolving political and personal spaces in post-ceasefire Northern Ireland through the lens of individual memories of prison artefact production, this chapter further substantiates the necessity to employ analyses of material culture in order to best comprehend the politics of place-making within transitional societies.

Erin Hinson is a graduate of the University of Pittsburgh and Queen's University Belfast, from which she graduated with an MA in Irish Studies in 2012 and a PhD in Irish Studies in 2017. Her MA and PhD research explored artefact production, identity formation, and prison experiences at sites of conflict. Her PhD examined the ways in which artefacts, through both production and use, facilitated the formation of identities within the prison experiences of the Ulster Volunteer Force and Red Hand Commando.

Notes

1. The Maze/Long Kesh prison has several labels. Long Kesh is the name of the army base, internment camp, and prison, however, the name was changed to Her Majesty's Prison (HMP) Maze in 1972 with the addition of sentenced prisoners, although the name is typically used to refer to the cellular system built from 1975 and housing prisoners from 1976 onwards (McAtackney 2014). The compound system under analysis existed under both names, and as such the joint name will be employed throughout.
2. The outbreak of violence between the Royal Ulster Constabulary (RUC) and civil rights marchers in Derry (Londonderry) on 5 October 1968 is the commonly agreed start of the conflict in Northern Ireland (McKittrick and McVea 2000). High level, intercommunal and ethno-national violence continued from 1968 to the paramilitary ceasefires in 1994 and the signing of the Good Friday Agreement in 1998. For further introductory information about the conflict, see the introduction to this volume.
3. The CLMC was an umbrella group, established in 1991, comprising the Ulster Defence Association, UVF and RHC (McKittrick and McVea 2000: 332).
4. One of the methods they established was through an exhibition of ex-prisoner handicrafts, which took place in 1998. Following this exhibition, EPIC produced a research document entitled 'The Prison Experience: A Loyalist Perspective', which was one of the first written documents to address the complex and diverse social and political environment of the UVF/RHC compounds (Green 1998). Included within this report was a section on the prison handicrafts. Although this exhibition and subsequent publication marked the reintroduction of these artefacts into the evolving political spaces of conflict transformation in loyalist communities, former prisoners and combatants would not significantly re-engage with the prison material culture for another decade.
5. Following the UVF and RHC's Statement of Intent in 2007, William designed ACT as a model of implementation to support this statement. With UVF support, and funding from the International Fund for Ireland, ACT's first programmes began in 2008. Within the statement the UVF claimed that after a three-year consultative process 'the Ulster Volunteer Force and Red Hand Commando will assume a non-military, civilianised role'. The document also encouraged their volunteers to 'embrace the challenges which continue to face their communities, and support their continued participation in non-military capacities', and also to 'show support for credible restorative justice projects so that they, with their respective communities, may help to eradicate criminality and anti-social behaviour in our society' – BBC News (2007), UVF statement in full, 3 May 2007, http://news.bbc.co.uk/1/hi/northern_ireland/6618365.stm (last accessed 4 September 2015).
6. Due to funding challenges, the ACT exhibition and offices moved from North Belfast to temporary premises in West Belfast in 2017. The ongoing suspension of the Northern Irish government (since January 2017) continues to negatively impact funding for programmes such as ACT; however, as of publication the exhibition and offices remain open.
7. In order to ensure the protection of all research participants, all names used in this chapter have been anonymized. Interviews with participants are cited using the initials of the given pseudonym and the date the interview occurred.
8. The UVF was formed in 1965 in response to the perceived threats of the liberal premiership of Terence O'Neill and of republican violence in connection to the upcoming fiftieth anniversary of the Easter Rising in 1966 (Garland 2001: 16). Most literature claims the RHC was formed in 1972; however, recent scholarship states that this occurred in June 1970 (Novosel 2013; Smith 2014). The leaderships of the two organizations formed an official alliance in July 1972, and the document included a section on the treatment of all UVF and RHC prisoners. See UVF/RHC

Agreement quoted in Balaclava Street blog post entitled, 'The Ulster Volunteer Force/ Red Hand Commando Agreement (1972), 1 February 2014, https://balaclavastreet.wordpress.com/?s=UVF+RHC+agreement+1972 (last accessed 8 April 2015).

9. Published accounts of UVF/RHC prison experiences describe the communal environment of the compounds as an intentional goal of the UVF's compound leaders (Snodden 1996; Green 1998; Garland 2001). Integral to the implementation and enforcement of this structure was the Officer in Command (OC) of the UVF/RHC compounds, Gusty Spence; however, given the restrictions of this chapter, Spence's influence cannot be appropriately addressed and a brief explanation has been left to this footnote. Presented with this unorthodox environment, Spence implemented a strict routine of military discipline, based on his previous service with the Royal Ulster Rifles (RUR) regiment of the British Army, in order to manage the prisoners' institutional life. He justified this approach by claiming that these activities diverted the mind from the reality of the prison environment and sentence (Garland 2001).
10. The 'special category status' included six concessions: one half-hour visit per week, one food parcel per week, unlimited incoming/outgoing mail, the right to wear personal clothing at all times, free association with other prisoners, and no requirement to perform prison work (Crawford 1982). Of the six concessions awarded, the right to freely associate with other prisoners and the removal of the requirement to perform prison work greatly impacted the prisoners' experiences within the compounds and enhanced their opportunities for material production.
11. The government utilized the remains of the Royal Air Force base located on the Long Kesh site in order to construct the prison. As a result, they positioned semi-circular Nissan huts alongside the runways of the former military base. An individual compound housed approximately eighty prisoners, and included four huts which were grouped in a 70 x 30-foot yard and enclosed by a 12-foot wire fence, effectively segregating prisoners within their own compound (Purbrick 2004). The prison authorities segregated compound populations based on paramilitary group, and a relatively free environment existed as the paramilitary leaderships were able to run the compounds with minimal daily interference from the prison authorities (Gormally, McEvoy and Wall 1993). Compound prisoners were usually limited to their own compounds, but did have access to all living quarters, canteens, and any exercise, educational and recreational facilities located within that compound (Snodden 1996).
12. Additionally, early scholarship on the institutional goals and psychological impacts of traditional confinement contend that the role of the prison authority is to simultaneously deprive the prisoners of their liberty while systematically dismantling their sense of self (Goffman 2006; Sykes 2006).
13. In this sense, the compound environment encourages comparisons with prisoner of war (POW) camps from the two world wars. Although no direct comparisons have been made between the two periods of imprisonment, accessing some scholarship about the POW camps can facilitate contextual understanding of the prisoners' lived experiences within those particular physical and social spaces (Saunders 2004, 2009; Carr and Mytum 2012).
14. Sykesian analysis of the five stages of deprivation argued stripping a prisoner of any material possessions attacks 'the deepest layers of personality' (Goffman 2006: 166).
15. Remand status refers to prisoners who are detained while awaiting preparations for trial (Casella 2007: 11).
16. YCV is the acronym for Young Citizen Volunteers, which at the start of the conflict was developed as the youth wing of the Ulster Volunteer Force. It also has historical connections to the Home Rule crisis prior to the First World War, as the YCV was also the youth wing of Carson's Ulster Volunteer Force circa 1912 (Taylor 2000: 92).
17. It should be noted that John was describing the level of military regime during the earlier years of the compound system. Within his narrative he continues to explain

how in later years, as leadership changed and numbers dwindled due to changing penal policies, the regime no longer operated on such a strict schedule. However, establishing the existence of this regime provides a specific context to the processes of 'locational socialization' taking place. Furthermore, as no new prisoners were admitted to the compounds after 1977 (due to the implementation of criminalization policies and the opening of the H-block cellular system in 1976), all compound prisoners recollect experiencing this strict regime at the start of their sentences.

18. For many prisoners, following the development of educational programmes in the Maze/Long Kesh in the late 1970s, the formal education included O and A level examinations and degree programmes offered by the Open University.
19. Through field research conducted for my doctoral thesis, I gained access to images of murals painted by UVF/RHC compound prisoners. As a part of my fieldwork methodology I showed these images to my interviewees in order to prompt rich textural memories regarding their production and significance. I received permission from the Northern Ireland Prison Service to reproduce these images *only* in my PhD thesis, and as such, I cannot include the image in this chapter. In light of this, I selected a participant narrative regarding a mural, which does not require the inclusion of the corresponding image.

References

Primary Sources (Interviews and Documents)

BBC News. 2007. UVF statement in full, 3 May 2007. Available at: http://news.bbc.co.uk/1/hi/northern_ireland/6618365.stm (last accessed 4 September 2015).
EPIC (Ex-Prisoners Interpretive Centre). 2015. Available at: http://www.epic.org.uk/ (last accessed 3 September 2015).
UVF/RHC Agreement (1972), quoted in Balaclava Street blog post entitled 'The Ulster Volunteer Force/Red Hand Commando Agreement (1972), 1 February 2014. Available at: https://balaclavastreet.wordpress.com/?s=UVF+RHC+agreement+1972 (last accessed 8 April 2015).
AJ, interview by Erin Hinson (19 November 2014).
AJ, interview by Erin Hinson (25 May 2015).
DS, interview by Erin Hinson (22 September 2014).
DS, interview by Erin Hinson (25 November 2014).
DS, interview by Erin Hinson (5 May 2015).
JC, interview by Erin Hinson (28 October 2014).
JW, interview by Erin Hinson (11 February 2015).
WM, interview by Erin Hinson (3 June 2015).
MT, interview by Erin Hinson (24 October 2014).
MT, interview by Erin Hinson (20 January 2015).
RW, interview by Erin Hinson (22 October 2014).
RW, interview by Erin Hinson (24 November 2014).

Secondary Sources

Belk, R.W. 1990. 'The Role of Possession in Constructing and Maintaining a Sense of Past', *Advances in Consumer Research* 17: 669–76.

Carr, G., and H. Mytum (eds). 2012. *Cultural Heritage and Prisoners of War: Creativity behind Barbed Wire*. London: Routledge.
Casella, E.C. 2007. *The Archaeology of Institutional Confinement*. Gainesville, FL: University Press of Florida.
Crawford, C. 1979. 'Long Kesh: An Alternative Perspective'. MSc thesis. Cranfield Institute of Technology.
———. 1982. 'The Compound System: An Alternative Penal Strategy', *The Howard Journal of Penology and Crime Prevention* 21(1): 155–58.
Ervine, D., and J.W. McCauley. 2001. 'Redefining Loyalism: A Political Perspective, an Academic Perspective', *Working Papers in British–Irish Studies* 4: 1–31.
Foucault, M. 1977. *Discipline and Punish: The Birth of the Prison*. Translated by A. Sheridan. London: Penguin Books.
Garland, R. 2001. *Gusty Spence*. Belfast: Blackstaff Press.
Goffman, E. 2006. 'Asylums: Essays on the Social Situation of Mental Patients and Other Inmates', in Y. Jewkes and H. Johnston (eds), *Prison Readings: A Critical Introduction to Prisons and Imprisonment*. Portland, OR: Willan Publishing, pp.174–80.
Gormally, B., K. McEvoy, and D. Wall. 1993. 'Criminal Justice in a Divided Society: Northern Ireland Prisons', *Crime and Justice* 17: 51–135.
Green, M. 1998. 'The Prison Experience: A Loyalist Perspective'. Research document no. 1. Belfast: EPIC.
Hummon, D. 1986. 'Place Identity: Localities of the Self', in J.W. Carswell and D. Saile (eds), *Proceedings of the 2nd International Conference on Built Form and Culture Research*. Lawrence, KS: University of Kansas Press, pp.34–37.
McAtackney, L. 2014. *An Archaeology of the Troubles: The Dark Heritage of Long Kesh/Maze Prison*. Oxford: Oxford University Press.
McAuley, J., J.J. Tonge, and P. Shirlow. 2010. 'Conflict, Transformation, and Former Loyalist Paramilitary Prisoners in Northern Ireland', *Terrorism and Political Violence* 22: 22–40.
McEvoy, K. 1998. 'Prisoners, the Agreement, and the Political Character of the Northern Ireland Conflict', *Fordham International Law Journal* 22: 1539–76.
———. 2001. *Paramilitary Imprisonment in Northern Ireland: Resistance, Management and Release*. Oxford: Oxford University Press.
McKittrick, D., and D. McVea. 2000. *Making Sense of the Troubles*. Belfast: Blackstaff Press.
Milligan, M.J. 1998. 'Interactional Past and Potential: The Social Construction of Place Attachment', *Symbolic Interaction* 21(1): 1–33.
Novosel, T. 2013. *Northern Ireland's Lost Opportunity: The Frustrated Promise of Political Loyalism*. London: Pluto Press.
Purbrick, L. 2004. 'The Architecture of Containment', in D. Wylie, *The Maze*. London: Granta Books, pp.91–110.

Rolston, B. 2007. 'Demobilization and Reintegration of Ex-combatants: The Irish Case in International Perspective', *Social & Legal Studies* 16(2): 259–80.
Saunders, N.J. 2004. 'Material Culture and Conflict: The Great War, 1914–2003', in N.J. Saunders (ed.), *Matters of Conflict: Material Culture, Memory and the First World War*. London: Routledge, pp. 5–25.
———. 2009. 'People in Objects: Individuality and the Quotidian in the Material Culture of War', in C.L. White, *The Materiality of Individuality: Archaeological Studies of Individual Lives*. London: Springer Press, pp. 37–55.
Shirlow, P., and K. McEvoy. 2008. *Beyond the Wire: Former Prisoners and Conflict Transformation in Northern Ireland*. London: Pluto Press.
Sinnerton, H. 2002. *David Ervine: Uncharted Waters*. London: Brandon Press.
Smith, W. 2014. *Inside Man: Loyalists of Long Kesh – the Untold Story*. Newtownards: Colourpoint Books.
Snodden, M. 1996. 'Culture behind the Wire', *Journal of Prisoners on Prison, Special Issue, Loyalist Prisoners of War* 7(2): 25–29.
Stokowski, P.A. 2002. 'Languages of Place and Discourses of Power: Constructing New Senses of Place', *Journal of Leisure Research* 34(4): 368–82.
Svašek, M. 2008. 'Introduction: Politics and Emotions in Central and Eastern Europe', in M. Svašek (ed.), *Postsocialism: Politics and Emotions in Central and Eastern Europe*. New York: Berghahn Books, pp. 1–33.
Sykes, G.M. 2006. 'The Society of Captives: A Study of a Maximum Security Prison', in Y. Jewkes and H. Johnston (eds), *Prison Readings: A Critical Introduction to Prisons and Imprisonment*. Portland, OR: Willan Publishing, pp. 164–73.
Tangen Page, M. von. 1998. *Prisons, Peace, and Terrorism: Penal Policy in the Reduction of Political Violence in Northern Ireland, Italy and the Spanish Basque Country 1968–1997*. London: Macmillan Press.
Taylor, P. 2000. *Loyalists*. London: Bloomsbury.

3

'Recalling or Suggesting Phantoms'
Walking in West Belfast

Elizabeth DeYoung

The First Step

In 2013, I began walking Belfast. My walks took me through a jigsaw of housing estates, past chip shops and corner stores, under flyovers and over stretches of vacant land. In negotiating the built environment, following twisting, bewildering routes, stopping to read memorial plaques and graffiti, running into barriers and brownfield sites, and nodding to people along the road, I came to develop a greater awareness of Belfast as a city. Immersion in one's surroundings is the first step to understanding the everyday realities of the landscape and the way in which the past is continually present within it.

I became interested in how the physical environment reflected broader narratives of remembrance: the memorial and material intertwined, and the streets as repositories of stories. Past and present were brought together as I pictured the invisible journeys of others who had walked the street, who had lived and worked and loved and died there (Solnit 2002: xv). In particular, I was fascinated and disturbed by the memorial plaques in many areas of Belfast. Here were physical clues to the cost of terrible violence, marking the presence of absence in a place and underlining the deeper consequences of the conflict known colloquially as the 'Troubles'.

For many in Belfast, memorial plaques have become part of the street furniture of the city. But as a newcomer, my first encounters with them brought a host of thoughts and images to mind, and this experience was one I wished to interrogate. In this chapter, I focus on the myriad functions and meanings attached to memorial plaques in West Belfast, but also on the relationship between past and present in the physical landscape – and on how much of it can be experienced by walking as an observer.

On some of the ethnographic walks that informed this chapter, I was accompanied by a university colleague with extensive knowledge of the streets of Belfast and the particularities of its history. At other times, I walked alone. My methodology relied in part on imagination, on the personal ruminations and speculations that come to mind through the act of walking (Edensor 2010: 70). I also researched the area beforehand – events that had befallen neighbourhoods during conflict, sites where someone had died – through a range of primary and secondary sources. Later, I engaged in conversations with Belfast residents regarding questions and observations that had arisen during my walks. However, my case study of the Falls Road in West Belfast[1] was researched largely on the sidelines, without the benefit of lived knowledge or experience.

Whilst exploring the landscape there, I came across one intriguing memorial that was affixed to a house. I went back to try to interview the residents, to find out more. I knocked – feeling clumsy and out of place – but the door remained closed, the house empty. As doors remain closed to us sometimes as researchers, as 'outsiders', particularly in strange places, there can be difficulties in connecting with an 'insider'. The estate in this chapter was located outside of my primary research field, explored as part of a side project. Without a 'gatekeeper' to this new environment, I remained on the periphery. As a result, my presence and my own perspective as researcher became a large part of the story.

This chapter draws on some of those experiences as a walker, observer and outsider. It has three principal aims: to explore the relationship between walking and the material environment in Belfast; to examine the intersection of death, remembrance and landscape as experienced whilst walking in the area of the Falls Road of West Belfast; and to situate this landscape of commemoration against the legacy of conflict in contemporary Belfast – what is remembered, and what is forgotten.

Space, Place and Movement in the Divided City

It starts with the first step. The balls of the feet push forward, arms swing, footsteps inscribe patterns on the footpath. The ground rises up and disappears beneath the feet; the air skims across the skin and through the lungs. One joins the 'sidewalk ballet' (Jacobs 2000: 45) of movement. 'The most anonymous man or woman, everything that speaks, makes noise, passes by, touches us lightly, meets us head on' – intertwining paths along the footpath compose a manifold narrative of the city, crossing and diverging (de Certeau 1988: 97).

Walking as methodology has been used by a variety of authors and researchers to examine the mutually constitutive relationship between human beings and our environment (de Certeau 1988; Solnit 2002; Benjamin 2002; Pink 2008; Edensor 2010; Vergunst 2010). As Jones et al. observe, walks can be used to interrogate the relationships between 'embodiment, landscape, place, experience, practice, mobility, materiality, and representation' (Jones et al. 2008: 6). From Benjamin's flâneur, meandering solitary through the streets of Paris, to the ethnographer following ritual processions and parades (Bryan 2000), the act figures prominently in studies of space, place and movement.

Low and Lawrence-Zúñiga (2003: 5) state that space derives from movement itself – it cannot exist without practice. People actively shape their surroundings through their use of and movement through environments, as their surroundings in turn shape them. As Lefebvre notes, 'the space in which we walk is a social product, a tool of thought, action, and expression' (Lefebvre 1991: 26). Cresswell (2004: 10) adds that when humans invest meaning in a portion of space and become attached to it in some way, it then becomes 'a place'. We take our surroundings and make them *mean* something to us. Place in this sense is a 'hybrid product of biography and location', each informing the other (Hall, Lashua and Coffey 2006: 2). The 'untidy, mundane, undesigned' streets and corners and routes of daily life are replete with layers of human histories and memories (Hebbert 2005: 583).

It is worth noting, however, that seeing the world through the lens of place can also lead to exclusionary or reactionary behaviour and bigotry – the notion that 'our place is threatened and others have to be excluded' (Cresswell 2004: 11). In many parts of Belfast, for example, there exists an overarching framework of sectarian division, fear and mistrust of the 'other', which moves people to delineate territory and identity, and maintain mental and physical boundaries (Jarman 2004: 5). Although the conflict has largely ceased, the use of urban space 'to include and exclude, to control, influence and express relationships of power' continues (Anderson and Shuttleworth 2003: 2). Material landmarks connote ethno-sectarian allegiance and paramilitary influence – from murals that adorn gable ends to flags fluttering on lamp posts, and impassive 'peace lines' of metal sheeting and brick that slice through neighbourhoods (see also chapter by Rush, this volume). This defensive, divided landscape is a legacy of the last forty years, which have compacted 'the performance of violence into space' (Feldman 1991: 28; Shirlow and Murtagh 2006: 58).

The spatialization of conflict in turn influences how people identify, classify and use space in Belfast. This recalls Bourdieu's notion of 'habitus', a system of routinized social practice and spatial meanings through which people experience and understand the world, often unconsciously (Bourdieu 1990: 52). For residents of Belfast, the paths that each person threads around the city are in accordance with 'an intricate text of norms' concerning spatial practice and perceived 'safe' and 'unsafe' spaces (Lysaght and Basten 2003: 15). According to Jarman, 'the journeys individuals make and therefore their understanding of place and sense of space are always marked by their ethnic background' (Jarman 2001: 36). The 'sidewalk ballet' of daily life takes on a more complex set of meanings. Other researchers have employed the methodology of walking in Belfast: it is the best way to gain a real understanding of space and place as an outsider, because by walking the divided streets one can start to appreciate people's lived experience of sectarianism, conflict and marginalization (Mitchell and Kelly 2011).

'Streets Become Battlefields'

Northern Ireland has a past riddled with political and religious discord (see Bardon 1992; McGarry and O'Leary 1995; Boal 1995; Coulter 1999; Allen and Kelly 2003). While it is not the purpose of this chapter to discuss this history in detail, it is necessary to explain, briefly, the background to the division of space in Belfast. This is to illustrate the way in which physical and mental divides are intrinsic to the life of the city and of many of its residents.

In 1921, Northern Ireland was partitioned to remain part of the United Kingdom. It is populated by two primary ethno-national groups: the Catholic/nationalist/republican population, who broadly favour Irish reunification; and the Protestant/unionist/loyalist grouping, who believe that Northern Ireland should remain part of the United Kingdom (Coulter 1999).[2] Historically, the struggle between the two was evidenced by episodic rioting, intimidation, and some degree of residential segregation in working-class areas. This was compounded by a one-party unionist government that discriminated against Catholics in housing, employment, and electoral rights (Hocking 2014: 23).

A civil rights movement began in the late 1960s, on a cross-community platform, to agitate for equal rights for Catholics within the framework of the United Kingdom. The empowerment of the Catholic population, however, caused insecurity amongst those Protestants who feared the spectre of a Catholic takeover and a united Ireland. Tensions erupted in August 1969 in the wake of a unionist parade in Derry (Melaugh n.d.). The rioting, burning of houses, gun battles and barricades that followed sparked further violence. The long-dormant IRA regrouped, and began an armed crusade against the British government and security forces, seeking Irish reunification through political violence.[3] Loyalist paramilitary groups were formed first to protect their own neighbourhoods, but this later extended to a campaign against the IRA. In 1972, as the crisis grew, Westminster reluctantly administered Direct Rule. Near thirty years of conflict, often referred to as 'the Troubles', followed.

The majority of violence occurred in urban space (Fay et al. 1999), in everyday, unremarkable places: pubs, sandwich shops, betting shops, taxi depots, on street corners and in alleyways. These were the sites of IRA bombings and assassinations, of sectarian killings, police and army brutality, and loyalist feuds. McDowell and Switzer have observed that, 'streets became battlefields' (2011: 83). Indeed, the street was the arena for violence, at the very centre of the Troubles, and this is written into the physical and symbolic geography of the city (Dawson 2005: 161). As Komarova and McKnight put it, space in Belfast is 'constituted and is itself constitutive of conflict and divisions' (2012: 5).

One could be forgiven, on their first visit, for thinking otherwise. Visually, the city centre of Belfast today is a very different place from when it was mired in conflict. Even before the first ceasefires, millions of pounds of investment concentrated on making the centre a neutral, normalized space. Walking through it, one experiences a bustling high street lined with globally recognizable retailers, cafes, bars and restaurants. Offices, hotels, and luxury apartments sit on the riverside along with the Titanic Experience, a multimillion pound signature building and tourist destination. To the untrained eye, Belfast appears to be a thriving city, shedding the cloak of conflict and moving into a new, globalized era.

As part of neoliberal-influenced economic strategy, heritage, culture and environment have become crucial in promoting investment, consumption and tourism (Strange and Davoudi 2009: 35). The television programme 'Game of Thrones' (filmed in part in Belfast), the city's industrial past, and opportunities for shopping and dining have become key in the marketing of Belfast. This is not dissimilar to other postindustrial cities. However, as part of a top-down peace-building strategy, government officials have sought to downplay the conflict in redeveloped public spaces. Thus, commemoration is largely absent in the city centre, despite the fact that for years it was the site of regular bombings. As Switzer and MacDowell (2009: 342) point out, 'the landscape is being divested of evidence of the conflict'. They note, for example, that nothing marks the spot of the Oxford Street bus station, blown apart in 'Bloody Friday', 1973. There are no sites to individual deaths that occurred in the centre, nor any collective memorial to the victims of the conflict as a whole. Rather than engaging with issues of the past, they have been moved out of sight (Boulton 2014: 111). This is also reflective of the politics of avoidance, which has shaped Northern Ireland since the 1998 Good Friday Agreement, with no genuine political consensus on either the meaning of the past or a vision for the future.

However, outside of the city centre, memorial plaques and gardens dedicated to remembering the victims (and the perpetrators) of the Troubles are much more visible on the streets (Graham and Whelen 2007: 477; Weidenhoft Murphy 2010: 547). These neighbourhoods bore the brunt of the violence, and local residents have invested the space with physical and symbolic reminders of the past. In contrast to the centre, here the dead are not forgotten, but stubbornly remain, placed within the landscape: 'Names map the past like ruins that haunt our present' (Dawe 2003: 204). And as memories are made material, stories come to the surface.

Landscapes, Deathscapes

Death and dying are intensely anchored in space and place, drawing attention to the significance we invest in our surroundings and the emotion and memories provoked by place (Kong 2010: xv). The intersection of memory and place often takes material form. Nora speaks of '*lieux de memoire*' (places of memory), which crystalize memory, deliberately 'materialising the immaterial' through the use of space, symbol and practice (Nora 1989: 19). The shaping of space becomes an instrument for the shaping of memory (Hebbert 2005: 592).

In Northern Ireland, there are myriad examples to draw upon. Physical artefacts and sites (monuments, gardens, murals) are constructed, and group practices (commemorative parades, vigils, festivals) take 'place'. These serve as contextual frameworks for individual commemoration and remembrance. For example, some nationalist murals draw on myths from an idealized Gaelic past to legitimize a sense of 'Irishness' and belonging. Unionist Orange Order parades, which commemorate particular battles and follow traditional routes, 'reaffirm territorial identities and confirm boundaries' through ritual and symbol (Jarman 1997: 258). This reflects Halbwachs' notion of 'collective memory': by participating in commemorative practice, group members reconstruct and reshape their understanding of the past within a present-day framework (Halbwachs 1992: 188). It is through these types of means that social groups can transmit a communal narrative through generations (Viggiani 2014a: 14). Dawson's theory of 'popular memory' also analyses how group narratives are created, particularly during conflict. Kinship groups and neighbourhoods share personal stories, and in doing so identify common experiences and themes. These narratives are then repackaged into a 'collective form and projected into a public arena' – like commemoration within the physical landscape (Dawson 2005: 154).

Places do not come with memories attached as if by nature; rather, they are 'the contested terrain of competing definitions' (Harvey 1996: 309). Practices of commemoration determine which events and people are reinforced as central to collective narrative, and which ones are allowed to fade over time. Nora (1989: 8) reminds us that 'memory, in so far as it is affective and magical, only accommodates those facts that suit it'. Commemorative practices insist on preserving people and their stories – but this may be in a particular way to reinforce particular beliefs or agendas, and may exclude other perspectives. Whatever the case, it is worth noting that these interpretations can then become covert exercises in power: sanctioning some voices while silencing others (Cronon 1992).

This can be said of *lieux de memoire* in Northern Ireland. Most memorial plaques were erected post-ceasefire, and the majority commissioned by paramilitary groups (Dawson 2005: 156). This suggests, perhaps, the construction and cementing of a particular narrative in regards to past conflict. For example, republican commemoration rests on a collective narrative of state oppression and the struggle for self-determination, on themes of heroism, sacrifice, martyrdom and liberty. The IRA traces its historical continuity to other republican uprisings in the past. Thus the placement of memorial plaques can represent a 'communal mediation of history' (Longley 2001: 223), physically marking the IRA as both defenders of the area and inheritors of past republican struggle in the fight for a united Ireland.

Memorial plaques are prevalent in urban working-class housing estates (predominantly though not exclusively nationalist/republican), which saw a disproportionate amount of violence (Viggiani 2014a: 50). Those killed in the conflict are remembered through their association with place, whether it is the site of their death or the neighbourhood in which they lived (Donnan 2005: 91). The plaques inscribe personal grief onto public space (Wells 2012: 154) and 'the familiar streetscapes with the names of those who once lived there' (Kelleher and Worpole 2010: 175).

Belfast's geography makes finding these plaques, as an outsider, somewhat challenging. They are often located away from the tourist track, in long loops of out-of-the-way cul-de-sacs, in little-known pockets of side streets. They can be found in spaces that are often highly segregated according to ethno-national identity, and cut off by visible or invisible barriers from the 'other' side. Thus, by locating plaques in specific areas, though technically accessible to the public, the spaces are actually highly defined. Viggiani (2014a: 51) notes that memorials in Belfast are often located at 'the heart of the estate', suggesting they are primarily oriented towards those whose identity they 'claim to represent and whose collective memory they attempt to reify'. They can also suggest paramilitary control of a particular area.

Using walking as research methodology makes it possible to find these places. However, for someone who does not 'belong' on the estate, standing in front of a plaque can evoke a feeling of being 'outside' the memorial – an intruder – balancing on a thin edge between the public and private. One resident said to me simply when I remarked on this: 'Maybe they're not for you, they're for the family' (Author fieldnotes 2013). The following case study of walking along the Falls Road explores some of these tensions and themes.

'You Should See What He Looked Like'

In April 2014, I went for a walk with a colleague through a housing estate off the Falls Road, a nationalist/Catholic area of West Belfast that had been seriously affected by the conflict. We often walked for hours through

Figure 3.1 Marking the presence of absence in a place. Photo by the author.

different areas of the city, as my colleague explained to me in great depth the material and historical nuances of the streets. On that day, we were in search of a string of memorial plaques that dotted the gable walls and odd corners of this particular neighbourhood.

In contrast to murals or memorial gardens, memorial plaques are significant because of their emphasis on the individual. They are unofficial and local expressions, usually enacted by paramilitary groups, but also sometimes by family, friends, or residents' groups. Often unassuming, modestly marking the sides of houses or side streets, they say little more than the name, age, date and manner of death of the deceased.

One house had a small black plaque above its front door. My friend commented that there used to be a small portrait on it, but it was gone. Underneath was written a man's name, his birth and death dates, and the legend 'Murdered by UVF'.[4] I furtively took a picture and we walked on.

Sometimes I feel embarrassed by my visibility in these estates – as one resident said to me, 'There's no reason to come here unless you live here' (Author fieldnotes 2013). The act of taking a photograph underlines my status as an outsider and draws attention. Walking the quiet streets, I sometimes wonder if I am being watched from windows, judged as odd for photographing examples of place-making – electrical boxes, murals,

Figure 3.2 'You should see what he looked like'. Photo by the author.

graffiti. I do not want to be seen as a voyeur, snapping pictures and then retreating comfortably back to my university life. This is an experience that other researchers in Northern Ireland have reported (Komarova and McKnight 2012).

On this occasion, a woman's yell split the silence: 'Hey! Come back here!' I groaned inwardly and slouched back. Maybe she did not want me taking pictures of her house? Perhaps I had offended her in some way? A woman in a printed dress and gaudy jewellery stood in the front garden, waving a porcelain oval in her hand. It was the missing portrait; she said it had fallen off in the strong winds. 'Are you tourists?' she asked. We nodded, not wanting to explain our weird hunt for memorials. 'Here, look at it, take a picture', she said emphatically, pushing it towards me, insistent. 'You should see what he looked like'. I snapped one, surprised at the turn of events. An older woman leaned against the doorframe, looking on with arms crossed. I thought this was possibly the deceased's widow, the younger woman his daughter. She looked like him. I was touched that she had felt so inclined to come out and show me the picture, and I thanked her.

Some memorial plaques feature a portrait of the deceased. The face 'makes moral claims upon us, addresses moral demands to us, ones that we do not ask for and are not free to refuse' (Wells 2012: 162). The eyes and smile are arresting, calling for the spectator to recognize that the deceased once lived and moved through this space, and that they now exist only in photographs and memories. The face also underlines that this person was once part of a social network with multiple identities: a sibling, a parent, a friend, a partner, a paramilitary. Given the context of conflict, many of these dead are reduced to other labels – terrorist, murderer – and some would not look favourably on their names.

These types of plaques, which can be found in many working-class areas of Belfast, call for acknowledgement that a certain person was part of and is remembered in the context of a particular place (Maddrell and Sidaway 2010: 9). Using material objects in commemoration is a means of realizing this presence and binding the living and the dead together, as Santino puts it, 'to put the dead back in the fabric of life' (Margry and Sánchez-Carretero 2011: 25). Leerssen (2001: 209) notes that, 'at the core of monuments and commemorations, there is death, absence, transience, a sense of loss resisted, denied, shouted down'. Memorial plaques insist on acknowledging real people, lives lost, and the presence of absence in a neighbourhood (Santino 2005: 12).

We walked away from the house. For a second, I had a glimpse into loss, the grief people have to bear every day, and the emptiness one person can leave. The woman had simply invited me to acknowledge and respond to a picture that clearly meant a great deal to her, and in that brief moment there was an exchange between us. Thus, memorial plaques, their context, the interaction between people and the material object – evoking empathy, shock, horror, anger – in this sense they have a performative quality attached to them, which I experienced in my role as a passer-by.

Later, at home, I went back and looked up the name, feeling compelled to research the inscription on the plaque. The man had been killed as he sat with his daughter on his knee in the front room of their home (McKittrick 1999: 1246). I considered the chain of events that this plaque emplacement had created. By stopping to notice it and take a picture, and then meeting a close relative in a chance encounter, I was moved to learn more and to reflect on the individual and the manner in which he died. I had been walking as a researcher, observing and analysing the surroundings. However, as a passer-by, I was drawn in by the plaque: affected by it, I experienced a range of emotions, and questioned the context and impact of the individual's death.

'Recalling or Suggesting Phantoms'

A few months later I found myself again walking down the Falls Road, imagining a world where armoured tanks roll past and clusters of soldiers stand on street corners clutching guns. I turned into the same housing estate to acquaint myself further with the environment. This time, I sought both the visible and invisible stories of the street.

In the physical landscape, there is the unspoken and unresolved: stories hidden beneath the surface, shadows invisible to the outsider (Doherty 2009). McKay describes a local resident narrating a tour of his neighbourhood: '[H]e pointed out the spot where someone was abducted, someone else shot, the lane where someone was stabbed . . . a pub where he'd been sitting as bullets flew' (McKay 2000: 196). For those who experienced the conflict, the ghosts of the past are entwined with particular spaces and places (Dawson 2005: 156): 'recalling or suggesting phantoms' (de Certeau 1988: 104).

Whilst walking, one can attempt to envision the imagined inscriptions of death on the landscape, traces of what might have happened, violence that has left no physical mark. Pile explores how various architectures of the city are haunted by multiple phantoms: as he puts it, 'the spirits of the dead become a part of the very fabric of the city, woven into its physicality, such that the sidewalks and stairwells become spectral' (Pile 2005: 139). But how can one experience this, as an outsider, a pedestrian in Belfast? It is not intuitive; without interacting with local residents, the stories remain hidden, the observer oblivious.

Before this walk, however, I had used an online database to pinpoint sites of death in the estate. I set out to find these sites, to examine the plaques that marked the spaces, and also to explore those places left unmarked. This was the only way I was likely to gain any perspective on the area's collective fashioning of history and its 'ghosts'. Indeed, on previous visits I had tried to set up an interview with one of the residents, but my lack of connections in the area at the time brought no results. However, I thought it would be important and interesting to capture the experience of walking through the estate from an outside perspective. What do these environments – these 'deathscapes' – bring forth for the casual walker or curious researcher (Maddrell and Sidaway 2010: 5)? What can we learn from the plaques themselves – or the lack of them – in terms of collective memory and individual loss, knowing how difficult it is to fathom, as outsiders, the burden of the past?

Following my research, I followed the twisting paths of the estate once more. I imagined gun battles in the alleyways and chases down the pokey rat runs, heart pounding and footsteps falling heavily on the pavement. It is difficult and disorienting to navigate this estate and would have provided good cover for those who knew the area during the conflict. I happened upon McDonnell Street, and a memorial plaque:

> Dedicated to the memory of Vol. Joe McDonnell born here in Slate Street 14th September 1950 and who died after 61 days on Hunger Strike in the H Block of Long Kesh 8th July 1981.[5]

His etched portrait was surrounded by larks and barbed wire. Underneath, a quote: 'A mother kneels in silent prayer, a flower clasped to her breast, she lays it on a lonely grave where her fallen son now rests. No tears blur

Figure 3.3 A means of mourning and a locus for protest. Photo by the author.

her deep blue eyes, they shine with loving pride, she knows he fought for freedom, for liberty he died.' Beneath the plaque, barbed wire coiled along the top of a fence.

This plaque speaks to how historical, political and economic forces shape space, and the ways that people think about and interact with their surroundings. According to Fregonese and Brand (2009: 20), individual behaviour has to be understood not only as a response to the immediate environment but also 'of history, the individual's socioeconomic condition and previous experience, the macro-political climate, and a myriad of other factors'.

McDonnell was a child here, playing in the street, going to the shop, coming home from school. But his surroundings shaped him as he interacted with them, in particular the violence that spilled forth with the onset of the conflict. As Sluka remarks in his ethnography of the area:

> People have been assassinated by Loyalist extremists and attacked by Protestant mobs; they have been killed by rubber and plastic bullets; they have been harassed, intimidated, interned, arrested, interrogated, and brutalised by soldiers and policemen . . . It is in this context that support for the IRA must be considered. (Sluka 1989: 63)

This social context would perhaps have encouraged McDonnell's involvement with the IRA, which ultimately led to his death. And his role in the conflict, his martyrdom as a hunger striker, has continued to shape the identity and galvanize the beliefs of the family and friends left behind. He was a son, a neighbour, a partner, a father – indeed, his daughter unveiled the plaque when it was erected in 2001 (Viggiani 2014b). Here the reciprocal relationship people have with their surroundings is evident, each shaping the other over time.

McDonnell's plaque is a means of mourning, but it is also a locus for protest. Whilst the death is first and foremost afforded its individual place, it is also linked to a wider framework and absorbed within a collective narrative of resistance (Viggiani 2014a: 173). By alluding to the 1981 hunger strike in Long Kesh, this plaque expresses social and political discontent. The message implies asking for an acknowledgment of an injustice ('This should not have happened') and of a sacrifice (that McDonnell and his fellow IRA members fought and died for their beliefs). It also intimates the seeking of an understanding of what happened, asking for responsibility: 'Look what happened to our neighbourhood and its people and Ireland under British rule' (Margry and Sánchez-Carretero 2011: 3). A lark in barbed wire functions as a symbol of oppression. The passer-by is then moved to think about the physical reality of the hunger strike, the dynamics of conflict and politics, and how it affected the people of the Falls Road area.

Turning into Servia Street, there were no plaques and it looked like any other street in any other housing estate: rows of terraced houses, concrete front gardens bedecked with ornamental statues and flowers, litter and gravel strewn here and there, graffiti scrawled on walls. However, this street was not ordinary at all, as it had been a regular foot-patrol route during the conflict and the site of death for several British soldiers (Wharton 2013: 193). I thought about how their bodies would have fallen on the pavement, arms splayed at odd angles, eyes shut, mouths open. The boots put on that morning now motionless, the uniform buttoned over bare skin bloodied – the last morning routine. They were individuals once, before becoming statistics, subsumed into the long, terrible narrative of the conflict. I wanted to walk the street whilst cognisant of these hidden stories.

British soldier Michael Murtagh was killed here aged twenty-two in an IRA rocket attack on an armoured car (Sutton 1999). Another soldier, John Ballard aged eighteen, was shot by a sniper not far from here whilst on patrol (ibid.). They died young in a conflict zone, as enemies in the streets. There is no memorial to them and no love for them in this winding estate. Here, they are invisible. Yet in another place, they were someone's son, or brother, or friend. Perhaps they came from similar-looking housing estates across the Irish Sea.

These are silenced voices, recalling that within a particular place some deaths are forgotten, some people erased from the landscape. The lack of memorialization evidences a particular narrative and an exercise of power over what is commemorated (McDowell and Switzer 2011: 100). As

McBride (2001: 4) says, 'whenever the past is evoked, we must ask ourselves not only by which groups, and to what end, but also against whom?' The British state, army, and security forces occupy a dark place in the memory of this estate, and their voices as individuals are lost in the landscape.

On this same street, two civilians, Vincent Hamilton and Harry McAleese, were killed in an explosion at their upholstery workshop (Sutton 1999). A ten-pound device, most likely stored there by the IRA, exploded prematurely (McKittrick 1999: 641). The two men had no paramilitary links. Walking along, I imagined the brief shining moment of silence before the blast shattered bricks and beams and bodies. The shop in the aftermath, a smouldering shell of its former self; the pop of paint blistering, crackling, wood cracking and collapsing; a charred door and flames dwindling to ash.

There is no plaque here – perhaps another route to forgetting. According to self-sanctioned memorials, the IRA are remembered as 'defenders of their community' and 'martyrs to the cause'. A situation like the upholstery works is more difficult to acknowledge, more uncomfortable – an accident, a faulty bomb placed in a small street, which killed civilian members of that same community. This incident, one of many such accidents, is harder to square with the enforced narrative of the IRA as protectors of the people.

As I moved on, the street held its secrets to itself. I felt inconsequential, understanding nothing of the horrors that this neighbourhood, these people, had endured.

Figure 3.4 The area's dead are 'placed' within the landscape. Photo by the author.

I walked up and down, trying to appear as if I knew where I was going, and eventually found Balkan Street. Three young IRA men had been accidentally killed in a premature explosion here (Sutton 1999). Again, there was no plaque marking the site. Earlier, I had stopped at the area's memorial garden on the main Falls Road. It is sometimes closed to the public, frustratingly locked, but it was open as I walked past. There, I found painted impressions of the three Volunteers involved – Patrick Maguire, Joseph McKinney and John Donaghy. McKinney had been just seventeen years of age. Their portraits were placed alongside those of their fallen neighbours next to a map of how the area used to look. This impressed me as a clear means of 'placing' these men within the neighbourhood, not only as defenders of it but also as residents.

Walking back towards the city centre, I passed Divis Tower. On the side of the tall, hulking block, once a centre of surveillance for the British Army, sat a plaque 'dedicated to the memory of Patrick Rooney and Hugh McCabe, who were murdered in this vicinity by the RUC on 15th August 1969'.[6] That night had rained bullets. Amidst the rioting and burning of homes taking place between the Shankill Road[7] and the Falls, police officers had opened indiscriminate gunfire on Divis Tower – this was what some would term 'the start of the conflict'.

Patrick Rooney's father was carrying him from his bedroom to the safety of the front room when he was hit. The heavy-calibre bullet had ripped through the walls of the apartment block and into his skull (McKittrick

Figure 3.5 Site of death at Divis Tower. Photo by the author.

1999: 34). He was nine years of age. Hugh McCabe was aged twenty, a British soldier home on compassionate leave (Sutton 1999). By marking the site of their deaths, the plaque emphasizes a sacred quality within the space, one changed into a highly emotional landscape, charged with meaning – 'it is the last place at which the person was alive' (Santino 2011: 99). I paused at the plaque for a moment, then headed to the city centre to lose myself in the lunchtime crowd.

A Negative Sign

By ending the walk in the city centre, I wish to reflect on the role of these plaques within the context of post-ceasefire Belfast. I want to briefly touch on other perspectives and viewpoints that challenge the importance of the plaques today. I will then conclude with a look at the studied blankness of the city centre and its implications for the legacy of conflict.

This chapter has used walking as a means to explore different aspects of memorial plaques – how people use the space around them to express notions of grief, identity, memory and protest, thereby turning it into 'place'. Plaque emplacements are an incorporation of material culture into communal space (Santino 2011: 106): materiality is central and critical to processes of individual and collective remembering (Graham 2011: 56). As a researcher and an outsider, my walk along the Falls begged interaction with the plaques. Afterwards, I was moved to add flesh to names and dates, to see what information could be gleaned later, huddled over the computer at home. Through the plaques, I became engaged with the stories of the dead. On my walks, I also concerned myself with what is hidden or silenced: the stories not marked by granite or marble, which live in the brick and concrete of the streets. These forgotten names and faces are also important.

This chapter has also reiterated the significance of historical context and of memory and meaning in relation to commemoration. However, in doing so, I do not wish to cut off the past from the present. The danger exists that by exploring these memorial plaques, we reify them, make them static, when indeed the sociopolitical and economic landscape around them is constantly changing. There is also the risk of essentializing the location and the people. According to Hall (1968: 84), 'people structure spaces differently and also experience them differently'. Place is uniquely encountered by each individual, and while meanings can be shared, they can also be 'competing or contested' (Low and Lawrence-Zúñiga 2003: 15). People's reactions upon seeing a memorial plaque will differ, depending on their individual perspective, past experiences, ties to place, and perceived identity. Indeed, in Viggiani's survey of residents in areas where there were murals and memorial plaques, over half of the respondents did not attach significance to these sites. Thus, even around the sites themselves, there is a multiplicity of engagement and detachment (Viggiani 2014a: 184).

Space and place must be reinforced, performed and practised to be maintained; if the processes and practices change, the physical and mental aspects of space and place will change as well (Castells 2003: 24). Today, Belfast is populated by a new generation of young people, some of whom are more concerned with moving forward than focusing on the past, and who have a different sense of identity and place. Post-ceasefire, there has been increasing space to identify with non-traditional identities, particularly for young people (Schubolz and Devine 2011: 26).

Some see the plaques as no longer relevant to a city moving away from conflict. For them, the plaques have a different significance, whether it be decidedly negative or apathetic. As one young person remarked: 'We want to forget about it, we want to move on . . . they're reminders of a past that no longer fits. They're a negative sign; people don't want to be brought back to that time'. Another related that their parents had carefully shielded them from the conflict, and the plaques meant little to them (Author fieldnotes 2013).

Others simply pass by the plaques without stopping – they go on with their day, inured to their presence (Viggiani 2014a: 66). 'Only tourists stop to look' (Author fieldnotes 2013). In many ways the plaques have become an unremarkable feature of the physical landscape, their significance faded by the passage of time. Certainly, demographic changes too will affect the plaques, as relatives move or pass away themselves in time, as neighbourhoods shift and new people move in and create their own sense of place.

These qualifications remind us that space and place are not static but dynamic and constantly changing. And so people are changing as well, responding to new contexts and environments. In the years to come, people will continue to interact with and impact the urban fabric in a reciprocal relationship. Space will be shaped differently, places will hold different meanings, and the secret stores of stories and memories will continue to evolve in Belfast's streets.

These qualifications remind us, however, that the city centre's 'deafening silence' regarding the past leaves commemoration in the hands of a fragmented and divided landscape (Switzer and McDowell 2009: 350). The plaques along the Falls Road, for example, record lives lost and individual grief on public space, but they also clearly delineate a collective narrative at the expense of the 'other' – security forces, loyalist paramilitaries, the British state – which all have their own nuances and stories. This in turn reinforces spatial segregation, polarizes perspectives, and hinders progress towards reconciliation.

Yet the studied blankness of city centre is equally troubling. Policymakers herald physical regeneration and economic investment as key strategies for building 'a shared future', and we see these at work in the centre. However, as Hocking notes, 'although international capital and global interconnectedness exert considerable sway over these new landscapes, the demands of place, with its residual troubled history and conflicted ethno-national groups, remain powerful forces' (Hocking 2014: 2). And these forces remain hidden under the surface of the 'new' Belfast. The past remains fundamentally disagreed, and as a result commemoration does not feature in the spaces of the city centre.

Yet to deny the conflict its place is to deny those hundreds of names and faces inscribed on memorial plaques, those countless hidden stories of the street. It is to deny the grief and injustice and anger that followed their deaths, and the impact on individuals, families and neighbourhoods. It highlights the structures of division that run through everyday life – from sectarian politics to spatial patterns, segregated bus stops, newspapers and names. Without tackling these divisions, without coming to terms with the past, 'a shared future' looks uncertain.

Elizabeth DeYoung is a graduate of Northeastern University, Boston (BA International Affairs/Modern Languages) and Queen's University Belfast (MA Irish Studies). She is at present completing her PhD at the Institute of Irish Studies, University of Liverpool. Her research examines the redevelopment of the Girdwood Barracks in North Belfast as a microcosm of power, politics and planning in post-ceasefire Northern Ireland, and of the ultimate failure of government to deliver a democratic, equal and civic society as envisioned by the Good Friday Agreement.

Notes

I would like to extend sincere thanks to my friend and mentor Paweł Romańczuk for introducing me to the streets of Belfast and their stories on our walks together.

1. The Falls Road is a nationalist/Catholic area of West Belfast, which was severely affected by the conflict.
2. For the purposes of this chapter, I will generally use the terms 'Catholic' and 'Protestant' to denote the two groupings. As with all generalizations and labels, there are many exceptions and contradictions. By using 'Catholic' and 'Protestant' I do not suggest that the past conflict has a primarily religious basis, as there are many more factors involved, ethno-national identity and allegiance included.
3. The Provisional Irish Republican Army (PIRA) was a major republican paramilitary group in the conflict. Their central aim was to end British control of Northern Ireland through political violence. This wing split from the 'Official' IRA, which had declared a ceasefire, at the start of the conflict. For this chapter, the term 'IRA' will be used to refer to the PIRA (http://cain.ulst.ac.uk/othelem/organ/iorgan.htm#ira).
4. The Ulster Volunteer Force (UVF) was a loyalist paramilitary group that aimed to defend Northern Ireland's link with Britain (http://cain.ulst.ac.uk/othelem/organ/uorgan.htm).
5. 'Special Category Status' for prisoners was withdrawn in 1976 as part of a process of normalization, meaning all political prisoners were to be treated as ordinary criminals. The following years saw prolonged protest from republican prisoners, culminating in a 1981 hunger strike in which ten men died (http://cain.ulst.ac.uk/events/hstrike/chronology.htm).

6. Royal Ulster Constabulary, the majority-Protestant police force in Northern Ireland from 1922 to 2001 (CAIN: http://cain.ulst.ac.uk/othelem/organ/rorgan.htm).
7. The Shankill Road is a Protestant/unionist/loyalist area of West Belfast.

References

Allen, N., and A. Kelly. 2003. *The Cities of Belfast*. Dublin: Four Courts Press.

Anderson, J., and I. Shuttleworth. 2003. 'Spaces of Fear: Communal Violence and Spatial Behaviour'. Cultures of Violence Conference, Centre for Research in the Arts, Social Sciences and Humanities (CRASSH), 9–10 January. Cambridge: University of Cambridge.

Author fieldnotes (Personal reflections and quotations). 2013. Belfast, Northern Ireland.

Bardon, J. 1992. *A History of Ulster*. Belfast: Blackstaff Press.

Benjamin, W. 2002. *The Arcades Project*. Cambridge: Harvard University Press.

Boal, F. 1995. *Shaping a City: Belfast in the Late Twentieth Century*. Belfast: Queen's University, Institute of Irish Studies.

Boulton, J. 2014. 'Frontier Wars: Violence and Space in Belfast, Northern Ireland', *Totem: The University of Western Ontario Journal of Anthropology* 22(1): 101–13.

Bourdieu, P. 1990. *The Logic of Practice*, trans. R. Nice. Cambridge: Polity Press.

Bryan, D. 2000. *Orange Parades: The Politics of Ritual, Tradition and Control*. London: Pluto Press.

Castells, M. 2003. 'The Process of Urban Social Change', in A. Cuthbert (ed.), *Designing Cities: Critical Readings in Urban Design*. Malden, MA: Blackwell, pp.23–27.

Certeau, M. de 1988. *The Practice of Everyday Life*, trans. S. Rendall. Berkeley, CA: University of California Press.

Coulter, C. 1999. *Contemporary Northern Irish Society*. London: Pluto Press.

Cresswell, T. 2004. *Place: A Short Introduction*. Oxford: Blackwell.

Cronon, W. 1992. 'A Place for Stories: Nature, History and Narrative', *The Journal of American History* 78(4): 1347–76.

Dawe, G. 2003. 'The Revenges of the Heart: Belfast and the Poetics of Space', in N. Allen and A. Kelly (eds), *The Cities of Belfast*. Dublin: Four Courts Press, pp.199–210.

Dawson, G. 2005. 'Trauma, Place and the Politics of Memory: Bloody Sunday, Derry, 1972–2004', *History Workshop Journal* 5(1): 151–78.

Doherty, W. 2009. 'Buried'. HD Video Installation, The Art of the Troubles, Ulster Museum, Belfast.

Donnan, H. 2005. 'Material Identities: Fixing Ethnicity in the Irish Borderlands', *Identities: Global Studies in Culture and Power* 12(1): 69–105.

Draft Google Map of Conflict Deaths. 2011. 'Remembering': Victims, Survivors and Commemoration. CAIN Web Service: http://cain.ulst.ac.uk/victims/gis/googlemaps/victims.html

Edensor, T. 2010. 'Walking in Rhythms: Place, Regulation, Style and the Flow of Experience', *Visual Studies* 25(1): 69–79.

Fay, M.T., et al. 1999. 'The Costs of the Troubles Study'. Report on the Northern Ireland Survey: The Experience and Impact of Violence. Derry: INCORE.

Feldman, A. 1991. *Formations of Violence: The Narrative of the Body and Political Terror in Northern Ireland*. Chicago, IL: University of Chicago Press.

Fregonese, F., and R. Brand. 2009. 'Polarization as a Socio-Material Phenomenon: A Bibliographical Review', *Journal of Urban Technology* 16(2–3): 9–33.

Graham, B. 2011. 'A Pair of Spectacles and a Lump of Coal: Objects of the Dead and the Stories They Tell', *Irish Journal of Anthropology* 14: 37–42.

Graham, B., and Y.F. Whelan. 2007. 'The Legacies of the Dead: Commemorating the Troubles in Northern Ireland', *Environment and Planning D: Society and Space* 25(3): 476–95.

Halbwachs, M. 1992. *On Collective Memory*, trans. L. Coser. Chicago, IL: University of Chicago Press.

Hall, E.T. 1968. 'Proxemics', *Current Anthropology* 9(2): 83–95.

Hall, T., B. Lashua and A. Coffey. 2006. 'Stories as Sorties', *Qualitative Researcher* 3(1): 2–3.

Harvey, D. 1996. *Justice, Nature and the Geography of Difference*. Cambridge: Blackwell.

Hebbert, M. 2005. 'The Street as a Locus of Memory', *Environment and Planning D: Society and Space* 23: 581–96.

Hocking, B. 2014. *The Great Reimagining: Public Art, Urban Space, and the Symbolic Landscapes of a 'New' Northern Ireland*. New York: Berghahn Books.

Jacobs, J. 2000. *The Death and Life of Great American Cities*. London: Pimlico.

Jarman, N. 1997. *Material Conflicts: Parades and Visual Displays in Northern Ireland*. Oxford: Berg.

———. 2001. 'Not an Inch', *Peace Review* 13(1): 35–41.

———. 2004. *Demography, Development and Disorder: Changing Patterns of Interface Areas*. Belfast: Institute of Conflict Research.

Jones, P., et al. 2008. 'Exploring Space and Place with Walking Interviews', *Journal of Research Practice* 4(2): 1–9.

Kelleher, L., and K. Worpole. 2010. 'Bringing the Dead Back Home: Urban Public Spaces as Sites for New Patterns of Mourning and Memorialisation', in A. Maddrell and J. Sidaway (eds), *Deathscapes: Spaces for Death, Dying, Mourning and Remembrance*. Farnham: Ashgate, pp. 161–180.

Komarova, M., and M. McKnight. 2012. 'The Digital Eye in Conflict Management: Doing Visual Ethnography in Contested Urban Space'. Conflict in Cities and the Contested State: UK Economic and Social Research Council. Divided Cities/Contested States Working Paper Series. Retrieved from www.conflictincities.org/workingpapers.html.
Kong, L. 2010. 'Foreword', in A. Maddrell and J. Sidaway (eds), *Deathscapes: Spaces for Death, Dying, Mourning and Remembrance*. Farnham: Ashgate, pp.xv–xvi.
Leerssen, J. 2001. 'Monument and Trauma: Varieties of Remembrance', in I. McBride (ed.), *History and Memory in Modern Ireland*. Cambridge: Cambridge University Press, pp.204–222.
Lefebvre, H. 1991. *The Production of Space*, trans. D. Nicholson-Smith. Oxford: Basil Blackwell.
Longley, E. 2001. 'Northern Ireland: Commemoration, Elegy, Forgetting', in I. McBride (ed.), *History and Memory in Modern Ireland*. Cambridge: Cambridge University Press, pp.223–253.
Low, S., and D. Lawrence-Zúñiga. 2003. 'Locating Culture', in S. Low and D. Lawrence-Zúñiga (eds), *The Anthropology of Space and Place*. Oxford: Blackwell, pp.1–47.
Lysaght, K., and A. Basten. 2003. 'Violence, Fear and the Everyday: Negotiating Spatial Practices in the City of Belfast', in E. Stanko (ed.), *The Meaning of Violence*. London: Routledge, pp.224–244.
Maddrell, A., and J. Sidaway. 2010. 'Introduction: Bringing a Spatial Lens to Death, Dying, Mourning and Remembrance', in A. Maddrell and J. Sidaway (eds), *Deathscapes: Spaces for Death, Dying, Mourning and Remembrance*. Farnham: Ashgate, pp.1–16.
Margry, P., and C. Sánchez-Carretero. 2011. 'Introduction', in P. Margry and C. Sánchez-Carretero (eds), *Grassroots Memorials: The Politics of Memorializing Traumatic Death*. New York: Berghahn Books, pp.1–48.
McBride, I. 2001. 'Memory and National Identity in Modern Ireland', in I. McBride (ed.), *History and Memory in Modern Ireland*. Cambridge: Cambridge University Press, pp.1–42.
McDowell, S., and C. Switzer. 2011. 'Violence and the Vernacular: Conflict, Commemoration, and Rebuilding in the Urban Context', *Buildings & Landscapes: Journal of the Vernacular Architecture Forum* 18(2): 82–104.
McGarry, J., and B. O'Leary. 1995. *Explaining Northern Ireland*. Oxford: Wiley.
McKay, S. 2000. *Northern Protestants: An Unsettled People*. Belfast: Blackstaff Press.
McKittrick, D. 1999. *Lost Lives: The Stories of the Men, Women and Children Who Died as a Result of the Northern Ireland Troubles*. Edinburgh: Mainstream Publishing Company.
Melaugh, M. n.d. 'The Civil Rights Campaign: A Chronology of Main Events'. CAIN Web Service. Retrieved from http://cain.ulst.ac.uk/events/crights/chron.htm.

Mitchell, A., and L. Kelly. 2011. 'Peaceful Spaces? "Walking" through the New Liminal Spaces of Peacebuilding and Development in North Belfast', *Alternatives: Global, Local, Political* 36: 307–25.
Nora, P. 1989. 'Between Memory and History: Les Lieux de Memoire', *Representations* 26(1): 7–24.
Pile, S. 2005. *Real Cities: Modernity, Space and the Phantasmagorias of City Life*. London: Sage.
Pink, S. 2008. 'An Urban Tour: The Sensory Sociality of Ethnographic Place-Making', *Ethnography* 9(2): 175–96.
Santino, J. 2005. *Spontaneous Shrines and the Public Memorializations of Death*. New York: Palgrave.
———. 2011. 'Shrines, Memorialization, and the Public Ritualesque in Derry', in P. Margy and C. Sánchez-Carretero (eds), *Grassroots Memorials: The Politics of Memorializing Traumatic Death*. New York: Berghahn Books.
Schubolz, D., and P. Devine. 2011. 'Segregation Preferences of 16-year-olds in Northern Ireland: What Difference Does Urban Living Make?' Conflict in Cities and the Contested State: UK Economic and Social Research Council. Divided Cities/Contested States Working Paper Series. Retrieved from www.conflictincities.org/workingpapers.html.
Shirlow, P., and B. Murtagh. 2006. *Belfast: Segregation, Violence, and the City*. London: Pluto Press.
Sluka, J. 1989. *Hearts and Minds, Water and Fish: Support for the IRA and INLA in a Northern Irish Ghetto*. Greenwich, CT: Jai Press.
Solnit, R. 2002. *Wanderlust: A History of Walking*. London: Verso.
Strange, I., and S. Davoudi. 2009. *Conceptions of Space and Place in Strategic Spatial Planning*. London: Routledge.
Sutton, M. 1999. 'Sutton Index of Deaths'. CAIN Web Service: http://cain.ulst.ac.uk/sutton/search.html.
Switzer, C., and S. McDowell. 2009. 'Redrawing Cognitive Maps of Conflict: Lost Spaces and Forgetting in the Centre of Belfast', *Memory Studies* 2(3): 337–53.
Vergunst, J. 2010. 'Rhythms of Walking: History and Presence in a City Street', *Space and Culture* 13(4): 376–88.
Viggiani, E. 2014a. *Talking Stones*. New York: Berghahn Books.
———. 2014b. 'McDonnell Joe – PIRA'. Talking Stones Online Database. Retrieved from http://northernirelandmemorials.com/database/283/mcdonnell-joe-pira-2.
Weidenhoft Murphy, W.A. 2010. 'Touring the Troubles in West Belfast: Building Peace or Reproducing Conflict?', *Peace and Change* 35(4): 537–560.
Wells, K. 2012. 'Melancholic Memorialisation: The Ethical Demands of Grievable Lives', in G. Rose and D. Tolia-Kelly (eds), *Visuality/*

Materiality: Images, Objects and Practice. Farnham: Ashgate, pp.147–165.

Wharton, K. 2013. *Wasted Years, Wasted Lives Volume 1: The British Army in Northern Ireland 1975–77*. Solihull: Helion and Company.

4

'Women on the Peace Line'
Challenging Divisions through the Space of Friendship

Andrea García González

> We said: 'Emma, it's a shame you're booking this fitness place. We're not using it. We're just going and sitting in the cafe and talking and laughing'. And we said: 'Couldn't we become a group then?

Claire, one of the Women on the Peace Line (WPL) members, recalled this quote from the moment in 2006 when a group of women from North Belfast, from mixed Catholic/nationalist and Protestant/unionist backgrounds, decided to establish WPL.[1] This chapter will analyse the space created by WPL as a 'talking space', a social space built on years of interactions that have developed into bonds of friendship. The socio-spatial dynamics of these encounters will be explored against the backdrop of the reconciliation process in Northern Ireland.

This chapter will also draw on theories of place and space to investigate the ideas and practices of friendship, an area insufficiently studied in social sciences and especially in anthropology (Paine 1969: 505; Beer 2001: 5806; Desai and Killick 2013: 4; Coleman 2013: 198). Several authors, in different disciplines, note that female friendship has been overly ignored, or even rejected (Uhl 1991; Cucó Giner 1995: 74; Derrida 1997a; Beer 2001: 5806; Still 2010), with the claim by some philosophers, such as Michelet and Nietszche, that women are incapable of friendship (Still 2010: 140).

The context where the space of friendship has been created by the women of WPL will firstly be analysed. Then, the chapter will explore how this space challenges both the division into two separate and strict communal identifications[2] of the people of Northern Ireland and the sexual division in a society, which, as McDowell (2008) states, has been deemed a 'gender regime' that 'places men above women ... in post-conflict Northern Ireland in almost every aspect of life'. Next, I will consider the difficulties that the participants of this group face and how they deal with their differences. This examination will lead to questions about the dualistic dimensions of the everyday and the political, the private and the public domains, friendship and reconciliation, which will be revealed as being intertwined in the path towards positive peace.

Everyday Encounters in Reconciliation Processes

The creation of 'relational spaces' where people can meet after the end of an armed violent conflict[3] has been highlighted as essential in peace-building and reconciliation processes (Lederach 2005). Negotiations and agreements can be carried out during peace processes at the so-called 'elite level' or 'macro-level' (McFarlane 2011). Actions taken at this level have been considered as 'a necessary but insufficient condition to move conflict societies from a state of transition, through transformation, and ultimately to reconciliation' (Knox and Quirk 2000: 196). It is at the societal level where everyday relationships develop with the potential to transcend hostilities and divisions. Lederach (2005: 96–97) highlights the importance of relationships that cross 'the lines of the conflict', and allow societies to 'move from interactions defined primarily by division and violence toward coexistence, cooperation, and constructive interdependence'. Some of these encounters may hold the capacity to contribute not just to the reduction of violence, but also to life enhancement. Galtung (1996: 30) conceptualizes this difference when he describes the ideas of 'negative peace' and 'positive peace'. The path towards the latter implies tackling not only direct armed violence, but also other kinds of violence going on in the society. This violence can be direct, structural or cultural, committed and suffered by different actors.[4] Galtung argues for an expanded concept of peace, which might be dynamic, and includes the actions taken to transform conflict in peaceful ways 'by people handling them creatively, transcending incompatibilities – and acting in conflict without recourse to violence' (ibid.: 265). In this sense, the elimination or reduction of violence is therefore a process more than a goal, arguably an everyday practice. The analysis of the WPL group in this chapter will contribute to the examination of the contributions that social spaces like this can make towards positive peace.

WPL was set in the context of Northern Ireland, where different kinds of violence have widely affected the society. The armed conflict that lasted from 1969 to 1998 (the year that peace agreements were approved) left 3,488[5] killed and 42,304[6] injured. Taking into account the small geographical size of Northern Ireland and the population of less than 2 million, there were few areas left unscathed (McWilliams 1995). Despite the peace agreements, violence is not over. In a documented article, Jarman (2004) reviewed 'the changing patterns of violence in post-ceasefire Northern Ireland'. This included paramilitary violence, violent criminal activity, sectarian violence and other forms of representative violence. In her analysis of the role of the women during the conflict in Northern Ireland and in Palestine, Sharoni (1998: 1085) affirmed that 'while the signing of peace agreements has triggered denunciations of political violence in both Israel/Palestine and the North of Ireland, to date little has been done to eliminate the structural conditions that breed violence, including violence against women'. Violence during war and violence in peacetime are not disconnected when looking at the roots of violence in a patriarchal system that uses violence to impose power, such as Woolf (1938) cleverly pointed out. This fact is encapsulated in the concept of a 'continuum of violence' used by Cynthia Cockburn (1998, 2004) as an analytical tool in different postwar contexts. The continuum of violence is explained by Cockburn (1998) as a continuum of time (pre-war, postwar, peacetime), place (home, street, battlefield) and scale. Although there has been little research done on the experiences of the women during the armed conflict,[7] the stories gathered by Fairweather, McDonough and McFadyean (1984) support that idea of the continuum of violence. Women not only suffered the direct violence inflicted by paramilitary groups or the British army, but also the violence committed by their husbands, the institutional control over their bodies, the imposition of fixed gender roles, and the cultural violence that legitimized that. As Galtung (1996: 40) states, 'Patriarchy, like any other deeply violent social formation, combines direct, structural and cultural violence in a vicious triangle'. The goal and the process of reconciliation must address the analysis of violence against women in its multiple dimensions (Strickland and Duvvury 2003: 6), and how that violence is sustained and also challenged. The mandates that the patriarchal system assigns to the women of WPL, and how they deal with them, will be part of the analysis in this chapter.

Space, Place and Community in Northern Ireland

Division and social polarization are part of deep-rooted violence contexts (Lederach 2005: 37). In Northern Ireland, segregation is one of the elements considered to have led to the 'protracted nature of the conflict' (McFarlane 2011: 1). Boundaries or 'interfaces', both physical and symbolical, have demarcated the areas of Protestants and Catholics in this society (Boal and Murray 1977, in Feldman 1991: 28). The demarcation of such areas has limited the contact between different groups, and it has also created a strict social categorization of 'us' and 'them'. Through the practice of 'telling',[8] people in Northern Ireland identify a person as belonging to one group or another, thus reproducing social identities and reaffirming social boundaries in the smallest mundane interactions (Jenkins, Donnan and McFarlane

1986: 26). Despite the peace agreement in 1998, division and sectarianism are still present. Nolan (2012) noted that the number of interface walls had increased from twenty-two in 1998 to forty-eight in 2012. In 2013, just before I started my nine months of fieldwork with WPL, new walls were still being erected: a so-called 'peace curtain' ('Peace Curtain' for East Belfast Church 2013) was built in East Belfast at an interface that has been considered a 'flashpoint for opposing factions in Northern Ireland for many years' (New 'Peace Fence' at St Matthew's Church in East Belfast 2013) and a place of regular rioting (Union Flag Dispute 2013; Rioting at Lower Newtownards Road – Short Strand Interface 2013).

Different discourses have sustained the representation of two opposing collective identities using a 'two communities' model approach to this society. Not only has this model been wielded in utilitarian political discourses, but it has also been fixed in government policy and legislation, in the media, and in academic research.[9] This model refers to two populations identified by religion, national beliefs and political ideology: as Protestant, British, unionist and loyalist, on the one hand, and as Catholic, Irish, nationalist and republican, on the other. The use of the concept of 'community' has been criticized for not questioning the existence of two separate cultures and cementing the division (Nic Craith 2002: 179; Bryan 2006: 605). Moreover, this community-model approach has been considered a neglection of historical and dynamic elements of the production of space and identities (McFarlane 1986; Wilson and Donnan 2006: 28). It has also been seen as homogenizing and trying to impose senses of belonging and affiliation (Shirlow 2003; Whitaker 2011: 58), and criticized for being instrumental in processes of political control (Nic Craith 2002; Jarman 2004; Bryan 2006; Curtis 2008). Drawing on these critiques, a link might be established between the concept of 'community' and the idea of 'place' as defined by de Certeau, and the concept of 'abstract space' as explained by Lefebvre. 'Place' is described by de Certeau as the order where 'the law of the "proper" rules', and where the elements within are situated in their own '"proper" and distinct location'; it thus implies stability (de Certeau 1984: 117). According to Lefebvre, 'abstract space' is a 'tool of domination', which destroys differences 'in order to impose an abstract homogeneity' (Lefebvre 1991: 370). The idea of community might also connect with the concept of 'place-identity', describing in this context identities intended to be fixed by physical and symbolical impositions.[10]

In contrast to the simplification implied in the community-model approach, the analysis of everyday spaces brings complexity to the study of the Northern Irish society. The analytical approach to be employed in this chapter follows de Certeau's concept of space, defined as 'the word when it is spoken' – an 'act of the present'; 'a practiced place' (de Certeau 1984: 117). De Certeau's meaning is the reverse of the terminology used by different contemporary ethnographers[11] and other scholars (Gray 2003: 240). This chapter will use the term 'space' in relation to everyday practices that are concrete, grounded in experience and embodied by the subjects of the action. Everyday practices that are called 'tactics' by de Certeau, meaning those that are used by 'ordinary' people, in contrast to the calculated 'strategies' sustained from the '"proper" place or institution' (de Certeau 1984: xix–xx). Space is neither ahistorical nor acontextual, as this chapter will suggest. As Massey (1994: 2) affirms, space is constructed out of social relations, which 'are never still; they are inherently dynamic'. In social spaces, unusual relationships cross and interact (Lederach 2005: 85).

This chapter will explore the challenges and contradictions that static notions of 'place-identity' generate in this society, through the analysis of the space of friendship created by WPL. When focusing on everyday socio-spatial activities, homogenizing conceptualizations of culturally distinct and spatially bounded social or political groups turns out to be inadequate as a tool of analysis.

The Creation of a Space of Friendship

The exploration of the social situations and cultural context in which particular forms of friendship develop has been highlighted as important (Santos-Granero 2007: 11; Coleman 2013: 295). In the context of social and territorial division, the participants in WPL had no contact with people belonging to the 'other' side of the conflict during many years of their lives. Of the twelve women that currently participate in WPL, six grew up in a Protestant/unionist/loyalist area (Louise, Lynda, Valerie, Rebecca, Caroline and Karen) and the other six in a Catholic/nationalist/republican area (Claire, Laura, Monica, Theresa, Suzanne and Eleonor). They lived in working-class neighbourhoods in Belfast, in areas most affected by the conflict. They witnessed or experienced displacement, associated with intercommunal violence and intimidation.[12] The division affected their everyday lives: they attended segregated schools; their leisure time was conducted within their respective religious communities. However, most of them had experiences that complicated the 'two-community' place-identity. That is particularly relevant from the women of Protestant background, who faced confrontations with members of loyalist paramilitary groups during the conflict, being threaten by them on different occasions. Moreover, the majority of the women of WPL referred to their families as having clear positions regarding unionism or nationalism, whereas they related well with people within and across the different social classes. Some of the interviewees raised the fact that their fathers had been involved in trade unions, and whose socialist stance was above the communal identification when dealing with social problems. Before joining WPL, some of the participants had met people of the other communal identification at the workplace, or in their extended family (particularly the women from Protestant background, meeting Catholic cousins).

The space of friendship of WPL started in the particular scenario of the promotion of peace-building initiatives. The first time some of the current participants of WPL met was due to a proposal made by a social worker, Emma, who secured funding with the aim of gathering Catholic and Protestant women together. Emma contacted Claire and Louise, who were active in community centres in North Belfast, one in a Catholic area and the other in a Protestant one. Both were asked by the social worker to find local women to join the activity, which consisted of a gym training session followed by a healthy meal. At that time, funding was coming from the EU Programme for Peace and Reconciliation 'Peace II – Extension'.[13] The only person who had previously participated in cross-community initiatives prior to WPL was Lynda, who distinguished this encounter from meetings with women from 'Southern Ireland' or the Catholic area of West Belfast, because, on this occasion, 'it was the next street to where you came from'. The 'patchwork' nature of social geography in Belfast[14] means that spatial proximity to 'the other' creates an intense sense of vulnerability and fear. In contrast to other societies where 'proximity serves as the principal facilitator for social interaction' (Froerer 2013: 149), the closeness of the territorial origins of the women forming WPL was an important symbolic wall to overcome.

The women of WPL have been meeting regularly since then, creating a space of shared experiences. They have participated in different activities together, such as Bollywood dance, handicrafts, Irish language and history classes, and workshops with other groups. They have enjoyed some activities more than others, but they look for activities to do as a justification for their meetings. These activities define the space of friendship in the sense that they share their memories about what they have done together and the expectations that these will continue in the future. Space and time are entangled: in the 'spacetime', 'memories and dreams are the stuff of such a fusion' (Harvey 2014: 14). Monica affirmed this idea, contrasting these memories with the ones which may be divisive: 'Our relationships are more built on our shared experiences we had since being together than what came before'. Activities have been deemed as a way to become 'interpersonally tied' in different contexts, as a way to develop friendship (Froerer 2013: 142). Beer states that friendship is based on sharing of 'time, problems, hopes and thoughts' (Beer 2001: 5806). During my nine months of fieldwork in the year 2013–14, I had the opportunity to meet and share weekly encounters and activities with these women. At that time their main activity involved attending Irish language classes. Initially that year, they were taking the classes in a building that belongs to a women's organization, and located in a working-class Protestant area in Belfast. This area is well known as the home of loyalist paramilitary groups who had a strong presence during the violent conflict. The Irish language teacher noted that he would not have dared to come to this area some years ago. Even so, the Irish language remains a controversial issue. For example, one mile away from the centre where the women were taking the classes, a senior Orangeman warned Protestants against learning Irish as they were serving a 'republican agenda' (Orangeman Says Protestants Should Not Learn Irish Language 2014). The women were not alarmed by this statement, and had had no intention of taking a political stance by carrying out this activity. They just enjoyed being there together.

Unlike other cross-community activities led by women in Northern Ireland (from the suffragettes at the turn of the twentieth century to the Northern Ireland Women's Coalition founded in 1996 in order to secure a place at the all-party peace talks), WPL was not created to make overt political claims. They decided to remain as a group because they valued meeting with no political intentions. When I asked Caroline, from a Protestant background, about the contribution of the group to the peace process, she affirmed: 'We are here for fun, more so than for politics'. The WPL women, who associate politics with the work of politicians, are more comfortable with the idea that they are just friends. Their aims are more related to McWilliams' idea that community projects and women's centres in Northern Ireland create 'safe, yet subversive, spaces where they can organize together around issues of concern [that] cross the sectarian divide' (McWilliams 1995: 32).

A Supportive 'Talking Space'

The everyday act of talking is an essential constituent in the creation and maintenance of relationships in WPL. Monica, one of the participants from a Catholic background, who has been in the group since the beginning, highlighted this activity as being at the heart of WPL, and described it as 'what normal friends do'. Nonetheless, the participants have experienced a significant transformation through the mere act of talking. Remembering the time when they were invited to join a cross-community activity, Louise expressed her concern about having nothing to say, while Claire worried about saying something wrong: 'This is what I said: "What are we going to talk to them about?" And I'll have to watch what I say'. This fear reduced when they realized they had 'more in common' than in what divided them, and some of them referred to housing, education, health and 'women's issues' as points of connection. The elements that helped them to overcome fears of cross-communal contact were those that made them feel comfortable with each other. After some sessions, they were more dedicated to talking than to the gym activity, and they decided to be constituted as a group '(b)ecause we got fond of each other', as Monica affirmed. The sharing of what some of them called 'private things' and the enjoyment of each other's company were elements also remarked on by the women who joined the group later.

Talking configures a space for sharing and having fun, where 'if you are down, that's the first thing to lift you up', as expressed by one of the participants. During the weekly Irish language classes I attended, they usually spent half of the class having breakfast and talking, and the other half regularly interrupting the teacher to start different conversations among themselves. Some of them expressed in the interviews that they did not really care about learning the language, either because they were already fluent, or because they found it too difficult. Planning a trip that they did with no funding in June 2014, Claire emphasized that they had to find somewhere where they could laugh as they 'usually do'. The day of the trip, for more than three hours they were just sitting in a park and eating, talking and joking. The closeness of the bonds, feeling happy with the others, the support, having fun and sharing jokes are some of the main motivations that the women of the group highlighted for choosing to be together.

De Certeau refers to the 'popular art of speaking' as a way to manipulate and appropriate imposed places and their 'proper' meanings (de Certeau 1984: 24, 33). WPL appropriates these places and creates surprises in them: for example, learning the Irish language in a staunchly Protestant community centre, which could be interpreted locally as serving a republican agenda; transforming a gym into a space for meeting, talking and sharing on a personal level, ignoring its proper use of getting fit; and appropriating the Irish classes themselves for building friendships, with the language element as secondary. It could be said that the 'talking space' created by WPL challenges the 'abstract space' described by Lefebvre (1991: 396) as relying 'on the repetitive, on reproducibility, on homogeneity'.

Challenges to the Fixed Place of Community

'Cross-community' encounters have been encouraged at the institutional level to put people from Protestant/unionist/loyalist backgrounds in touch with people from Catholic/nationalist/republican backgrounds. Not all of those encounters have had the same continuity as WPL has had. The decision of these women to keep this space alive is a choice, an election that entailed a rupture with the fixed place of the 'community'. The creation of a space of friendship may imply a 'mutation' (de Certeau 1984) that leads to problematizing imposed divisions in Northern Ireland. According to de Certeau, 'mutations' are everyday practices that manipulate the established order; tactics that make use of the cracks in places and poach in them (de Certeau 1984: xix–xxi, 24, 37).

Friendship is differentiated by the participants of WPL from family bonds and from the communal group. Considering the definition of friendship in Western culture as a volunteered relationship (Allan 1979: 17; Cucó Giner 2004: 137) in opposition to kinship relations (Beer 2001: 5805; Whitaker 2011: 63), *having* Catholic cousins is not the same as *choosing* Catholic friends. The women of the group remarked extensively on this distinction. For example, discussing ways of describing the group for a photography exhibition that I set up with them as part of the fieldwork, they decided to write at the end of the introductory text: 'This is friendship for life'. They believed that 'friendship' suited them better than 'family', because, as Claire affirmed, 'you don't get on with some of your family'. Moreover, they regard friendship as a commitment that fosters situations where those involved do not act according to the expectations of the communal group. They say that they are proud of their friendship 'before religion' difference. According to the participants, they would protect other group members even if they had to confront members of their communal group in the process. Furthermore, when it came to a potentially divisive issue, such as the Orange parades,[15] gratitude and friendship were expressed across religious divides. For instance, Lynda stated that she appreciated that Claire, despite being annoyed about the band that passed through her son's Catholic neighbourhood during the Ulster Protestant celebration of the Twelfth of July, had phoned Lynda to confirm that her son, a band member, was safe after the riots that happened that day.

The space of WPL may also imply a sense of freedom from the restrictions of their communal groups. Some of the women have engaged in activities that are not necessarily highly regarded in their communities. Lynda, for example, likes the Irish language, but has faced opposition from her son. She started Irish classes in a Protestant/unionist/loyalist area of West Belfast twenty years ago but was threatened by a paramilitary group. When she explained it in class, the Irish teacher seemed impressed with her courage. Furthermore, through the 'art of manipulating and enjoying' (de Certeau 1984: xxii), they reappropriate the imposed place of the 'community' while allowing themselves to joke about their communal identifications. In the photography workshop I delivered to them, one of the pictures selected included oranges in the foreground, and they titled it 'Too much orange, not enough green';[16] Monica stated that they could laugh about that. Theresa referred to the 'banter' in the group as the quality she enjoyed the most, as they 'can laugh at each other, and this is acceptable'. In doing that, they mutate the 'vocabularies of established languages' – as the 'consumers' described by de Certeau do – and 'trajectories trace out of the ruses of other interests and desires that are neither determined nor captured by the systems in which they develop' (de Certeau 1984: xviii).

Moreover, the members of WPL affirmed that their perception of the 'other' had changed through their participation in the group: 'Being in the group', commented Lynda, 'you look at people differently'. Some of them have started another group of cross-community women in their area, claiming that this has been possible due to their experience in WPL. Through the social and mutual obligations that friendship entails (Killick 2013: 64), the participants of WPL have opened themselves to some aspects of the other communal group, mainly regarding their religious practices. In her fieldwork about friendship in a Lebanese town, Obeid highlighted that 'social obligations are epitomized in two basic life events: marriage and death' (Obeid 2013: 105). The women of WPL attended the churches of the other group for weddings and funerals. Caroline, a woman of Protestant background, stated that 'years ago we would never have done that'. Furthermore, they appreciate the rituals carried out by the others: Lynda commented that she was grateful when Catholics prayed for her daughter who had cancer. Participants confirmed that membership in WPL is not only changing them, but also affecting their families.

Their encounters challenge the perpetuation of a division that they feel no interest in sustaining, by contrast to politicians and paramilitaries. 'Every time Catholics and Protestants are getting together, politicians will put something in, to put distance in', expressed one of the members of WPL. According to Rebecca, meeting with the 'other' is the reason why paramilitaries 'go against women big time' and 'want to keep us apart', because she believed that the division is a business for them. This statement fits with Owens' gender analysis about 'the masculine desire to fix the woman in a stable and stabilising identity' (Owens 1985, in Massey 1994: 238). The women of WPL have broken away from these limitations and moved from own place-identities to the dynamic space of friendship. The division is seen as something that sustains sectarian political discourse, and as a problem that they hope will not exist for future generations. Talking of their sons and daughters, some participants were proud to say that their children did not care about religion, while others admitted that their descendants preferred not to live in Belfast because it 'all seems terribly petty and silly and all of that. And there is no engagement in politics here other than if you are green or orange'. They do not want to perpetuate the division, and they are acting as a means of safeguarding voluntary bonds of friendship.

Gender Dynamics

This section explores the ways in which the space of friendship of WPL not only challenges the rigid communal identifications, but also societal gender relations. Places and spaces are charged with gendered meanings, as different feminist and anthropologist scholars have pointed out (Massey 1994; Low and Lawrence-Zúñiga 2003: 8). The cultural construction of place 'carries certain understandings of what the permissible roles and behaviours of each sex are' (Pellow 2003: 162).

On the onc hand, the women of WPL sustain gender stereotypes when representing men and women in their discourses. When I asked them why they decided to be a women-only group, they explained that they felt 'more comfortable' and relaxed, that they enjoyed 'each other's company', and they could 'have more of a laugh and talk about things better'. Some members perceived men as driven by money, 'troublesome' and the cause of 'friction', in contrast to women, who like to 'mix more' and are 'more adaptable'. Valerie explained that women do so in the name of their kids. Lynda recalled a situation that had occurred some years before, when 'the IRA shot soldiers' and how the women unanimously rejected such behaviour because 'they thought the same, that they were somebody's son'. Empathy and understanding were being linked with motherhood. Also, in the domestic sphere, the participants of WPL reproduced gender roles in the labour division of their everyday lives, babysitting their grandchildren or cooking for their husbands on the assumption that this is what women do.

In addition to those embodied gendered understandings, it is important to highlight their consideration about the activity of WPL as something not 'political'. This appears to maintain the division of the public sphere, regarded as a masculine domain where politics are carried out, and the private sphere, regarded as the space of women. This dichotomy is criticized by some feminist scholars for reinforcing 'the view that women have no power or political agency, and that they are totally dependent on the existing social and political structures' (Sharoni 1998: 1062). Moreover, many scholars (such as Pitt-Rivers 1973, Paine 1999, and Carrier 1999, in Torresan 2011: 238) characterize friendship as a relationship comprising emotions that belong in a private domestic sphere.[17] This idea may shed light on the perception by the women of WPL that their friendship is non-political, and hence non-public.

On the other hand, there have been transformations in their attitudes towards how they are expected to perform as women. Firstly, weekly meetings provide 'time for themselves' and participants are fully committed to such occasions, regardless of family demands. Secondly, during their conversations they talk about what they used to keep for themselves. When being together, they criticize the marriage institution or complain about their own family. Rebecca highlighted that WPL changed her a lot because it made her 'more assertive'. Being in the group, she commented, had allowed her to express her anger or annoyance with her own family. Thirdly, gender roles and attitudes are transformed through their meetings. Louise was provided as an example of a role change with the support of the others in that she had adopted a more assertive stance towards her husband. Some of the women remembered the first time she had gone on a trip with the group: she had never previously left her home for a night, and cried when she got onto the bus, worried for her husband and daughter whom she had left alone. This changed, however, the moment that the women gave her a drink, and then she 'never looked back' – as Louise affirmed. Monica connected the idea of supporting each other with challenges to gender roles. She explained how men react against that 'level of support' as a way of 'trying to undermine that we have friendships', saying to them that 'you're like a bunch of lesbians down there'. Relationships, in this sense, create a space for sharing and support that allows them to confront and explore gender expectations.

In the 'talking space' of WPL, by creating intimacy in order to share their concerns, the women of WPL are breaking with the constrictions of the 'private' or 'domestic' sphere. The house, as the place where the roles of women are fixed (Pellow 2003: 162), may find its walls shaken by the airing of these encounters. The participants of WPL are generating what anthropologist Teresa del Valle Murga calls 'bridge spaces': spaces that are configured by bridging traditional demarcations of the domestic space and the outside, the private and the public – that is to say, spaces for change in relation to gender models (del Valle Murga 1997: 164–65). Through the trust and support developed in this space, they defeat some gender rules. Nonetheless, gender roles and behaviours do not completely disappear. As Aretxaga reflects, the tension between the transgression and reproduction of gender ideology is a dynamic process, which is part of the actions of women in Northern Ireland as in other parts of the world (Aretxaga 1997: 78). Since space is created by bodies in motion, interacting with others and the environment (Low 2014: xxiii), the place of the 'proper' – where gender norms rule – and the space of the encounter – where gender roles are both performed and challenged – are linked. Contrary to the dismissal of the body in the 'abstract space' (Lefebvre 1991: 310, 395–96), in the everyday gendered bodies interact and may reinforce cultural norms, while at the same time transforming them.

Dealing with Differences

The process of constant creation of the social space of WPL entails tensions and negotiations. The space of friendship is by no means 'a new plane of perfection, a new tabula rasa, onto which all that matters in human experience comes to be written' (Casey 1996: 46). Contradictions and challenges in dealing with different place-identities are part of the space.

The participants of WPL recognized that members harbour oppositional stances in relation to religion, nationalism and politics. Nonetheless, the women of WPL fluctuate between a belief in respect for such differences, and silence about their implications. They referred to themselves and to the others as 'Catholics' or 'Protestants', although not all of them practice religion. These terms are categories linked with nationalism, understood as an 'imagined community' (Anderson 1983). They include feelings of British-ness and Irish-ness, or – as Jenkins (1997: 119) points out – of the constitutional 'membership of the United Kingdom and the reunification of Ireland'.[18] They called 'differences' to those communal identifications, and they claimed they were proud to maintain them. Theresa drew attention to this when asked about the contribution of the group to the peace process: 'They can learn a lot from us because we are very comfortable with the differences'. Most of the interviewees made reference to the idea raised by Monica in a workshop about the WPL's refusal to be considered a 'rainbow'. Monica had explained that the group is 'not a merging of colours: I'm green and Lynda is orange, and I'm very happy for Lynda to be orange, but I'm green'. They agree that they can deal with differences: 'We just have to respect each other's opinions, to agree to disagree'. However, they consider that not talking about the past or about controversial issues such the Orange parades is a way not to offend others. Their standpoints are kept for their own communal group. Silence is a tool for dealing with differences, and it hides some of the women's beliefs. This is hardly surprising in a society dominated by fear of letting the 'other' know who you are, famously and poignantly captured in Seamus Heaney's poem on silences and ways of 'telling' – 'whatever you say, say nothing' (Moloney 2014: 202).

The avoidance of confrontation is an important aspect in WPL. Karen affirmed that they decided to close the group three years ago because they did not want to take the risk of including someone who could be 'bitter'. They used this concept when alluding to someone who confronts the other community, and who displays their identity however problematic this may prove. Lynda described her son as 'pretty bitter', and she justified his attitude by claiming that '[h]e has seen a lot of murder'. Caroline referred to her grandmother as a 'bitter woman' because she lived surrounded by Catholic families and chose to display a Union flag outside her home. 'Bitterness' was explained by McFarlane as the opposite of a general agreement in Northern Irish society to act 'decently' towards any person (McFarlane 1986: 96). That attitude is not welcome in the group. A significant example elicited in order to illustrate such bitterness is a situation that occurred in a WPL Irish language class when Lynda wore a badge with the initials of a loyalist paramilitary organization ('UVF', Ulster Volunteer Force) in a community centre of a Catholic area. During the class following this event, Claire mentioned the incident, and Lynda said she wore it because of the memorial she had been to the day before for the centenary of that organization. The other participants found it inappropriate nevertheless. In an interview, Lynda referred to the UVF badge stating: 'It's my culture, it's my history, and I'm not gonna be ashamed of that'. According to another participant, she 'put us all in danger there'. This anxiety was caused not just by the object itself, but by the place where it was shown, a place 'where you can meet an IRA man'. The fact that the UVF badge and the Irish community centre represented opposed places was significant. The situation revealed a clash between place-identities, and gave visibility to those boundaries that are still not easy to cross. Space as a set of social relations is about interaction, which 'is likely to include conflict' (Massey 1994: 139) – a conflict that could be deemed as 'part of life and as a motor of change' (Lederach and Maiese 2003: 1), but which the WPL aimed to avoid in order to keep relationships fluid.

Rodman (2003: 209) affirms that 'the contests and tensions between different actors and interests in the construction of space should be explored'. Examining these controversies allows the analysis not to offer an idealization of the space of friendship, and also to explore the constraints faced in a reconciliation process. The difficulties detected in the analysis of WPL may provide important clues about the problems of overcoming years of hatred, hostility, confrontation, isolation and reinforcement of communal identifications. Recognizing the differences that exist among the group and respecting such differences is regarded by some scholars as essential in the improvement of democracy (Derrida 1997a; Cockburn 1998; Bloomfield, Barnes and Huyse 2003). Derrida advocates the inclusion of the concept of 'hospitality' as a route to redefining democracy, welcoming the 'other' not by means of assimilation or acculturation, but through negotiating 'at every instant' and with rules 'invented at every second with all the risks involved' (Derrida 1997b). In WPL, silence and concealment may be an implicit norm for preventing conflictive situations, but the space of friendship is also a space for negotiation in the face of unexpected issues. The situation when Lynda wore a UVF badge in an Irish class was managed through the reinforcement of silence, but it was also a reminder of the differences that broke the ideal, 'relaxed' and 'enjoyable' space created at WPL and delivered such differences in their context. This space of friendship within WPL, as Lefebvre states about the concept of space, is not a passive or pre-existing void, but is created by that action (Lefebvre 1991: 11, 90, 170).

The Imagination of the Political

Even though the women of WPL do not regard themselves as political, it can be argued that the space of friendship might be seen as a space of politics. This follows the propositions raised by authors such as Magnusson (2013: 1) who suggests 'the possibility of a new politics, no longer centred on the state but instead on everyday life'. Different venues and activities are seen as the everyday site of politics in the city, where unanticipated transformations may happen (ibid.: 9). Paying attention to those spaces may lead us to imagine politics and transformation differently (ibid.: 10; Stephens 2013: 109, 117). Moreover, social spaces are key in peace building, for they might be the locus of social change that may allow to transcend violence (Lederach 2005: 86).

The space of WPL implies a transformation. Firstly, it challenges dualistic polarities that are deemed as driving cycles of violence (Lederach 2005: 35). Secondly, it questions some gender impositions through their relationships, contributing to slowly breaking with the violence sustained by patriarchy, and thus walking towards positive peace as a context where multiple inequalities must be tackled. Thirdly, the development of elements like trust, care and cooperation are part of the space of friendship, but also regarded as important components in reconciliation processes. Bar-Siman-Tov defines the process of reconciliation as a long-term endeavour that will require former enemies to 'form new relations of peaceful coexistence based on mutual trust and acceptance, cooperation, and consideration of each other's needs' (Bar-Siman-Tov 2004, in Aiken 2013: 18). Furthermore, friendship provides emotional support – a key element of healing after war-related violence (Miller and Rasmussen 2010: 14).

The 1960s feminist slogan 'the personal is political' seems appropriate to refer to the elimination of definitive lines of demarcation between these dimensions. Two poles of a dichotomy connected with categories of the private and the public, which are employed as ideological weapons (Magnusson 2013: 50), as part of the patriarchal social and cultural construction. The social space of friendship requires and promotes the participants to be in relation. Through this relationship – based on trust, enjoyment, support – they are transformed, also transforming their environment in their everyday. This is a space for the unexpected to happen, for constant negotiations, which may have the potential to 'shift the boundaries of the familiar' (Ahmed 2000: 7, in Stephens 2013: 110), challenging in diverse ways the foundations of violence in the context of Northern Ireland. For reconciliation studies, it is important to break assumptions about what is considered political, and to bring ethnographic detail and the political impact of 'the everyday' into focus.

Conclusions

In this chapter, the space of friendship created by 'Women on the Peace Line' has been analysed in relation to the challenges it poses in the established and divided order of the Northern Irish society. The 'talking space' where bonds of friendship are developed breaks into the 'proper', and goes beyond imposed meanings and homogenizing conceptions of place and space in Northern Ireland.

The transgression and reproduction of embodied identities of place and gender has been revealed as significant in the analysis. The participants in WPL create a space that allows them to joke and relax, away from the constraints of their family and their communal group, challenging overarching communal identifications and gender roles. However, at the same time, they bring cultural norms from the place of the 'proper' to the space of encounter. In that intersection of place and space, identities are revealed as fluid, heterogeneous, and in constant formation. This is part of the rich tapestry of everyday practices, and the evidence of the numerous and intertwined layers that a space is composed of. WPL is not a model to follow, but it is an experience of life. The women of WPL express and perform multiple and contradictory interpretations of the heterogeneity they aim to live in. This 'talking space', which also includes silences, detours and constant negotiations, is transformed in the walking, creating its own unpredictable path.

The exploration of groups like WPL might broaden reconciliation analyses. The analysis of reconciliation processes should include not just those groups that situate themselves in the traditional political domain, but also the initiatives that are contributing to a positive peace under the banner of privacy and enjoyment. The importance of friendship in reconciliation processes has been highlighted, with the need to break with the traditional division of private and public spheres. Dichotomies like domestic/public, personal/political, or even conflict/post-conflict are abstractions that may not correspond to everyday experiences. The slash sign here might represent a symbolic fence that, in perpetuating binaries, impedes the analysis of everyday transformative spaces and the exploration of different kinds of violence and experiential and structural inequalities. Going beyond those slashes, paying attention to relational spaces, to transformative relationships, will allow us to incorporate and give value to different initiatives that are part of the constantly changing map of reconciliation.

Andrea García González graduated with an MA in anthropology at Queen's University Belfast, after completing a BA in anthropology and a BA in journalism at Universidad Complutense in Madrid, and different post-graduate courses in gender and equal opportunities. At present, she is completing a PhD in arts and humanities in the University of Brighton. Her research focuses on the role of women in reconciliation processes, studying the case of Northern Ireland for her MA, and the case of the Basque Country for her PhD.

Notes

1. 'Women on the Peace Line' is a pseudonym. It was the name suggested by the participants in order to anonymize their identities.
2. I will use the term 'communal identification' and 'communal group' in this chapter to refer to ascriptions in Northern Ireland that include religion, nationalist beliefs and political ideologies. In this way, I avoid employing the term 'community', which, as we will see later, has been used to reduce the complexity of this society (see García González 2016).
3. This 'end of an armed violent conflict' is usually referred to as 'post-conflict'. I find this latter term problematic, since conflict is part of human life and not necessarily negative in itself. What makes a conflict harmful is when it is addressed with violence – and the conflict in Northern Ireland was intended to be resolved through the use of violence, specifically through armed violence.
4. Direct violence includes physical and verbal violence and is intentional; structural violence describes the indirect violence that comes from the social structure itself; cultural violence serves to legitimize direct and structural violence, motivating actors to commit direct violence or to omit counteracting structural violence (Galtung 1996: 2, 31).
5. Calculation based on the Sutton database (Sutton 2002).
6. Calculation based on Melaugh, McKenna and Lynn 2014.
7. In Northern Ireland, scholars and women's organizations have denounced the omission of women when considering the past. The little archival material generated during the violent conflict that covers the political events involving women (McWilliams 1995: 16), or the misrepresentation of women in the remembrance of the conflict (McDowell 2008) are part of the institutionalized ignorance about women's contributions to a more peaceful Northern Irish society (Ward 2013).

8. 'Telling' was explained by Burton as 'the pattern of signs and cues by which religious ascription is arrived at in the everyday interactions of Protestants and Catholics' (Burton 1978, in Aretxaga 1997: 35).
9. See Wilson and Donnan (2006: 22) in their analysis of the use of the 'tribal conflict model', which dominated the discipline of anthropology up to the 1990s.
10. 'Place-identity' is defined by Proshansky, Fabian and Kaminoff (1983: 59) as part of the 'self-identity' of the person, consisting of 'memories, ideas, feelings, attitudes, values, preferences, meanings and conceptions of behaviour and experience' in relation to the physical world. In a society where 'place is inextricably linked to the formation and re-creation of ethnic identities', as Aretxaga (1997: 24) claims, the definition of 'place-identity' needs to be expanded to the 'strategic construction' of collective identities, such as Low and Lawrence-Zúñiga (2003: 24) describe it.
11. Such as Ingold, who prefers the idea of place rather than space, considering the latter as 'detached from the realities of life and experience' (Ingold 2011: 145).
12. The population movement due to the violent conflict in Belfast was, up until the Balkan conflicts, 'the most significant shift of people attributed to violence within Europe since the conclusion of World War II' (Shirlow 2003: 79).
13. Since 1995, Northern Ireland has received money from that programme, in its different stages. The 'Peace II' Programme ran from 2000 to 2006 with a budget of €1,155 million (Potter and Egerton 2011). The beneficiaries were 'sectors, fields, groups and communities hardest hit by the conflict', and projects were 'expected to prioritize a cross-community approach' (European Council Regulation 1999). Young people, women and older workers were given particular consideration (Harvey 2003: 36).
14. The 'patchwork pattern', as Allen Feldman calls it, is especially significant in North Belfast, where most of the women that joined WPL lived. Due to that geographical distribution of the neighbourhoods, that area suffered '[o]ver half the doorstep murders that took place in Belfast in 1969–77' (Feldman 1991: 71–72). For Feldman, those killings at people's front doors were acts of breaking the 'sanctuary space' or 'no-go areas', which ceased to 'fully protect or insulate the community' (ibid.: 41).
15. These parades have constituted a historically disputed point in Northern Irish society – see Bryan 2000.
16. In Northern Ireland the terms 'green' and 'orange' are used as synecdoches alluding to the Catholic/nationalist/republican 'community' and the Protestant/unionist/loyalist 'community' respectively.
17. This viewpoint might have led to the neglect of the study of friendship, as this has been assumed as a 'personal matter' (Allan 1979: 2) or 'informal' when referring to female friendship (Abrahams 1999, in Bell and Coleman 1999: 13).
18. Nationalist sentiments, however, are not always analogous with the communal group. Lynda and Rebecca provide evidence of this rupture with the homogeneity of nationalism and the concept of territory:

    L: If anybody says to me 'What's your nationality?', I'm Northern Irish.
    R: No, I would say British.
    L: I love it, because I can take a wee part of Britain and a wee part of Ireland, and I can have what I want. Northern Ireland is six counties, but to start being proud and working as if our own country is Northern Ireland, rather than Britain.
    R: Excuse me, but we are not a country. We are a province.

References

Aiken, Nevin. 2013. *Identity, Reconciliation and Transitional Justice: Overcoming Intractability in Divided Societies*. London: Routledge.

Allan, Graham. 1979. *A Sociology of Friendship and Kinship*. London: Allen and Unwin.
Anderson, Benedict. 1983. *Imagined Communities: Reflections on the Origin and Spread of Nationalism*. London: Verso.
Aretxaga, Begoña. 1997. *Shattering the Silence: Women, Nationalism and Political Subjectivity in Northern Ireland*. Princeton, NJ: Princeton University Press.
Beer, Bettina. 2001. 'Anthropology of Friendship', in Neil J. Smelser and Paul B. Baltes (eds), *International Encyclopedia of the Social & Behavioral Sciences*. Vol. 11. Amsterdam: Elsevier, pp. 5805–5808.
Bell, Sandra, and Simon Coleman (eds). 1999. *The Anthropology of Friendship*. Oxford: Berg.
Bloomfield, David, Teresa Barnes and Luc Huyse. 2003. *Reconciliation after Violent Conflict: A Handbook*. Stockholm: International Institute for Democracy and Electoral Assistance.
Bryan, Dominic. 2000. *Orange Parades: The Politics of Ritual, Tradition and Control*. London: Pluto.
———. 2006. 'The Politics of Community', *Critical Review of International Social and Political Philosophy* 9(4): 603–18.
Casey, Edward S. 1996. 'How to Get from Space to Place in a Fairly Short Stretch of Time: Phenomenological Prolegomena', in Steven Feld and Keith H. Basso (eds), *Senses of Place*. Santa Fe, NM: School of American Research Press, pp. 13–52.
Certeau, Michel de. 1984. *The Practice of Everyday Life*. Berkeley, CA: University of California Press.
Cockburn, Cynthia. 1998. *The Space Between Us: Negotiating Gender and National Identities in Conflict*. London: Zed Books.
———. 2004. 'The Continuum of Violence: A Gender Perspective on War and Peace', in Wenona Giles and Jennifer Hyndman (eds), *Sites of Violence: Gender and Conflict Zones*. Berkeley, CA: University of California Press.
Coleman, Simon. 2013. 'Making Friendship Impure: Some Reflections on a (Still) Neglected Topic', in Amit Desai and Evan Killick (eds), *The Ways of Friendship: Anthropological Perspectives*. New York: Berghahn Books, pp. 197–206.
Cucó Giner, Josepa. 1995. *La amistad: Perspectiva Antropológica*. Barcelona: Icaria Editorial.
———. 2004. *Antropología Urbana*. Barcelona: Ariel.
Curtis, Jennifer. 2008. '"Community" and the Re-Making of 1970s Belfast', *Ethnos: Journal of Anthropology* 73(3): 399–426.
Derrida, Jacques. 1997a. *Politics of Friendship*. London: Verso.
———. 1997b. 'Politics and Friendship'. Conference at the Centre for Modern French Thought, University of Sussex, 1 December. Retrieved 28 January 2016 from http://hydra.humanities.uci.edu/derrida/pol+fr.html.

Desai, Amit, and Evan Killick (eds). 2013. *The Ways of Friendship: Anthropological Perspectives*. New York: Berghahn Books.

European Council Regulation. 1999. *Northern Ireland: PEACE II Programme (2000–2006)*, No. 1260/1999 of 21 June 1999. Retrieved 28 January 2016 from http://europa.eu/legislation_summaries/regional_policy/provisions_and_instruments/g24201_en.htm.

Fairweather, Eileen, Roisin McDonough and Melanie McFadyean. 1984. *Only the Rivers Run Free. Northern Ireland: The Women's War*. London: Pluto.

Feldman, Allen. 1991. *Formations of Violence: The Narrative of the Body and Political Terror in Northern Ireland*. Chicago, IL: University of Chicago Press.

Froerer, Peggy. 2013. 'Close Friends: The Importance of Proximity in Children's Peer Relations in Chhattisgarh, Central India', in Amit Desai and Evan Killick (eds), *The Ways of Friendship: Anthropological Perspectives*. New York: Berghahn Books, pp. 133–53.

Galtung, Johan. 1996. *Peace by Peaceful Means: Peace and Conflict, Development and Civilization*. London: Sage.

García González, Andrea. 2016. '"Out of the Box": Punk and the Concept of "Community" in Ireland', *Liverpool Postgraduate Journal of Irish Studies* 1(1): 39–52.

Gray, John. 2003. 'Open Spaces and Dwelling Places: Being at Home on Hill Farms in the Scottish Borders', in Setha M. Low and Denise Lawrence-Zúñiga (eds), *The Anthropology of Space and Place: Locating Culture*. Malden, MA: Blackwell, p. 224–44.

Harvey, Brian. 2003. *Review of the Peace II Programme*. York: The Joseph Rowntree Charitable Trust.

Harvey, David. 2014. 'Spacetime and the World (2005)', in Jen Jack Gieseking et al. (eds), *The People, Place, and Space Reader*. New York: Routledge, pp. 12–16.

Ingold, Tim. 2011. *Being Alive: Essays on Movement, Knowledge and Description*. New York: Routldege.

Jarman, Neil. 2004. 'From War to Peace? Changing Patterns of Violence in Northern Ireland, 1990–2003', *Terrorism and Political Violence* 16(3): 420–38.

Jenkins, Richard. 1997. *Rethinking Ethnicity: Arguments and Explorations*. London: Sage.

Jenkins, Richard, Hastings Donnan and Graham McFarlane. 1986. 'Social Anthropology and the Sectarian Divide in Northern Ireland', Royal Anthropological Institute of Great Britain and Ireland, Occasional Paper 41.

Killick, Evan. 2013. 'Ayompari, Compadre, Amigo: Forms of Fellowship in Peruvian Amazonia', in Amit Desai and Evan Killick (eds), *The Ways of Friendship: Anthropological Perspectives*. New York: Berghahn Books, pp. 46–68.

Knox, Colin, and Padraic Quirk. 2000. *Peace Building in Northern Ireland, Israel and South Africa: Transition, Transformation and Reconciliation*. London: Macmillan Press.
Lederach, John Paul. 2005. *The Moral Imagination: The Art and Soul of Building Peace*. New York: Oxford University Press.
Lederach, John Paul, and Michelle Maiese. 2003. *The Little Book of Conflict Transformation*. Intercourse, PA: Good Books.
Lefebvre, Henri. 1991. *The Production of Space*. Oxford: Basil Blackwell.
Low, Setha M. 2014. 'Introduction. Embodied Space: The Ethnography of Space and Place', in Jen Jack Gieseking et al. (eds), *The People, Place, and Space Reader*. New York: Routledge, pp.22–23.
Low, Setha M., and Denise Lawrence-Zúñiga (eds). 2003. *The Anthropology of Space and Place: Locating Culture*. Malden, MA: Blackwell.
Magnusson, Warren. 2013. *Politics of Urbanism: Seeing Like a City*. New York: Routledge.
Massey, Doreen B. 1994. *Space, Place, and Gender*. Minneapolis, MN: University of Minnesota Press.
McDowell, Sara. 2008. 'Commemorating Dead "Men": Gendering the Past and Present in Post-conflict Northern Ireland', *Gender, Place & Culture: A Journal of Feminist Geography* 15(4): 335–54.
McFarlane, Graham. 1986. '"It's Not as Simple as That": The Expression of the Catholic and Protestant Boundary in Northern Irish Rural Communities', in Anthony Cohen (ed.), *Symbolising Boundaries: Identity and Diversity in British Cultures*. Manchester: Manchester University Press, pp.88–106.
McFarlane, Peter. 2011. 'Community-Based NGOs in Grassroots Peacebuilding and Reconciliation in Northern Ireland', *E-International Relations Journal*. Retrieved 28 January 2016 from http://www.e-ir.info/2011/09/24/community-based-ngos-in-grassroots-peacebuilding-and-reconciliation-in-northern-ireland/.
McWilliams, Monica. 1995. 'Struggling for Peace and Justice: Reflections on Women's Activism in Northern Ireland', *Journal of Women's History* 6(4): 13–39.
Melaugh, Martin, Fionnuala McKenna and Brendan Lynn. 2014. 'Background Information on Northern Ireland Society: Security and Defence', CAIN Web Service – Conflict and Politics in Northern Ireland. Retrieved 28 January 2016 from http://cain.ulst.ac.uk/ni/security.htm#05.
Miller, Kenneth E., and Andrew Rasmussen. 2010. 'War Exposure, Daily Stressors, and Mental Health in Conflict and Post-conflict Settings: Bridging the Divide between Trauma-Focused and Psychosocial Frameworks', *Social Science & Medicine* 70(1): 7–16.
Moloney, Michelle. 2014. 'Reaching Out from the Archive: The Role of Community Oral History Archives in Conflict Transformation in Northern Ireland'. PhD dissertation. Belfast: University of Ulster.

'New "Peace Fence" at St Matthew's Church in East Belfast'. 2013. *BBC News*, 8 November. Retrieved 28 January 2016 from http://www.bbc.co.uk/news/uk-northern-ireland-24856275.

Nic Craith, Máiréa. 2002. *Plural Identities – Singular Narratives: The Case of Northern Ireland*. New York: Berghahn Books.

Nolan, Paul. 2012. *The Northern Ireland Peace Monitoring Report*. Belfast: Community Relations Council.

Obeid, Michelle. 2013. 'Friendship, Kinship and Sociality in a Lebanese Town', in Amit Desai and Evan Killick (eds), *The Ways of Friendship: Anthropological Perspectives*. New York: Berghahn Books, pp. 93–113.

'Orangeman Says Protestants Should Not Learn Irish Language'. 2014. *BBC News*, 1 February. Retrieved 28 January 2016 from http://www.bbc.co.uk/news/uk-northern-ireland-26000146.

Paine, Robert. 1969. 'In Search of Friendship: An Exploratory Analysis in "Middle-Class" Culture', *Man, New Series* 4(4): 505–24.

'"Peace Curtain" for East Belfast Church'. 2013. *UTV News*, 8 November. Retrieved 28 January 2016 from http://www.u.tv/News/Peace-curtain-for-east-Belfast-church/d7bb5dcf-03ab-4c5a-a0ec-3e1c674631e0.

Pellow, Deborah. 2003. 'The Architecture of Female Seclusion in West Africa', in Setha M. Low and Denise Lawrence-Zúñiga (eds), *The Anthropology of Space and Place: Locating Culture*. Malden, MA: Blackwell, pp. 161–83.

Potter, Michael, and Leigh Egerton. 2011. 'The EU PEACE and INTERREG Programmes in Northern Ireland'. *Northern Ireland Assembly*, Research and Information Service Briefing Paper. Retrieved 28 January 2016 from http://www.niassembly.gov.uk/globalassets/Documents/RaISe/Publications/2011/OFMdFM/12611.pdf.

Proshansky, Harold M., Abbe K. Fabian and Robert Kaminoff. 1983. 'Place-Identity: Physical World Socialization of the Self', *Journal of Environmental Psychology* 3(1): 57–83.

'Rioting at Lower Newtownards Road – Short Strand Interface'. 2013. *The Wild Geese*, 13 July. Retrieved 28 January 2016 from http://thewildgeese.irish/video/raw-footage-rioting-at-lower-newtownards-road-short-strand.

Rodman, Margaret C. 2003. 'Empowering Place: Multilocality and Multivocality', in Setha M. Low and Denise Lawrence-Zúñiga (eds), *The Anthropology of Space and Place: Locating Culture*. Malden, MA: Blackwell, pp. 204–24.

Santos-Granero, Fernando. 2007. 'Of Fear and Friendship: Amazonian Sociality beyond Kinship and Affinity', *The Journal of the Royal Anthropological Institute* 13(1): 1–18.

Sharoni, Simona. 1998. 'Gendering Conflict and Peace in Israel/Palestine and the North of Ireland', *Millennium: Journal of International Studies* 27(4): 1061–90.

Shirlow, Peter. 2003. '"Who Fears to Speak": Fear, Mobility, and Ethno-sectarianism in the Two "Ardoynes"', *The Global Review of Ethnopolitics* 3(1): 76–91.

Stephens, Angharad Closs. 2013. *The Persistence of Nationalism: From Imagined Communities to Urban Encounters*. New York: Routledge.

Still, Judith. 2010. *Derrida and Hospitality: Theory and Practice*. Edinburgh: Edinburgh University Press.

Strickland, Richard, and Nata Duvvury. 2003. *Gender Equity and Peacebuilding. From Rhetoric to Reality: Finding the Way*. Washington, DC: International Centre for Research on Women (ICRW).

Sutton, Malcom. 2002. 'An Index of Deaths from the Conflict in Ireland', *CAIN Web Service – Conflict and Politics in Northern Ireland*. Retrieved 28 January 2016 from http://cain.ulst.ac.uk/sutton/book/index.html.

Torresan, Angela. 2011. 'Strange Bedfellows: Brazilian Immigrants Negotiating Friendship in Lisbon', *Ethnos* 76(2): 233–53.

Uhl, Sarah. 1991. 'Forbidden Friends: Cultural Veils of Female Friendship in Andalusia', *American Ethnologist* 18(1): 90–105.

'Union Flag Dispute'. 2013. *BBC News*, 15 January. Retrieved 28 January 2016 from http://www.bbc.co.uk/news/uk-northern-ireland-21020296.

Valle Murga, Teresa del. 1997. *Andamios Para una Nueva Ciudad: Lecturas desde la Antropología*. Madrid: Cátedra.

Ward, Margaret. 2013. 'Excluded and Silenced: Women in Northern Ireland after the Peace Process', *Open Democracy Online*. Retrieved 28 January 2016 from www.opendemocracy.net/printpdf/77473.

Whitaker, Robin. 2011. 'The Politics of Friendship in Feminist Anthropology', *Anthropology in Action* 18(1): 56–66.

Wilson, Thomas M., and Hastings Donnan. 2006. *The Anthropology of Ireland*. Oxford: Berg.

Woolf, Virginia. 1938. *Three Guineas*. New York: Harcourt.

5

'You Have No Legitimate Reason to Access'

Visibility and Movement in Contested Urban Space

Milena Komarova

> The mere fact that you . . . were able to stand on the Springfield Road and *observe* the parade and the gate is one of the issues that remain today . . . I live on the inside of that gate and on that particular day every single year I am denied *access* to the very point where YOU were . . . [W]hen the Police or the Parades Commission say to me, 'You have no *legitimate reason to access* the Springfield Road at that time', very often we would say, 'Ok, so what legitimate [reason] have the world's press to be on the outside of that gate? What legitimate right have academics to be on that road? . . . And, with the greatest respect, what right has a researcher to be at that space if someone who lives there can't access that space?'
>
> —Interview, 12 January 2016

Introduction

In the early afternoon of 25 June 2011, two university colleagues and I arrived at the site of Workman Avenue gate. This was a solid, non-see-through structure, made of corrugated iron, in one of Belfast's 'peace walls' (Figure 5.1). The wall runs along a large portion of the Springfield Road in the west of the city, dividing unionist communities on its north side from nationalist communities on the south. Upon our arrival the site was barren and, in the absence of many others, we felt vulnerably visible, caught in the middle of the 'stare down' between the wall and the few 'nationalist' houses directly facing it from across the road (Figure 5.2). Our 'standing out' created a certain feeling of discomfort. However, this was soon to

Figure 5.1 The solid gate. Photo by the author.

Figure 5.2 Housing across the road. Photo by the author.

change as more people, media and the police began arriving to observe, photograph and video the contentious annual Whiterock (Orange Order) Parade, and the nationalist protest against it. We knew that the gate itself was solidly welded for most of the year but for a small pedestrian entrance on its side, only open to let people through during daylight hours. The occasion of our observation was one of the mere two times a year when the larger gate was un-welded and opened for a few short minutes, if not seconds, in order to allow a small party of Orange Order members to ceremonially march through, under the hostile gaze of the protesters and the irreverent digital eye of the media.

This was the first of a series of visits that we have since conducted to the site, to observe the parade and protest, but also the everyday life practices of people using the gate as a pedestrian entrance. During that first observation we felt that what we noticed, and in equal measure what we omitted, was strongly driven by our own experience of being visible. Our visibility was shaped by the social geography of the area, composed of small juxtaposing 'unionist' and 'nationalist' communities divided by a wall, where outsiders are clearly recognizable in public space. It was also shaped by the contentious nature of the events taking place, for which opposing crowds had congregated. This was in sharp contrast to the mundane emptiness of the space, only sparsely used for pedestrian purposes.

As the small Orange Order party was walking through, marchers and protestors engaged each other with photographic and video gazes from across the line of digital 'fire' presented by the opening gates. Media and researchers, like ourselves, jostled and pushed for a good viewing position, broadcasting, popularizing and later analysing images from the events (Figure 5.3). We felt that the intense use of digital image technologies by everyone present communicated contestation, threat and resistance to the presence and actions of various parties, including us – the researchers. While we were keenly aware of the subjectivity of our perceptions, the opening quote in this chapter, from a more recent interview with a local resident legitimizes our intuition. It also confirms the affective power of 'the visual' in inter-subjective communication, territorialization, and the positioning of self and others (Brighenti 2010).

Returning to Workman Avenue in June 2015, a week before the annual Whiterock Parade was due, and after a long period of not having observed the area, we were struck by a highly visible change: the solid iron gate in the interface wall had been replaced by a see-through structure, such that the immediate vicinity on either side was now in plain sight at all times (Figure 5.4). This change impressed us immediately. What would it mean, when the parade and protest were under way, for both sides to be able to observe each other all the while, as opposed to only for the few brief seconds as the gate opened and closed? Furthermore, how (if at all) had this change in visibility affected the mundane uses of the gate, the accessibility of space on either side, and movements through and around it? Finally, what was

Figure 5.3 Photographing the parading procession. Photo by Katy Hayward, reproduced with permission.

Figure 5.4 The new see-through gate. Photo by the author.

the relationship between this newfound visibility in the everyday and its strategic uses during contentious events? These were the questions that we now wanted to explore, believing them pertinent to the effectiveness of government approaches to gradually remove 'peace walls' through redesigning physical structures (OFMDFM 2013).

We spent the next few months making regular visits back to the site and interviewing local residents, community workers, and representatives of the Department of Justice.[1] The ceremonial and confrontational forms of usage and (not) walking through the gate, that we had observed during contentious events, had highlighted its role as a deterrent of movement, and as an active border for place, community and identity. We hoped, therefore, that an exploration of its everyday uses by residents of divided communities, after its redesign, would reveal the conditions under which the gate's function as a border might be changing.

In what follows, I discuss our research findings and consider how contested urban space is produced, experienced and accessed through strategic uses of visibility. In doing so, I build upon Brighenti's (2010) observations on the capacity of the 'socio-technical' and 'bio-political' field of visibility to shape and produce public space and territoriality. I query how within this field of visibility, the movements, materialities and technologies associated with contentious parades and protests, and with everyday life at the research site, intersect, constituting a dynamic process of place-making.

Movement and Visibility: Producing Public Space and Territoriality in the City

Andrea Brighenti notes that public space is often defined in relation to both accessibility and visibility. Being visible and accessible are such 'tightly knotted together' elements that the public 'is by definition what is open and visible to everyone, as opposed to the private, which is restricted, concealed and protected' (Brighenti 2010: 111). The question of movement in particular is often considered definitive within this framework. As Sheller (2008) states, the publicness of space is defined by the degree of *physical* and *informational* mobility that it enables. Space is only public when people can *access* it. It is thus, ideally, the opposite of territoriality[2] – a condition of free and unhindered mobility. In reality, of course, the criteria for accessibility are not equally set at all times and for all those that comprise 'the public'. Indeed, a growing interdisciplinary group of scholars stress that different social groups have unequal capacity for movement through geographic space (Sheller 2008; Cresswell 2011). A complex interweaving of social practices, cultures and patterns of social inequality, on the one hand, and highly embedded material infrastructures, on the other (Ohnmacht, Maksim and Begman 2009; Lucas 2011) have unequal impact on the physical mobilities of young and old, women and men, rich and poor, and on people from different ethnicities and races.

Visibility, on another hand, is also regarded as essential to definitions of 'the public'. Indeed, attention to visibility has increased in relation to the growing capacities for technological surveillance in contemporary urban environments (Koskela 2000; Greer and McLaughlin 2010). Brighenti (2010) defines visibility as a complex 'field of social action' through which social territoriality is established, resisted and explored. By separating 'the perceptible or noticeable from the imperceptible or unnoticeable', visibility constitutes territories within the 'flesh' of social life (ibid.: 186). To attain an enlarged definition of the field of visibility, he suggests:

> It is necessary to understand the act of looking and the phenomenon of the gaze from the point of view of the social forces that are unleashed in these processes. Both looking and being looked at are . . . far from restricted to a merely cognitive or informational dimension. Looking is also a *making-do*: it is affective and haptic, it is a grip on objects and especially on bodies. (ibid.: 5, my emphasis)

Crucially, Brighenti suggests, visibility is both 'socio-technical' and 'bio-political'. This means it is produced through space, materiality and technology on the one hand, and through social practice, the positioning of bodies, gestures, interactions, and social meanings, on the other. Taking the context of Belfast, and of the Workman Avenue gate case study below, I first discuss the relationship between 'socio-technical' aspects of visibility (e.g. how it is moulded by divisions in the built environment, such as walls) and government-led attempts to transform territoriality in a post-conflict context. I then turn to a discussion of its 'bio-political' aspects (e.g. spatial practices and performances of political conflict), as seen in three 'models' of visibility proposed by Brighenti (2010) of 'recognition', 'control' and 'spectacle'. Following this, I consider how these models apply to the case study, and conclude with a discussion of the role of visibility in (de)territorializing the 'divided city'.

Visibility as a 'Socio-Technical' Production: The Built Environment

Debates on the role of spatial and material form in social processes have often revolved around power relations and their perpetuation by the built environment. Dovey (2005 and 2008), for instance, focuses on the architectural form of buildings and sees them as 'inherently coercive [as] they enforce limits to action and enable social practice to 'take place' (2005: 291). The built environment as a whole, he argues, 'frames everyday life by offering certain spaces for programmed action, while closing other possibilities' (ibid.). Built form shapes perception and cognition, and makes spatial order appear 'natural' or 'unchangeable' through both concealing and revealing social relations (ibid.); for example – in the terms of our discussion – through its function of in/visibilization. It is through visibility, adds Brighenti (2010: 120), that 'basic architectural artefacts', such as walls, 'can radically reshape publicness . . . creating specialized enclosed

Figure 5.5 The wall surrounding the Crumlin Road Gaol regeneration site. Photo by the author.

spaces endowed with affordances that foster a specific grammar and practice of interaction'. Such an understanding has had a specific manifestation in Belfast. Here, spatial intervention has often served as an instrument of securitization, demarcation and division of communities. The most obvious example at the macro-level of urban structure is residential segregation, supported and maintained not simply through the positioning of housing but through that of services, amenities, employment sites and leisure. Furthermore, individual built environment elements such as walls, buffer zones and roads (Figure 5. 5) have helped to maintain this status quo, often supported by micro-level design and landscaping techniques (Brand 2009).

Conversely, in the 'post-conflict' city, the built environment is understood as an instrument of 'spatial conflict transformation' (Gaffikin et al. 2012). A case in point can be seen in strategic policy visions for the removal of 'conflict architecture', such as 'peace walls'. 'Peace walls' first began to be erected by local communities at the outset of 'the Troubles' in 1969 as temporary, improvised defences in areas of the city where street violence was erupting. They have since proliferated and become more permanent institutionalized forms of division, planned for, built, extended and fortified in a variety of ways by central and urban authorities. While such walls have imposed and sustained direct physical changes to the geography of the city, and have shaped 'socio-technically' both visibility and movement, they are more than physical manifestations of division. Instead, they also set afoot complex intersecting social processes, ranging from disinvestment in divided areas, physical and social deprivation, out-migration, anti-social behaviour, sectarian violence, lack of positive social interaction and, for newer generations, even a lack of curiosity regarding who or what can be found on the 'other side' (Leonard and McKnight 2011; Jarman 2012).

More recently, however, conscious effort is applied to reversing this process. The 2011 'Executive Programme for Government' and the 2013 'Together Building a United Community Strategy' of the Office of the First Minister and Deputy First Minister (OFMDFM) have committed to removing the 'peace walls', as the latter document suggests, by the year 2023. In practice, this intention is executed by the Department of Justice (DoJ), whose approach has been to probe opportunities for introducing new and 'lighter' security structures in peace walls, while making this process conditional on local agreement. One example is our case study site, where the security gate was replaced in 2014 with a lighter see-through structure, with extended opening hours of the pedestrian entrance, and a variety of other measures for improving visibility around the gate. The DoJ recognize the insufficiency of an exclusive focus on urban design (Department of Justice 2014). Nevertheless, they rely extensively on the idea that physical design renewal measures can improve safety and security, with the ultimate aim 'to create spaces that are for the community as a whole and which the community feel safe using or passing through' (ibid.: 5). Thus, it is clear that whether for the purposes of division and securitization or for transforming communal territoriality and extending the public nature of urban space, the material environment of the city serves as a powerful instrument of managing visibility and movement.

Visibility as a 'Bio-political' Production: Models of Visibility

The material environment, however, does not solely shape public encounters, practices and movements. Instead, as Brighenti (2010: 123) suggests, 'public space on the ground is constantly made by acts of territorialisation, which are themselves processes made up of different thresholds and dynamics of visibility, carving the environment through acts of boundary-drawing'. Pertinently to this case study, the social experience of visibility in contested space is not only a logical effect of the physical layout of segregated areas but also of mundane and annual commemorative cultural practices, such as parades. Such practices compound different intersecting models of visibility – as 'recognition', 'control' and 'spectacle' (Brighenti 2010) – each of which can be discerned, and has a particular role to play, in our case study.

The model of 'visibility as recognition' builds upon Goffman's notion of 'face work' (Goffman [1967] 2005), which denotes practices for the reciprocal management of gazes between social actors. In such practices, as

Goffman notes, acknowledging the visibility of others legitimizes them as participants in a social situation. Therefore, failing to acknowledge others' visibility may be a form of withholding or refusing recognition. Moreover, one's active avoidance of visibility may signal a search for anonymity, particularly in politically contested environments where invisibility may be equated with safety. The search for visibility by different sides of the local 'sectarian divide' in our case study, while constituting different demands for recognition, may produce varied effects. For instance, it is not per chance that a local voluntary organization, Forthspring, have set up their offices at the literal physical interface, immediately next to the gate itself. The visibility of their physical positioning represents their neutrality vis-à-vis sectarian conflict and a search for recognition of their cross-community orientation and work. Conversely, the Orange Order parade and the protest against it, which both happen at the site annually, while representing reciprocal demands for recognition of own cultural identities and rights by unionists and nationalists, are also a form of refusing positive recognition of the cultural and political identity of 'the other'.

Brighenti (2010) himself suggests that visibility does not always produce effects of recognition in a direct or linear way. Rather, degrees of 'correct visibility' intervene, shaped by socio-spatial and temporal contexts, by forms of direct visual communication, or mediated by visual technologies. For example, Zurawski's (2005), research of 'interface' areas in Belfast and Derry (Londonderry), describes a common cultural practice of 'people watching'. Stemming from the ability of local residents to know by sight many of their own community, the practice serves as a form of non-technological surveillance and is linked to the legacy of 'The Troubles', when survival could depend on knowing 'who somebody is and what side he or she may possibly belong to' (ibid.: 499). While for those who 'belong', visibility can serve as a mechanism for reassurance, being watched in segregated space if one 'does not belong' can be experienced as a threat. The dimensions and effects of visibility, therefore, can fluctuate, producing not only forms of recognition, but of control.

This second model of 'visibility as control' builds on Foucault's thesis on the formation of the disciplinary society. It is based on the notion that the act of looking inherently entails power for those who look, and thus implies a 'hierarchization of different gazes' (Brighenti 2010: 150): 'The subject produced by this model of visibility is obliged to be visible but does not struggle for recognition through visibility' (ibid.: 49). In this process, one's actions are impacted upon by the very knowledge or suspicion of being observed. This is so because '[t]he gaze creates affects; it is an affective machine, just like the threat. . . . a threat is not a punishment but a visibility device' (ibid.: 58).

The model of 'visibility as control' is thus particularly pertinent to the social practices and interactions that happen at the 'sectarian interface'. For instance, the act of walking through the Workman Avenue gate, which is a territorial border between two divided communities, often makes those who cross identifiable by communal belonging, and therefore deprives them of anonymity. This is demonstrated by the vignette at the beginning of this chapter: finding oneself in the immediate vicinity, on either side of the gate or wall, makes one an object of non-technological surveillance and, if not a member of the respective community, exposes one to potentially hostile 'others'. Conversely, the installation of CCTV cameras at the study site, demanded by local communities and discussed further below, demonstrates how technological surveillance can be put to use for the purposes of security and safety.

Finally, the model of 'visibility as spectacle' is directly linked to the typical for Northern Ireland forms of collective ritual, represented by Orange Order parades. Parades are a celebration of unionist cultural and religious identity which are perceived by some nationalists as a commemoration of the historical military and political ascendancy of Protestants over Catholics in Ireland. A small number of parades are contentious because their routes pass through predominantly Catholic/nationalist residential areas, engendering resentment and protest by local communities. The intertwining of visibility and movement in parades is both a form of Protestants seeking recognition and of claiming space in the face of perceived present-day territorial losses (Cohen 2007). Again, however, visibility as spectacle does not directly produce effects of recognition or of control over territory. Instead, these effects depend on both technological and non-technological forms of performance and spectatorship, on socio-spatial context, on degrees of visibility, and on who event-participants are.

For instance, the intense mediatization of such collective rituals in contested space may result in visibility being effectively 'highjacked' by observers, protestors or even the police, and used for the purposes of control. Our case study, the Whiterock parades and protests, routinely involve reciprocal and complex forms of control and resistance through the use of photography and video. One of the striking features of these events, when we first observed them in 2011, was the manner in which the photographic gaze was employed in a 'digital shooting' by both paraders/supporters and protesters as they faced each other directly, for a few brief moments, when the gate opened to let the parading party onto the Springfield Road (see Figure 5.3).

Through interviews we learned that protesters photograph paraders to 'create a living documentation of what actually occurs during the day', or to document any breaches in 'the determination by the Parades Commission which should be upheld by the PSNI [The Police Service of Northern Ireland]' (interview with a member of North Belfast Interface Network, 21 May 2013). We have often observed this practice since, noting that, as well as controlling for breaches of regulation, it can also appear to express a judgment or a 'stance' against the practice of parading as such, its symbolism and value content. However, what surprised us more during that first observation was to see paraders themselves pointing cameras back at protesters in what, to us, appeared to be a breach of ritual code. Having positioned ourselves around the gate from which the paraders emerged, and ostensibly at one with the crowd of protesters and other observers, we also became subjects of the paraders' digital gazes. We intuitively interpreted these as a stance against being treated through such intense scrutiny, being subject of control, and having to comply with the regulations imposed on the parade. To our minds this was resistance to being observed, 'over-visibilized', and 'seized through a haptic gaze' (Brighenti 2010: 66). By contrast, our observations of the biggest annual unionist parade, the Twelfth, in other central shared areas and uncontested communal territories in Belfast, have demonstrated that media and observers' attention there is a sought after and a much enjoyed by paraders effect. In such spaces, visibility becomes a simple aspect of celebration, and a sign of recognition of Protestant/unionist cultural identity.

The Case Study: Visibility and Movement at a Belfast 'Interface'

Visibility as Control: The Built Environment

An Institute for Conflict Research (ICR) report (2010: 14), commissioned by Forthspring, suggests that the area surrounding Workman Avenue bears the distinct legacy of 'the Troubles', manifested in communal residential and educational segregation, socio-economic and health deprivation, low educational attainment, and a 'lack of sustained economic development'. According to the Northern Ireland Statistics and Research Agency's 'Multiple Deprivation Measure' (NISRA 2010), both Clonard (nationalist) and Woodvale (unionist) electoral wards, surrounding the physical 'peace wall', rank among the top 3 per cent of the most deprived wards in Northern Ireland. There is also a visible degree of underinvestment in the built environment and a lack of service and amenity infrastructure in the immediate surroundings of the wall. The lack of social activities that this social and physical geography presupposes has resulted in little pedestrian movement in and around the gate. This gives a distinct appearance of bareness for most of the time, contrasting with the regular passing of motorized traffic through the Springfield Road, a major arterial route in the city. As a local man, a resident and a regular observer of the parade, affirmed:

> [T]here isn't a huge amount of interaction . . . because it's not as if it's a bustling shopping area . . . You access the road for a very specific purpose and that purpose could be dog walking, taking children to and from primary school, could be to the E3 campus but there's usually a reason why. You're not going out the gate to cross over into your neighbour's house on the Springfield Road. (12 January 2016)

Thus the social and physical geography of the wider area, together with individual built environment elements at the site, shape forms of everyday movement and visibility, broadly along lines of communal belonging and gender. Those who cross the gate are largely residents of unionist-inhabited Woodvale who need to use the nationalist-inhabited Springfield Road to access local amenities. Additionally, Woodvale parents (mostly mothers) bring their young children to the nearby state primary school in the Springfield Road, Woodvale older residents walk their dogs in Springfield Road, and young people (from both sides of the wall) attend the youth club at the premises of Forthspring, the entrance to which is in the Springfield Road. While mothers we spoke to suggested that this type of visibility does not result in a sense of threat during their everyday 'crossings', their reticence to our attempts to recruit them as participants in walk-along interviews and observations of these daily movements was to us one of the clearest indications of their discomfort at the consciousness of being watched. To us this demonstrated that visibility 'at the interface' is a form of social control.

That visibility here is important as a controlling mechanism is also reflected in the previously referred to ICR Report (2010). The report suggests that Forthspring's physical positioning puts it 'in a unique and somewhat unenviable geographical position', requiring care 'in the language they employ [in] public consultations and discussions on the future of the interface', and that they maintain neutrality 'in relation to parade-related disputes' (ibid.: 3). The report then makes a direct link between everyday physical visibility at the site and processes of subject positioning and identification (or 'taking sides'). This understanding was confirmed when speaking to a female staff member of Forthspring, who stated: 'On the Twelfth I would really just go and watch the parade in the city centre . . . I won't come up here in case there is any trouble or anything, because I work here [and] in case some of the young people coming here would see me standing there' (1 October 2015). That visibility, as recognition at the physical 'interface', is not easily achievable is testified by the conclusion of the ICR report: that, despite being watched for 'taking sides' in relation to parades, the cross-community work of Forthspring is not well known to residents in the area. Moreover, in speaking about the publicity that the change of the security gate received in 2014, a male Forthspring staff member suggested that visibility as recognition may not always be desirable: '[T]here wasn't a big hype. David Ford arrived one day and there was a photo opportunity, but it was all kept very low key that the gate had changed . . . because [otherwise] it just becomes a magnet' (23 September 2015). The allusion to violence in this quote, whether sectarian or defined as 'anti-social behaviour', directly links visibility to experiences of threat and safety at the study site.

The Practice of Everyday Life: (In)visibility as 'Fear' and 'Safety'

While the physical parameters of space were revealed as foundational to shaping the effects of (in)visibility, conversations with local residents also demonstrated the extent to which strategic uses of visibility depend on everyday and annual rhythms of life. The time of year, for instance, was seen as helping sectarian attacks and anti-social behaviour, emanating from the Springfield Road: 'As soon as the evenings start growing longer, and it gets darker, there seems to be more . . . anti-social stuff on the other side. . . . It creates this sense that perhaps they can get away with more because of the nights drawing in' (female resident, 24 November 2015). Similarly, the very rationale for, and process of, changing the security structure of the gate was directly linked to attacks on houses on both sides of the wall, which had ebbed and flown over the years but had intensified in 2012. As a result, the DoJ began discussions with both communities regarding a strategy for reducing such incidents at the interface. The discussions were particularly focused on what people from both communities could *not* see behind the gate and, therefore, feared:

> If you were trying to go to the Springfield Road, people with small children were fearful because the pedestrian gate was almost like a chicane type, and that was just designed to stop motorbikes because from both communities motorbikes were used to carry out murders . . . But the bottom line was that you couldn't physically see outside. So people were attacked when they stepped outside the gate, and on occasion people were attacked when they stepped inside the gate. (male resident 12 January 2016)

Thus the invisibility resulting from the physical structure of the gate is linked to feelings of threat, suspicion and fear. As a the previously quoted resident suggested, 'If you can't see what *themuns*[3] are doing over there and they can't see what *themuns* are doing in there, then there's always a fear about what *themuns* are up to'. While these emotional responses have indeed often been justified by actual sectarian attacks, carried out under the night-time cloak of invisibility, perception itself would induce intense states of fear, particularly when organized events, such as vigils, parades and protests, would result in masses of people congregating on both sides of the wall. A male community worker from the area commented that, at such times, perception and imagination of what may be going on, invisibly, across the wall may itself serve as a trigger for violence:

> There was a vigil held on the Workman Avenue side of the gate in February 2014, and the Catholic community (who were against all the stone throwing and the window breaking, and the sectarian attacks) [actually] found this very difficult because they wanted to stand shoulder to shoulder and [shout] 'this is wrong' – but it was on the other side of the gate, and because it was the old gate they couldn't see. And so there were all those [cameras] flashing when you were standing on the other side of the gate, and you were going, 'What's going on there!?' . . . And we worked with young people in the Springfield Road that night because they were obviously also going, 'What's going on, what's going on here?!' (23 September 2015)

As a result of the process begun by the DoJ, the PSNI produced a report around community safety in the area, recommending a number of measures, to include instalment of security cameras, improvement of street lighting and transforming the gate into a 'see-through' structure. According to a representative of the DoJ (7 December 2015), the main rationale for the latter change concerned the capacity of CCTV cameras to capture movement through the gate. The importance of these changes from a community point of view, as a measure of calm, security, safety and reassurance, was repeatedly stressed by a local man:

> While security cameras aren't the panacea, what they do, in a very subtle way, is they give residents confidence that . . . the police can . . . identify whoever came in and attacked a house, and [they] would be arrested and charged and taken to court for that offence. . . . [B]oth communities, we stood our ground – No cameras no deal! . . . So it was almost a deal breaker for us. There has to be cameras here for the reassurance they provide. (12 January 2016)

At the same time, as well as the need for reassurance and security, there was an anticipation that widening the field of visibility around the gate would facilitate movement through it, increase accessibility and bring a measure of 'normality', of 'softening images' and of 'changing the norm' (male community worker, 23 September 2015). This argument was more focused on a concern with improving the public nature of space by changing the content of social interaction and social practices at the 'interface'. Indeed, such expectations proved, to no small degree, to be correct:

> We believe that . . . there are more people now using the gate in darkness hours, especially in the winter. . . . [This is] for a number of reasons: you can see that there's no one outside that gate standing waiting for you, maybe to attack you or do you harm, because the improved lighting around the whole area means that from far away from the gate you can clearly see if there's anything you're uncomfortable about; [if] so, then you can change your mind and you don't go out [of] the gates. . . . It's confidence, you know. (Male resident, 12 January 2016)

Furthermore, the sensory and affective impact of this change of visibility, especially for residents living immediately next to the gate in Workman Avenue, can hardly be overestimated:

> I suppose I spent a long time longing to hear that gate close, and it gave me a sense of ease. But the moment we got the new gates I didn't listen out for it anymore. We became very relaxed because we went through a long spell of maybe a year when there was nothing happening. (Female, 24 November 2015)

The visibility resulting from the sheer redesign of the security structure has clearly also positively altered perceptions of place. Residents suggested that after the change 'it just felt more open. You didn't feel as hemmed in' (Female, 30 September 2015), and that 'as we [now] open the door there's a kind of brightness in the street, which wasn't there before' (Female, 24 November 2015). However, the question of whether or not this change represents or indeed drives a move towards transforming territoriality at the interface, or whether it changes the function and role of the gate and wall as a border, is a more complex one. It is clear, for instance, that the type and meaning of social relationships and interactions across the interface, which create the social context to visibility effects and experiences, are not substantially transformed. Just as much as providing the feeling of safety, visibility continues to serve the purpose of mutual surveillance, and it manifests a sense of mutual suspicion. A female resident of Workman Avenue commented, for instance, on the erection of a see-through metal fence around the front of 'nationalist' houses directly facing the security gate from across the Springfield Road:

> We actually had a bit of a giggle – we got this lovely gate up and it's easy on the eye, and then all of a sudden houses facing . . . started getting hemmed in . . . this fence went up so it was like. . . they got locked in. I don't know if that was for their safety. . . . It's a whole fence job right down the back. . . . It looks as if actually they are hemming themselves in. (30 September 2015)

While it appears that the fence commented upon was erected by the Housing Executive for the purposes of safety (DoJ interview, 7 December 2015), what this quote demonstrates is that practices of mutual surveillance at the interface continue the logic of 'visibility as control'. Ultimately, the physical redesign of the gate and the concomitant measures around it to increase visibility, while assessed very positively by local residents, mainly because of allowing a sense of 'normality' and freer access to the Springfield Road, also continue to perpetuate, a securitization agenda and rationale.

Parades and Protests: The Spectacle of Visibility

Our observation of the contentious Whiterock parade and protest in the summer of 2015 similarly highlights the extent to which these events both add to the positive effects of increased visibility, and continue to serve as a ground of contestation through visibilization. Our main focus during this observation was to gauge the effects of the new gate on these performances of political conflict. In this respect, a local community worker commented:

> Just as much as [on a daily basis] being able to see through reduced an awful lot of the fear, equally there were a lot of people telling me it was going to be an awful lot more interface trouble [during the marching season], because people could see and antagonize each other. (Male, 23 September 2015)

These expectations did not necessarily realize in terms of spurring more physical violence during, or in the aftermath, of the Whiterock parade in 2015. However, our observation suggests that improved visibility between contenders during the event enables both a multiplication and an intensification of forms of contestation. In the past, invisibility between paraders

Figure 5.6 Confrontation, resistance and control through the see-through gate. Photo by the author.

and protesters on opposite sides of the solid non-see-through gate was consciously and successfully harnessed by both the police and local community stewards to minimize conflictual engagement. Presently, however, contenders were able to engage each other through direct stares, shouting, taunting, and waving flags and other symbols for a prolonged period. They were also now able to direct cameras at each other for the whole duration of the event, irrespective of whether the gate was open or not (Figure 5.6).

Moreover, supporters of the parade and local residents, standing in Workman Avenue, were able to directly confront the police (speaking to them through the iron bars of the gate) to demand what, they argued, was their right to be let through to the Springfield Road, while the protest on the other side was still going on. This was then, clearly, a moment when the very visibility, the gazes, and the communicative discourses enabled by the new see-through security structure, intersected with, and produced in new ways, the contentious question of the 'right to access'. The words of the following interviewee demonstrate the multiplication of layers of mutual control enabled by increased visibility:

> Well, this year I think it caused the police a lot more work, the fact that you could see through the gate and I'll tell you the reason why. If the Parades Commission issue a determination, it states that you or your group must congregate at Point A. It will also say when . . . but it also specifies that during that period of time

> your protest is a static one and you are not allowed to move from Point A whilst the determination is in place. [This year] . . . everybody witnessed . . . that protestors . . . quite clearly lifted their placards and followed the parade from Point A to Point B at the centre of the Springfield Road. . . . In previous years that may well have been the normal thing . . . but the fact that people could see it taking place . . . many people were able, quite rightly, to report a breach of this determination. So huge pressure has now been placed on the police to publicly deal with the complaints that have been lodged before them, and in my opinion, it has huge implications for the protests in the future. (Male, 12 January 2016)

What we see in the above is an appropriation of digital photography by parade supporters to monitor and record a parade's breach of the Parades Commission's determinations. Here, it is the new visibility at the site that enables such a proactive position. Visibility also reveals more clearly the role of the police in actively managing and shaping forms of contestation during such events. Indeed, our observations also speak to the question of strategic uses of digital media and online technologies, astutely understood by participants in contentious events as procedures for visibilization. The previously quoted participant repeatedly highlighted the existence of abundant online documentation of his argument with a police officer across the bars of the redesigned gate:

> I think it's actually on YouTube. If you check for [date], you will see a number of people, myself included, going to the gate and speaking to the [name of police officer], and whilst I am not very good on camera you will find me saying to the policeman: 'Sorry, I'm just trying to go over to the corner there to observe the parade'. 'I'm sorry, you're not allowed out here'. And the conversation then went, 'Why am I not allowed out there?' 'I have instructions that you and you are not allowed out onto this road'. . . . So he singled us out for special attention. . . . There's another video . . . of me arguing the case. And it's funny, as I realized that while at the time it was embarrassing to us, it was more embarrassing to the police . . . It was important to embarrass the police. (12 January 2016)

The above quote chimes with Brighenti's argument that '[v]isibility over the Internet represents a peculiar prolongation of the logic of recognition' (2010: 97). Through Internet visibility, parade supporters are drawing attention to both their 'right to access' and to the forms of control exercised by the police over those who are granted or denied such a right. On the one hand, therefore, the use of technologically aided visibility can be a form of empowerment for contending parties at such events, helping them to produce information that challenges both the opposing side and the 'official' version of events by police or other public authorities (Greer and McLaughlin 2010: 1041). This observation resonates with Soares' work in this volume on the role of social media as a space of political expression and exchange.

Yet, peculiarly, this process does not appear to challenge the logic of territorial contestation at 'the interface'. Indeed, direct visual surveillance at the site continues to serve as a means of control by the police just as much as by protesters and supporters of the parade, while the 'right to access' is denied, or only granted on the basis of who or what one is identified as. In the above quote the participant emphasizes that he was singled out by the police as someone who should not be let through the gate. By contrast, when interviewing him, I was able to point out that my colleague and I had been let though the gate under similar circumstances in previous years of observation. Thus, the capacity for both technological and direct non-technological surveillance and identification during contentious events, extended by the new visibility created by the see-through gate, continues to reproduce, at the same time as it appears to challenge, the territorialist logic of control at the 'interface'.

Conclusions

Changes in the design of a security gate have altered visibilities at a Belfast sectarian 'interface'. These changes are executed in the context of a wider policy vision for the removal of 'peace walls', relying on the idea that physical design renewal can improve safety and security, and 'create spaces that are for the community as a *whole*' (Minister of Justice 2014). However, to understand the effects of this change on the surrounding area, attention is required to the nuances of how visibility works 'socio-technically' and 'bio-politically' at the intersection of space, time and social practice (Brighenti 2010). With this in mind, this chapter interrogated how different 'models of visibility' (ibid.), intersect with movement, materiality and technology during contentious events and in everyday life in the locality of 'the interface'.

The case study demonstrated that models of visibility as 'recognition', 'control' and 'spectacle' are not mutually exclusive. Each can be (and often are) used as a means to achieve the desired effects of another. Such effects intertwine within the city as a complex socio-spatial terrain and are shaped by degrees of 'correct visibility', spatial and temporal context, forms of direct visual communication, mediatization, and use of visual technologies. A model of 'visibility as recognition', for example, is used to demand, attain, withhold, refuse or resist acknowledgement of the cultural and political identity of 'the other', and of their respective cultural practices. Visibility as recognition at 'the interface' more often serves as a form of social control, particularly as it is experienced affectively through feelings of fear or threat, stemming from the knowledge or suspicion of being watched. A model of 'visibility as control', at the same time, is often consciously and strategically wielded for the purposes of surveillance. It communicates that 'the other' is watched for observing the rules of 'the game'. It is also used to express ridicule or resistance, or for creating a sense of security and safety. Finally, 'visibility as spectacle' is strategically used by both paraders and protesters to modify the broader field of visibilities relating to conflict, contestation and 'right of access', and to demonstrate 'an ongoing attachment to critical places' (Cohen 2007: 951).

I suggested that from the point of view of the social processes unleashed and implicated in practices of (in)visibilization on the ground, visibility is still largely used to maintain, rather than transform, territoriality. On the one hand, locally, both accessibility and visibility have been improved and extended. In the everyday this has resulted in greater mobility for ordinary people who no longer fear the possibility of a sectarian attack, or of becoming victims of anti-social behaviour while passing through the gate. At the same time, during contentious events being visible/noticed at the gate by itself sets the limits to accessibility. Thus, in the case study, both visibility and accessibility still represent, enact, and are experienced as, forms of territorialization and of boundary-drawing. Changing the social meaning and content of these fields of social action will require a longer-term process of challenging the broader socio-spatial geography of the city that conditions the social phenomenology of visibility and accessibility of individual public spaces.

Milena Komarova is a research officer at the Centre for Cross Border Studies, Armagh, and a visiting research fellow at the Senator George J. Mitchell Institute for Global Peace, Security and Justice, Queen's University Belfast. Her work spans the fields of conflict transformation, urban sociology and border studies, exploring the intersections between public space, place, identity and bordering practices, within and without ethno-nationally 'divided' cities. Milena has published on the spatial aspects of conflict transformation in Belfast, such as urban regeneration, the development of 'shared space', the management of contentious parades and protests, and on the role of visibility and movement in 'post-conflict' and 'post-socialist' cities. Her publications include 'Imagining a "Shared Future": Post-Conflict Discourses on Peace-Building', in K. Hayward and C. O'Donnell (eds), *Political Discourse and Conflict Resolution: Debating Peace in Northern Ireland* (2010); and (with Liam O'Dowd) 'Belfast, the "Shared City"? Spatial Stories of Conflict Transformation', in A. Björkdahl and S. Buckley-Zistel (eds), *Spatializing Peace and Conflict: Mapping the Production of Places, Sites and Scales of Violence* (2016).

Notes

1. Owners of the security structure at the site.
2. Territoriality, as Sack (1986) notes, is the establishment of control over access for people, things and interactions across borders.
3. A colloquialism meaning 'those ones'.

References

Brand, R. 2009. 'Urban Artifacts and Social Practices in a Contested City', *Journal of Urban Technology* 16(2–3): 35–60.

Brighenti, A.M. 2010. *Visibility in Social Theory and Social Research*. Basingstoke: Palgrave Macmillan.

Cohen, S. 2007. 'Winning While Losing: The Apprentice Boys of Derry Walk their Beat', *Political Geography* 26(8): 951–67.

Cresswell, T. 2011. 'Mobilities I: Catching Up', *Progress in Human Geography* 35(4): 550–58.

Department of Justice, NI (DoJ). 2014. Minister of Justice Communication with Northern Ireland Assembly. Available from: http://www.niassembly.gov.uk/globalassets/documents/ofmdfm/inquiries/building-a-united-community/written-submissions/department-of-justice.pdf.

Dovey, K. 2005. 'The Silent Complicity of Architecture', in J. Hillier and E. Rooksby (eds), *Habitus: A Sense of Place*. Aldershot: Ashgate, pp.283–96.

———. 2008. *Framing Places: Mediating Power in Built Form*. London and New York: Routledge, 2nd edition.

Gaffikin, F., et al. 2012. 'Planning for Spatial Reconciliation. Project Outline'. Available from: https://www.qub.ac.uk/research-centres/PlanningforSpatialReconciliation/FileStore/Filetoupload,279174,en.pdf.

Goffman, E. (1967) 2005. *Interaction Ritual: Essays in Face-to-Face Behavior*. New Brunswick, NJ and London: Transaction Publishers.

Greer, C., and E. McLaughlin. 2010. 'We Predict a Riot? Public Order Policing, New Media Environments and the Rise of the Citizen Journalist', *The British Journal of Criminology* 50(6): 1041–59.

Institute for Conflict Research. 2010. 'Baseline Indicator Evaluation for Forthspring Inter-Community Group'. Report. Available from: http://www.forthspring.org/uploads/1/3/0/5/13051643/forthspring_final_evaluation_and_monitoring_document.pdf.

Jarman, N. 2012. *Belfast Interfaces: Security Barriers and Defensive Use of Space*. Belfast: Belfast Interface Project. Available from: http://www.conflictresearch.org.uk/.

Koskela, H. 2000. '"The Gaze Without Eyes": Video-Surveillance and the Changing Nature of Urban Space', *Progress in Human Geography* 24(2): 243–65.

Leonard, M., and M. McKnight. 2011. 'Bringing Down the Walls: Young People's Perspectives on Peace–Walls in Belfast', *International Journal of Sociology and Social Policy* 31(9–10): 569–82.

Lucas, K. 2011. 'Transport and Social Exclusion: Where Are We Now?', in M. Grieco and J. Urry (eds), *Mobilities: New Perspectives on Transport and Society*. Farnham: Ashgate, pp.207–22.

NISRA (Northern Ireland Statistics and Research Agency). 2010. 'Northern Ireland Multiple Deprivation Measure'. Belfast. Available at: www.nisra.

gov.uk/deprivation/archive/Updateof2005Measures/NIMDM_2010_Report.pdf.

OFMDFM. 2013. *Together Building a United Community Strategy*. Available at: http://www.ofmdfmni.gov.uk/together-building-a-united-community-strategy.pdf.

OFMDFM. nd. 'Programme for Government 2011–15'. Available at: http://www.northernireland.gov.uk/pfg-2011-2015-final-report.pdf.

Ohnmacht, T., H. Maksim and M. Begman. 2009. 'Mobilities and Inequalitiy: Making Connections', in T. Ohnmacht, H. Maksim and M. Begman (eds), *Mobilities and Inequality*. Aldershot: Ashgate, pp.7–26.

Sack, R. 1986. *Human Territoriality: Its Theory and History*. Cambridge: Cambridge University Press.

Sheller, M. 2008. 'Mobility Freedom and Public Space', in S. Bergmann and T. Sager (eds), *The Ethics of Mobilities: Rethinking Place, Exclusion, Freedom and Environment*. Aldershot: Ashgate, pp.25–38.

Zurawski, N. 2005. '"I know Where You Live!" Aspects of Watching, Surveillance and Social Control in a Conflict Zone', in *Surveillance and Society* 2(4): 498–512.

6

'LIFTING THE CROSS' IN WEST BELFAST

ENSKILLING CRUCICENTRIC VISION THROUGH PEDESTRIAN SPATIAL PRACTICE

Kayla Rush

In the spring of 2014, traffic on the Falls and Shankill roads in West Belfast slowed at noon every day, as a lone man or woman wearing a yellow safety vest walked down the centre of those busy streets, carrying a large and visibly worn wooden Cross bearing the inscription 'John 3:16'.[1] Shortly after, at one o'clock every afternoon, small groups of people appeared with identical Crosses at three local interfaces. These events occurred daily for forty days, with the final 'Cross walks' and 'Cross vigils' taking place on Good Friday, a day that holds both religious and historical significance for Christian residents of Northern Ireland.[2]

These women and men were participants in 'Lift the Cross' (LTC), an initiative of River of Hope Pentecostal Fellowship (RHPF), a Pentecostal Christian church in West Belfast. Located within sight of Belfast's longest 'peace wall', an 'immense steel fence' separating the primarily Protestant Shankill Road from the predominantly Catholic Falls Road (Tate 2013: 73), River of Hope billed LTC as a spiritual solution for these divided neighbourhoods: the initiative's slogan ran, 'Can a nation be changed in a day? Who can believe it?' (a rough paraphrase of Isaiah 66:8).[3]

This chapter examines Lift the Cross as a process of spatial enskillment, in which participants' knowledge of place in West Belfast was refashioned through distinctly Christian, street-level interactions with local geographies. It draws on my own experiences as a regular (twice weekly) participant in the Cross walks and Cross vigils, during seven months of participant-observation at River of Hope. I begin this chapter with a brief examination of the notion of 'skilled vision', and of urban walking as a way of knowing. I then look at the variety of ways in which this enskillment was enacted through strategic uses of visuality and movement. Following that, I look at the enskillment of interpersonal interactions and the engagement of an international online spectatorship through Facebook. I conclude with a brief look at an instance in which these enskilled visions were shown to be enduring, as they were brought into play in response to local events months after LTC had ended.

Pedestrian Practice and Skilled Vision

> Their story begins on ground level, with footsteps. . . Their swarming mass is an innumerable collection of singularities. Their intertwined paths give their shape to spaces. They weave places together.
>
> —M. de Certeau, *The Practice of Everyday Life*

For de Certeau, space and place in the city are created through pedestrian movement; as urban walkers' paths intersect and diverge, the city takes form (see also DeYoung, this volume). He calls these people *Wandersmänner*, 'whose bodies follow the thicks and thins of an urban "text" they write without being able to read it' (de Certeau 1988: 93). De Certeau and his successors (e.g. Gray 1999; Ingold and Vergunst 2008; Pink et al. 2010) speak to the materiality, sensuality and embodiedness of spatial knowledge, as well as the ability of memory to break in on present experiences and 'disrupt' linear understandings of place (Edensor 2008: 136–37).

We hear echoes of de Certeau in Grasseni's (2007: 4) discussion of 'skilled visions'. The two authors share an emphasis on movement in and through space, on the embodied nature of spatial knowledge and experience, and on a specific type of vision. De Certeau (1988: 92–96) connects this vision, whose vantage point rests at street level, to his notion of the *Wandersmänner*, writing, 'The ordinary practitioners of the city live "down below", below the thresholds at which visibility begins' (ibid.: 93). Similarly, Grasseni (2007: 5) discusses a multiplicity of '*visions*, meant in the plural as local and shared practices, naturally connected to the other senses' (emphasis in original). She further reminds us that vision is learned – or, to use the language I will employ throughout this chapter, 'enskilled' – within communities and through practice (ibid.: 5–10; Grasseni 2008: 152–57; see also Herzfeld 2007: 207). Both authors juxtapose this pedestrian, experiential vision with what de Certeau (1988: 92–93) calls the 'voyeur-god's-eye view', enabled by the map, the urban landscape painting or the top floor of a skyscraper. Grasseni (2007: 3–5) calls this latter type 'panoptic vision'.

The skilled visions these authors discuss are fundamentally material, 'embedded in multi-sensory practices, where look is coordinated with skilled movement, with rapidly changing points of view, or with other senses, such as touch' (Grasseni 2007: 4; see also Pink 2008: 180–81). The slap of footsteps on pavement, the sound of passing traffic, the rough grain of the Cross beneath one's fingers and its heft against one's body, the glossy smoothness of the tracts in one's pocket: these were all integral to the visions that were shaped by Lift the Cross.

Grasseni draws her understanding of 'enskillment' from the work of Ingold (1993: 153), for whom enskillment is 'an education of attention', whereby residents learn to live and move within the landscape.[4] As the individual's attention is educated, both by listening to others and by observing and learning the landscape herself, she becomes more knowledgeable, and more skilled. Walking is one such mode of education, and it engenders a vision of place that 'more closely resembles storytelling than map-using' (Ingold 2000: 219; see also de Certeau 1988: 115–18). However, Ingold (2010: 15–16) argues against the equation of vision exclusively with images, noting that walking 'involve[s] the exercise of both eye and mind' and is every bit as much an 'imaginative' practice as painting or writing: '[T]he mental and the material, or the terrains of the imagination and the physical environment, run into one another to the extent of being barely distinguishable' (ibid.: 17; see also Vergunst 2012: 19).

Thus, urban pedestrianism is more than simply journeying between two points. Walking in the city is an act of both skill and enskillment, in which the walker simultaneously draws upon existing knowledge and learns new ways of being, interacting, moving, sensing and seeing within the urban landscape. These acts of spatial enskillment are closely entwined with, and mutually inform, memory, myth and narrative, structures of power and emotional and sensory input (de Certeau 1988: 96, 108–9; Aretxaga 1997: 24–25, 37–40). It is within this framework that I examine the case of the Lift the Cross initiative.

The Visuality of Division

The most common and best-known 'vision' of Belfast is that of a divided city, and the spaces of West Belfast reflect this vision. The Belfast Interface Project (2011: 31–44) identifies nine walls or fences and five fortified gates along the border between the Shankill and Falls areas. The earliest of these were built in 1969 (ibid.), the year in which the conflict known as 'the Troubles' began (McKittrick and McVea 2001: 53–75); the most recent was constructed in 2009–10 (Belfast Interface Project 2011: 31–44). These barriers, which draw the attention of even the most unskilled eye, such as that of the tourist,[5] to the city's divisions, exist alongside myriad 'tacitly understood boundaries' between Belfast neighbourhoods, where interfaces are indicated to more skilled pedestrians 'by vacant lots, by abandoned homes, by sectarian flags or symbols or by other markers' (Tate 2013: 73; see also Radford 2001: 37).

Pedestrian mobility in West Belfast is heavily circumscribed by these boundaries, both physical and symbolic. This is not to say that residents never cross these barriers; they do so frequently, but in strategic and informed ways (Lysaght 2005: 128–29). As Jarman (1992: 148–49) points out, 'Urban living, which demands that one constantly move in and out of one's residential area in order to shop, work, visit, makes geographical knowledge of Belfast a political knowledge, and physical movement a political enactment of that knowledge'. In an interview, Gavin, a man of Scottish origin who had lived in Belfast for seven years, described this sort of skilled movement to me:

> [I]t's a case of just getting to know where you should be, and what time, 'cause like now they shut the gates at seven o'clock. If I was on the other side there at seven o'clock I'd say, Ooh how am I gonna get back home. So I try and make sure, if I *am* on the Falls Road, not to be there too late.

Local images and discourse, recent history, everyday practice, and even tourist experiences thus point to the pedestrian landscape of West Belfast as divided. It is the aspect of the landscape most quickly learned by the newcomer, as illustrated by Gavin's statement. Skilled knowledge of geographical divisions is crucial to moving within and through these spaces.

The sites chosen for the Cross vigils emphasized this sense of place through strategic engagements with the visuality of division. The three locations were not among the subtle or 'tacitly understood' (Tate 2013: 73) interfaces mentioned above. Rather, two of the three sites, located at 'Church Street'[6] and Lanark Way, respectively, are overshadowed by fortified gates. The third Cross vigil location, situated at the roundabout where the Crumlin Road intersects with Twaddell Avenue and Woodvale Road, has no such structural dividers; however, recent events have made it a site of well-known sectarian contention, and occasionally violence. From July 2013 to October 2016, this interface was the site of a longstanding protest against a Parades Commission decision preventing loyalist marchers from passing through a stretch of the Crumlin Road identified with the largely Catholic Ardoyne area (DeYoung 2016). During Lift the Cross, Twaddell Avenue was bedecked in Union Jack flags, along with banners from Orange Order lodges and loyalist groups that had spent time at the protest site, nicknamed 'Camp Twaddell'.[7]

Lift the Cross reinforced the divided visuality of these sites through the strategic use of photography. Cross walks and vigils were photographed daily, and church leaders uploaded the photos to the church's Facebook page, creating a new Facebook album for each of the forty days. Several locations feature conspicuously in these albums: the gates on Church Street and Lanark Way, the Sinn Féin offices on the Falls Road and paramilitary murals and memorial gardens on both the Falls and the Shankill roads were among the most popular. Photographing the flags at Twaddell Avenue was also a daily task. When assigned to that location, my fellow participants and I would typically position ourselves against a low concrete wall facing the roundabout, as this gave us a surface on which to lean or sit, and it provided the best vantage point from which to display the Cross to passing motorists. However, when the day's appointed photographer arrived to photograph us, he (the photographer was always male, and usually one of the church's leaders) would invariably instruct us to move so that we could be photographed in front of the flags. This made for more striking photographs in which it is obvious that we were located at a place of sectarian conflict.

Interacting physically with these symbols of division thus reinforced participants' everyday experiences of circumscribed place, as did viewing the photos online after the day's events had finished. Furthermore, the photographs broadcast digitally on Facebook allowed both church members who did not participate in LTC in person and RHPF's wider international network of supporters to share in this vision of a divided West Belfast. (This is discussed at greater length below.) And yet, the vision with which River of Hope sought to enskill participants is more complex than that: while the divided nature of the city was an important aspect, it was not the only one.

The Mobility of Unity

Tony, one of River of Hope's assistant pastors, described LTC's aims to me as 'publicly lifting the Cross up as a symbol to our society and across the divide, to show that we may not have the answers to our situations, either individually or as a society, but God has'. This movement 'across the divide' enacted spatial practices that were out of the ordinary. While crossing boundaries in West Belfast is a common affair for residents, as mentioned above, the type of movement involved in the Cross walks is unusual, particularly the elements of carrying the Cross and taking a circular route. Moving across the boundaries between the Shankill and Falls neighbourhoods in this intentionally atypical manner is an example of what Eliade (1959: 32) calls the 'cosmicization' of territory, a 'ritual taking possession' which 'repeat[s] the cosmogony' of a group. According to Eliade, an act of cosmicization 'is always a consecration' (ibid.). Giving the example of the conquistadors in South and Central America, he writes, 'The raising of the Cross was equivalent to consecrating the country . . .' (ibid.)

In his examination of Pentecostal Christian prayer walks in contemporary Belfast, Murphy (2010: 52–53) states, 'In an important sense, [prayer walking] is also seen as a means of reclaiming for God land that had long since been "lost" to terrorism and the "evils" of social division', echoing Eliade's language of cosmicization and consecration. RHPF's walks differed from those discussed by Murphy in two ways – their use of a physical Cross and their decision to walk in the centre of the road – but otherwise the two practices and their goals are largely the same. By 'publicly lifting the Cross', as Tony put it, over their immediate surroundings on both sides of the wall, participants claimed that territory in the same manner as the conquistadors, only the kingdom for which they laid claim is a heavenly realm rather than an earthly one.[8]

A key element of the vision articulated and enskilled during the LTC walks is the idea that the geographical area traversed by Cross walk participants is one 'community',[9] rather than two. Jack, the church's senior pastor and the driving force behind the project, explained this perspective in an interview: '[W]hen I say community, I don't mean Protestant community or Catholic community. I see them all as one community. We have a wall that divides us, but we have a church that reaches out to both communities'. By 'lifting the Cross' along a pedestrian route encompassing the areas on either side of the peace wall, participants enacted, and were simultaneously enskilled with, the vision Jack described: that of a single, unified 'community' without barriers to mobility, one that is joined together by River of Hope itself ('we have a church that reaches out to both communities'). Eileen, a church member and regular participant in the Cross vigils, spoke to me about the ways in which LTC had affected her own understandings of space in West Belfast:

> Somehow I find myself praying about one community that River of Hope is right in the middle of. Instead of bridging two. That the Lord would have one community, neither Protestant nor Catholic but children of *God* who are totally surrendered and submitted to the Holy Spirit.

Murphy (2010: 138–47) provides further insight into the ways in which LTC's Cross walks subverted prior knowledge of space and enskilled a new type of vision. He likens prayer walking to the parading tradition in Northern Ireland, as both are 'action[s] that inscrib[e] sovereignty into the landscape' (ibid.: 128–30). In Northern Ireland, '[p]arades and the associated visual displays have been a vibrant feature of political life . . . for over two hundred years' (Jarman 1997: 79), though the history of the practice stretches back much longer, at least to the late 1400s (Jarman 1999: x–14). The tradition is dynamic and changing, and today '[p]arading remains the most prominent means of asserting collective identities and claiming political dominance over territory' (Jarman 1997: 79). While parades are held by a variety of groups for a multitude of reasons (Radford 2001: 38–40),[10] around 59 per cent of parades in Northern Ireland are 'organised by the loyal orders and broad Unionist tradition' (Parades Commission for Northern Ireland 2014: 8). As such, parades are typically associated with (primarily unionist/loyalist) sectarian displays, and thus with the dominant vision of Belfast as a divided, conflicted city.

However, by incorporating certain elements from this, Northern Ireland's best-known pedestrian practice, and strategically altering others, the Cross walks subverted the narrative of spatial division; enskilled participants with an alternative, distinctly Christian vision of the city; and practised a religiously inspired politics of hope. Their vision is one in which the neighbourhoods on either side of the 'dividing wall' are united under the Cross – 'one community, neither Protestant nor Catholic but children of *God*', as Eileen put it. The next sections of this chapter build on the latter portion of Eileen's quote, examining more closely the distinctly Christian nature of this vision.

Inscribing Crucicentric Vision onto Places and Bodies

Participants in Lift the Cross viewed the initiative as a Christian intervention targeting a variety of local issues. In our interview, Jack summarized the point he wanted to communicate through LTC: 'If you've got issues and problems in life, issues and problems in the society, there is a better way and now for us the better way is Christ and the better way is the Cross'. For members of River of Hope, Christian faith and practice are a 'better way' – and for most participants the only way – to bring about a peaceful and prosperous city.

The act of walking or standing with the Cross was perceived as a direct solution to conflict, and in particular to the protest at the Twaddell Avenue–Woodvale Road–Crumlin Road interface. Church members consistently referred to the ongoing protest as a 'stand-off', discursively highlighting the elements of conflict at play while also implying that there was an unnecessary stubbornness on the part of the protestors. This choice in terminology was no accident; rather, it reinforced the vision of West Belfast as divided and conflicted, and by extension emphasized the necessity of LTC as a remedy for that situation.

Furthermore, participants viewed LTC as an intervention targeting a variety of other social issues as well. The Falls and Shankill areas are consistently listed among the 'most disadvantaged and deprived' neighbourhoods in Northern Ireland (Belfast Education and Library Board 2013: 8; see also NISRA 2010). Research participants listed high rates of suicide and drug use, joblessness, mental health issues and paramilitary involvement, especially among young people, as concerning and in need of intervention. Their discourse around economic deprivation was particularly interesting, as while participants generally agreed that it was a negative thing, a few saw something of a 'silver lining' in it. In one exchange I witnessed during a Cross vigil, two participants, Patrick and Susanna, were discussing the current state of the Shankill neighbourhood. Susanna, who does not live in West Belfast, expressed regret that the area is not doing well, as evidenced by the many boarded-up shops visible on the Shankill Road. Patrick agreed, but remarked that one positive aspect of the current economic state is that, where there used to be 'a bar on every corner', a fact he had 'prayed against' for years (RHPF members are generally opposed to drinking alcohol), now there are very few.

Patrick's language here illustrates a vital point: for participants in Lift the Cross, none of these problems are merely earthly in nature. Rather, they are seen as having spiritual dimensions as well. One of the key narratives utilized during LTC was that of a spiritual war being waged over the places of West Belfast. Church members frequently commented that they saw themselves as engaging in spiritual battles through their participation in the initiative, considering their actions direct acts of warfare against 'principalities' that control various negative aspects of society, each of which is attributed to a demonic influence – a 'curse', a 'spirit' or a 'demon' (cf. Csordas 1994: 41).[11] Meanwhile, minor illnesses, car troubles or lethargy during the forty days were attributed to the work of evil spirits, who were seen as attempting to distract participants or prevent them from fulfilling God's work.

This notion of the Cross as the answer to all social ills, and of societal problems as a type of spiritual warfare, underlies the ultimately crucicentric vision that LTC sought to enskill. In their acts of carrying or standing with the Crosses, participants quite literally inscribed the image of the Cross over the places of West Belfast on a daily basis. This was intentional: in the LTC kick-off event, Jack stated that the daily repetition of the walks and vigils would 'etch the Cross into the minds' of those who saw it.

This inscription, or 'etch[ing]', though, is not only imaginative, but embodied as well. Gray (1999: 449) writes that 'in doing things with objects people abolish the distance between themselves and the things they use, thereby bringing them into a spatial relationship', while Edensor (2010: 8–9) adds: '[T]he accumulation of repetitive events . . . becomes sedimented as individuals, through familiar bodily routines in local space, for instance, walk on tarmac pavements, patches of grass and wood'. By physically interacting with the Crosses – holding them, carrying them, touching them, standing with them – participants brought themselves into relationship with those objects, 'abolish[ing] the distance' between themselves and the Crosses, and 'sedimented' within their minds and bodies a distinctly crucicentric vision of West Belfast.

In Figure 6.1, for example, the Cross is physically inscribed over both the places of the Falls Road and the participant's own body. This act of inscription was highlighted for both participants and spectators (especially digital spectators who interacted with LTC primarily through photographs) by the central positioning of the Cross ('crucicentric' in the literal sense) in the images created, both the physical tableaux of participants standing or walking with the Crosses and the photographs published online. Furthermore, these images symbolically rearrange the hierarchy of skilled visions of West Belfast. In Figure 6.1, the Christian vision, symbolized by the Cross, supersedes competing visions of place: the vision of a 'new Belfast' as a thriving tourist destination (as evidenced by the sign in the lower right corner, which was placed there by the group Visit Belfast and contains tourist information about the Falls Road; cf. Tate 2013: 69–72; Hocking 2015: 33–36); the 'surveillance' vision of 'panoptic

Figure 6.1 A woman walks in front of a mural paying tribute to hunger striker Bobby Sands. This mural is located on the side of the Sinn Féin offices on the Falls Road. Photo by Kayla Rush, March 2014.

administration' (de Certeau 1988: 96; there are several security cameras on and around the Sinn Féin offices); and the sectarian – in this case republican – political vision evidenced by the mural of hunger striker Bobby Sands (in the centre of the photo). The daily repetition of images similar to Figure 6.1, and the sheer volume in which they were published, served to enskill participants with this vision of West Belfast, in which the Cross supersedes all other visions. The following section discusses the ways in which this crucicentric vision spilled into interactions with other pedestrians.

Bounding Souls: Enskilling through Interpersonal Interactions

The first Cross walks and vigils were held on a cold, windy Monday afternoon. I was assigned to stand at the Church Street vigil with several other women and men. Shortly after we hefted the wooden Cross to the curb and faced it towards the street, one of the River of Hope pastors walked by and handed us each a stack of glossy tracts – short pamphlets with religious messages, often used in street evangelism – with the words 'John 3:16' on the cover. The pastor instructed us to hand these out to pedestrians who passed our vigil. This was an aspect of Lift the Cross of which I had not previously been made aware. The presence of the tracts made me profoundly uncomfortable, as I, while a professing Christian, do not like to be given tracts and try to avoid street proselytizers of all faiths. I deposited the tracts in my coat pocket and volunteered to hold the Cross, busying my hands elsewhere.

My fellow participants were more eager, offering the literature to pedestrians, and even to drivers in cars parked or waiting at the nearby intersection. After offering a tract to someone, participants would typically speculate as to the state of that person's soul. This was done privately, after the recipient had walked or driven away. Those who declined to take the tracts were characterized as 'blind' or spiritually 'closed off', and more vehement rejections – hurling the tract back in the giver's face or making rude hand gestures – were occasionally interpreted as signs of demonic influence. Conversely, anyone who took a tract, or any passing motorists who honked, waved, shouted support or gave the thumbs-up sign, were either assumed to already be Christian or were considered to have spiritual eyes that were 'open'.

Harris (2006: 52) describes Christianity as 'a religious system that wishes to maintain clear boundaries between what is acceptable and what is not'. LTC became a tool with which to enskill these boundaries: it gave participants tools with which they might discern who is 'acceptable' and who is not. While sharing the Christian message with individual passers-by was not one of the officially stated goals of the event, these tracts were the primary way in which participants engaged with fellow pedestrians. Even as the Cross walks worked to break down the physical separation between the Falls Road and the Shankill Road, the distribution of tracts cemented a new type of barrier, one based not on physical geography but rather on individual attitudes toward the tracts themselves.

One story in particular illustrates the ways in which these interpersonal interactions were shaped and enskilled. During one of LTC's early weeks, a male pedestrian in his thirties stopped by one of the Cross vigil locations, where Jack spoke with him and gave him a tract. The man, who accepted the tract and expressed concern for the participants' safety, was found murdered in a neighbouring area later that day. Jack identified him from a photo on television and visited the deceased's parents, encouraging them to take comfort in the fact that their son had heard the Christian message hours before his death and responded so positively. This story, more than any other from LTC, has been told again and again by participants and church leaders.

It has, of course, a certain sensational quality that makes it a compelling tale. But its draw for participants goes beyond sensationalism, as the story also illustrates the centrality of receptivity in determining 'insiders' and 'outsiders' in this skilled vision. While they do not know whether this man chose to become a Christian before his death – a fact they admit openly – the people of RHPF take this man's receptivity as a positive indicator when they retell the story. Further, the story both reinforces the idea of a troubled society in need of the church's message and underscores the potential of the Cross to change individual lives. While the official narrative behind LTC presented the event as a force for widespread societal change, the sharing of the Christian message through tracts and conversation reveals another side of the event: that of the Cross as a force for personal, individual change. As the story was told and retold, the discourse developed: 'Can a nation be changed in a day? It was for that man'.

The act of carrying the Cross during LTC was viewed as a powerful signification of this sort of change, and of radical departure from a previous way of life (see Toulis 1997: 168; Harris 2006: 53). In our interview, Tony told me about a woman who had become a Christian shortly before LTC began. He said, 'And the same girl, as a public declaration, walked the Cross on the Falls Road [her home neighbourhood]. And this was just literally, a couple of weeks after she gave her life to the Lord. That's God having an impact on somebody's life'. The following year, RHPF began a monthly event in which a church member would share her or his conversion story in front of the congregation. Each event was advertised with a photo of the speaker, and nearly every photograph used showed the man or woman in the act of holding or carrying the John 3:16 Cross during LTC. These images, in which the Cross is inscribed over participants' bodies (as discussed above), echo this idea of the Cross as life changing, and in turn as a signifier of individuals who fall within these boundaries between 'insider' and 'outsider'.

Cyber-Pedestrianism and the Facebook Gaze

These interpersonal, street-level actions, while important to the processes of enskillment taking place, were few in number. Despite its rather grandiose goals of urban transformation, LTC struggled to engage local residents on a one-to-one, pedestrian-to-pedestrian level, simply because the Cross vigil locations were not areas of heavy foot traffic. The roundabout near Twaddell Avenue, for example, is a site of fairly heavy car traffic, but pedestrians are far less numerous, especially in the centre of the roundabout, where participants were stationed. Foot traffic was just as unusual at the Church Street gates, and I never encountered another pedestrian at the Lanark Way gates, outside of my fellow LTC participants.[12]

There is, however, another group that RHPF engaged much more successfully during Lift the Cross. These were the online spectators of the events, who viewed LTC with what we might call the 'Facebook gaze'. The *flâneur*, the urban walker traditionally associated with the writings of Baudelaire and Benjamin, is a useful concept with which to examine these spectators.[13] In keeping with Ingold's (2010: 15–16) assertion that walking 'involve[s] the exercise of both eye and mind' (discussed above), Turner (2003: 28–29) writes that the *flâneur*'s interaction with the city is fundamentally visual, with watching being just as central as walking to the *flâneur*'s activities. Non-participating viewers of LTC might be appropriately described through this lens, as the *flâneur* is above all a passive spectator: '[H]is is a life of visual encounters, all the while maintaining a detached, anonymous and essentially distant relationship to the urban landscape he moves through' (ibid.: 29).

The concept of the *flâneur* is not a particularly useful way to describe the pedestrians with whom LTC participants engaged, as local residents would not be 'detached' from the spaces of their home neighbourhoods. However, the concept can usefully be applied to those distant spectators who only viewed these spaces online. Several authors (Valentine 2001: 245; Hartmann 2004: 123–25, 160–65) have suggested the rise of a new, contemporary type of *flâneur*: 'the electronic *flâneur* who browses online space' (Valentine 2001: 245). While these writers view the 'cyberflâneur' as 'walking' through virtual spaces – an act not so different from the 'mind-walking' described by Ingold (2010) – I would like to raise another possibility: that of the cyber-pedestrian, the virtual *flâneur* who interacts with physical, geographical space through online means. The Google Maps 'Street View' feature, for example, allows the user to 'travel' virtually up and down city streets, viewing the city from 'down below' (de Certeau 1988: 93), from the same perspective as the physical, non-virtual pedestrian. Photos, videos and a host of other digital resources can also be means by which cyber-pedestrians 'walk' virtually in the spaces of the city (cf. Kelley 2013).

In their study of an annual Orange Order parade in West Belfast (whose route passes quite close to that of the LTC walks), Komarova and McKnight (2012: 4) argue that 'the use of digital image technologies, incorporated into often highly regulated and ritualised bodily performances, plays an integral part in how urban space is claimed or contested'. They later add: 'A pervasive element of these embodied performances was the taking of photographs and video footage of the events themselves' (ibid.: 7). As LTC participants 'claimed' and 'contested' urban space through physical pedestrianism, they simultaneously took part in a digital negotiation as well, presenting images of their pedestrianism – and thus their claims about the spaces in which they walked – for a virtual audience.

River of Hope boasts an extensive international network, and as such the potential audience for these photos was quite large.[14] As mentioned above, photographs of the Cross vigils and Cross walks were uploaded to the church's Facebook page daily, and each day was given its own separate album. During LTC, a virtual *flâneur* would have seen hundreds of photos of the Crosses at various points in West Belfast. Both local and international viewers acknowledged and interacted with the photos by 'liking' the albums or making supportive comments, such as 'God bless you', 'Well done' and 'I'm praying for you'.

Now, imagine for a moment looking at these images with the Facebook gaze, and seeing these sorts of photos repeated day after day for forty days. The photos repeat a series of images that, if not already familiar, will soon become recognizable to the cyber-pedestrian: gates, walls, flags and murals, alongside more mundane features of city life, such as traffic and industrial buildings. Much like walking the same route over and over, the daily repetition of these representations gives these cyber-pedestrians a certain image of place: groups of men and women, nearly all of them white, smiling and crowding together as they stand with, hold or carry a Cross. Consider as well the consistent centrality of the Crosses: in the same way that places were inscribed with the image of the Cross for participants, these virtual *flâneurs*' knowledge of the city is also inscribed with this crucicentric vision.

The cyber-pedestrians who interacted with these photos were not necessarily enskilled with this vision of place, at least not according to the definition I have been using. Enskillment is fundamentally a bodily activity, and while interacting with places online can be something like 'walking', as noted above, these cyberflâneurs did not partake in the material or sensorial elements of Lift the Cross, thus missing some of the key elements of enskillment. Rather, those looking with the Facebook gaze are presented with an aggregate of the visions enskilled in bodily participants, a managed vision (managed by the gatekeepers who uploaded the photos), seen through the eyes of those participating 'on the ground', in the physical city spaces themselves.

Conclusion: Enskilled Visions in Action

In retrospect, Lift the Cross did not manage to bring about the sort of large-scale urban transformation its early discourse promised. The group of people with whom LTC engaged in a lasting manner has proven small, with little impact evident outside of the limited in-group of active participants in the Cross walks and vigils. And yet, these participants' knowledge and modes of interacting with these places were significantly and lastingly altered.

The initiative's success in shaping these participants' visions of the city more permanently became evident several months later. In autumn 2014, a police vehicle was attacked with a grenade at one of the former Cross vigil locations. Two days later several members of RHPF, once again led by Jack, began another vigil on the site. This vigil ran for four consecutive afternoons. On the final day of the vigil, participants affixed the Cross to the site permanently, planting it in concrete (Figures 6.2 and 6.3).

The speed of the church members' response to the attack illustrates the way in which skilled visions become more permanently embedded in understandings of space and serve as resources for current and future

Figure 6.2 The Cross in cement at the interface. Photo by Kayla Rush, July 2015.

interactions with and in the urban landscape. 'Lifting the Cross' has become the church's go-to response to incidents of violence. The vision of the Cross as a solution to Belfast's 'divisions' has taken root – literally so in the case of the Cross in concrete – and it continues to be acted out through street-level, pedestrian practices in West Belfast, in circumstances both everyday and out of the ordinary.

Kayla Rush recently completed her PhD in social anthropology at Queen's University Belfast, researching community arts in contemporary Northern Ireland. She also holds an MA from Queen's, where her MA dissertation was awarded the 2014 John Blacking Prize. Her research interests include performance studies, the senses and the body, pedestrian practices and the political economy of arts funding. Her work has been published in the *Irish Journal of Anthropology*, and online in the research blog *Women Are Boring*.

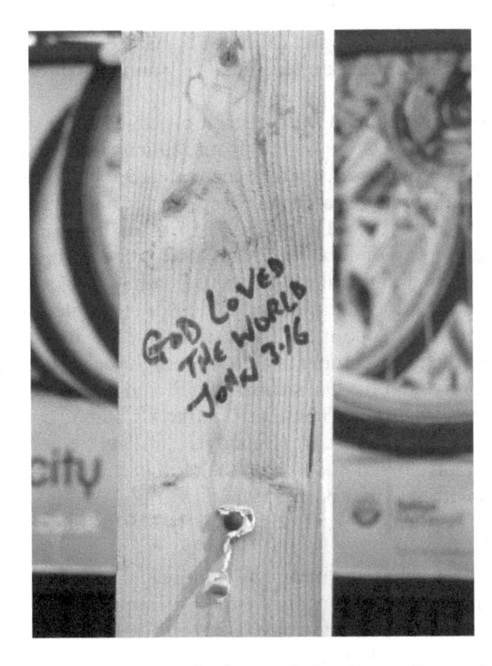

Figure 6.3 A handwritten note on the base of the Cross. Photo by Kayla Rush, July 2015.

Notes

1. John 3:16 is a verse in the Bible. It reads, 'For God so loved the world that he gave his one and only Son, that whoever believes in him shall not perish but have eternal life'. Many Christians consider this verse to summarize the central message of Christianity.
2. In Christian religious practice, Good Friday marks the observance of the death of Jesus. In Northern Ireland, 'Good Friday' is the name given to the 1998 Agreement that generally marks the end of 'the Troubles', so named for the day on which it was drawn up by lawmakers (McKittrick and McVea 2001: 219).
3. This was not the first time a Christian group had performed a Cross walk in this area. Other Christian groups have performed prayer walks on the Falls and Shankill roads (Murphy 2010: 52–53, 147), and one of my interviewees described a Cross walk that had taken place in the town of Dromore, County Down, several years earlier. On Good Friday 2013 a group from nearby Clonard Monastery carried several wooden Crosses 'in Belfast's Fall [*sic*] Road ("Catholic") district through the Shankill Road ("Protestant") district and back' (Kennedy 2013). The Clonard Cross walk's route overlapped significantly with that of RHPF's. Unfortunately, the scope of this chapter does not allow for a discussion of the relationships between Lift the Cross and these prior initiatives.
4. Ingold (1993: 156) defines landscape as 'the world as it is known to those who dwell therein, who inhabit its places and journey along the paths connecting them'.
5. As part of a broader trend of 'conflict tourism' in Northern Ireland, the peace walls in West Belfast have become a popular tourist attraction (Hocking 2015: 97). In an interview, Jack, RHPF's senior pastor and a vocal supporter of removing the wall,

conceded: 'If they wanna keep part of the wall, just as a memorial to our past, sadly the wall between us is a tourist attraction. We wanna encourage tourism, so let the tourists have the wall'.

6. 'Church Street' is a pseudonym for the street on which River of Hope is located.
7. 'Camp Twaddell' itself was not visible from the intersection where the Cross vigil was held, and LTC participants rarely encountered loyalist protesters. I only witnessed two nationalist/republican displays at that location during my research, both occurring on St Patrick's Day (17 March) 2014: a bar hung an Irish tricolour flag in the window, and a group of adolescent girls, one with a tricolour draped around her shoulders, strolled up and down the Crumlin Road.
8. Although, of course, the conquistadors' actions were rooted in spiritual language, and RHPF's practices have political implications in the 'earthly' realm as well.
9. Participants used the term 'community' as shorthand for both geographical area (the 'Shankill community' and the 'Falls community') and ethno-religious background or identification (the 'Protestant community' and the 'Catholic community'). Given the challenges of defining 'community' (Delanty 2003: 3–4), especially in the Northern Ireland context, I have opted not to used the term in this chapter, save when quoting from interviews with research participants.
10. See, for example, Cullen 2011; Curtis 2013: 147–50; Culture Night Belfast 2014; and Boyd 2015.
11. When I asked Eileen what she meant by a 'principality', she responded: 'The Bible talks about principalities and powers, it's a prince demon, it's a huge, powerful demon . . . One with a lot of authority'. The term 'principality' comes from biblical passages such as Romans 8:38 and Ephesians 6:12.
12. Participants encountered more pedestrians during the Cross walks, as stretches of the Shankill Road and the Falls Road experience more foot traffic due to the presence of shops, parks, leisure centres, etc. However, the mobile nature of the walks meant that participants did not have time to speak at length to those they met, but rather handed them the tracts and moved on fairly quickly.
13. The *flâneur* as a concept is only cursorily related to de Certeau's *Wandersmänner*, in that both are pedestrians in the city. While some authors have successfully combined the two ideas (e.g. Jenks 1995: 156; Kuftinec 2001: 200; Pink 2008: 180–83), de Certeau (1988) does not mention the *flâneur* in his book.
14. See Murphy (2002: 26) and Coleman (2006: 167) on the role of transnational connections among Pentecostal churches, particularly in Europe.

References

Aretxaga, B. 1997. *Shattering Silence: Women, Nationalism, and Political Subjectivity in Northern Ireland*. Princeton, NJ: Princeton University.

Belfast Education and Library Board. 2013. *Northern Ireland Education & Library Boards' Youth Services: West Belfast Area Plan, April 2013–2016*. Retrieved 15 May 2015 from http://www.belb.org.uk/downloads/y_west_needs_analysis.pdf.

Belfast Interface Project. 2011. *Belfast Interfaces: Security Barriers and Defensive Use of Space*. Retrieved 15 May 2015 from http://www.belfastinterfaceproject.org/sites/default/files/publications/Belfast%20interfaces.pdf.

Boyd, D. 2015. '"Let's Party" Parade – Saturday 20th June'. Retrieved 15 May 2015 from www.beatcarnival.com/news-archives/2015.

Certeau, M. de. 1988. *The Practice of Everyday Life*, trans. S. Rendall. Berkeley, CA: University of California.
Coleman, S. 2006. 'Materializing the Self: Words and Gifts in the Construction of Charismatic Protestant Identity', in F. Cannell (ed.), *The Anthropology of Christianity*. Durham, NC: Duke University, pp. 163–84.
Csordas, T.J. 1994. *The Sacred Self: A Cultural Phenomenology of Charismatic Healing*. Berkeley, CA: University of California.
Cullen, T. 2011. 'Contesting St Patrick's Day in Downpatrick', *The Canadian Journal of Irish Studies* 37(1/2): 208–22.
Culture Night Belfast. 2014. 'The Methane Mardi Gras'. Retrieved 15 May 2015 from http://www.culturenightbelfast.com/e.php?e=1158.
Curtis, J. 2013. 'Pride and Prejudice: Gay Rights and Religious Moderation in Belfast', *The Sociological Review* 61(S2): 141–59.
Delanty, G. 2003. *Community*. London: Routledge.
DeYoung, E. 2016. 'Lest We Forget: Observations from Belfast's Twaddell Avenue', *Streetnotes* 25: 179–93.
Edensor, T. 2008. 'Walking through Ruins', in T. Ingold and J.L. Vergunst (eds), *Ways of Walking: Ethnography and Practice on Foot*. Aldershot: Ashgate, pp. 123–41.
———. 2010. 'Introduction: Thinking about Rhythm and Space', in T. Edensor (ed.), *Geographies of Rhythm: Nature, Place, Mobilities and Bodies*. Farnham: Ashgate, pp. 1–18.
Eliade, M. 1959. *The Sacred and the Profane: The Nature of Religion*, trans. W.R. Trask. Orlando, FL: Harcourt.
Grasseni, C. 2007. 'Introduction', in C. Grasseni (ed.), *Skilled Visions: Between Apprenticeship and Standards*. New York: Berghahn Books, pp. 1–19.
———. 2008. 'Learning to See: World-Views, Skilled Visions, Skilled Practice', in N. Halstead, E. Hirsch and J. Okely (eds), *Knowing How to Know: Fieldwork and the Ethnographic Present*. New York: Berghahn Books, pp. 151–72.
Gray, J. 1999. 'Open Spaces and Dwelling Places: Being at Home on Hill Farms in the Scottish Borders', *American Ethnologist* 26(2): 440–60.
Harris, O. 2006. 'The Eternal Return of Conversion: Christianity as Contested Domain in Highland Bolivia', in F. Cannell (ed.), *The Anthropology of Christianity*. Durham, NC: Duke University, pp. 51–76.
Hartmann, M. 2004. 'Technologies and Utopias: The Cyberflâneur and the Experience of "Being Online"', PhD dissertation. Westminster: University of Westminster.
Herzfeld, M. 2007. 'Envisioning Skills: Insight, Hindsight, and Second Sight', in C. Grasseni (ed.), *Skilled Visions: Between Apprenticeship and Standards*. New York: Berghahn Books, pp. 207–18.

Hocking, B.T. 2015. *The Great Reimagining: Public Art, Urban Space and the Symbolic Landscapes of a 'New' Northern Ireland*. New York: Berghahn Books.

Ingold, T. 1993. 'The Temporality of the Landscape', *World Archaeology* 25(2): 152–74.

———. 2000. *The Perception of the Environment: Essays in Livelihood, Dwelling and Skill*. London: Routledge.

———. 2010. 'Ways of Mind-Walking: Reading, Writing, Painting', *Visual Studies* 25(1): 15–23.

Ingold, T., and J.L. Vergunst. 2008. 'Introduction', in T. Ingold and J.L. Vergunst (eds), *Ways of Walking: Ethnography and Practice on Foot*. Aldershot: Ashgate, pp. 1–19.

Jarman, N. 1992. 'Troubled Images', *Critique of Anthropology* 1(2): 133–65.

———. 1997. *Material Conflicts: Parades and Visual Displays in Northern Ireland*. Oxford: Berg.

———. 1999. *Displaying Faith: Orange, Green and Trade Union Banners in Northern Ireland*. Belfast: Institute of Irish Studies, Queen's University Belfast.

Jenks, C. 1995. 'Watching your Step: The History and Practice of the *Flâneur*', in C. Jenks (ed.), *Visual Culture*. London: Routledge, pp. 142–60.

Kelley, M.J. 2013. 'The Emergent Urban Imaginaries of Geosocial Media', *GeoJournal* 78: 181–203.

Kennedy, J. 2013. 'Bearing the Cross on Good Friday, Belfast NI' (video). Retrieved 8 July 2015 from https://www.youtube.com/watch?v=bdn1et nhRrY.

Komarova, M., and M. McKnight. 2012. 'The Digital Eye in Conflict Management: Doing Visual Ethnography in Contested Urban Space'. Conflict in Cities and the Contested State, Electronic Working Papers Series, no. 28. Retrieved 27 June 2015 from http://www.conflictincities.org/PDFs/DigitalEyeWP28Revised.pdf.

Kuftinec, S. 2001. 'Staging the City with the Good People of New Haven', *Theatre Journal* 53(2): 197–222.

Lysaght, K.D. 2005. '"Catholics, Protestants and Office Workers from the Town": The Experience and Negotiation of Fear in Northern Ireland', in K. Milton and M. Svašek (eds), *Mixed Emotions: Anthropological Studies of Feeling*. Oxford: Berg, pp. 127–43.

McKittrick, D., and D. McVea. 2001. *Making Sense of the Troubles*, revised edn. London: Penguin.

Murphy, L.D. 2002. 'Demonstrating Passion: Constructing Sacred Movement in Northern Ireland', *Journal of the Society of the Anthropology of Europe* 2(3): 22–30.

———. 2010. *Believing in Belfast: Charismatic Christianity after the Troubles*. Durham, NC: Carolina Academic.

Northern Ireland Statistics and Research Agency (NISRA). 2010. 'Northern Ireland Multiple Deprivation Measure 2010, May 2010'. Retrieved 15 May 2015 from http://www.nisra.gov.uk/deprivation/archive/Updateof2005Measures/NIMDM_2010_Report.pdf.

Parades Commission for Northern Ireland. 2014. 'Annual Report and Financial Statements for the Year Ended 31 March 2014'. Retrieved 13 May 2015 from https://www.gov.uk/government/uploads/system/uploads/attachment_data/file/327936/9781474108058_PRINT.PDF.

Pink, S. 2008. 'An Urban Tour: The Sensory Sociality of Ethnographic Place-Making', *Ethnography* 9(2): 175–96.

Pink, S., et al. (eds). 2010. *Visual Studies* 25(1), special issue.

Radford, K. 2001. 'Drum Rolls and Gender Roles in Protestant Marching Bands in Belfast', *British Journal of Ethnomusicology* 10(2): 37–59.

Tate, S. 2013. 'Tinkering with Space: Heterotopic Walls and the Privileged Imaginary of the "New Belfast"', in M.O. Stephenson, Jr., and L. Zanotti (eds), *Building Walls and Dissolving Borders: The Challenges of Alterity, Community and Space*. Farnham: Ashgate, pp. 69–95.

Toulis, N.R. 1997. *Believing Identity: Pentecostalism and the Mediation of Jamaican Ethnicity and Gender in England*. Oxford: Berg.

Turner, M.W. 2003. *Backward Glances: Cruising the Queer Streets of New York and London*. London: Reaktion.

Valentine, G. 2001. *Social Geographies: Space and Society*. Harlow: Pearson Education.

Vergunst, J. 2012. 'Seeing Ruins: Imagined and Visible Landscapes in North-East Scotland', in M. Janowski and T. Ingold (eds), *Imagining Landscapes: Past, Present and Future*. Farnham: Ashgate, pp. 19–37.

7

Engaging amid Divisions

Social Media as a Space for Political Intervention and Interactions in Northern Ireland

Augusto H. Gazir M. Soares

The BBC Northern Ireland television programme *The Nolan Show*, and its usually heated debates, generated more controversy than normal on Wednesday 28 May 2014. On that night, Pastor James McConnell was one of the guests of the live audience show presented by Stephen Nolan. The pastor had become news for describing Islam as 'satanic' in a sermon, and for saying he did not trust Muslims. That day, the story got bigger. The *Irish News* published an interview by the Northern Ireland first minister, Peter Robinson, in which he gave his support to the pastor. Robinson said he had known the pastor for more than twenty years and that McConnell was a good man. The first minister added that he himself would not trust Muslims for spiritual advice, but would 'trust them to go down the shops'. The condemnation of Robinson's remarks was immediate and wide. On social media, the anonymous satirical online profile Loyalists Against Democracy (LAD) was one of the main protest voices against the unionist first minister and the pastor. The previous week, LAD had broken the story about McConnell's comments, having mined the video of the sermon on the internet and posted it on its YouTube page.[1] On the night of the 28th, I watched the *Nolan Show* and followed LAD's simultaneous postings and conversations on Twitter about the programme, as part of my research for a social anthropology MA dissertation about the internet profile, presented in 2014 at Queen's University Belfast.

Live on television, McConnell repeated his views that he would not trust Muslims because they follow Sharia Law. Meanwhile, on Twitter, LAD expressed its sarcasm and indignation. Such feelings were shared by others on the platform through original posts, comments and retweets. A target for LAD and its interlocutors, for example, was McConnell's peculiar pronunciation of 'Sharia'. LAD referred to it in a photomontage exploiting the physical similarity between the pastor and the actor Tom Oliver, who plays Lou Carpenter in the soap opera *Neighbours*. In the image, the pastor's lookalike is being shoved by a masked man. The inserted caption says: 'It's pronounced "Sharia" you mad Pastord ye!'. On the following day, LAD would circulate a video collage of all the times the pastor pronounced 'Sharia' during the programme.[2] Stephen Nolan also interviewed the Respect MP George Galloway, who criticized the pastor. In the studio, a man in the audience supported the preacher and attacked Galloway. He would be mocked on Twitter and identified on the platform as a candidate for the UUP in the Belfast local election, which had taken place in the previous week. A Twitter user asked LAD if the profile did not have anything to report on the man. LAD responded that it was working on it and then made available electoral material of the candidate, including a photo of him with UUP MEP Jim Nicholson. The unionist UUP would go on to suspend the candidate, and he then decided to leave the party. 'George Galloway', '#nolanshow', '#bbcnolan' and 'Sharia' were all listed by Twitter as trending topics for Belfast in the early morning of the 29th, whereas LAD was one of the Twitter profiles with most traffic in Northern Ireland on the previous night, according to the website Trendsmap, specialized in this kind of data.

LAD's activity on Twitter during the *Nolan Show* illustrates the particularities of interaction on social media.[3] Such mediation has involved the fast-paced and potentially expansive circulation of different kinds of content among users, and the possible reconfiguration of this material as part of the process (Jenkins 2006; Shifman 2011; Jenkins, Ford and Green 2013). I described, for instance, how LAD selected a scene from a soap opera on the web, reworked it in a derivative piece, and circulated the result to ridicule Pastor McConnell. The posts by LAD evidence how the online increases the possibilities to combine visual and textual discourses in everyday communications, and to play with intertextuality – the practice of decontextualizing a speech or a speech element and reinserting it in another situation (Spitulnik 1997: 162; Peterson 2005: 130–31). The account above of the *Nolan Show* also draws attention to the possibility of co-present conversations on social media, the simultaneous sharing of an online space (Miller 2011: 212; Miller 2012: 149). Moreover, Harrington (2014) notes that Twitter has offered audiences the chance to engage in real-time conversations, beyond their homes, about a television programme. The platform works as a 'virtual loungeroom', where viewers from different physical locations meet and discuss the television experience while it happens (ibid.: 241).

Based on my fieldwork carried out in 2014 about the digital politics and satire of LAD in Northern Ireland, this chapter will analyse how practitioners of the online – to paraphrase de Certeau's 'practitioners of the city' (1984: 93) – have been able to craft on social media spaces for political expression and interactions related to the region. Posts, comments, shares, likes, retweets, favourites and memes, among other acts of circulation, have defined such spaces, at the same time as these modalities of intervention are defined by the possibilities of the online. These are actions that relate to the offline, but could not happen outside the virtual. My research involved the online tracking of LAD, an effort inspired by Postill's 'media epidemiographic' approach (the term comes from the combination of epidemiology and ethnography), which aims to pursue and reconstruct trajectories and movements on social 'viral' media (Postill 2014: 51–69). I undertook research for three months, mostly on Twitter, but the tracking took me to other websites as well, such as Facebook and YouTube. I conducted semi-structured interviews with followers of LAD and with the creator of the profile, and I observed political events in Belfast in loco, simultaneously following the related social media traffic through a smartphone. As I intend to show below, the case of LAD provides an opportunity to assess online political engagement and circulation in Northern Ireland, to ponder on the role of these communications in the region and to consider the connections and distinctions between the online and offline settings of social practices.

The 'Schizophrenic Character'

Loyalists Against Democracy (LAD) was made possible by the internet. An anonymous internet profile with a coordinated presence on social media platforms, LAD was created in December 2012, during the so-called flag protests in Northern Ireland, which consisted of weeks of loyalist/unionist demonstrations against the Belfast City Council decision to fly the British flag at City Hall only on designated days, and no longer during the whole year. LAD's mocking of the protestors became a hit on social media in the region. Almost three years later, LAD was reaching eighteen thousand followers on Twitter and had around thirty-five thousand likes on Facebook. It continues to spotlight loyalism/unionism, but, beyond that, the profile has made fun of everyday aspects of the region's divisions. It has attacked mainstream politicians and campaigned for equality policies in Northern Ireland. The profile divides opinions. It is celebrated for exposing bigotry and at the same time accused of raising tensions and stereotyping the loyalist/unionist working class.

LAD can be understood as part of a constant social media flow of interactions, where the spreading of one's pieces – one's impact – are crucially dependent on the acts of circulation of other users, their retweets, comments, likes, shares, remixes and so on (Fattal 2014: 321; Jenkins, Ford and Green 2013: 9–16). Social media allowed an individual to circulate jokes anonymously about the flag protests and led to the quick sharing of these posts, attracting dozens of followers and contributors. As LAD got bigger, its creator invited early engagers to form a non-paid administrative group for the profile. The group has kept in touch online, through a Facebook chat page. Each administrator enjoys relative autonomy in the task. Users' feedback and contributions (tips, ideas and digital material, for example) have been feeding content production and, therefore, circulation.

The movement and transformation of content is not by any means exclusive to the online. Edbauer (2005) analyses, for instance, the 'shared contagion' of a motto created by local shop owners in Austin, Texas in the United States (ibid.: 16–18). They launched a sticker against the establishment of large chain stores in the centre of the city. The sticker 'Keep Austin Weird' became very popular. The motto was quoted on public radio, and printed on T-shirts and mugs by different people. Its spread led the local library to rework the phrase and print stickers with the message 'Keep Austin Reading'. In the end, even a corporate giant used the motto in its marketing. In another example, Strassler (2009) discusses the refashioning of money in Indonesia as a medium of political communication. A sticker of a 50,000Rp bill that replaced the face of the former president Suharto with that of the then candidate Megawati Sukarno Putri became one of the most popular materials of the 1999 electoral campaign (ibid.: 87–93). Spitulnik (1997) points out the 'detachability' and 'transportability' of 'media fragments', examining how listeners in Zambia negotiated the meanings of radio expressions in employing them in varied situations (ibid.: 181). The widespread availability of content creates, according to her, possibilities for circulation (ibid.: 162).

In the online, circulation and content production become more deeply intertwined (Fattal 2014: 321). The internet and its tools give greater speed and scope to the exchanges of the circulatory flow (Jenkins, Ford and Green 2013: 12), and the heightened interactivity makes the paths of circulation less predictable and more contingent (Fattal 2014: 321–22). Interactivity intensifies circulation at the same time that interactive production is impacted by the possibilities of internet mediation. The YouTube parodies of the film *Downfall* (2004), 'one of the web's most enduring memes' according to *The Telegraph Online* (6 October 2009), illustrate the phenomenon. The German film is about the defeat of Nazism, and its memes, discussed by Ray (2013) and Shifman (2011), have applied a scene of a rant by Hitler to address a number of situations. Each author/user recontextualizes the excerpt in a particular way by changing the film's subtitles. Through this manoeuvre, Hitler has been portrayed in a number of roles. He has complained about a videogame, about Michael Jackson's death, about the signing of Ronaldo by Real Madrid (Shifman 2011: 188). He was used to criticize the awarding of the Nobel Peace Prize to Barack Obama, to lampoon a councillor in Colorado Springs (U.S.) and in a metaprotest to attack the parodies of *Downfall* on YouTube (Ray 2013: 187–89). LAD has its version of the meme as well, in which Hitler reacts to a parade restriction in Ardoyne, in North Belfast.[4] The *Downfall* videos demonstrate the reach that online circulation can achieve and the variety of reconfigurations that are ignited by this movement, in the 'interplay between flows and forms' (Gaonkar and Povinelli 2003: 388). More and more, circulation represents constitutive acts of meaning (Jenkins, Ford and Green 2013: 44; Lee and LiPuma 2002: 192) – and meaning, therefore, becomes increasingly unstable (Gries 2013: 338).

Recent anthropological work has been drawing attention to the political significance of such acts of circulation, a relevant aspect for the debate about LAD in Northern Ireland. Fattal (2014) studies the 'recombinatory circulation' – the reconfiguration of content as part of its circulation among users – of YouTube videos about the Colombian conflict. According to him, the conflict 'plays out through likes, favourites, shares, comments and re-edited videos' (ibid.: 320). Internet remixing, for Fattal, is a locus of politics (ibid.: 321). Postill (2014) shows how the *indignados* in Spain turned social media into viral media, setting the tone and the agenda of their protest movement and enlarging mobilization through specific practices of online interaction (ibid.: 51–69). The introductory vignette has already made clear the political charge of the circulation around LAD and indicated how Northern Irish politics plays out in the online, as in Fattal's case. An unintentional contribution that I made to LAD during my fieldwork corroborates that. With the intention to build rapport with LAD's administrators, I sent one of them a link to a news item about a satirical party in Ukraine which had launched Darth Vader for president. LAD reworked the link to tease a unionist politician, suggesting that he would be worse than the villain of *Star Wars*.

The episode illustrates the potentialities of digital circulation, and offers a small example of how LAD and its operation should be seen as part of a social media engagement, which moulds and is moulded by the profile's intervention. Social media engagement is understood here as the communications and interactions that the profile, through acts of circulation, is able to provoke, take part in and sustain within the online. My research on LAD revealed a constant initiative by the profile to maintain and enlarge this social media engagement and its repercussions. As seen above, LAD can be considered an engagement in itself, having been developed through the contacts among users and their collaboration. The profile has shown entrepreneurship oriented towards acknowledging the suggestions and reactions of followers, addressing in the best way, and with the best timing, an event, piece of news or circumstance, tailoring digital content in the most attractive way, and using the structure of social media platforms to promote its content and increase traffic. The creator of LAD, William H. Smyth,[5] defines 'being good at social media' as 'engaging, updating'. He goes on: 'People spend a lot of time on social media, so you have to be refreshing, you have to be giving them content'.[6]

At the same time, for Smyth, LAD is also the result of 'pure chance': 'it was truly just an organic experience'.[7] It involves users with different motivations and perspectives ('even people who really hate us follow us', Smyth says),[8] which is reflected in diversified content, an output that can sometimes puzzle users. LAD alternates satirical and sincere messages without warning. It posts about the Northern Irish conflict, gay marriage, the football World Cup, fictional television series and the Glastonbury Festival. It ridicules loyalist/unionist protestors and celebrates historical loyalist leaders. It is politically correct in relation to some issues, but not to others. It can be seen as abusive, and it apologizes when it judges that it has gone too far. William H. Smyth defines the profile as a 'schizophrenic character'.[9] LAD can provoke conversations with varied people, but the dynamics of social media circulation do not allow its administrators to keep control over the ramifications and outcomes of these exchanges, as Smyth himself recognizes.[10] LAD's regime is not an improvised one, but it has improvisation as a resource, and unpredictability as a component. The emergence and unfolding of the engagement and its 'schizophrenic character' entangle intentionality and spontaneity. The character is built live.

LAD's interaction indicates how acts of circulation can, in a Lefebvrian sense, produce social space within the online. After all, it could be argued that these social media spaces 'attain "real" existence by virtue of networks and pathways, by virtue of bunches or clusters of relationships' (Lefebvre 1991: 86), being 'the outcome of past actions' and 'what permits fresh actions to occur' (ibid.: 73). Such connectivity can be observed in LAD's movements on Twitter during the *Nolan Show* programme, when it composes, sustains and inhabits the 'virtual loungeroom' (Harrington 2014: 241), linking with other users through its statements and jokes, and tying together different narratives and subjects through its digital recycling. For instance, after its exchange of posts with a user about the candidate who supported the pastor in the *Nolan* audience, LAD framed the man's old electoral campaign material to the then present context in order to bring to the arena the candidate's party, and embarrass it.

In his formulation about space, de Certeau (1984) emphasizes the role of practices and movements in its constitution. For him, space is 'composed of intersections of mobile elements. It is in a sense actuated by the ensemble of movements deployed within it' (ibid.: 117). He uses the metaphor of walking in the city, in which the planned city is made into lived space by walkers, the 'practitioners of the city', and their everyday 'ways of operating' (ibid.: 91–110). In comparison to the 'practitioners of the city', the practitioners of the online undergo different possibilities in their acts of circulation. Moving and interacting within and/or between social media platforms is different from the physical displacement and interaction in the offline world. Staying with the *Nolan Show* example, socializing about a television programme in a living room with friends or relatives is a very different experience from discussing it on Twitter.

Following Boellstorff (2008, 2011, 2012), this chapter argues that, despite the connections it maintains with the offline, the online can be considered an integral space of culture to the extent that it results from interactions and harbours experiences proper to the web. Boellstorff has been warning against the conceptual blurring of the actual and the virtual spheres, criticizing a literature that treats the latter as a mere derivative of the former. In his view, 'virtual worlds' are specific 'places' to the extent that people interact in them (Boellstorff 2008: 180). Places, according to him, are made meaningful through the engagement of human 'techne' (the action that engages with the world, transforming it). They are not places per se, but place-making. Place and the activities within it are mutually constituted (ibid.: 55; Boellstorff 2011: 511–12). The author's notion of place relates in this way to the concepts of 'space' by Lefebvre (1991) and de Certeau (1984). For Boellstorff, what is distinctive about virtual worlds is that for the first time techne can take place within a world that is, itself, a product of this engagement. Techne becomes recursive (Boellstorff 2008: 58; 2011: 510–11). The 'gap' between the two dimensions of techne does not mean that they are sealed off (Boellstorff 2011: 509; 2012: 41–43). Boellstorff (2008: 201) notes that users reconfigure in virtual worlds many aspects of the actual-world sociality. The 'traffic' from one sphere to other can be constant in social life, but this movement does not erase their boundaries. Instead, it makes clear the differences between both dimensions, and between the experiences that they propitiate (ibid.: 200).

Boellstorff bases his discussion on his research within Second Life, a 3D world accessed and inhabited through avatars. In the book about his research, he considers this kind of environment 'virtual worlds', and differentiates them from 'social networking websites like MySpace and Facebook' (Boellstorff 2008: 238, 247). In fact, 3D virtual worlds, where users can go to parties and decorate houses, provide a distinct experience of immersion compared to social media. However, years later, Boellstorff (2012) brings evidence presented by Miller (2011) about the use of Facebook in Trinidad to reinforce his case about the gap between online and offline socialities (Boellstorff 2012: 50–52). For example, Miller (2011, 2012) points out that Facebook can provide 'an additional space for personal expression' for introverted people (2011: 169). It can be a 'buffer' for those who feel awkward in the company of strangers, enabling users to find out more about potential offline friendships (ibid.: 165).

It is important to note that there are important distinctions between the works of Miller and Boellstorff. The latter has conducted ethnography within the virtual. The former has assessed the offline context of social media use and discussed the complementarity between the two dimensions. Having said that, according to Miller, it is 'possible to start thinking about SNS [social networking sites] as places in which people in some sense actually live' (Miller 2012: 155–56). He quotes the portrait of a user who, disabled, does not leave his house, but spends most of the time socializing on Facebook, 'liv[ing] as much as possible within' the platform (ibid.: 156). Miller observes that Facebook is a place where someone can aggregate all the people that she or he knows privately, open to each other, in co-present connections through texts and photos, that differ greatly from conventional conversation with particular individuals (Miller 2011: 174–75).

The Online and Offline Engagement of LAD

The case study of LAD permitted the observation of the different possibilities of the online and offline, and also the movements between the two. One of the main surprises of my fieldwork was the realization that LAD's engagement was not strictly confined to the internet. The profile's interactions crossed to the offline in meetings maintained by its administrators with certain followers and supporters. These contacts tended to be arranged online, took place in public spaces, and involved a cautious approach by the administrator in question. A follower of the profile provided me with a valuable account of these offline incursions. This interviewee of mine had given informal online advice to LAD's administrators in 2013, when the profile's Facebook page went down. Allegedly, loyalist/unionist users reported it to Facebook, leading to automatic closures. Later, the page was definitively restored. Months after the episode, LAD launched a campaign against the cancellation of a play in Northern Ireland, which, according to local politicians, disrespected Christianity. The profile asked for the support of my interviewee, who is a member of a political party. He discussed the topic with LAD, this time in a face-to-face meeting with the profile administration. My informant was not prepared to deal with 'political issues' without knowing who LAD was.[11] When the exclusively online contact ceased to be appropriate for my interviewee, it seems that LAD's administrators decided to reveal themselves in order to strengthen their campaign. In the end, after social media outrage instigated by the profile and public pressure, the play was reinstated. Despite the obvious crossing and complementarity between online and offline socialities in this situation, the distinctions between both in the perception of my interviewee were significant. The creator of LAD suggests that he also distinguished between the two dimensions, and pondered about his movements across them. Regarding these offline meetings, Smyth told me he would go to these events 'out of curiosity', since he did not 'want to get locked in this virtual world'.[12]

Another episode of my fieldwork that related to the boundaries and crossings between the online and offline was the Rally Against Racism, held in Belfast city centre on 31 May 2014. The rally was a response to the so-called Pastorgate, mentioned at the beginning of this chapter. The morning after the *Nolan Show* I described, Anna Lo, a member of the regional assembly, condemned in an interview first minister Peter Robinson's defence of Pastor McConnell's comments about Islam, and threatened to leave Northern Ireland because of the discrimination against minorities. Lo, from a Chinese background, had been a victim of racism on social media. The hashtag #IstandwithAnna soon became

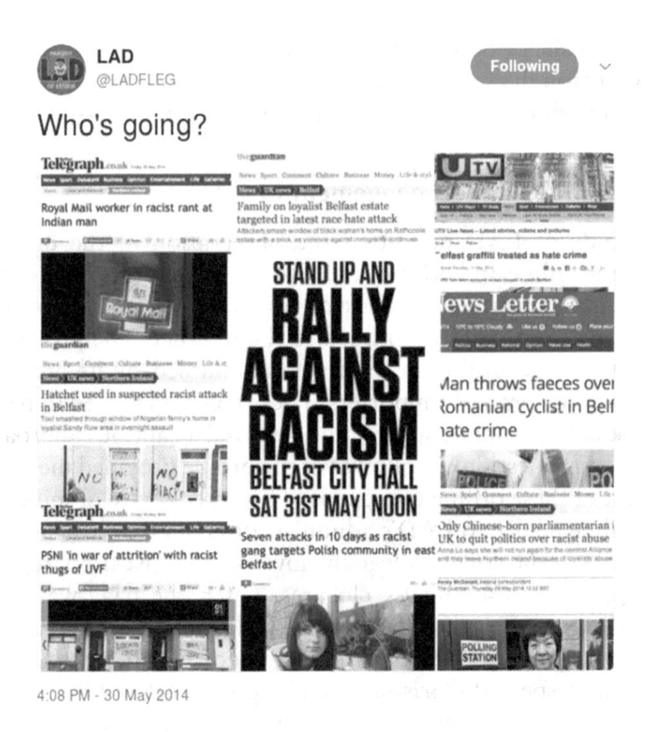

Figure 7.1 LAD/Promotional material. Screenshot by the author.

viral on Twitter, with help from LAD. At lunchtime, a page on Facebook inviting people to attend an 'Emergency Rally Against Racism' on the following Saturday was set up, and gained quick and large adhesion. LAD was not organizing the event, but encouraged participation and produced its own promotional material, combining news pieces about racism in Northern Ireland (see Figure 7.1).

On that Saturday, a sunny morning in Belfast, my online tracking of LAD took me to the offline, to the Rally Against Racism at the main gates of City Hall. I attended the event with my smartphone connected to Twitter in order to concomitantly follow LAD's online steps. The event was scheduled for noon, and I arrived around one or two hours earlier. I was among the first to get there and I positioned myself right in front of City Hall. There was no stage set up or sound equipment for the rally. I watched the arrival of the participants. Among them, there were plenty of adults, families, children, old people, couples and groups of friends. Gradually, it became difficult to move on the large pavement in front of City Hall. The police closed the street in front of the building and opened the gates to accommodate everybody. Despite the squeezing, friends and relatives continued to chat together, giving an impression that they were simply having a good time on a sunny Saturday. Many children carried placards apparently drawn by themselves. 'Be kind', read one. A man carried a big photo of his father with the phrase: 'My father, an awesome Muslim'. A lot of posters made critical and ironic reference to the first minister's remarks about trusting Muslims to 'go down the shops'.

A girl who I recognized from social media as being one of the creators of the rally page on Facebook got things going with the sole help of a megaphone. At the fringes of the crowd, it was possible to catch sight of big banners from mainstream organizations and parties. Representatives of ethnic groups addressed the rally. The Belfast mayor, local politicians and activists also spoke. Anna Lo was the most celebrated. It appeared that the chance to speak was given to anyone who claimed some kind of representativeness. I was around ten or twenty metres from the gate and could hardly hear the speeches. People further away were clearly clapping without hearing properly, maybe because they saw the applause of others in front of them. Close to one o'clock the rally had to disperse, because of the weekly protest that loyalists/unionists have been staging in the same spot since the restrictions on flying the British flag at City Hall were introduced. The crowd of four thousand people dispersed peacefully, being immediately replaced by dozens of protestors. Three days later, the first minister publicly apologized for his comments.

During the rally, I was double-tracking off- and online developments using my smartphone. Around me, people took photos, and read and wrote messages on their phones. On Twitter, under the hashtag #rallyagainstracism, the demonstration appeared as a succession of users, their comments and pictures – a lot of pictures – about the collective experience. Squeezed in the centre of the multitude, I felt as if there were no individuals around me – only the mass of people. When I switched to Twitter, the rally was dissected into a mosaic of individuals/profiles and their posts. The tweeting was intense, but the interaction was minimally traceable, different from the diffuse offline crowd. The social media circulation, which had already been crucial in aggregating people in the demonstration, reinforced the sense of solidary connectedness and co-presence at City Hall (Juris 2012: 267; Postill 2014: 60–61). At the same time, Twitter could communicate the event to a broader public, extending it beyond the crowd (Rafael 2003: 405). The online and offline offered me two experiences of the rally. Being there, I could associate both, but I perceived them as being clearly distinct. I was witnessing the same event in two different settings, each one with its own forms of interaction and expression, but with the two linked by social reality (Boellstorff 2008: 245–46). I underwent in practical terms Boelstorff's thesis about the boundaries and traffic between the online and offline. Meanwhile, LAD, despite having broken the Pastorgate story, discussed and promoted it for days and encouraged its thousands of followers to go to the rally, made itself present on the streets as any other Twitter user: an anonymous administrator, among the participants, tweeting photos and comments (Figures 7.2 and 7.3). The presence of the profile was revealing

Figure 7.2 LAD/City Hall. Screenshot by the author.

of its absence. In the offline, LAD could not be as visible or outspoken as it is on social media. It did not bring banners to promote itself, like parties and conventional organizations. It did not ask to be included in the list of speakers. The occasion did not allow the cautious approach that LAD's representatives tend to adopt in the actual world. At the rally, the crossings between the virtual and the actual contrasted the online potentialities and offline limits of the social media profile.

Molnár (2014) uses the term 'back-and-forth dramaturgy' to discuss the movements between 'online and offline modes of operation' in her analysis of flash mobs (ibid.: 53). Like the Rally Against Racism, these offline events are mobilized online. Taking place in different cities around the world, they are sudden and brief gatherings with a variety of motives. The flash mobs are recorded in video by their participants and exhibited on the internet, promoting the practice and attracting new adepts to it (ibid.: 53). For Molnár, flash mobs show the possibilities of intersection between new media and physical space (ibid.: 44). In the case of the Belfast rally, the 'dramaturgy' referred to by her exposes these intersections and also the differences of the online and the offline. It would be difficult to conceive events like the flash mobs and the rally in Belfast without the far-reaching and agile summoning capacities of the virtual space. To the same extent, it would not be possible to reproduce in the online the excitement or sensorial experience of dozens or even hundreds of people concentrated in a physical place, and the statement that such a public gathering may represent. As noted before, the crossings of the online and offline, rather than weakening the boundary between them, strengthen it. The border that separates is the same one that connects.

Figure 7.3 LAD/Anna Lo. Screenshot by the author.

The distinctions between the online and the offline were also made clear by the interviews that I conducted with the creator of LAD and twelve followers of the profile. Their testimonies add to an understanding about the production on social media of a space for political intervention and interactions in Northern Ireland. The interviewees were selected during my tracking of LAD on Twitter. I followed all of them on the platform. They showed on their timelines an interest and/or involvement in Northern Irish politics, and most of them had exchanged tweets with LAD. I made an effort to pick interviewees with different professional profiles and political perspectives, from distinct ethnic backgrounds and social classes. One of them was not living in Northern Ireland at the time, and I interviewed him by email. I did one more interview by email, and I did one by phone. The rest were conducted in separate meetings in Belfast. One of my lines of questioning to them was about their views on the impact of social media in the politics of Northern Ireland.

Most of the interviewees acknowledged the potential of the online as a space for dialogue across the ethnic and political divisions in Northern Ireland. Some had even experienced such engagement. Moreover, users tended to describe this potentiality by comparing the online and the offline. Some perceived social media, especially Twitter, as a sphere in which understandings and ties beyond their own social groups could be more easily established. Having said that, this chapter does not intend to jump to general conclusions about the impact of social media on Northern Irish politics – particularly because my research did not have the duration or scope to allow that. If some of my interviewees emphasized the positive consequences of these platforms, there are studies pointing out circumstances in which the online can reinforce divisions. Reilly (2011, 2012), for instance, discusses the role of social media in organizing antisocial behaviour and increasing tensions in the interfaces. A report by him and Young (2015) distinguishes between positive aspects (intergroup contact, among them) and negative ones (spreading of rumours, among others) in the use of social media in relation to parades and protests in Northern Ireland (ibid.: 24–34). In another example, Ó Dochartaigh (2007) describes how online interaction on loyalist/unionist and nationalist/republican websites and the platforms' guestbooks diversified and heightened hostile contacts and attitudes in an interface area in Belfast.

If, in the case studied by Ó Dochartaigh, the online can reinforce physical territorial divisions, the author also detects differences between the offline confrontational exchanges and the new ones taking place through the internet. The online brings new modes for conducting and experiencing such hostilities. For example, if the new technologies have facilitated the communications of 'surveillance' and 'penetration' between communities, intensifying and extending intimidatory territorial strategies, they have also provided an opportunity to directly challenge them (Ó Dochartaigh 2007: 483–88). Surveillance, for instance, can become 'a process of interchange' (ibid.: 484). Like any other social process, online place-making, as discussed by Boellstorff (2011: 511–12), can lead to diverse and non-anticipated outcomes. The social media engagement involving LAD and the online space carved out by these interactions can, according to the circumstances, attitudes and points of view, deepen or tackle polarization, be interpreted as positive or negative. My interviewees' observations about beneficial consequences of social media are insightful for this chapter, especially because they are founded on the differences perceived by these informants between the online and offline.[13] The attention to these distinctions is integral to comprehending the production of space within the online, and to address the constant traffic between both spheres.

An interviewee who identified himself as 'unionist working class' exemplified these differences in his description of his personal dramaturgy between the virtual and the actual. He said that social media 'allows conversations to happen that otherwise wouldn't', because in Northern Ireland 'there's still very much a physical barrier ... there's still a social, even an economic barrier'. On Twitter, he 'got to speak with a lot of... not just republicans, but ... with different kinds of unionists'. Moreover, he has met some of these people in person and 'essentially made friends out of it'. According to him, social media 'can take the sting out of speaking to someone'. Referring to the Rally Against Racism, the interviewee identified a new 'political' scene in Northern Ireland, which involves social media in its making and connects people from different perspectives. That 'wasn't here during the conflict . . . there was no debate, there was war. I often think to myself, had we had Twitter and Facebook thirty years ago, would conflict have been so easy to enter into?'[14] In wondering if the contemporary online engagement could have impeded the Troubles, the interviewee suggests that he notices in the online potentialities not seen in the offline. In speculating about the possible effects of the online exchanges on the conflict, he also recognizes that the two dimensions can connect.

A nationalist interviewee corroborated the working-class unionist's view. He also emphasized the potential of social media to allow conversations that would not otherwise happen, and illustrated this by recalling an interaction that he had had with a member of the PUP, a unionist party. Another interviewee, from a mixed background, agreed: 'People who never engage before, they may have very, very strong views, but they're now talking, they're arguing' on Twitter.[15] The argument of Dr Francis Teeney[16] is along the same lines. He acknowledges that social media can be used to increase tension in the interfaces and to direct hate speech, but, he says, online engagement has been a good experience for Northern Ireland, a way for people to interact. The contact may be 'very, very rude', but 'at least it is a communication of sorts': 'It's very hard to challenge a brick or a bottle . . . but it's much easier to challenge . . . hate speech'.[17] Making the reference to 'a brick or a bottle', Teeney contrasts the online and the offline as settings for engagement: as long as the challenges are within social media, there is no immediate risk of physical aggression.

Like Teeney, William B. Smyth, creator of LAD, implies that exchanges online can be worthwhile even when stormy. Regarding the criticism that LAD receives for supposedly stimulating sectarian tensions in its targeting of loyalism/unionism, I asked Smyth once if the initiative was not feeding polarization. He refuted this: 'No, I think that we're providing a platform for people to come and talk to each other. And yes, that might be angry, heated conversation, but then sometimes you'll see beautiful moments where people from two opposing traditions realize that they've got something in common'.[18] Tracking LAD on Twitter, I witnessed on some occasions two or more users disagreeing, for shorter or longer periods, in the comment section of a post made by the profile. If offences were a possibility, and concessions rare, these users clearly had to acknowledge the other's points of view in order to articulate responses. Through their conversation, a space for political expression and exchanges was drawn on social media, an interaction that would not have been possible if not for the online.

Conclusion

Through their acts of circulation on social media, practitioners of the online have produced spaces for political interventions and conversations related to Northern Ireland politics and its conflictive context. These spaces are in constant connection with the offline, but, nevertheless, they encompass and are defined by specific possibilities and social practices. The case study of LAD offers a chance to assess the interactive making of these virtual spaces and the crossings between them and the actual world. This chapter has shown, for instance, how users could establish an environment through content circulation on Twitter, and dialogue in real time and in a co-present way about a live television programme. It has discussed how LAD itself is the result of a social media engagement, having developed and consolidated its status through exchanges that sometimes reached the offline. In another example, with the crucial participation of LAD, social media interaction snowballed into a major political rally in Belfast, an escalation that highlighted the online potentialities and offline limits of the profile. In addition, interviewed users saw possibilities within the online for conversations and understandings that, according to them, offline barriers usually impede in Northern Ireland.

As Boellstorff (2012) suggests, 'social realities are no longer limited to the physical world; the process of moving though [*sic*] space and establishing common grounds can now take place online as well as offline' (ibid.: 52). This understanding and approach can add new elements to the analysis of Northern Ireland's contemporary conflict. This chapter has indicated the political significance and consequences that social media interaction can have in the region. It has showed how Northern Irish politics also play out in the online (Fattal 2014: 320–21). The issues discussed here invite further analysis of this everyday online political engagement. For example, what are the impacts of this engagement for the conflict in Northern Ireland? Can such an interaction make a difference? What can scholarship about digital politics and the online, whether in conflictive contexts or not, offer to the case of Northern Ireland, and vice versa?

In relation to Northern Ireland, authors have been pointing out the importance of the use of public space for defining and exercising identity in the region, and highlighting the role that space and territorial limits play in the divisions (Bryan [no date], 2000, 2004, 2009; Bryan and Connolly 2009; Bryan and Stevenson 2009; Stevenson 2010; Byrne and Gormley-Heenan 2014; Cunningham 2014; Rallings 2014). This chapter indicates the emergence of new complexities for this analysis. In times of offline and online events and offline and online engagement, such as the Rally Against Racism in Belfast, how can social media interaction interfere in the perception and use of public space? Are there distinctions between, for example, the experiences of antagonizing in the offline and antagonizing in the online, or building ties in the offline and in the online? What are they?

The present assessment is an initial contribution and may serve as a starting point for future investigation to address these questions. As technological tools and resources advance, as they become more and more accessible, and people appropriate and make use of them in diverse ways, the topics of the online and of digital politics gain increasing relevance for the understanding of Northern Ireland divisions, the current peace process and its challenges.

Augusto H. Gazir M. Soares is a journalist and a PhD candidate in social anthropology at Queen's University Belfast. He holds an MA in social anthropology (2014) from the same university. His PhD explores online political sociality in Northern Ireland, and builds on his MA dissertation, that was entitled 'The Case of Loyalists Against Democracy (LAD) in Northern Ireland: A Contribution to an Anthropology of Digital Politics and Political Satire'. In 2015, he published 'The Parodic/Sincere Political Satire of Loyalists Against Democracy (LAD) and its Digital Remixing of Northern Ireland', *Queen's Political Review* 3(2): 36–53.

Notes

1. https://www.youtube.com/watch?v=Mx2EP-6he-0.
2. https://www.youtube.com/watch?v=zDjI9nluAZ4&index=5&list=PLnTFuV_YJKw510MkkJSLvdsBs5G2qapZB.
3. I use 'social media' here as a general term to refer to sites such as Twitter, Facebook and YouTube, despite being aware that these websites can be classified in different categories. According to Murthy (2013), Facebook is a social networking site. It allows users to coordinate relationships with a group of other users, in a 'friend-centred' model (ibid.: 8). Twitter is defined by him as a microblog, a blog of short messages. Social media's emphasis would be on the circulation of content, that is, social media are 'publishing-oriented' media (ibid.: 7–8). However, Murthy recognizes the overlap among these categories (ibid.: 8–9). In my research, for instance, I observed prominent content circulation on Facebook, and the use of Twitter, to build relationships. In my field, people used the term 'social media' to refer to all these sites. I am also aware that these platforms present different features and, in use, can result in distinct settings of interaction, but here I will discuss them in a more general way as online spaces of social practices.
4. https://www.youtube.com/watch?v=mSgoR3JMOoo.
5. William H. Smyth is the pseudonym used by the creator of LAD. He asked to be identified in my work by the pseudonym. Smyth is not originally from Northern Ireland. He told me that LAD was definitely influenced by his point of view as an 'outsider', as he puts it. It was a way to engage with what he called the 'absurdity' of the disarray because of a flag.
6. Interview with the author on 1 August 2014.
7. Interview with the author on 12 August 2014.
8. Interview with the author on 1 August 2014.
9. Interview with the author on 12 August 2014.
10. Interview with the author on 12 August 2014.
11. Interview with the author on 21 July 2014.
12. Interview with the author on 12 August 2014.

13. It is interesting to note that the only interviewee who was categorical in saying that social media has been negative for Northern Ireland's politics also differentiated in his testimony between the online and the offline: 'You and I are speaking here face-to-face, and it makes it harder for me to insult you . . . but if we're on social media it is a lot easier for me to insult you' (interview with the author on 14 July 2014).
14. Interview with the author on 15 July 2014.
15. Interview with the author on 15 July 2014.
16. Dr Francis Teeney authorized the identification of his interview. He is an academic at Queen's University Belfast, and editor of the blog *Compromise after Conflict* in Northern Ireland. The blog publishes contributions of people from different backgrounds and political perspectives.
17. Interview with the author on 9 July 2014.
18. Interview with the author on 1 August 2014.

References

Boellstorff, T. 2008. *Coming of Age in Second Life*. Princeton, NJ and Oxford: Princeton University Press.

———. 2011. 'Placing the Virtual Body: Avatar, Chora, Cypherg', in F.E. Mascia-Lees (ed.), *A Companion to the Anthropology of the Body and Embodiment*. Oxford: Blackwell, pp.504–20.

———. 2012. 'Rethinking Digital Anthropology', in H.A. Horst and D. Miller (eds), *Digital Anthropology*. London and New York: Berg, pp.39–60.

Bryan, D. [no date]. 'Parades, Flags, Carnivals and Riots: Public Spaces, Contestation and Transformation in Northern Ireland'. Retrieved 9 May 2015 from https://ugc.futurelearn.com/uploads/related_file/file/4136/5993f14f524ede5b769658f3e8157a0d-Byran__Parades__Flags__Carnivals_and_Riots_Public_Space.pdf.

———. 2000. *Orange Parades: The Politics of Ritual, Tradition and Control*. London: Pluto Press.

———. 2004. 'Parading Protestants and Consenting Catholics in Northern Ireland: Communal Conflict, Contested Public Space, and Group Rights', *Chicago Journal of International Law* 5(1): 233–50.

———. 2009. 'Negotiating Civic Space in Belfast or The Tricolour: Here Today, Gone Tomorrow', Divided Cities/Contested States Working Paper 13. Belfast: Institute of Irish Studies/Queen's University Belfast, pp.3–16.

Bryan, D., and S. Connolly. 2009. 'Identity, Social Action and Public Space: Defining Civic Space in Belfast', in M. Wetherell (ed.), *Theorizing Identity and Social Action*. New York: Palgralve Macmillan, pp.220–37.

Bryan, D., and C. Stevenson. 2009. 'Flagging Peace: Struggles over Symbolic Landscape in the New Northern Ireland', in M.H. Ross (ed.), *Culture and Belonging in Divided Societies: Contestation and Symbolic Landscapes*. Philadelphia, PA: University of Pennsylvania Press, pp.68–84.

Byrne, J., and C. Gormley-Heenan. 2014. 'Beyond the Walls: Dismantling Belfast's Conflict Architecture', *City* 18(4–5): 447–54.
Certeau, M. de. 1984. *The Practice of Everyday Life*. Berkeley and Los Angeles: University of California Press.
Cunningham, T. 2014. 'Changing Direction: Defensive Planning in a Post-conflict City', *City* 18(4–5): 455–62.
Edbauer, J. 2005. 'Unframing Models of Public Distribution: From Rhetorical Situation to Rhetorical Ecologies', *Rhetorical Society Quarterly* 35(4): 5–24.
Fattal, A. 2014. 'Hostile Remixes at YouTube: A New Constraint on Pro-Farc Counterpublics in Colombia', *American Ethnologist* 41(2): 320–35.
Gaonkar, D.P., and E.A. Povinelli. 2003. 'Technologies of Public Forms: Circulation, Transfiguration, Recognition', *Public Culture* 15(3): 385–97.
Gries, L.E. 2013. 'Iconographic Tracking: A Digital Research Method for Visual Rhetoric and Circulation Studies', *Computer and Compositions* 30: 332–48.
Harrington, S. 2014. 'Tweeting about the Telly: Live TV, Audiences, and Social Media', in K. Weller et al. (eds), *Twitter and Society*. New York: Peter Lang, pp. 237–47.
Jenkins, H. 2006. *Convergence Culture*. New York and London: New York University Press.
Jenkins, H., S. Ford and J. Green. 2013. *Spreadable Media: Creating Value and Meaning in a Networked Culture*. New York and London: New York University Press.
Juris, J.S. 2012. 'Reflections on #Occupy Everywhere: Social Media, Public Space, and Emerging Logics of Aggregation', *American Ethnologist* 39(2): 259–79.
Lee, B., and E. LiPuma. 2002. 'Cultures of Circulation: The Imaginations of Modernity', *Public Culture* 14(1): 191–213.
Lefebvre, H. 1991. *The Production of Space*, trans. D. Nicholson-Smith. Malden, MA: Blackwell Publishing.
Miller, D. 2011. *Tales from Facebook*. Cambridge: Polity.
———. 2012. 'Social Networking Sites', in H.A. Horst and D. Miller (eds), *Digital Anthropology*. London and New York: Berg, pp. 146–61.
Molnár, V. 2014. 'Reframing Public Space through Digital Mobilization: Flash Mobs and Contemporary Urban Youth Culture', *Space and Culture* 17(1): 43–58.
Murthy, D. 2013. *Twitter*. Cambridge: Polity.
Ó Dochartaigh, N. 2007. 'Conflict, Territory and New Technologies: Online Interaction at a Belfast Interface', *Political Geography* 26: 474–91.
Peterson, M.A. 2005. 'Performing Media: Towards an Ethnography of Intertextuality', in E.W. Rothenbuhler and M. Coman (eds), *Media Anthropology*. Thousand Oaks, CA, London and New Delhi: Sage Publications, pp. 129–38.

Postill, J. 2014. 'Democracy in an Age of Viral Reality: A Media Epidemiography of Spain's Indignados Movement', *Ethnography* 15(1): 51–69.

Rafael, V.L. 2003. 'The Cell Phone and the Crowd: Messianic Politics in the Contemporary Philippines', *Public Culture* 15(3): 399–425.

Rallings, M. 2014. '"Shared Space" as Symbolic Capital: Belfast and the "Right to the City"', *City* 18(4–5): 432–39.

Ray, B. 2013. 'More than Just Remixing: Uptake and New Media Composition', *Computers and Compostion* 30: 183–96.

Reilly, P. 2011. '"Anti-social" Networking in Northern Ireland: Policy Responses to Young People's Use of Social Media for Organizing Anti-social Behavior', *Policy and Internet* 3(1): 1–23.

———. 2012. 'Community Worker Perspectives on the Use of New Media to Reconfigure Socio-spatial Relations in Belfast', *Urban Studies* 49(15): 3385–401.

Shifman, L. 2011. 'An Anatomy of a YouTube Meme', *New Media and Society* 14(2): 187–203.

Spitulnik, D. 1997. 'The Social Circulation of Media Discourse and the Mediation of Communities', *Journal of Linguistic Anthropology* 6(2): 161–87.

Stevenson, C. 2010. 'Beyond Divided Territories: How Changing Popular Understandings of Public Space in Northern Ireland Can Facilitate New Identity Dynamics', Working Papers in British-Irish Studies 102. Dublin: Institute for British–Irish Studies/University College Dublin.

Strassler, K. 2009. 'The Face of Money: Currency, Crisis and Remediation in Post-Suharto Indonesia', *Cultural Anthropology* 24(1): 68–103.

Young, O., and P. Reilly. 2015. 'Social Media, Parades and Protests'. Retrieved 9 May 2015 from http://www.community-relations.org.uk/wp-content/uploads/2015/03/Social-Media-Parades-and-Protests.pdf

8

BELFAST'S FESTIVAL OF FOOLS
SHARING SPACE THROUGH LAUGHTER

Nick McCaffery

Belfast's Festival of Fools (FOF) is an annual street performance festival that, each May, brings internationally renowned performers and artists from around the world to the streets of Belfast. The festival has been running since 2004 and records high audience numbers, mostly people who look for family-oriented entertainment. In 2004 the Festival of Fools' audience was estimated at thirty thousand, watching about one hundred performances across five locations, including a small number of walkabout acts taking in the breadth of the city centre (McBride 2012: 7).

In 2012 and 2013, audience figures – using head counts at venues and estimates of interactions with walkabout acts – were 46,600 and 40,162 respectively (McBride 2012, 2013). In 2015 and 2016, the audience figures were estimated at 36,000 and 38,000 respectively (personal communication, Sarah Kelly, FOF coordinator). According to figures collected at the 2012 festival:

> Of the 43,569 audience members, 50% were from Belfast, 32% were from the rest of Northern Ireland and 18% were from out of state.[1] Of those surveyed, there were representatives from every Belfast postcode except BT3.[2] 12% of the Belfast-based audience was from the top 25% most deprived Super Output Areas (McBride 2012: 6)

Throughout the festival it is common to see families consult the brochure in town and set out on journeys to parts of the city they would not ordinarily visit on those days when shows are not taking place.

The festival uses a format that is global in nature; it has been adopted in many different cities in Europe, and is thus a fine example of a cultural festival in a contemporary European city. Having performed in, and conducted research on, the festival over a twelve-year period, I argue in this chapter that it has successfully introduced a specific kind of interactive spatial sociality amongst local audiences that transcends practices of Protestant/loyalist and Catholic/nationalist ethno-political place-making. My main aim is to explore to what extent this spatial sociality has been shaped by intentional policies of creating 'Shared Space'. Although understood as a 'physical and social landscape that is welcoming and inclusive to everyone' (Belfast City Council 2015: 66), this is often interpreted, in the context of Belfast, as a spatial form of conflict transformation – a space that can be used together by people from the traditionally opposed ethnonational local communities. I ask, in what ways, if at all, have the festival organizers, performers and audiences engaged with these reconciliatory aims? How has the festival created new ways for people to act in, and react to, specific sites within the city centre? And, if the festival crowd has come to the city to laugh and enjoy themselves, is this a result of an intentional local post-conflict spatial policy, a by-product of the global genre of circus festivals, or a combination of the two?

In what follows, I first provide a brief analysis of the discourse of 'Shared Space' in Belfast, and place the Festival of Fools in its local *political* context. I then show how the festival exists in a local and international *cultural* context that places it amongst both Belfast-based cultural events and global street performance. Since my research is based on my own immersion in the field of circus studies, both as researcher and circus practitioner, I also build on the concept and practice of 'social circus', defined as an intentional intervention to improve areas of well-being amongst individuals and communities.[3] Using the approach of social circus, I argue that the Festival of Fools is not necessarily *intentionally* 'healing the scars of a divided city'; rather it is one of many events that is contributing to the positive well-being of its audiences by the *effect* participation has on them. By gathering together to laugh with each other, the festival creates a sense of place that is a less divisive and more positive expression of a shared future.

Shared Space in Belfast

The dynamics of civic space in Belfast city centre have changed considerably over the past century. In the early twentieth century it was dominated by unionist state and political practices. During 'the Troubles' it was a central theatre of conflict, hosting the physical structures and militarized practices of security and conflict management that earned it the name of the 'ring of steel'. In more recent years, however, the city centre has become a civic place with the potential for cross-community interaction. Drawing upon ethnographic data from the Lord Mayor's Parade and the St Patrick's

Day celebrations in the city in the early 2000s, Bryan (2015: 571) argues that whilst a considerable amount of division and conflict is still evident in and around Belfast city centre today, there is increasing evidence to suggest that 'public, civic space in Belfast is being shared'.

The increased presence of an ethnically and religiously diverse population in the city centre itself reflects the political and institutional rhetoric of 'Shared Space', originating from a post-conflict policy that seeks a 'Shared Future'. These ideas have been defined as:

> The establishment over time of a normal, civic society, in which all individuals are considered as equals, where differences are resolved through dialogue in the public sphere, and where all people are treated impartially. A society where there is equity, respect for diversity and recognition of our interdependence. (OFMDFM 2005: 7)

However, the generic way in which the concept of Shared Space has been utilized and interpreted in public and policy discourse has led to some dispute as to how space – or rather the actions and activities of people who inhabit that space – can be seen as truly 'neutral' or 'shared' (see Komarova and Bryan 2014). Researchers who have explored the role of distinct public spaces (or types of public space, particularly the city centre) for conflict transformation have focused on public civic events and the cultural and political symbolism that they enact and represent (e.g. Nagle 2009; Bryan 2009; Nagle and Clancy 2010; and O'Donnell et al. 2015). Such events, it is noted, offer space for the expression of opposing, marginal or alternative cultural and political identities through staged performances and have, over time, moved from being marginal to being officially enabled and sponsored by local authorities (Bryan 2009). In creating Shared Space, public policy has focused on ensuring equal access to the city centre by neutralizing its political symbolism. Such neutralization has involved removing contentious symbolic markings from public space and the careful management of material symbols used in civic events (OFMDFM 2005, 2010 and 2013; Belfast City Council 2005). However, Rallings (2014) argues that such an approach misses the complexity contained in the relationship between people and place, and sidelines broader elements of the accessibility of public space. These could include, but are not limited to, psychological perceptions of space, everyday life sense-making spatial practices, such as movement (walking, driving, cycling, parading, etc.) and the manner in which social inequalities associated with age, class and gender shape access to space or even to cultural capital. As I argue further in the chapter, it is these latter aspects of accessibility that are addressed through the concept and practice of 'social circus' adopted by the Belfast Festival of Fools. The next section explores this notion of social circus, and asks how its features resonate with Northern Irish political strategies of 'Shared Space'.

Social Circus: The Belfast Festival of Fools

'Social circus' is the use of circus arts (most commonly the *teaching* of circus skills) to enable a positive impact upon the well-being[4] of individuals and communities. Most social circus programmes are designed with the intent to enable a positive impact, and as such can be seen as therapeutic in their nature, even if most of these programmes are run by circus tutors rather than by trained therapists.[5] I draw upon the term here in order to argue that the Festival of Fools, although it has never been explicitly defined by organizers as a 'social circus' enterprise by intent, does have a positive impact on the well-being of its audiences. I argue that this impact on well-being is implicitly connected to the festival's convergence with the concept of 'Shared Space' in Belfast.

My approach to studying the Festival of Fools has come from several years as an observer of the festival through the lenses of both performer and anthropologist. In addition, I have drawn upon interviews with local artists involved in the festival over the years, and the festival's director, Will Chamberlain.[6] This 'dual role' as professional performer/participant and as professionally detached anthropological observer has led me to focus on the ways that different actors within the festival interact in different ways (if at all) with the political dialogue of Shared Space. I have been a street performer in Northern Ireland for over twenty years, and performed in the 2015 Festival of Fools as one half of the double act 'Jim and Dr Nick'. Throughout this time, I have developed shows that incorporate circus skills such as juggling and unicycling with comedy and clowning. This style of show is rooted in the type of street show most commonly associated with buskers and performers seen at Covent Garden in London. It is a style of show designed to have an impact on as many people as possible, by gathering them together in a space and getting them to stay there for the duration of the show. The logic of developing this style of street show is elaborated upon below by the Belfast-based performer Grant Goldie. Of course, it goes without saying that a street show such as this relies upon the temporary transformation of a civic space into a performance space; a street show is performed on the street.

As a performer I appreciate the ways in which my colleagues over the years have made audiences laugh together, shocked them with feats of danger and risk, or challenged the ways that street theatre is perceived in Northern Ireland. As an anthropologist, I am fascinated by the way these inherent qualities of street performance relate to and support a policy-led concept of Shared Space that has been developed in a context far removed from the world of street performers. However, it is the areas of convergence that are most interesting in this case. My own observations and participation in the Festival of Fools suggest that areas in the city where performances take place are temporarily transformed into places of shared fun and laughter. In this sense, the festival differs from those uses of 'cultural reimaging' (Hocking 2015) or cultural events in the city that,

Figure 8.1 The author (on the unicycle) performing in Belfast as '2 flaming idiots' in 2013. Photograph by Brian McKinley, published with permission.

albeit ostensibly 'neutral' in their symbolism, are ultimately an expression of the political project of conflict transformation.[7] By contrast, the main intention of the organizers of the festival is not to make permanent visible changes to the city, or to bring conflicting groups together.[8] Instead, they aim to put on attractive and spectacular shows that entertain anyone coming to the festival, and introduce them to the art of street performance. This makes the Festival of Fools an event that is radically different to the Lord Mayor's Parade and the St Patrick's Day celebrations (cf. Bryan 2015). Despite efforts to engage in a notion of Shared Space and transcend associations with 'one side or the other', the latter two events are ultimately emanating from one or other of the two main ethno-political communities in Northern Ireland. After all, while the Lord Mayor's Parade began as a largely Protestant/unionist celebration, St Patrick's Day is historically associated with a Catholic/republican population. By comparison, the Festival of Fools is more cosmopolitan in nature, as the kinds of circus skills on display are not associated with either 'side'.

But whilst it is tempting to omit any reference to the city's divided past, and frame the festival as a completely unrelated endeavour, notions of Belfast's conflict history linger in the background. Even though the festival's director denies that this event is a reaction to ethno-political 'claims' to the city (personal communication), one cannot assert that it exists in a socio-historical or spatial vacuum. This is, after all, *Belfast's* Festival of Fools. Indeed, one of the key aims of the festival is to 'promote a positive image of Belfast at home and abroad' (McBride 2013: 5), which assumes that there are negative images of Belfast in circulation that need to be challenged by the city's inhabitants. This supports Quinn's concept of one of the formative elements of festivals in various cities:

> For a long time, festivals have been understood to be cultural expressions of people living in particular places, but in addition, they have always had an overt outward orientation, which saw communities of people generate cultural meanings expressly to be read by the outside world. (Quinn 2005: 238)

Although the festival claims to ignore ethno-nationalist stereotypes of a city based on being on either one side or the other, it does seem to exist as a reaction against these stereotypes, and therefore is just one example of a number of cultural events in Belfast that seeks to provide an alternative and less contested way of celebrating the city centre. This idea was reflected in the original formulation of the aims of the festival, back in 2004:

> The Festival of Fools started out as a way to help create shared celebration in the heart of what has been a divided city in the recent past. To have a street festival where people could share some moments with strangers and to help change people's relationship with the city centre was our ambition in 2004, and since then we have created an event [that] really does transform the city centre for tens of thousands of people – for a few days a year at least. (Festival of Fools 2015)

The Festival of Fools as a Cultural Event

The Belfast Festival of Fools is not a unique event as there are similar street performance and circus festivals, events and gatherings across the world. Whilst larger arts festivals, such as the Edinburgh Fringe, often have an element of street theatre or circus as part of the programme, many festivals across the UK, Ireland and the rest of the world are devoted solely to street theatre and outdoor art. A brief search of festivals close to home shows that these include: Winchester Hat Fair, 'the UK's longest running festival of street theatre';[9] Surge, which each July 'brings new Scottish work and cutting-edge international performances to the streets, theatres and unusual spaces of Glasgow';[10] and Stockton International Riverside Festival, which bills itself as 'the world's best international festival of outdoor art'.[11] In Ireland there is the Waterford Spraoi, which takes place each August, attracts huge numbers of people to the city, and provides music, street theatre and a large parade. Further afield we find events in such places as

Auvergne in France (the Aurillac Festival of street theatre), Graz, Austria (La Strada), the 'Imaginarius' in Portugal, and the Open Street Festival in Milan – the list goes on. With such a booming worldwide street art sector, it is perhaps more difficult to find a major city that does not host some form of street entertainment. Belfast is now one of many cities and large towns across the world where street art is celebrated and encouraged. But, of course, the Festival of Fools is not the only cultural event in Belfast. The local context for Belfast's Festival of Fools is one of many arts events across the city throughout the year. According to Belfast City Council:

> Belfast is a city of festivals, staging the equivalent of at least one festival for every week in the year. Festivals are part of Belfast's cultural lifeblood, and provide substantial social and economic benefits for our city . . . Major festivals attract visitors from all over the world, while the many community festivals celebrate and boost local communities, encouraging social interaction, cross-community participation and shared enjoyment.[12]

One immediately comparable event in Belfast is the annual Culture Night – 'Belfast's biggest and boldest cultural celebration'.[13] In just one night in 2015, Culture Night hosted over fifty thousand people at over two hundred events at over one hundred venues. Many of these venues are outdoors, and my own exploration of the streets of Belfast on an evening where so much artistic expression is on display (for free) certainly produced a feeling that Belfast was much more than the stereotype of a 'divided city'. In addition to Culture Night, Belfast hosts a Pride Festival in July/August, a Mela in August, and the Belfast Festival each autumn. There are also comedy festivals, film festivals, several music-based festivals (from opera to folk) and a host of other smaller community festivals dotted around the city throughout the year. In short, the cultural landscape of Belfast is certainly more varied than a series of public displays of identity belonging to either 'one side or the other', and the Festival of Fools is one aspect of this increasingly cosmopolitan landscape.

While the benefits of many of the events above have often been seen in commercialized terms – for example, as big attractors for tourism and vehicles of consumerism (Frost 2015) – my argument for focusing on this particular festival[14] is based on my assertion that street performance is an immediately accessible art form that is broad enough and varied enough to appeal to a very wide audience – often at the same time. Data from the festival organizers shows the diversity of its audience in terms of age, assumed social/economic background (based on postcode analysis), ability and ethnicity.[15] Being a performer myself, I also agree with the statement made in the festival's evaluation reports (McBride 2012, 2013) that street theatre is audience-led – if a show is not good enough, or if a member of the audience simply does not like a show, they are free to walk away at any time. Street performances also tend towards more audience interaction than many other art forms, and so the tendency is for audiences to feel more connected to the performers. Street performers openly engage with the people in front of them, rather than merely perform for them, or in front of them. This is evident in the way that street performers draw a crowd around them in order to entertain them, as illustrated in the following photograph.

Veteran street performer and 'gentleman juggler' Mat Ricardo (who performed at the festival in 2007 as part of the comedy juggling double act 'Married Men') writes of the way that this genre of performance relies upon an intimate understanding of, and communication with, the audience:

> See, the thing about a good street performer is that by the very nature of how their living is earned, they have to craft work that appeals to as many people as possible. If you have a family watching your show on a sunny Saturday afternoon, you had better make sure that every member of that family sees something they like. If you bore the kids, they're going to start tugging on their parents' sleeves to go do something else. If you just play to the kids, then the parents are going to get eye glaze and start to want to drift away to Starbucks-fuelled shopping. (Ricardo 2016)

When discussing with a fellow performer (interview with Hillas Smith, June 2015) the good awareness among performers of Belfast as a city with a troubled history, Hillas suggested that performers did not really need to raise the issue of Belfast's history, at least not directly. Although it is difficult to ascertain without further research amongst the range of performers who have visited the festival over the past twelve years, Hillas and I agreed that many of the performers who have been hired to work at the festival (both from Belfast and abroad) consider this to be 'another gig'. Performers are in Belfast merely to do the job that they do in any other city or festival in the world. I would contend this attitude alone can be seen as a potentially positive change in the perception of Belfast as a cultural destination, rather than as a 'divided city' that has led to the 'Dark Tourism' industry over recent years (Lisle 2000; Leonard 2011; Skinner 2016). This implies that street theatre is an art form that contributes to an experience of Shared Space in Belfast because of its existing format. This experience, in other words, is inherent in the art form and not the result of Belfast City Council's policy aims.

'A Real Festival Crowd'

If the performers at the Festival of Fools are 'just doing their job', this suggests that audiences who come to watch the shows enjoy them for what they are, independent of Shared Space policies. As someone who has worked as a street performer in Northern Ireland for almost twenty years, I can say with some certainty that the Festival of Fools has played a major part in creating an audience who have a better understanding of street performance now than was the case when I started.[16]

In 2015, I was hired to perform in the Festival of Fools as one half of the double act 'Jim and Dr Nick'. My performing partner and I performed in two pitches: St Anne's Square and Cotton Court (see map at Figure 8.5). Whilst travelling from one to the other we met with another double act whom we knew well – the Cork-based 'Lords of Strut'. In the conversation that followed we talked about the pitch at Cotton Court where we were headed towards to perform, and where the Lords of Strut had already performed. 'You'll like it there,' we were informed, 'you get a real festival crowd there'. Thanking the duo for this perspective on our upcoming pitch we proceeded on to Cotton Court to get ready to perform. I did not really take much notice of this comment at the time, but upon reflection I began to ponder what my colleague had meant by a 'festival crowd' and why he felt it necessary to distinguish this kind of audience. In an interview with festival director Will Chamberlain (June 2015) we discussed this concept of a 'festival crowd' in Belfast city centre. Will sees the festival as one of the contributing factors towards the 'normalization' of Belfast city centre, where even post-ceasefire, it was used solely for commerce, for shopping. Will asserted that 'there was no sense of belonging, no reason to dwell in the city centre'. Indeed, the opening ceremony for the inaugural festival of 2004 was intentionally held on a Thursday evening in order to coincide with late night shopping, and therefore relied upon the fact that there would actually be an audience in the centre itself. Clearly at this time, there

Figure 8.2 Dansko Gida performing in Cotton Court. Photograph by Dave Powell, published with permission.

Figure 8.3 Mario Queen of the Circus performing outside Castlecourt Shopping Centre. Photograph by Dave Powell, published with permission.

Figure 8.4 Fatt Matt performing in St Anne's Square. Photograph by Dave Powell, published with permission.

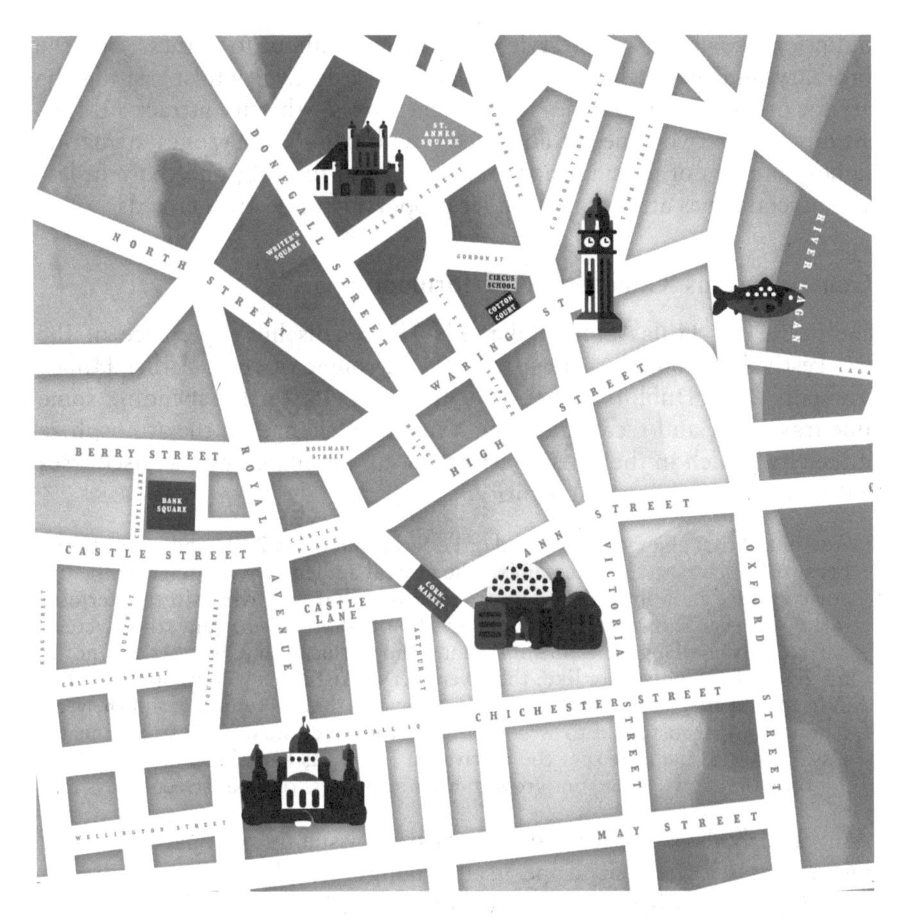

Figure 8.5 Festival map. Designed by Nic Charlton Jeffers, Nic Charlton Design. Published with permission.

was no such thing as a festival audience waiting in the wings for a festival to appear – this 'following' had to be created and nurtured.

The acts perform in various locations across the city, and each of these sites has a different feel to it, hence the comment that our pitch in Cotton Court was more likely to host a 'festival crowd' – that is, an audience who were aware of the acts due to perform at this space throughout the day and who would choose where to be at a certain time. This would be in contrast to pitches at Rosemary Street or Victoria Square, where there would be a higher number of passing shoppers and tourists who would not necessarily have travelled to the centre to visit the Festival of Fools, but who would be able to engage with the shows, so long as they saw something that was interesting enough to distract them from their shopping.

The Festival of Fools has developed over the twelve years to accommodate this split between a 'festival crowd' armed with their programme, and prior knowledge of the style of act they are about to witness, and the 'ordinary audience' who become aware of the festival whilst visiting the city for other reasons. Pitches in different parts of the city attract a different mix of the two types of audience – with commercial zones attracting higher numbers of passing shoppers, or general footfall; and those in less commercial zones attracting a higher proportion of 'festival crowds'.

'Generic' versus 'Conceptual' Performances

The performer Hillas Smith (aka 'Mr H') recalls his experience of the first Festival of Fools in Belfast in 2004. A couple of years earlier Hillas, originally from Dublin, had come to live in Belfast after spending some time travelling, and recalls noticing a tangible 'change' in the atmosphere of the city, which in the recent past had been dominated by the discourses and symbols of tension and security:[17]

> And out of that change the Festival of Fools kicked off in 2004 and it was funny because at that first year I remember the festival audiences were quite small, and you could see a lot of the crowd were very unfamiliar with what street entertainment was; even though a lot of the shows that first year were quite, they weren't particularly challenging. Some of the later shows that Will [Chamberlain] got in for Festival of Fools were like, they were very artistic, very conceptual . . . But even in that first year, 2004, the audience were, they were quite kind of, yeah they were unaccustomed to what street performance was, what street theatre was . . . But in the time that the Festival of Fools has been here, and watching not only the crowd grow, but grow in their awareness of what street shows are.

In its early days, the festival addressed the issue of an apparent lack of engagement with the cityscape itself amongst people who were already using the city for other purposes. By introducing acts that used aerial dance against upper stories of city centre buildings, performances way above eye level intentionally drew shopper's attention up above the shop fronts, above the facade of commerce and up to a level of architectural heritage. Here was a reason to dwell in the city again; here was a chance for shoppers to be aware of the space in which they were living, but not engaging – at least not in the eyes of the festival organizers:

> In the aftermath of the conflict, people were using the city centre in a purely business-like fashion – to shop, to work, etc. But not to play, not to enjoy the landscape and architecture, and certainly not to enjoy themselves for free. The festival has been an attempt to help create a new relationship with the city centre [that] promotes a sense of ownership and empowerment (in part a unique response to street theatre specifically, rather than 'arts activity' generally). The festival owes more to a sense of anarchy and socialism as positive motivators than to sectarianism as negative provocation. (Will Chamberlain, personal correspondence)

By introducing the medium of street performance, the festival gave people in Belfast an excuse to pause from their relationship with the city on commercial terms, and engage with the city and other inhabitants of it by forming an audience and, ideally, spending half an hour in the company of a crowd of people who are enjoying themselves and laughing out loud. As an expression of Shared Space, the process of gathering to enjoy oneself without feeling the need to express a contested public identity, a street show seems to tick all of the boxes. Indeed, as the festival director pointed out in his interview for this research in 2015, 'it's quite hard to turn round and punch someone in the face when you've spent half an hour standing next to them laughing together at a show'.

But, over the years the festival has developed in various ways, including entertainment designed to entertain existing users of the city, shows that are appreciated by audiences increasingly aware of the genre of street performance, and acts targeting a now established 'festival crowd'. The latter consist of individuals who are able, as Mr H pointed out above, to distinguish between shows that are 'not particularly challenging' and those that are more 'conceptual'. This distinction between types of show is addressed by another Belfast-based performer who has taken part in the Festival of Fools several times over the past few years, Grant Goldie (aka 'That Man'). Grant, who has performed in festivals around the world, refers to the former as 'generic' street shows:

> A generic street show in my mind, and in a lot of other performers' minds that I kind of speak to ... is designed to pull money out of people's pockets ... So you've got a build, you've got a middle bit which makes them laugh and you've got the stunt at the end. And so generally it's on three tricks; the first trick is the build and whatever you're doing, it might be a routine, it might be anything – it could just be standing there picking your nose – but whatever it is that's your build, that's your first trick. Your middle trick is an entertaining 'getting to know your audience' and building the crowd, ... then your third bit is your final trick, which could be a routine or it could be a unicycle, or a ladder, or a rola-bola or anything that gets you up high so you can see more people and more people can see you, and therefore you get money out of their pockets when you hat it.

As a street performer I understand the distinction between generic and conceptual shows very clearly and I have noticed it in my own approach to working in different contexts. In the late 1990s I was one half of a double act called 'Double Trouble'. My working partner 'Weee John' was also a solo performer; he was one of the only performers in Belfast at that time actively busking his shows in the city centre on a Saturday afternoon. Unlike several other cities (e.g. London, Dublin, Edinburgh), Belfast had not developed a 'busking culture', where street performers could congregate to develop regular performance pitches in the centre. On several occasions when we were developing our act we would travel to the city centre to 'test things out' on a live audience. At that time, there were a number of professional performers based in Belfast who would have been hired to work at events across the country to perform their acts at fetes, or tourist destinations such as the seaside towns of Portrush and Portstewart on the North Antrim coast. These acts had emerged from the early days of Belfast

Community Circus, founded in 1985, and the later emergence of Streetwise Community Circus, but would rarely, if ever, consider busking in town.

The logic that 'Weee John' had for trying things out in Belfast was not based so much on financial return – a booked gig at a fete for a fixed fee was always a better option than busking in town, risking little to no earnings – but this did give us the opportunity to develop skills on working with an audience that could not be learned in a rehearsal space. John assured me that if we could 'survive' a show in Belfast on a Saturday afternoon, we could thrive in the more tranquil settings of a seaside resort or a country fete. Getting people to stop was the first part of the battle, getting them to stay the next part, and getting them to part with the money was the ultimate reward, and yes, we did develop a 'generic' street show that followed the logic described by Grant Goldie above.

The 'generic' street show is designed to be sturdy and fairly uncomplicated – it is based on a small number of high impact pieces that often include a good amount of comedy and clowning, and some danger thrown in – fire, high unicycles, tightrope, etc. The humour and clowning are rarely subtle, and the entire show is designed to stop people for long enough to part with their money. This was the kind of show that would work in Belfast in the late 1990s for an audience who were quick enough to let you know whether you were any good or not! Whilst most people voted with their feet, and walked away if you were not entertaining enough, the most obvious indication was seen in the 'hat' at the end of the day – if the hat was scant, you needed to rethink the show. But the Festival of Fools is not an event where performers are reliant upon collecting money from the audience for their shows. Although collections are made by volunteers which helps to reduce the running costs of the event, the Festival of Fools attracts support and funding from a range of sources. As such, performers are hired and paid by the festival organizers. To some extent, this gives them the freedom to relax, and provide a show that is unburdened from the need to focus on collecting money.

With a wider variety of styles of street performance on offer, Belfast audiences have become more open to stopping to watch these varied styles of show; and the festival now hosts a number of acts that are more, in Mr H's words, 'artistic' or 'conceptual'. In 2015 the festival provided a mix of acts, from those more busking-based street shows (such as my own act, which involves fire juggling on very tall unicycles as a finale), to the more conceptual (e.g. Dot Comedy's 'Lost on Earth' which, rather than relying upon circus skills such as acrobatics and juggling, involved an alien attempting to return his stolen and crash-landed space ship to his host planet). By incorporating shows that are perhaps more innovative or conceptual than the generic style of street show, the festival is providing a diversity of performance styles that do not in any way reinforce Protestant/loyalist–Catholic/nationalist oppositions, but cross-cut them. Thus, the festival is providing a form of entertainment on the streets of Belfast that may challenge audiences on purely artistic or aesthetic terms, rather than in an ethno-political context.

The Festival of Fools as an Inclusive Space of Social Circus?

I have suggested that the Festival of Fools in Belfast contributes to the well-being of people who move through the city centre by providing accessible, high quality street performance that is appealing to a diverse audience and does not rely upon a dialogue of conflicting identification. People from a range of social and cultural backgrounds (local, national and international) come together in the city to enjoy seeing something dangerous, or funny, or awe inspiring, or just silly. The shows at the festival are rarely controversial, and are never associated with Protestant/loyalist or Catholic/nationalist territorial practices. Through the medium of street performance, the festival is contributing to the idea of Shared Space in Belfast, even if it is not a direct result of the local statutory discourse of Shared Space emanating from a host of government departments. Interestingly, another unique way in which the festival contributes to Shared Space in Belfast is its interconnection with the concept and practice of social circus. A definition of the philosophy and practice of 'social circus' is necessary to distinguish it from other forms of circus: tented/traditional circus (e.g. Barnum and Bailey, Duffy's), contemporary circus (e.g. Cirque du Soleil, Archaos), and recreational circus (e.g. the many juggling clubs and societies around the world; and the recent examples of fitness regimes drawing upon circus techniques). But definitions are not always so neat and tidy, and there is often some disagreement amongst practitioners as to the basic tenets of a social circus programme.[18] For some, social circus is a form of therapy that targets specific psychological or physiological conditions; for others it focuses solely on working with young people at risk of exclusion from society; some work with individuals living with disabilities, others work with homeless adults.[19] Some social circus programmes focus on specific areas of training, such as aerial or acrobatics, whereas others tend to focus more on the balance and equilibristic disciplines, such as juggling and stilt-walking. Whilst the diversity within the approach is often confusing, it is also one of the strengths of this practice in that social circus is an inclusive approach that can be tailored to an extraordinary range of participants.

The following definition of this global movement, as set out by one of the key proponents 'Cirque du Monde', is perhaps the most precise:

> Social circus is an innovative social intervention approach, based on the circus arts. It targets various at-risk groups living in precarious personal and social situations, including street or detained youth and women survivors of violence . . . In this approach, the primary goal is not to learn the circus arts, but rather to assist with participants' personal and social development by nurturing their self-esteem and trust in others, as well as by helping them to acquire social skills, become active citizens, express their creativity and realize their potential

> ... Social circus is a powerful catalyst for creating social change because it helps marginalized individuals assume their place as citizens within a community, and enrich that community with their talents. (La Fortune 2011)

The effects of social circus projects on individuals can be seen across four areas of well-being: physical, social, emotional and cognitive (see Maglio and McKinstry 2008). These changes can be subtle (e.g. a gentle improvement in physical fitness) or life changing (e.g. one of our own tutors came to us as a participant on a project with an Autism charity, and he is now both a circus teacher and professional performer). But how does this approach relate to the ideals of the Festival of Fools?

In 2015, the Festival of Fools presented shows from several social circus organizations based in Ireland alongside the professional acts; Belfast Community Circus School, Streetwise Community Circus (Belfast), Lisburn Community Circus, North West Circus School (aka In Your Space, Derry/Londonderry) and Cloughjordan Circus Club (Tipperary). I was involved as a tutor for Streetwise Community Circus, and we presented a show from our 'Evergreen' performance group, which consists of individuals living with Autism Spectrum Disorders and/or learning disabilities and/or accessing mental health services in Belfast. The opportunity for members of this group to publicly show off the circus skills that they had been learning, some for over ten years, was welcomed by the group, and we relished the chance to perform as part of this festival. By designing this social circus element, the festival actively enabled several groups of performers from marginalized sections of society to share a pitch with other performers from around the world, and were supported in their reception as people with the ability to entertain an audience in a public space. The individuals in these groups were all, in various ways, positively affected in terms of the areas of well-being that each project had designed in their social circus programmes. In the case of Streetwise's Evergreen group, the key aims of our project related to challenging public perceptions of disability, and enabling individuals to develop and show off the kind of circus skills that most members of the public are unable to do. The 'social circus' element of the festival intentionally provided a space, a pitch, for social circus groups to publicly showcase their work, which not only reflects the festival's close connection to Belfast Community Circus School, but also the connection to a larger scene of social circus practitioners, locally and internationally. But, of course, this was only one aspect of the festival – the rest of the programme was devoted to professional performers who are not necessarily connected to the world of 'social circus'. How can these shows be classed as a social circus enterprise rather than solely as professional street performers?

If a traditional touring tented circus provides an occasional circus workshop for local at-risk children, then I would argue that they are not a social circus enterprise, although they do have an element of social circus practice. This circus would exist, as most other touring circus groups do, as a small business in the entertainment industry. So how is the Festival of Fools, a public street performance festival, showcasing professional acts from round the world, any different? Surely this is just a street festival with a social circus element to it? The key here, I argue, lies in both the intent and effect behind the actions. Social circus organizations use the same props as professional circuses, they teach the same skills, and recognize a shared history in the art of circus. But social circus organizations exist primarily to use circus as an intervention that aims to have a positive impact on the well-being of the individuals with whom they work. By stating that the festival arose from the need to create 'shared celebration in the heart of what has been a divided city', and to 'have a street Festival where people could share some moments with strangers; and to help change people's relationship with the city' suggests to me that the *intent* of this festival lies more in social intervention and outcome than in making money. What makes the Festival of Fools so effective in this regard is the way that the artists who perform throughout the city centre, and the audiences who stop to watch them, are engaging with each other without reference to each other solely as political actors, but rather as an example of the richness of society. My own experience as a street performer in Northern Ireland over the past twenty years certainly suggests that there is little time or space to consider an audience as a group of political agents, when the immediate aim is to find a common bond between performer and audience that will result in a group of people coming together to laugh at me.

If the intent of the festival is social intervention and impact, then is it actually doing so? Does the Festival of Fools actually have an effect on a sense of Shared Space amongst audiences in Belfast? Supporters of the festival certainly seem to think so:

> Festival of Fools exposes the general public and the wider arts sector to a quality artistic experience, demonstrating the potential of the arts and specifically circus and street theatre to engage the public with the arts and artists from a local, national and international background. It positively challenges perceptions or experiences that the arts are limited to certain communities or groups belonging to specific social or cultural backgrounds. (Gavin O'Connor, ACNI arts officer, in McBride 2013: 9)

Belfast's Festival of Fools is providing an opportunity for access to public space to individuals and populations who are rarely considered in discourse of Shared Space in the city, even though these are the people whose lives have been transformed by the conflict here (see e.g. Bunting et al. 2013; Breen-Smyth 2013). The processes of marginalization and deprivation in Northern Ireland are not unrelated to political conflict; they are in many ways its legacy (see Bamford 2005). By working with such groups, the Festival of Fools celebrates the work of social circus organizations and provides an alternative to forms of developing Shared Space in Belfast city centre that concern themselves with either the question of recognition of various political and cultural identities or with the question of neutralization through commercialization. The festival therefore addresses multiple aspects of Shared Space as space that accommodates safe interaction, engagement between, and social inclusion of, people of multiple backgrounds – not only with particular political or religious identities, but still addressing issues of conflict transformation that pertain to political conflict.

Conclusion

As we have seen, the ways in which the festival resonates with the concept of Shared Space is central to its success. When the Festival of Fools began in 2004, the logic behind the event was rooted in an idea of 'normalization' of the city in an era of post-conflict. The director of the festival states clearly (personal communication) that he wanted to instigate an engagement with the public space in Belfast that was more than just a commercial or occupational endeavour. The festival aimed to have a positive impact upon the way that those people who use the city relate to the city itself – its architecture, its spaces, and the other people who inhabit those spaces – even if this habitation is only temporary. In this sense, it is fair to suggest that both the medium of street performance and the format of the Festival of Fools dovetail with the concept of developing the city centre as a Shared Space: after all, its intention is to bring people together to share moments of joy and awe and wonder via the medium of high quality performances from internationally renowned street performers.

However, whilst it is certainly possible to define the festival as a shining example of Shared Space in action in a divided city, what has thus far been less clear is the extent to which, as well as the ways in which, the activities of the festival (both the performances themselves and the choice of their locations) are *contributing to the development* of Shared Space. Is the festival just one of a number of similar local and global festivals that address the concept of Shared Space by their nature (Picard 2015)? Is the way that Shared Space is created at the Festival of Fools a result of intentional local post-conflict spatial policy, a by-product of the global genre of circus festivals, or a combination of the two? Addressing these questions is potentially revealing of the increasingly important concept of Shared Space, often used within and beyond the context of Belfast to denote the civic character of urban public space. The question of intentionality, on the other hand, demonstrates the de facto role and effect of the practice of cultural festivals, especially when entwined with that of social circus, in making the city an inclusive stage and desirable destination of civic urban life.

Belfast's history as a contested space has resulted in a festival that exists as a 'social circus' that aims to affect the well-being of a very large group of individuals – the audiences who come to see the shows. Unlike many other social circus projects, the festival does not teach circus arts to vulnerable or at-risk populations. Rather it provides accessible, professional performances, to anyone, for free. This has been so effective that the festival now attracts its own 'festival crowd' who continue to support it. In addition, new audience members discover the festival each year, simply because it is located in areas of the city that are ordinarily associated with shopping. These audiences come together from across the political and economic strata of the city (and beyond) to inhabit those spaces in the city where the festival exists, simply in order to laugh together. More recently, by incorporating performances from social circus organizations, the festival has also enabled a means to positively impact the well-being of its performers as well as its audiences. By providing a space dedicated to local performers who represent the variety and richness of the city, the festival presents an image that goes beyond stereotypes of a 'contested city' in terms of political agents. This means that Belfast's Festival of Fools is an example of an event in which people from around the world come to a city that has for so long been framed in terms of conflict and political space-making, simply to laugh, to be entertained, and to share the space around them. It is, I argue, a fine example of a 'social circus' enterprise that arose from an intent to impact local and global perceptions of the city centre, and has had the additional effect of enabling a diverse audience to come together and share a brief moment of fun in an ever-evolving city.

Nick McCaffery is an independent researcher based in Belfast. He graduated in 2005 with a PhD in social anthropology from Queen's University Belfast. His research explored global flows of knowledge based on New Age interpretations of Hopi culture; and local Hopi reactions to these flows. He has also explored research ethics and the ethnographic interview, and interpretations of history and identity amongst young people in Northern Ireland. His current research investigates the phenomenon of 'social circus' – an intervention-based approach that uses circus arts as a way of engaging with at-risk and socially excluded populations.

Notes

1. Out-of-state visitors surveyed included those from England, Scotland, Wales, the Republic of Ireland, France, Germany, Holland, Spain, Poland, Italy, the Netherlands, Latvia, USA, Mexico, Canada, South Africa, New Zealand and Australia (McBride 2012).
2. BT3 is a largely industrial area in East Belfast, with few residential dwellings, which may explain the paucity of visitors from this area.
3. The term 'social circus' is hereby distinct from other forms of circus – traditional, contemporary and recreational. I expand on this definition below.
4. The areas of well-being can include social, physical, emotional and/or cognitive (see, e.g., Maglio and McKinstry 2008; McCaffery 2014).
5. However, there are examples of trained therapists who do use circus arts in their work (e.g. Carrie Heller at the Circus Arts Institute, Atlanta, GA).

6. As such, I have used a methodology that combines several years of informally observing the festival's artists and audiences with a more recent and detailed ethnographic approach, drawing upon interview data and archival research to investigate this convergence of policy and apparent folly.
7. E.g. the reimaging of Belfast's murals away from icons of violence and paramilitaries to more celebratory images – local sports celebrities, artists or musicians (see Hocking 2012). Similarly, the processes used by Belfast City Council to make St Patrick's Day celebrations in the city an event designed to appeal across cultural barriers.
8. As would happen in the discourse of 'Shared Space' propagated by central and local authorities (e.g. OFMDFM 2005; Belfast City Council 2011).
9. http://www.hatfair.co.uk/.
10. http://www.conflux.co.uk/.
11. http://sirf.co.uk/about/.
12. http://www.belfastcity.gov.uk/tourism-venues/culture/festivals.aspx.
13. http://www.culturenightbelfast.com/.
14. That is aside from my background as a street performer and as a participant in the festival, and therefore as someone who has a close understanding of the nature of the event.
15. Although there are certain assumptions that I disagree with from these observations of audiences attending shows, in particular the method of counting 'visible' signs of disability or ethnicity (wheelchairs and dark skins one assumes), it does give some idea of the diversity of audiences who attend.
16. Whilst either discussing my work as a performer with non-performers, or when performing at venues across the country, I have often been asked by audience members whether I have been a part of the festival, which infers a broad awareness of both the festival and the type of performance that it promotes. I believe that it has developed an audience that is either travelling to the city to attend the shows, or (and perhaps more pertinently) willing to stop and engage with the festival whilst in the city for other reasons.
17. The aforementioned 'ring of steel' approach to the city, where security guards used to be employed at shop fronts, and armed police and army personnel patrolled the streets on a regular basis.
18. E.g. at the 2010 American Youth Circus Organisation's Educators' Conference, there was a heated and ultimately unresolved debate as to where the boundaries lay between youth circus, social circus and community circus. In my own career I have fought to have inclusive circus projects that work with disabled participants defined as social circus, rather than the existing label of 'Handicirque'.
19. See, for example, the proceedings of the 2013 conference on social circus in Tampere, Finland: http://www.uta.fi/cmt/index/Studying_Social_Circus.pdf.

References

Bamford, D. 2005. 'Equal Lives: Review of Policy and Services for People with a Learning Disability in Northern Ireland'. Research Report available at http://www.dhsspsni.gov.uk/learning-disability-report.

Belfast City Council. 2005. *Your City, Your Space: Belfast City Council Strategy for Open Spaces*. Belfast.

———. 2011. *Good Relations Plan*. Belfast. Available at www.belfastcity.gov.uk/nmsruntime/saveasdialog.aspx?lID=2803&sID=2200.

———. 2015. *Belfast City Centre Regeneration and Investment Strategy*. Belfast. Available at http://www.belfastcity.gov.uk/buildingcontrolenvironment/regeneration/Regenerationandinvestmentplan.aspx.

Breen-Smyth, M. 2013. 'Injured and Disabled Casualties of the Northern Ireland Conflict: Issues in Immediate and Long-Term Treatment, Care and Support', *Medicine, Conflict and Survival* 29(3): 244–66.
Bryan, D. 2009. *Negotiating Civic Space in Belfast or The Tricolour: Here Today, Gone Tomorrow*. Economic and Social Research Council. Available at http://www.arct.cam.ac.uk/conflictincities/PDFs/WorkingPaper13_7.1.10.pdf.
———. 2015. 'Parades, Flags, Carnivals, and Riots: Public Space, Contestation, and Transformation in Northern Ireland', *Peace and Conflict: Journal of Peace Psychology* 21(4): 565–73.
Bunting, B., et al. 2013. 'Trauma Associated with Civil Conflict and Posttraumatic Stress Disorder: Evidence From the Northern Ireland Study of Health and Stress', *Journal of Traumatic Stress* 26(1): 134–41.
Festival of Fools. 2015. 'Artist Welcome Information' letter, personal correspondence.
Frost, N. 2015. 'Anthropology and Festivals: Festival Ecologies', *Ethnos: Journal of Anthropology* 81(4): 569–83.
Hocking, B. 2012. 'Beautiful Barriers: Art and Identity along a Belfast Peace Wall', *Anthropology Matters* 14(1): available at https://www.anthropologymatters.com/index.php/anth_matters/article/viewFile/273/488
———. 2015. *The Great Reimagining: Public Art, Urban Space, and the Symbolic Landscapes of a 'New' Northern Ireland*. New York: Berghahn Books.
Komarova, M., and D. Bryan. 2014. 'Introduction. Beyond the Divided City: Policies and Practices of Shared Space', *City* 18(4–5): 427–31.
La Fortune, M. 2011. *Community Worker's Guide: When Circus Lessons Become Life Lessons*. Montreal: Cirque Du Soleil.
Leonard, M. 2011. 'A Tale of Two Cities: "Authentic" Tourism in Belfast', *Irish Journal of Sociology* 19(2): 111–26.
Lisle, D. 2000. 'Consuming Danger: Reimagining the War/Tourism Divide', *Alternatives: Global, Local, Political* 25(1): 91–116.
Maglio, J., and C. McKinstry. 2008. 'Occupational Therapy and Circus: Potential Partners in Enhancing the Health and Well-being of Today's Youth', *Australian Occupational Therapy Journal* 55: 287–90.
McBride, C. 2012. *Evaluation of the Festival of Fools 2012*. http://www.belfastcircus.org/gallery/FOF_Evaluation_12_Web.pdf.
———. 2013. *Evaluation of the Festival of Fools 2013*. Unpublished manuscript. . .
McCaffery, N. 2014. 'Social Circus and Applied Anthropology: A Synthesis Waiting to Happen', *Anthropology in Action* 21(1): 30–35.
Nagle, J. 2009. 'Sites of Social Centrality and Segregation: Lefebvre in Belfast, a "Divided City"', *Antipode* 41: 326–47.
Nagle, J., and M. Clancy. 2010. 'Constructing a Shared Public Identity in Ethno-nationally Divided Societies: Comparing Consociational and Transformationist Perspectives', *Nations and Nationalism* 18(1): 78–97.

O'Donnell, A.T., et al. 2015. '"Something That Unites Us All": Understandings of St Patrick's Day Parades as Representing the Irish National Group', *Journal of Community and Applied Social Psychology* 26: 61–74.

OFMDFM. 2005. *A Shared Future: Policy and Strategic Framework for Good Relations in Northern Ireland*. https://www.niacro.co.uk/sites/default/files/publications/A%20Shared%20Future-%20OFMDFM-Mar%202005.pdf.

———. 2010. *Programme for Cohesion, Sharing and Integration Consultation Document*. http://cain.ulst.ac.uk/issues/politics/ofmdfm/ofmdfm_270710_sharing.pdf.

———. 2013. *Together: Building a United Community Strategy*. https://www.executiveofficeni.gov.uk/sites/default/files/publications/ofmdfm_dev/together-building-a-unitedcommunity-strategy.pdf.

Picard, D. 2015. 'The Festive Frame: Festivals as Mediators for Social Change', *Ethnos: Journal of Anthropology* 81(4): 600–616.

Quinn, B. 2005. 'Changing Festival Places: Insights from Galway', *Social & Cultural Geography* 6(2): 237–52.

Rallings, M. 2014. '"Shared Space" as Symbolic Capital: Belfast and the "Right to the City"?', *City* 18(4–5): 432–39.

Ricardo, M. 2016 'Circus Got Sexy... But at What Cost?', *Chortle*. http://www.chortle.co.uk/correspondents/2016/05/31/24981/circus_got_sexy..._but_at_what_cost%3F.

Skinner, J. 2016. 'Walking the Falls: Dark Tourism and the Significance of Movement on the Political Tour of West Belfast', *Tourist Studies* 16(1): 23–39.

9

Criss-crossing Pathways
The Indian Community Centre as a Focus of Diasporic and Cross-Community Place-Making

Maruška Svašek

With her back to a colourful background of Hindu gods, a middle-aged Northern Irish interviewer looks into the camera with a broad smile directed at her imaginary audience. She explains that she is visiting the Hindu Temple in Belfast, and introduces her first guest as the 'ex-vice chancellor of the Over Fifties [50+] Group'. The interviewee, a lady of Indian descent, points out that the group was established some years ago by Indian migrants like herself who felt the need to meet up on a regular basis. Mostly retired, many of them had moved to Great Britain and Northern Ireland as children or young adults. They had worked, set up businesses, made friends, raised children, cared for dependent family members and stayed in touch with their relatives in India. Having reached old age, many faced physical ailments, illness, and in some cases had become widows or widowers. Some of them felt quite lonely and isolated. Their weekly gatherings on Monday mornings at the Indian Community Centre (ICC) gave them the opportunity to exchange news, participate in various activities, share an Indian meal, and enjoy each other's company. Most of all, the meetings provided a much-needed space in which they could support each other as elderly migrants who shared a link to their Indian homeland.

Nodding her head, the interviewer remarks that elderly people all over Northern Ireland are indeed at risk of being lonely and marginalized. Her Indian-background interviewee agrees: 'If no initiative is taken,' she emphasizes, 'people don't come out of their isolation. This is the same for Irish people'.

Figure 9.1 The Indian Community Centre in Belfast, 2011. Photograph by Maruška Svašek.

This opening vignette, constructed from fieldwork notes taken on 24 October 2011, introduces the main theme of this chapter, namely that gatherings in a particular spatial setting can create a sense of community and well-being. The filmed exchange brings several aspects of spatiality and sociality into focus. First, human life is essentially spatial: people cannot but be in, move through, and act in 'locations', concrete settings in the landscape that are identifiable through specific geographical coordinates and that are 'related to other sites or locations because of interaction, movement and diffusion between them' (Agnew 2011: 23). In the case above, elderly people had travelled from their homes in Belfast and other locations in Northern Ireland to gather in the ICC building, situated north of the city centre in Clifton Street, just off the A4, close to an Orange hall (see Figure 9.1).

The architectural structure was a momentary setting of their social interaction, a Diwali celebration which included the production of a short television feature about ageing for a local broadcaster. The site was shaped by what the political geographer John Agnew calls 'locale', the spatial and material aspects of place-specific sociality; in his own words, 'the where of social life and environmental translation' (Agnew 2011: 23). The ICC building was a former Methodist church hall that had been adapted for new purposes to serve the needs of Indian migrants and their offspring. One of the main new features was the physical transformation of one of the spaces into a meeting hall and a Hindu temple (see Figure 9.2).

Figure 9.2 The Hindu temple at the Indian Community Centre in Belfast, 2011. Photograph by Maruška Svašek.

In addition to 'location' and 'locale', Agnew (2011: 24) has used the term 'sense of place' to refer to people's affective experiences of site-specific physical and social engagement. The vignette clearly alludes to the particular sense of place created in the ICC setting by elderly Indian migrants during their weekly meetings.

A second important aspect of sociality and spatiality, equally central to the analysis in this chapter, is that people's situated experiences are often marked by space–time 'entanglements' (Harvey 1991: 14). This concept draws attention to the fact that people's past, present and future movements are interconnected through recurrent arrivals at, occurrences in, and departures from specific sites, and that long-distance communication and rapid travel has greatly increased rapid translocal movement. Very dense entanglements occur, for example, when an employee works in similar employment for many years, boundaries between work and leisure become blurred, and spatial distances between workplaces (at 'home' and at 'work') shrink through frequent movements and extensive use of communication technology. To explore concrete cases of entanglement, it is also useful to turn to the anthropologist Tim Ingold (2011: 148), who has used the terms 'pathway' and 'meshwork' to explore how individual people's trajectories emerge and interweave at different frequencies and in different spatial patterns. In his theoretical perspective, 'the lines of the meshwork . . . are the paths along which life is lived. And it is in the binding together of lines, not in the connecting of points, that the mesh is constituted' (ibid.: 151–52).

Evidently, there are myriad ways in which sites of (locally and translocally) criss-crossing pathways and movement gain significance and emotional resonance. Consider, for example, a train commuter who interprets her daily travels as 'route from home to work', and most likely experiences the frequent train journey as an uneventful repetitive activity. Compare this to a situation in which two passengers start a conversation, get to know each other, fall in love, and come to see the train ('our train') as a highly personalized place. Melinda Milligan (1998: 2) used the term 'place-attachment' to refer to such dynamics, defining it as an 'emotional link formed by an individual to a physical site that has been given meaning through interaction'. This chapter focuses on the ways in which the ICC has become not only a place of affective diasporic attachment, but also of temporary interaction and identification between 'Indian' and 'Irish' individuals.

Sharing a sense of commonality in the same location can generate a strong sense of group identity. This brings us to a third aspect of spatiality: the fact that place-making practices are never indifferent, often politically charged, and never isolated in time. This also implies that newly visited locations have always already been shaped and interpreted before by groups or individuals whose earlier and on-going spatial practices may influence the experiences and practices of new arrivals. In line with this argument, the next section will explore how Indian migrants who settled in Northern Ireland in the 1960s and 1970s were confronted with forms of territorial place-making that shaped the heavily politicized environment of Northern Ireland.

Traces of Territorial Place-Making

The reference made by the Indian interviewee in the opening vignette to 'Irish people' hides complex histories of inequality, territorial competition and violence (Coulter 1999; Murtagh 2002). As widely reported in the international media, the clashes over questions of territoriality and nationhood came to an extreme during 'the Troubles' – a euphemistic name for the period of violent conflict between 1968 and the 1994 paramilitary ceasefires. At the time, unionists and loyalists (from a Protestant background) generally supported the continued inclusion of Northern Ireland in the United Kingdom, and nationalists and republicans (from a Catholic background) called for its accession to the Republic of Ireland. The British government played a complex political and military role, too complicated to discuss in this chapter. During the Troubles, over 3,600 people were killed, around 50,000 people were injured, and many others ended up being severely traumatized. While people of Indian descent were relatively unaffected as they tended not to take sides, some entrepreneurs faced the destruction of warehouses and shops as a result of bombings (Kapur 1997: 178).[1]

The ceasefires were followed by the Good Friday Agreement of 1998, which marked the start of a process of peace building, also known as the 'peace process'. While occasional instances of violence have continued to hamper the reconciliation process in the past fifteen years, ongoing territorial contestations have mostly been played out through symbolic spatial politics (Bryan and McCartney 1994; Jarman 1997). Such politics include, for example, frequently recurring demonstrations for or against annual parades and ongoing 'flag-protests' that started in December 2012 after Belfast City Council decided to stop permanently flying the Union Jack from City Hall (see Soares, this volume). Many locations in Northern Ireland are visual reminders of ongoing paramilitary influence and territorial tensions (Boal 1995; Coulter 1999; Murtagh 2002; Jarman 2004; Lysaght 2007; Bryan and Stevenson 2009; Connolly 2012). As I write in 2016, one only needs to walk a few minutes away from Belfast city centre to find flags, murals, memorials and painted kerbstones that signal opposing political alliances.

To get back to the reference to 'Irish people' by the Indian interviewee at the start of this chapter, it will now be clear that the word 'Irish' has a particular political meaning when used by Irish nationalists and republicans, and can antagonize those opposing the inclusion of Northern Ireland in the Republic of Ireland. The interviewee in the opening vignette, however, did not employ it to position herself as a supporter of an Irish nation state. By contrast, her reference meant to point out that *all* 'indigenous' Irish people[2] living on the island (including both Protestants and Catholics) share the predicament of old age, not only with each other but *also* with migrant groups. The underlying political message was that, in a rapidly ageing society, the need to deal with issues around ageing concerned everybody. Her statement can be read as a critique not only of loyalist–nationalist antagonism, but also of a failure by many commentators and analysts to acknowledge the presence of other groups on Northern Irish soil.[3]

A Limited 'Two-Communities' Model

Scholars analysing Northern Irish society have been slow in acknowledging the presence and place-making activities of migrants and their families, as research into loyalist–nationalist conflict and reconciliation has dominated the field. Until recently (see, for example, Connolly and Khoury 2008), the result has been a persistent 'two-opposing-communities' discourse, not only in academic circles but also in the public imagination. This is clearly reflected by the following joke, frequently told to me during various spells of fieldwork amongst Indian migrant families in Belfast: 'A Belfast man meets an Indian migrant in the street. 'Are you a Catholic or a Protestant?', he asks. 'A Hindu', he replies. 'Catholic Hindu or Protestant Hindu?'

The inability to look beyond the two identity markers 'Catholic' and 'Protestant' is highly problematic, not only because it ignores the increasing ethnic and religious diversification of the Northern Irish population, but also as it denies the complex dynamics of the personal histories and pathways of many Irish Catholics and Protestants living in the region[4] (see Mazzetti, this volume). Nevertheless, the two-community discourse has strongly influenced the dominant 'social imaginaries' in and about Northern Ireland, defined as 'the ways in which people imagine their social existence, how they fit together with others, how things go on between them and their fellows, the expectations that are normally met, and the deeper normative notions and images that underlie these expectations' (Taylor 2002: 106).

From an analytical perspective, 'community' discourse is problematic for two main reasons. First, it assumes that certain groups of people are single units whose members all share the same outlook and identity. As Dominic Bryan (2006) has convincingly argued, this view ignores any internal hierarchies, tensions or conflicting loyalties within groups, and tends to present them as relatively static, ahistoric entities. Second, the discourse overlooks the complex dynamics of multiple identification, whereby people may perhaps identify themselves as members of this or that community at certain moments, but also, at other times or in other places, emphasize other identifications, such as gender, occupation, age and position within kin groups, or foreground their unique, individual trajectories and predicaments (Amit and Rapport 2002). These analytical objections do not have any impact, of course, on the ways in which the discourse of 'community' is often appropriated by individuals and groups for political reasons. As noted earlier, territorial behaviour in Northern Ireland has often been justified through overlapping claims to specific community identity, history and territory.

Interestingly, 'two communities' discourse has also informed policies aimed at the promotion of interaction between Catholics and Protestants, defined as 'communities' that need to 'reconcile'. Cross-community work aimed at these antagonistic groups began in the mid-1970s during the height of the conflict, and continues today (Schubotz and Robinson 2006; Schubotz and McCartan 2008). Highly relevant to the focus of this chapter, organizers of Northern Irish 'cross-community' projects have also started to include groups with roots outside the UK. Their more inclusive cross-community work, in other words, has built on the 'two-communities' imaginary, first of all by adding other named migrant groups as additional 'communities'. Secondly, concerned by rising numbers of hate crimes against migrants and refugees, people involved in these projects have also extended the existing discourse of reconciliation (between Catholics and Protestants) to address issues of (mutual) cultural bias and racism.

Concrete projects have brought together populations of different backgrounds, producing what are, in Ingold's terminology, entirely new meshworks. In 2006, for example, the project 'Shared History' was aimed at Protestant, Polish and Chinese residents living in the Donegall Pass area of Belfast. The aim was to reinforce positive relations between groups of existing residents and newcomers with relatively longer (the Chinese) and shorter (the Polish) histories of migration to the area. The outcome was an exhibition of photographs and stories of life in Belfast that comprised personal stories of movement, mobility and migration. The project provided insights into historical changes at the Donegall Pass location, and changes of locality and sense of place. As with many other projects, the anti-racist aims resonated with reconciliatory intentions aimed at Protestants and Catholics (Svašek 2009: 145).

The 'community' label has been embraced by Northern Irish ethnic minority organizations, such as the Chinese Welfare Association, the Polish Association of Northern Ireland, and the ICC. The discourse has specific spatial connotations, referring to the countries of origin as geopolitical entities – for example, 'China', 'Poland', 'India'. Ignoring the ethnic, religious, economic and other diversities within these states, the suggestion of diasporic unity (such as the 'Indian' community in Northern Ireland) helps them to identify their internal and shared interests as minority groups, and to present a united front when tackling anti-foreigner hostilities. For similar reasons, the Northern Ireland Council for Ethnic Minorities, an independent non-governmental organization that monitors racism and racial inequality, has also frequently used the terms 'community' and 'communities', for example describing its members as 'representative[s] of the majority of black and ethnic minority *communities* in Northern Ireland' (NICEM; italics mine).

Diasporic Spatial Politics: Securing a Location

Highly significant for the focus on place-making in this chapter, the larger migrant organizations in Northern Ireland have all bought or rented particular buildings in Belfast that serve as spatial foci for group activities. The ICC, for instance, was founded in the late 1970s by Hindu migrants who had arrived from the Punjab, searching for economic opportunities in the United Kingdom. The majority came from a group of villages situated in the Jalandhar district, and many arrived through intermarriage and chain migration. As the number of Hindu Indian families in Northern Ireland increased, a need arose for a communal space that could be used for larger-scale social and religious activities (Kapur 1997). In 1981, the organization decided to buy Carlisle Methodist Memorial Church's church hall, which marked the site as 'Protestant' territory. This happened at the height of 'the Troubles', when the location of the hall was a major interface area between Catholic and Protestant populations and saw many instances of violence. A year after the purchase, as a result of ongoing violence in the area, the church building itself, next door, was also closed and became derelict. This was still the case at the time of my fieldwork in 2012.[5]

In a sense, the ICC had taken advantage of the existing territorial tensions in Northern Ireland, appropriating a location that had become unusable to the locals and cheaply available as a result of the conflict. They transformed the building into a site that was neither 'Catholic' nor 'Protestant', turning it into a location that was central to their own politics of diasporic place-making. The transformation shows that, while existing spatial discourses and practices often serve as fundamental ideological and interpretative frameworks that structure individual experience and impose limits on action and meaning, place-making is always an ongoing process, and is therefore changing and diverse (Cresswell 1996).

Responding to, and participating in, policies of integration and anti-discrimination, the ICC building has now also become a location where cross-community activities and lectures about Indian society and culture are frequently organized. The ICC emphasized this through its website, proclaiming that it is 'a voluntary organization which encourages people to learn about all aspects of Indian culture. Set up in 1981 and located on Clifton Street, its community development and outreach programmes promote integration between the Indian and the wider community' (http://www.iccbelfast.com/, last accessed 1 March 2015).

Over a period of three years between 2009 and 2012, I saw the temple and the two larger halls being transformed in numerous ways to accommodate the needs of specific social, religious and political gatherings.[6] In all cases, spatial practices were vital to diasporic and/or cross-community place-making.

Cross-Community Place-Making: Creating Common Ground

The remainder of this chapter zooms in on an outreach event that took place in the ICC on 24 October 2011. As noted at the start of this chapter, on that occasion the building was housing a Diwali celebration organized by the 50+ Group in which several invited groups of senior citizens participated. During the day, I was accompanied by co-researcher Amit Desai, a London-born anthropologist of Indian descent who worked with me on a collaborative project that explored creative practices in the ICC and India. Highlighting the fact that researchers are always bound by their own limited pathways, it was useful to combine our research efforts. This enabled us to speak to a larger number of participants and, at crucial moments, be in the hall and the temple at the same time.

When we arrived in the morning, we entered the main hall on the ground floor, using the back entrance of the ICC building. The room was more elaborately decorated than normal, largely because a wedding had been held there over the weekend and members of the 50+ Group had rearranged some of the decorations, thus producing space for a new purpose. Rows of tables were decorated with red paper and stars, and on the stage an altar had been set up. It included a picture of Lakshmi, one of the female Hindu Goddesses who is of central importance during Diwali celebrations. While the altar marked the occasion as a Hindu religious event, a lottery table placed next to it promised light entertainment. As we came in, some Indian ladies were busy making final preparations, setting out drinks and snacks. Sitting at two of the long tables were about twenty people from other invited senior citizens community groups who were quietly chatting to each other and observing the activities in the hall. Most of the 50+ Group members, also about twenty people, were sat down at a third table.

The start of the celebration was marked when Chandra,[7] an enthusiastic female spokesperson of the 50+ Group, opened the meeting, welcoming everyone to the event. Addressing the visitors in a familiar Northern Irish accent, she explained that Diwali was a 'festival of lights' and that '*Pandiji*, a Hindu priest', would first perform a short ritual for which a light had to be lit. Her translation of the word 'Pandiji' exemplified the aim of the occasion: to create understanding between groups that had different cultural backgrounds, finding expressions that were comprehensible to both. Chandra then asked one of the Indian ladies who happened to be celebrating her birthday that day to light the lamp on the altar. As Sai lit the lamp, the *Pandit* chanted in the microphone in Sanskrit and performed a brief *puja*. For the Hindu participants of the 50+ Group, this was a familiar moment of sacred place-making, and an activity that tied them not only to the location but also to each other, to India and to the divine. While the *puja* performance was thus reassuring to them and reinforced their Hindu identity, it had a different effect on the Irish guests, most of whom had never visited a Hindu temple and had little or no knowledge of Hindu philosophy. When I asked some of the invitees later during lunch what they had made of the ritual, I got various responses, from 'different' through 'exotic' to 'a bit like Catholic rituals'. Whatever their perception, the action had gained relevance through Chandra's reference to the birthday, which associated the lighting of the lamp with the lighting of a birthday candle, and thus transformed the sacred act into a shared experience accessible to non-Hindus. This experience was enhanced by the subsequent joint singing of 'Happy Birthday'. Even the *Pandit*, whose English was limited and did not know the words that well, chanted the melody.

The reframing of the ritual as a birthday celebration had the intended outcome: it broke the ice and lightened the mood. This effect was heightened when someone called out '21 again!', an action that triggered much laughter and eye-contact between hosts and visitors. The joke confirmed why they had gathered in the same location: all were visibly senior citizens, having to cope with ageing and wanting to protect the rights of the elderly in Northern Ireland. The joke also brought out another commonality. All were familiar with age-related humour and the play pretence of being much younger than one really is.

Diwali as 'Hindu Christmas': Performing People and Things

A spatial approach to sociality and movement brings out interrelated dimensions of material, affective and linguistic performance. During the first ten minutes of the visit, a dynamic space of social performance had been created in which moving bodies produced speech, listened to each other, handled artefacts, and were engaged in emotional interaction. While the first task of the 50+ Group had been to make the visitors feel welcome and relaxed, enabling mutual communication, the second undertaking was part of the wider ICC policy, namely to 'reach out', beyond the 'Indian community', teaching the visitors something about 'Indian culture'. What followed was a short talk by Priya, another female member of the 50+ Group, about the meaning of Diwali. Trying to find more common ground with the visitors, she explained that Diwali was 'about lights, just like Christmas'. In addition to the earlier reference to birthday candles, the image of Christmas lights evoked embodied memories of a celebration familiar to the Irish guests. This was reinforced when Priya stated that Diwali was 'one of India's most famous festivals and as important as Christmas in Ireland'. There were various reasons for its significance, she explained. First, it marked the bringing in of the harvest before the winter, so Diwali celebrated having plenty of food in the home. Several people in the audience nodded and smiled as the image of an abundance of celebratory food was evoked. Second, Priya continued, Diwali was a celebration of 'good wealth, health, prosperity and happiness', and, she emphasized, 'we need all of these'. Looking around, she made eye contact with the members of her own group and the Irish guests. The simultaneous act of saying 'we' and the movement of her gaze included and connected hosts and guests, defining all as vulnerable co-humans who needed protection against poverty, ill health and misery.

Priya then returned to the particularity of the Hindu ritual, explaining that Hindus regard Lakshmi as the goddess of wealth and that this is why she is worshipped during Diwali. She explained that the Diwali celebrations welcome Lord Rama 'back home to his kingdom after fourteen years of exile, after he has vanquished the forces of evil'. A brief version followed of the story of Ram and Sita's exile in the forest, the encounter with Ravana's sister, Laxman's rejection of Ravana, and Ravana's consequent abduction of Sita. Soon, the Irish visitors looked puzzled, getting lost in the details of the unfamiliar story, visibly losing concentration. When Priya noticed this, she quickly acknowledged that it was 'all very complex' and that the most important part of the story was when the three gods 'came back home from the forest and were welcomed with lights lit alongside the path'. She ended with 'the moral of the story', namely that 'evil must be destroyed' resulting in 'no envies', and that 'everybody must be welcomed . . . so today we welcome you here!' The light of Diwali, earlier associated with birthday candles and Christmas lights, was now related to guidance, protection and the need for cross-community acceptance.

In the Diwali story, the metaphor of 'home' referred to Ram's return to his kingdom and a restoration of harmony. Priya skilfully linked the idea of home to her act of welcoming the Irish guests to the ICC building. Interestingly, this reversed the more common imaginary of majorities needing to welcome disembedded minorities, which highlights the importance of ownership over a physical site, allowing minority groups to exercise control over the management of proceedings inside. The words of welcome were meant to encourage a relationship of mutual trust, a central trope in cross-community discourse in Northern Ireland.

The message was reinforced through the logo 'equity, diversity, interdependence', printed on a Community Relations Council poster that hung on one of the walls of the hall. The poster further proclaimed the necessity to 'promote a peaceful, inclusive and fair society based on reconciliation and mutual trust'. As noted earlier, these words had an important local meaning, as policies aimed at migrants in Northern Ireland have been framed as extensions of the Troubles-related policies of cross-community reconciliation. As Catherine Nash (2005) has argued, cultural policy-makers and community activists in Northern Ireland have employed the discourse of equity, diversity and interdependence 'in relation to specific controversies about culture in Northern Ireland and wider debates about pluralism and multiculturalism'. This means that the trope of cultural dialogue in Northern Ireland has connotations that differ from those in the rest of the UK (Eyben et al. 2002).[8] Cross-community policy aimed at migrants also emerged from laws that countered discrimination, including the discrimination of Irish Travellers. These laws included the 1976 Race Relations Act, the 1997 Race Relations (NI) Order and the 2003 EU Framework Employment Directive that outlawed discrimination on grounds of colour, race, nationality and ethnic or national origin. The 2009 Race Relations Order Regulations also ruled that segregation on racial grounds constituted discrimination.[9]

Framed as a 'cross-community event', the shared Diwali celebration has to be understood against the background of these interlinking Northern Irish, UK and EU legal frameworks. It shows that the very specific discourse of anti-sectarianism in Northern Ireland has broadened out to address issues around the tolerance of 'others'. The trend to define an overall aim of 'social cohesion' has continued more recently with the introduction of the Racial Equality Strategy 2015–2025.[10]

The Ease of Structured Fun

So how was the Diwali event further performed as 'cross-community engagement' as the day progressed? Smooth interaction between the hosting group and their visitors was assured by a well-structured programme that offered activities that were both familiar and new. After the talk, food and drinks were offered during a short break, which stimulated informal interaction and movement through the hall. The Indian migrants and their Irish guests intermingled as they walked to a table where some of the 50+ Group members served tea and coffee, and the latter encouraged the guests to eat not only conventional biscuits but also to try Indian sweets and nibbles. The visitors seemed to feel at ease, queuing up for their beverage, standing around and chatting with each other and their hosts. They were clearly acquainted with this mode of socializing, typical of other community and cross-community events, and their sense of familiarity increased their experience of the event as an opportunity to reach beyond their usual socio-spatial networks.

Later in the day there was a quiz, another familiar format of interaction, meant to entertain the visitors and test them in a playful manner on their knowledge of 'Indian culture'.[11] I had already experienced similar quizzes organized by 50+ Group members during earlier cross-community events, so it did not surprise me that it was performed with much ease and flair. For the occasion of the Diwali celebration, the questions were customized, and included some questions about Diwali – for example, 'What is the name of the goddess worshipped during Diwali?' The visitors were placed in the position of learners, their knowledge being tested by their more knowledgeable hosts. The interaction was highly organized as the 50+ Group continued to lead the entertainment. One of the Indian ladies read out each of the questions that were also printed on the sheets, her voice bridging the spatial divide between the different tables. When talking to Amit, some of the male hosts made fun of the quiz, telling him that the questions 'didn't really make any sense' and that the answers proposed by the quizmaster were 'wrong'. They were, however, happy enough to mark the answer sheets and decide on the winner. So while the quiz was being used as a tool of instruction by the quiz master and was received as such by the Irish guests, some of the Indians downplayed its pedagogical worth. The purpose of the game was clearly not educational, but to create a relaxed atmosphere in which the groups could interact and create rapport, getting to know each other so that they could find solutions to 'shared problems'.[12]

Bodies in Space: Physical Interaction

So far, the use of the hall adjacent to the temple had reflected the fact that most of the hosts and guests had not met before. The tables had remained divided, with the 50+ Group members sitting around one table and the guests around the other two. The next, hands-on activity stimulated more intermingling and physical interaction, a process that contributed to a sense of mutual identification. Chandra, who had welcomed the visiting groups at the start of the day, announced a sari demonstration, calling an 'Irish volunteer' up to the front to show the audience how to wear the outfit, naming the different folds and parts of the cloth, as she draped it on her live mannequin. The act of dressing someone in public produced feelings of homeliness and intimacy. The model willingly cooperated, and the activity caused much giggling and laughter. The visitors admired the beauty of the colours, the quality of the material and the shape of the final result, and the women in particular seemed fascinated by the way the garment twisted and turned around the body and emerged as a sari. Ratna, another Indian host, then called a male volunteer from among the Irish guests and proceeded to dress him in a green waistcoat, lungi and red turban. The green colour was instantly picked up on, and there followed a bit of joking about the outfit 'coming in handy for St Patrick's Day'. In the context of the cross-community event, the reference to the possible use of an Indian cultural item as a marker of Irish identity increased a sense of mutual identification.

The organizers of the day then announced a sari contest, and six Irish women were called to the front. The challenge was to tie a sari correctly in five minutes. Music played and people shouted out instructions as the women tried desperately to remember what they had been taught. People laughed and joked. Once the music stopped, Chandra asked Sai to judge each sari and announced a winner who was given a prize. The music was put back on and the Irish women in saris together with a few Indian women danced in a procession around the hall, creating a festive atmosphere. The competition and the dancing allowed a more intimate interaction between hosts and guests and, as such, were crucial to practices of cross-community performance. Though temporary and highly context bound, the activity produced embodied memories of an enjoyable day, giving the Irish visitors an increased (though still limited) experience of 'Indian migrants', beyond their more familiar encounters with waiters and doctors in restaurants and medical facilities. Ironically, the dressing up session played with stereotypical images of 'Indianness' and 'Irishness', which arguably questioned the possibility of actual transformation. The phrase 'It'll come in handy for St Patrick's Day' was funny exactly because it expressed the awkward recognition that the elderly Irish man would never decide to wear something like this for St Patrick's Day.

Filmed Performance: Reaching Wider Audiences in Other Locations and Times

There was another reason why the Indian and Irish participants had come together, namely their concerns about issues related to ageing. While the elderly people were busy with the saris in the main hall of the ICC, in the adjacent temple space, Community Television made preparations to do some filming for a documentary that would address this matter.[13] The intention of this particular television item on ageing was that, watching the documentary from the familiarity of their own sofas, individual viewers in Northern Ireland would understand that they shared specific predicaments with people of other social, political, religious and ethnic backgrounds, namely the need to tackle ageism and develop support networks for isolated and ailing elderly people.

To create a film that would be visually interesting, the film crew chose the Hindu temple as the interview location. Making preparations for the filmed performance, the cameraman set up the camera and a few chairs, moving things around with the help of the *Pandit* who in normal, everyday circumstances, controlled the sacred space. The cameraman's eyes were attracted by the shrine and the colourful statues that, in his view, presented an excellent filmic background for the interviews. His perception clearly differed from that of the *Pandit*, who intimately knew the statues as consecrated statues of Krishna, Ganesh and other Hindu gods (Svašek 2016: 225). In the context of the film, however, the sacred deities, who were central to his own devotional practices and those of most members of the 50+ Group, were basically reframed as props.

As the camera was being prepared, I spoke with Margaret, the interviewer, a blonde lady who had brought her teenage grandson along for the day. She explained that Community Television was working on a series of programmes for and about the elderly, 'so from *all* the communities'. Stressing the word 'all', she reiterated Northern Vision's intentions to empower people with different backgrounds and abilities. When filming started, Margaret first spoke with six members of the 50+ Group and then interviewed five representatives of the invited senior groups. She strongly orchestrated the interviews, clearly aiming to bring the message that old people from all communities have things in common. Some of her questions drew attention to the ICC building and the functioning of the group. Their answers indicated that having an actual community space increased their sense of homeliness and well-being, and made it easier to organize social events. I knew from earlier research that engagement in social activities in the ICC building was crucial to their identification as a diasporic group, an identity that reinforced transnational connections with India as geographical, cultural and to some sacred place (Svašek 2012, 2016). In the context of the documentary, this identity was underemphasized as it was more important to draw attention to shared experiences with the indigenous population, namely the challenges of old age. Kalpana, in her seventies, noted that quite a few members of the 50+ Group lived in isolated areas. She said that they 'enjoy [the Monday meetings], they talk with each other, about family life, about problems, they share joys'. She added that they could also ask advice about benefits, and that, 'sometimes specialists are invited to tell us how things work. Some people think you get a pension automatically, they don't know that you have to apply, when you have go to the council'. The problem of isolation was also mentioned by the next Indian interviewee, the treasurer of the ICC, who was briefed to talk about 'the mingling of Irish and Indian groups over the years'. He mentioned that being able to come together in a familiar space boasts elderly people's well-being: 'People are lonely, during the 50+ Monday meetings they get an

Indian meal. It is hard to meet up in larger groups; but buses are provided once a month to participate in events. The over 70s often cannot drive anymore. They get free bus passes but going by bus can be difficult too if they have physical problems'.

Margaret mentioned that social isolation was also a problem in the 'Irish community', as it was in the 'Indian and Chinese communities'. The two agreed that being able to meet up in an appropriate space such as the ICC made all the difference. Another 50+ Group member noted that when people are lonely and depressed they end up in a nursing home. Being able to come to a community centre helps, she said; it improves health and mind. Margaret agreed, saying that 'a bit of *craic* lifts you up and does you good'. Pradeep, in his early seventies, picked up on the theme of shared activities. Referring to the Diwali celebration, he said that 'it's good to meet friends and exchange views', and it is useful to exchange 'cultural views, learn about each other. It takes people out of isolation, you can solve each other's problems, find solutions'. He explained that Indian migrants had celebrated Diwali 'ever since we arrived'. He said that he enjoyed 'the festival, the food; you dance, it is part of Indian history'.

Keen to lead him back to the 'cross-community' focus of the documentary, Margaret asked about 'the changes in the *two* communities, and what about their amalgamation?' Her question presented a social imaginary that opposed the indigenous population, construed as one community, to a second community of Indian migrants. As noted earlier, the use of the 'two-community' terminology tends to reflect a habit of talking about reconciliation efforts between Protestants and Catholics, and Margaret's reframing shows how anti-sectarian discursive constructions have been used to advocate interaction between all residents in Northern Ireland. Pradeep understood that she meant mutual engagement. 'We [in our turn] go to other [Irish] centres', he replied politely; 'we exchange ideas, have dances'. Tellingly, his answer did not reflect some of the grumbles I had heard on an earlier occasion, when two 50+ members complained that their group only 'occasionally' received return invitations from the Irish groups they host. I am not sure whether Pradeep shared these concerns. For obvious reasons, he did not express them in front of the camera. Equally telling, nobody mentioned in front of the camera that diasporic community groups have easier access to funding when they can demonstrate active engagement with the majority population.

The Limits of Cross-Community Place-Making

Rada, the last Indian interviewee, mentioned the importance of the ICC as a location of community and cross-community building, but emphasized the significance of the temple as a focus of religious practice. A pious lady in her early eighties, she explained that she had participated in the Indian community for the past thirty-six years: 'I always come. I like the spiritual part, the temple'. Her words reminded viewers that this part of the building was in fact a place of religious devotion, a sacred environment where the gods both inspired and demanded love and respect. As with other active Hindus who regularly frequented the temple in Belfast, her routine behaviour had produced a strong emotional attachment to the place, generated by years of experiences that were much more formative than any kind of sporadic cross-community activity. Her activities included *darshan*, an intense visual engagement with representations of named gods whose statues are believed to give direct access to the divine, and *puja*, the act of showing reverence through invocations, gifts and prayers. Visits to the temple offered an escape from the hustle and bustle of everyday Belfast, and produced a joyful multi-sensorial experience, being surrounded by colourful gods, smelling incense, and hearing the sound of religious chanting (Eck 1998; Pinney 2001; Packert 2010; Svašek 2016).

None of these details could be shared with the members of the other senior citizen groups, whose interpretations of the Hindu temple environment were, most of all, shaped by cross-community discourse. For them this was a place to perform commonality. When Margaret started her interviews with her Irish interviewees with the question 'What do you think of this Diwali event?', all repeated the mantra 'Diwali is like Christmas', a view that had been presented to them that morning by their Hindu hosts. It was also a view that had allowed them to experience, at least to some extent, a shared sense of place.[14] In their filmed self-performance, the location of the temple space most of all functioned as visually interesting backdrop and signifier of cross-community engagement.

There were also allusions to further intersecting pathways. When asked why she had come to the ICC, Jane said she had 'wanted to see a different culture', and that 'this was the first time coming here, but I hope it is not the last'. Patricia, a member of the Shankill Forum, had already been to the ICC before; this was her third time on site. She stressed that it was good to mix with the 50+ Group because ageing people had very similar problems. She claimed feeling 'completely at ease here', and said that elderly people all just 'want to get on with life'. In the context of the Northern Irish peace-building process, 'to get on with life' mostly means not to be distracted or affected by continuing loyalist–nationalist tensions and hostilities. But here, the utterance was stretched to refer to problems of racism, xenophobia and ageing. Margaret ended the interview agreeing that, over the years, senior citizens from *all* backgrounds had started to cooperate, tackling age-related problems together.

The day did, however, have a surprising finale when, after the Irish guests had left, the members of the 50+ Group critically reflected upon the ways in which 'togetherness' had been performed in front of the camera. As Amit and I were helping to clear the tables, one of the elderly men mentioned his uneasiness with the film crew, who had taken over the temple space and had placed interviewees in a position in which they had their backs turned to the gods. He was embarrassed that none of the group, including himself, had objected (or perhaps even noticed) because this was a sacred Hindu place, and turning one's back to the gods was unacceptable. He pointed out that he did not expect the non-Hindu film crew to have known this, but they themselves should not allow this behaviour again. There were clearly certain limits to cross-community place-making. All others agreed, and a decision was taken to never permit an unknowing film crew to enter the temple again.

Conclusion

Drawing on theories of place-making, place-attachment and movement, I investigated the dynamics and limitations of 'community' and 'cross-community' making in Northern Ireland. I argued that concrete spatial processes, considered as dynamics of location, locality and sense of place, are always influenced by multiple histories of spatial engagement and mobility. The analysis made clear that the policies of reconciliation between Protestants and Catholics, central to the Northern Irish peace process, have partially shaped policies of interaction between majority and minority populations.

The chapter has zoomed in on a specific event at the Indian Community Centre where various senior citizen groups had gathered to meet up and draw attention to the plight of all Northern Irish elderly people. The analysis considered it as a temporary meshwork of criss-crossing pathways, and explored the social, material, discursive and affective dynamics of the concrete act of 'cross-community' place-making. Some practices, normally associated with Diwali, were appropriated in specific ways to create a locale that transformed the physical space into a place of positive affective movement, interaction and senior citizen activism. Discourses of cross-community dialogue and reconciliation framed the ongoing event as politically relevant engagement, and specific activities helped to assure smooth socio-spatial interaction.

The shared aim of the participants was to draw attention to the social and physical needs of elderly citizens in Northern Ireland and, presenting the issue of 'ageing' as a shared human challenge, they strongly criticized both sectarianism and racism. To reach a wider audience, the temple space was transformed into a performative setting in which common predicaments of elderly people in Northern Ireland were discussed in front of a camera. The medium of television intended to broaden their campaign. The digital mediascape, in other words, produced new time–space entanglements with possible wider political outcomes beyond the production setting. Their united appearance on screen also meant to stimulate others to think about age-related problems and change policies through cross-community activism.

The sense of commonality was, however, time and place specific, as the evolving pathways of the individual participants were shaped by different histories and conditions of movement. For the Indian 'hosts', the location carried memories of the lives of four generations of Indian migrants, which added to their emotional attachment to the building. Over the years, their frequent visits to the hall and the temple had resulted in a strong sense of belonging to the ICC. Their criss-crossing movements had also produced many shared memories, for example of the arrival of the *murtis* (statues depicting the gods) from India, and of recurrent participation in many rituals, including the annual reconsecration of the temple (Kapur 1997: 133). In addition, since the establishment of the 50+ Group, they had also frequently gathered as elderly Indian migrants. The resulting dense meshwork had produced a strong sense of 'growing old together'. In addition, their place-attachment had transnational dimensions, as many of the social activities in the building increased, and were informed by, their sense of connectedness with India.

By contrast, most of Irish 'guests' (the members of the Irish senior citizen groups, the interviewer and the cameraman) had not frequented the ICC location before the 2012 event. Their pathways had been strongly shaped by territorialism and ethno-political violence during the Troubles. In spatial terms, their main consideration was to redefine Northern Ireland and be engaged in peaceful community and cross-community making, and their experience as ageing citizens strongly motivated them to be involved in such politics. In a changing demographic situation in which they had witnessed the rise of anti-foreigner sentiments, this also meant involvement in cross-community projects with ethnic minority groups. The novelty of their appearance in the ICC framed them as outsiders who had specifically travelled to the location to discuss shared problems of ageing and marginality. Unlike their 'hosts', their life trajectories did not connect them to India and they were unfamiliar with most Hindu practices. Their hosts had anticipated this, but had not foreseen the possibility of a faux pas – namely the disturbance of the sacred temple space when the cameraman 'placed' the interviewees in a disrespectful position relative to the Hindu gods. This moment revealed the constructed nature of community and cross-community making, exposed the transitory politics of place-making and place-attachment, and uncovered the complex affective dimensions of multiple identity formation through space and time.

Acknowledgements

This chapter is one of the outcomes of the collaborative research project Creativity and Innovation in a World of Movement (CIM) that I led from 2010 to 2012. CIM was financially supported by the HERA Joint Research Programme Cultural Dynamics, which was co-funded by AHRC, AKA, DASTI, ETF, FNR, FWF, HAZU, IRCHSS, MHEST, NOW, RANNIS,

RCN, VR and the European Community FP7 2007–2013, under the Socio-economic Sciences and Humanities programme. I would like to thank all involved for their generous financial and organizational support. I am also extremely grateful for the input of my co-researcher Amit Desai, and would like to thank the participants of the ICC event described in this chapter for allowing us in their midst. Last but not least, thanks to Milena Komarova for her very perceptive comments on earlier drafts of this chapter.

Maruška Svašek is reader in anthropology at the School of History, Anthropology, Philosophy and Politics at Queen's University Belfast, and fellow at the Senator George J. Mitchell Institute for Global Peace, Security and Justice. Her major publications include *Anthropology, Art and Cultural Production* (2007), *Emotions and Human Mobility: Ethnographies of Movement* (2012), *Moving Subjects, Moving Objects: Transnationalism, Cultural Production and Emotions* (2012), and (with Birgit Meyer) *Creativity in Transition: Politics and Aesthetics of Cultural Production across the Globe* (2016). She is co-editor (with Birgit Meyer) of the Berghahn Books series Material Mediations.

Notes

1. Narinder Kapur (1997) described some of these events in his book *The Irish Raj: Illustrated Stories about Irish in India and Indians in Ireland* – for example, the destruction of the first Indian-owned wholesale clothing warehouse in Belfast in 1977 (ibid.: 180). Around six families decided to leave Northern Ireland because of the violence (ibid.: 184).
2. 'Indigenous' includes groups with longer histories of migration to Ireland, such as the Ulster Scots. Ultimately, of course, all 'indigenous' groups in Ireland are offspring of people who have arrived from elsewhere.
3. Over the last three decades, various political and economic factors have contributed to an increasing presence of migrants, asylum seekers and refugees on Northern Irish soil, namely the Northern Irish peace process, the end of the Cold War, the enlargement of the European Union, the growth of rich middle classes in China and India, and continuing political instability and economic deprivation in various parts of the world.
4. As Tim Cresswell (1996) has argued, while existing spatial discourses and practices serve as fundamental ideological and interpretative frameworks that structure individual experience and can impose limits on action and meaning, place-making is always an ongoing process and is therefore changing and diverse. In line with this argument, it is important to realize that, while to some extent comparable to diasporic processes of place-making and place-attachment in other parts of the United Kingdom, the Northern Irish case has particular local features, and it has to be investigated against the background of the wider socio-spatial and political context of conflict and peace building.
5. The area continues to be occasionally the stage for clashes and territorial contestation, particularly during the marching season when demonstrations are staged around the adjacent Orange Order Hall, while parades and protests pass or take

place in the immediate vicinity of all three buildings. Simultaneously, the ICC is also associated with Catholic–Protestant 'cross-community' activities, as the Indian society often rents it out for various events addressing 'post-conflict' cooperation between the two long-standing local communities. This reinforces the theoretical point made in this chapter, namely that space is both constructed in the moment of experience and, at the same time, 'framed' by existing discourses and practices of place. On the one hand, there are the 'dynamic insides' of the ICC and the event central to this chapter. On the other, the ICC building is materially 'encased' by the adjacent buildings and surroundings that are an active stage of both conflict and aspects of 'peace-building' practice. I would like to thank Milena Komarova for these important insights.

6. I attended several religious celebrations in the Hindu temple, where the *Pandit* and other invited Hindu Swamis took an active role (Svašek 2016: 235). I was also present during many meetings of the 50+ group, when the halls were used for art and computer workshops, chair-based exercise sessions, and the consumption of an Indian lunch, prepared in the kitchen. At other times, the space was transformed for the purpose of cross-community events. In 2012, I witnessed, for example, a celebration of St Patrick's Day in the hall on the ground floor, when groups of non-Indian senior citizens had been invited and most of the decorations (table cloths, balloons) were green. A few Indian hosts were dressed in green saris and some wore green cowboy hats, emblazoned with the words 'St Patrick's Day'. Ironically, none of the Irish visitors had put on clothes referring to St Patrick's Day. On another celebratory occasion, namely that of the 2012 Queen's Jubilee, the red-white-blue of the Union Jack dominated the colour scheme in the hall, and images on cups, plates and masks showed symbols and portraits of Queen Elizabeth and other members of the Royal Family. These material interventions clearly aimed to create a sense of shared 'Irishness' or 'Britishness' in a playful, non-antagonistic manner (Svašek and Desai 2012).
7. All names have been anonymized.
8. The Equity, Diversity and Interdependence Framework had a history of its own, as it had emerged from various attempts in the 1990s to tackle sectarianism. The Counteract and Understanding Conflict Project and the Future Ways Programme, for example, challenged sectarianism at work, the workplace being one of the few places where Catholics and Protestants met at the time, and thus provided an interactional setting with 'a potential for change absent in many other areas in society' (Eyben et al. 2002; http://uir.ulster.ac.uk/3972/, last accessed 1 April 2016).
9. http://www.equalityni.org/ECNI/media/ECNI/Publications/Individuals/RaceDiscrimShortGuide2010.pdf and https://www.nidirect.gov.uk/articles/racial-discrimination, last accessed 12 May 2016.
10. The Racial Equality Strategy 2015–2025 established 'a framework for government departments (and others) to tackle racial inequalities, to eradicate racism and hate crime and, along with Together: Building a United Community, to promote good race relations and social cohesion' (https://www.executiveoffice-ni.gov.uk/publications/racial-equality-strategy-2015-2025, last accessed 5 January 2017).
11. For the activity to take place, quiz sheets were handed backwards and forwards between the two 'communities'. The action of handing out, filling in, checking and marking the papers created a momentary sense of common purpose, culminating in the handing over of the prize. Some questions referred to more general cultural themes, such as 'What is the length of a sari?'; others concerned the history of Indian migration to Northern Ireland, for example, 'When was the ICC established?'.
12. The guests seemed to be happy with the entertainment. When I asked them why they had decided to come to the ICC, an elderly Northern Irish man, his wife and their female friend replied that they had never visited the building before and had been

'curious'. Just knowing the church building from the outside, they had been keen to gain a sense of the interior, and learn how the Indian migrants had transformed it. They also had never met 'Indian Irish' people, apart from as customers in an Indian restaurant, so this was a good way of 'getting to know them a bit better'. They also liked to 'get out of the house', found it important to meet elderly people from 'other communities', and find solutions to 'shared problems'. The latter aim was central to the activities in the adjacent Temple space.

13. The broadcasting organization had been set up in 2004 by Northern Vision, a Belfast-based non-profit media centre involved in community media and arts projects since 1986. During the launch, David Hyndman, Northern Vision's community media development director, had said that, '[w]hile the local output from BBC and UTV is of a very high standard, we aim to widen viewers' choices by providing a range of alternative programmes that are made with and by all the various communities in Belfast'. His comment again reflects a perception of the Northern Irish population as a conglomerate of diverse communities, and identifies television as a medium that allows people to project their voices both within and outside their day-to-day social circles, allowing people to reach out to other spaces and times.
14. None of them elaborated on religious elements of either Diwali or Christmas, but mentioned supposed cultural commonalities instead, such as its festive mood, the special food dishes and the playing of games.

References

Agnew, J. 2011. 'Space and Place', in J. Agnew and D. Livingstone (eds), *Handbook of Geographical Knowledge*. London: Sage, pp. 316–30.

Amit, V., and N. Rapport. 2002. *The Trouble with Community: Anthropological Reflections on Movement, Identity and Collectivity*. London: Pluto.

Boal, F. 1995. *Shaping a City: Belfast in the Late Twentieth Century*. Belfast: Queen's University, Institute of Irish Studies.

Bryan, D. 2006. 'The Politics of Community', *Critical Review of International Social and Political Philosophy* 9(4): 603–17.

Bryan, D., and C. Stevenson. 2009. 'Flagging Peace: Struggles over Symbolic Landscape in the New Northern Ireland', in March Howard Ross (ed.), *Culture and Belonging in Divided Societies: Contestation and Symbolic Landscapes*. Philadelphia, PA: University of Pennsylvania Press, pp. 68–84.

Castells, M. 2003. 'The Process of Urban Social Change', in A. Cuthbert (ed.), *Designing Cities: Critical Readings in Urban Design*. Malden, MA: Blackwell.

Connolly, P., and R. Khoury. 2008. 'Whiteness, Racism, and Exclusion: A Critical Race Perspective', in C. Coulter and M. Murray (eds), *Northern Ireland after the Troubles: A Society in Transition*. Manchester: Manchester University Press, pp. 192–212.

Connolly, S.J. (ed.). 2012. *Belfast 400: People, Place and History*. Liverpool: Liverpool University Press.

Coulter, C. 1999. *Contemporary Northern Irish Society*. London: Pluto Press.

Cresswell, T. 1996. *In Place/Out of Place: Geography, Ideology and Transgression*. Minneapolis, MN: University of Minnesota Press.

Eck, D.L. 1998. *Darsan: Seeing the Divine Image in India*. New York: Columbia University Press.

Edensor, T. 2010. 'Introduction: Thinking about Rhythm and Space', in T. Edensor (ed.), *Geographies of Rhythm: Nature, Place, Mobilities and Bodies*. Farnham: Ashgate, pp.1–18.

Equality Commission for Northern Ireland. 2010. 'Racial Discrimination Law in Northern Ireland: A Short Guide'. Belfast. Retrieved 12 May 2016 from http://www.equalityni.org/ECNI/media/ECNI/Publications/Individuals/RaceDiscrimShortGuide2010.pdf (see also https://www.nidirect.gov.uk/articles/racial-discrimination, last accessed 12 May 2016).

Eyben, K., et al. 2002. *The Equity, Diversity and Interdependence Framework: A Framework for Organisational Learning and Development*. Belfast: University of Ulster.

Gordon, G. 2013. 'Corner of Belfast Where It Is Always the Twelfth of July', *BBC News*, 3 October. Retrieved 15 July 2015 from http://www.bbc.co.uk/news/uk-northern-ireland-24388338.

Harvey, D. 1991. *The Condition of Postmodernity: An Enquiry into the Origins of Cultural Change*. Cambridge, MA: Wiley-Blackwell.

Ingold, T. 2011. *Being Alive: Essays on Movement, Knowledge and Description*. London: Routledge.

Jarman, N. 2004. *Demography, Development and Disorder: Changing Patterns of Interface Areas*. Belfast: Institute of Conflict Research.

———. 1997. *Material Conflicts: Parades and Visual Displays in Northern Ireland*. London: Bloomsbury.

Kapur, N. 1997. *The Irish Raj: Illustrated Stories about Irish in India and Indians in Ireland*. Vancouver: Greystone Books.

Lysaght, K.D. 2007. 'Catholics, Protestants, and Office Workers from the Town: The Experience and Negotiation of Fear in Northern Ireland', in H. Wulff (ed.), *The Emotions: A Cultural Reader*. Oxford: Berg, pp.93–100.

Meredith, F., and R. Black. 2014. 'Northern Ireland after 37 Years Here, Says Belfast Mela Founder', *Belfast Telegraph*, 23 August 2014. Retrieved 8 August 2016 from http://www.belfasttelegraph.co.uk/news/northern-ireland/racist-attacks-make-me-want-to-leave-northern-ireland-after-37-years-here-says-belfast-mela-founder-30529819.html.

Milligan, M.J. 1998. 'Interactional Past and Potential: The Social Construction of Place Attachment', *Symbolic Interaction* 21(1): 1–33.

Murtagh, B. 2002. *The Politics of Territory: Policy and Segregation in Northern Ireland*. London: Palgrave.

Nash, C. 2005. 'Equity, Diversity and Interdependence: Cultural Policy in Northern Ireland', *Antipode. A Radical Journal of Geography* 37(2): 272–300.

Northern Ireland Council for Ethnic Minorities (NICEM). Retrieved 3 May 2013 from https://www.nidirect.gov.uk/contacts/contacts-az/northern-ireland-council-ethnic-minorities-nicem.

Packert, C. 2010. The Art of Loving Krishna: Ornamentation and Devotion. Indiana University Press.

Pinney, C. 2001. 'Piercing the Skin of the Idol', in: Pinney, C and Thomas, N, (eds.) *Beyond Aesthetics: Art and the Technologies of Enchantment.* Berg: Oxford, pp.157-80.

Schubotz, D., and C. McCartan. 2008. 'Cross-community Schemes: Participation, Motivation, Mandate', *ARK Research Update* 55.

Schubotz, D., and G. Robinson. 2006. 'Cross-community Integration and Mixing: Does it Make a Difference?', *ARK Research Update* 43.

Taylor, C. 2002. 'Modern Social Imaginaries', *Public Culture* 14(1): 91–124.

Svašek, M. 2012. 'Affective Moves: Transit, Transition and Transformation', in M. Svašek (ed.), *Moving Subjects, Moving Objects: Transnationalism, Cultural Production and Emotions*. New York: Berghahn, pp.1–40.

———. 2016. 'Undoing Absence through Things: Creative Appropriation and Affective Engagement in an Indian Transnational Setting', in B. Meyer and M. Svašek (eds), *Creativity in Transition: Politics and Aesthetics of Cultural Production across the Globe*. New York: Berghahn, pp.218–244.

———. 2009. 'Shared Histories? Polish Migrant Experiences and the Politics of Display in Northern Ireland', in Kathy Burrell (ed.), *Polish Migration to the UK in the 'New' European Union*. Farnham: Ashgate, pp.129–148.

Svašek, M., and A. Desai. 2012. 'Creativity and Improvisation among Indian Migrants in Northern Ireland'. Retrieved 7 November 2015 from http://www.qub.ac.uk/sites/CreativityandInnovationinaWorldofMovement/ResearchFindings/CreativityandimprovisationamongIndianmigrantsinNorthernIreland/.

10

Sushi or Spuds? Japanese Migrant Women and Practices of Emplacement in Northern Ireland

Naoko Maehara

Let me begin with one of my own experiences. It was on a Saturday afternoon in September 2006 that my husband and I joined one of the events organized by the Japan Society, Northern Ireland for the first time. Arriving at the Canyon Guest House in Newtownabbey, Co. Antrim, one hour and a half from our house in Derry, we were welcomed into a friendly atmosphere. More than half of the crowd were Japanese women, the rest were men and women of different nationalities, while children of various ages were playing in the garden. I found some familiar faces, but most people were new to us. We introduced ourselves to each other, and had little chats. In the meantime, plates of sushi rice and a number of other beautifully presented dishes were brought out to a long table. It was supposed to be a '*temaki sushi* party', in which people pick their favourite ingredients and wrap them in rice and seaweed. But the dishes were fantastic – in Okinawa I had never seen a *temaki sushi* party like this before. More than twenty kinds of fillings had been prepared, using ingredients which would be hard to find in Northern Ireland. The scarcity of Japanese ingredients in Northern Ireland shaped the emotional significance of the Japanese dishes. Most of us stopped chit-chatting while we tucked in and enjoyed the taste of home.

Throughout the afternoon, English and Japanese could be heard around the room. There were couples, like us, made up of Japanese women and 'local' men. The local men usually spoke some Japanese, while the women switched more skilfully between Japanese and English. On closer inspection of the Japanese-looking children playing outside, I noticed that many had light-coloured hair and eyes, denoting their mixed parentage. Inside in the kitchen, more Japanese women were preparing tea. My son, who was then only ten months old, was crawling all over the room, while I mixed with new people. Meantime, there was a musical performance. A Japanese woman was playing some songs on a lyre. Some women, presumably regular members of Japan Society, joined in with singing the Japanese folk songs. These songs, however, reminded me that this was 'the *Japan* Society', not 'the *Okinawa* society'. I wondered if I would have felt more at home if these songs had been Okinawan folk songs and this had been the Okinawan society. A little later, another young Japanese mother arrived with her Irish-looking husband and a newborn baby, and was delighted to see that so many other Japanese people also lived in Northern Ireland. I could empathize with her. I too was glad to see other women who had married local men, and realized that I was not on my own. I also felt it was good for my husband and son to have some experience of Japanese language and food, experiences we hardly ever had in our daily life in Northern Ireland.

This event was what sparked my interest in this research, and what started me meeting other Japanese women living in Northern Ireland. In this chapter, I will focus on the spatial experiences and place-making practices of these women who had migrated from Japan to Northern Ireland. They constitute one of the smaller (and hitherto largely unstudied) migrant populations that have settled in this area over the past two decades. As such, this study offers an important contribution to the study of multiple processes by which recent globalization and population movements in Northern Ireland have been transforming social-cultural spaces and places. The questions that I will explore echo some of the questions raised by recent studies on space/place: how do people transform 'an unfamiliar physical space into a personalized, socialized place'? (Hommond 2004: 3); and 'what sorts of efforts, strategies and affects are involved in making a home?' (Obeid 2013: 368). Since this study also examines the Japanese women's changing social-cultural positions as wives and/or mothers, it also builds on research into the links between gender and migration, particularly 'the role of cognitive processes, such as the imagination, as well as substantive agency' (Mahler and Pessar 2001: 447).

In this chapter, I will use the work of Henri Bergson on the dialectical relationship between memory and perception to take a processual approach to how the women experience the new spaces in Northern Ireland, and how they transform unfamiliar spaces into personalized and concretized places. I will discuss how migrants build up a sense of familiarity and authenticity, while the disruption of their authentic sense of self may lead to a sense of loss or confusion. In existentialist philosophy, authenticity and inauthenticity are different modes of existence that are dynamic and socioculturally situated. The authentic self is defined as an emotionally appropriate mode of self, and it 'seizes itself and defines itself' (Sarvimäki 2006: 6). The inauthentic self can be a consequence of 'drifting along with the others', and 'can be disclosed by anxiety, and [an] ever-latent primordial state of mind' (ibid.). As I will describe, the women's different modes of being – authenticity and inauthenticity – reflect their perceptions of the present, the past and the future, and their place-making processes.

Japanese Women in Northern Ireland

As an analysis that is partly autoethnographic,[1] this chapter features thirteen women, including myself, who came from different parts of Japan to live in Northern Ireland in the 1990s and the 2000s.[2] The women's journeys and migration processes happened in different ways. Three women met their husbands while studying in Northern Ireland and decided to stay. In one case, the couple first interacted as penfriends. Other women met their husbands in Japan or in other places (including Britain and Ireland) while studying, working or on holiday, and eventually migrated to Northern Ireland together. All the women are married to Irish and/or British nationals.[3] They retained their Japanese nationality and have spouse or permanent visas.

The 1990s and the 2000s, in which our migrations happened, saw major changes in Northern Ireland as well as in the Republic: the former underwent a major political development in the shape of the Good Friday Agreement, which was signed in 1998, while the latter was undergoing rapid economic growth in the late 1990s. In Japan, the economic bubble came to an abrupt end in the early 1990s, and growth slowed markedly in the following ten years. The end of the Cold War was followed by an acceleration of economic globalization. It was during these so called 'Lost Decades' that the flows of people, things and information between Japan and Northern Ireland began to increase significantly. There was an increase in the number of Japanese tourists venturing abroad, and Northern Ireland (as well as the Republic) became a more popular destination. Across Japan, there was an increasing number of cultural events to introduce Irish music, dance, films and cooking, while a rash of Irish pubs opened in cities throughout the nation.

In the study of intercultural marriages/relationships, various scholars have investigated the role of gendered imaginary, asking 'who marries out' and 'who moves' (Breger and Hill 1998; Constable 2005). Intercultural marriages, as researchers indicate, show certain gendered patterns that are shaped and limited by existing and emerging cultural, social historical and political-economic factors (Constable 2005). In exploring the spatial experiences and practices of the women in this study, Kelsky's work on Japanese women's feelings about the West (i.e. *akogare*, translated as longing, desire or idealization) is useful. Kelsky (2001) discusses how media representations of the West circulated globally and locally, and helped to shape their cosmopolitan identities, however brittle. Throughout the postwar period, Japanese women have been excluded from the dominant urban white-collar employment environment; and many married women in Japan cannot continue working because it is difficult to combine the demands of a full-time job (which often requires overtime and a long commute) with the heavy demands of raising a family. Driven by their discontent and frustration, many began a quest for 'alternative lifestyles (*ikikata*) that reference a Western-derived "individualism" (*ko toshite no ikikata*) as an emancipatory project (ibid.: 33). They had invested in study or work abroad, or regarded romances with Western men as opportunities to circumvent what they considered oppressive corporate and family structures in Japan. This phenomenon, however, reflects long-standing relations of power, not only between men and women within Japanese society but also between Japan and the West in a global context. As I will discuss below, the women's experiences and practices involve their embodied images associated with 'the West' and 'Japan', images that classify areas of the world, placing them into a cultural hierarchy.

This research took place during the period between January 2007 and March 2010. As one of the Japanese migrant women married to a Northern Irish husband, I consciously engaged in relationships with these women whom I met in online communities, the Japan Society, and through personal networks. I conducted interviews with them mostly during 2007. The subsequent two years and two months were spent on follow-up conversations, often mixed with other encounters; I attended events organized by the Japan Society; and I became a regular face at smaller gatherings of Japanese people and their families in Co. Derry and Donegal, which took place nearly every month. The women lived in different parts of Northern Ireland (in most cases in their husband's home town or village), mostly in nuclear family households, except for Miho who lived with her husband and his mother. Tami was a widow with young children, having lost her husband two years before I first met her. The ages of the women varied from late twenties to early fifties, but the majority were in their late thirties and early forties. Of the thirteen women interviewed, ten were mothers. Some of these mothers worked part-time (as Japanese teachers, interpreters, a tour guide, and a cook), while the women who were not mothers had professional jobs (as a teaching assistant, a researcher, and an accountant). The data used in this chapter mostly comes from my encounters and interactions with them.

Encountering New Spaces: Migration and Disruption of Embodied Past

How do we perceive, feel and think about our surroundings? Bergson views the process of perception neither as a means of getting the world 'inside' the brain, as if it were some form of storehouse or container, nor as a means for the nervous system to shape representations of the world. Think for instance of the burning sensation in your fingers as you touch the stove. If you burn your fingers your brain gets the message to withdraw your hand very quickly. Through the nervous system we receive stimulation, transfer and interpret impulses, which send appropriate instructions to the muscles. The brain is thus to be regarded as an instrument that receives information, interprets the eventual action from a number of possibilities, and executes movement. In this sense, for Bergson, the emergence of conscious perception is the means by which 'the fluid and mobile continuity of the real' is divided and selected in relation to the lived body. Bergson also argues that '[t]here is no perception which is not full of memories' (Bergson 2004: 33). Our neural pathways develop through experience, and remain bound up with the rest of the material world. In processing sensory information, we mingle a thousand details from our past experience. In this way, memories are not conserved in the brain; but they are 'in' time and are linked to creative duration and to perception.

Bergson's views on memory and perceptions can be a good starting point to explore the experiences of individuals who are embedded in, or move through, multiple spaces. How do adult migrants, who have already embodied certain expectations of reality that have shaped cognitive and affective forms, perceive the new spaces in Northern Ireland? A Japanese woman, Maki, in her early forties, reflected on her first encounter with the Northern Irish environment when she visited her husband's home village in Co. Down in the summer of 1999: 'I was brought here on a Sunday. It was so quiet, as no shop was open. It was so dark'. The summer in Tokyo, where she was from, was much hotter and brighter than the one in Northern Ireland, and no shop was ever closed on Sunday in Japan. She felt the new surroundings were quiet, subdued and isolated. Sae, a 48-year-old Japanese woman, who came to live in Co. Derry/Londonderry in 1996, had a rather different story to tell. She described her early experiences as follows: 'It was before the Agreement. Burning cars and police with guns were everywhere'. She felt it was not safe like Japan. On the other hand, Yoko, who came to live in Belfast (her husband's home town) in 1998, had another distinct impression: 'When I first arrived, I was lost on the street, so I asked somebody. The old lady held my hand and brought me to the destination . . . I felt, these are such nice people'. For Yoko, such a kindness would have been unusual in Tokyo where she used to live, and it left a warm feeling.

Recently arrived migrants encounter numerous objects, events and relationships which, while not always being unfamiliar, may have unfamiliar features, values and attitudes. Unsure about how to interpret and react to certain social and material environments, the disruption of embodied memories of previous situations may lead to a sense of loss or confusion. I remember myself, in the winter of 2004, I was climbing the snowy Mourne Mountains for the first time with the man who would become my husband.

I realized how we perceived the same icy, all-white landscape completely differently. A Belfast-born, seasoned hillwalker, he looked like he was really enjoying the view, often exclaiming, 'oh, how beautiful!' Coming from a sub-tropical island in the south of Japan, however, I had never walked on snow. My feet were almost numb with the cold. Apart from us, there was not a sound of any living creature. The landscape was totally unfamiliar to me. It was literally just a gentle, snowy hill: no trees, and no flowers. It did not evoke any meaningful memories or emotional associations for me, as it clearly did for him. The language we spoke (mainly he spoke) was also not my own – I was still not confident enough to express my emotions in English, if at all. I did not know how to react, what to feel, apart from feeling lost in this unfamiliar space.

Building up bodily relationships with, or emplacing themselves in, the new environment, are important ways in which migrants grasp new realities and take control of them. This is what Bergson calls 'the correspondence to environment – adaptation, in a word – which is the general aim of life' (2004: 96). Without this coordination of memory-images and a present perception by the adaptive consciousness, our life would be inexplicable and less meaningful. In my case, when it comes to hillwalking in Northern Ireland, I have learned that it is too cold for me to do it in winter. However, in summer I have tried different hills with my husband. Sometimes, the landscape (often with few trees and few flowers) has come to evoke in me some pleasant refreshing feelings, while at other times it has just appeared to me as a bleak, desolate scene. The different feelings I came to associate with certain places suggest the different state of my mind/body at given times. As Bergson writes, a lived body is embedded in the flux of time, and in the requirements of the present that inform its constant movement within the dimensions of the past and the horizon of the future.

The experiences of some of the Japanese women who migrated relatively recently (within the previous five years) show how difficult it is to coordinate a present perception with memory-images and with the horizon of the future. For Yukiko, my friend who had lived in Belfast, her husband's home town, for four years, it was difficult to adapt not only to the physical environment but to the social environment more generally. She said, 'I don't mind the weather, I don't mind local food either, but the most difficult thing to live here is to develop relationships with local people'. She sighed over her lack of local friends; 'My friends are only those who are from Japan like you'. She and I had known each other since we studied at university in Belfast. She graduated from a Master's course, married a Belfast man, and started working at an after-school club for local youngsters. She said that while, generally, she 'did not have any problem with communication', small everyday episodes always made her realize that her English was not the same as the other teachers: at the primary school where she worked, her students often told her that she made grammatical mistakes, that her pronunciation was 'funny', and asked why she was speaking a 'different English'. Although she had become quite fluent, she still felt frustrated:]/t[

> I don't have any problem with communication. But at work, in school, when I am asked something, I have to really concentrate. I sometimes need to ask them to tell me again . . . and sometimes I misunderstand. Other people say to me, I am adapting to life here quite well. But the fact is I'm often a listener rather than a speaker . . . I'm often a speaker in chatting with Japanese people, but a listener at work. I don't talk much. I'm overwhelmed by. . .their knowledge of things. . .which I'm not sure about. . .TV programmes and many other things they know about because they have lived here for a long time.

Her imperfect linguistic competence restricted her from accessing 'the local knowledge of things'. She said, 'There are still many things here I'm not sure about. . . and this is bothering me'. Her frustration arose from her inability to interpret and react to specific spaces, being unable to mingle them with her past experiences. Her comment, 'I'm often a listener rather than a speaker', suggested how her previous, authentic sense of self was disrupted in the new space. This was also disempowering for her, as she said: 'I often have to rely on other people'; and 'I would be independent in Japan, but here, I always have to depend on someone'. Such an experience was, however, not what she had expected when she came to Northern Ireland. Before her arrival, her first trip outside Japan was to Australia in her twenties with her friend. She described her positive feelings associated with the size of the land and the people: 'It was a different place. People were really big. The land was enormous. I was particularly impressed by their shoe size!' She explained, laughing, that her own shoe size was so big compared to average women in Japan that she always had trouble finding the right size in Japan. Yukiko, whose height was above average for a Japanese woman, felt comfortable: 'In Australia there were many people who were better built and taller than me'. Her Japanese friend who spoke fluent English also left a good impression, as she noted: 'I couldn't speak English at all at that time. My friend spoke good English. She looked to be enjoying herself very much. Since that holiday, I have always wanted to go abroad'. So she went back to Japan, worked as a dance teacher for a while but quit it to study English in the UK. She explained: 'I wanted to live abroad anyway. I worked in Japan for a long time and was feeling frustrated . . . I hadn't married yet, hadn't changed my job. Maybe I wanted to change my life. My work wasn't great. I was having difficulty with my relationship with the boss. I was going to quit that job anyway'.

She did not expect to marry someone in Northern Ireland. She said, 'I used to tell my parents that I'm a strong person, I wouldn't need (to marry) anyone, and I would live by myself independently'. She said her parents were happy about her unexpected marriage, and of course she was happy herself with her husband. However, as her father had died of cancer the previous year, she talked about how she regretted not being able to spend more time with him: 'My dad never wanted me to go abroad. He used to ask me every year when I would be coming back to Japan. When I married, he told me "congratulations", but I think he really missed me. Now I regret I couldn't spend more time with him'. Concerned about her mother who was now left alone at home, Yukiko wondered about her marriage:

> When I married my husband, I wasn't thinking about the future at all. But my parents became older and I realized I couldn't do anything for them. Even if something happens to my parents, it takes a long time to be able to get there. Which sometimes makes me think about my marriage . . . If I had married a Japanese person (in Japan), it would have been much easier.

While Yukiko's perceptions of her marriage and of her new surroundings were shaped under certain circumstances at a particular period in time, her inability to connect her present, the past and the future images was shared by some of the other women in this study. The new spaces in Northern Ireland were perceived as alienating from their authentic selves and their meaningful past experiences, while they were not able to picture any positive future there. For Chie, who had lived in her husband's home village in Co. Down for four years, the future was vague. She said, 'I might go back to Japan if my husband died . . . because he is ten years older than me, and women would generally live longer than men'. She and her husband had met each other on holiday when she was travelling around Ireland. After they had engaged in a long-distance relationship for a couple of years, she decided to come to live with him in Northern Ireland. She quit her managerial career as a scientist at a multinational company to 'choose a personal life'. However, her previous expectations or images of migration were disconnected from her ongoing sense of discontent regarding the new spaces in Northern Ireland. She was clearly experiencing some frustrations:

> Many things are annoying me here. Poor public services. For example, there's not a periodic medical check-up, etc. Customer service is also bad. People (in shops) are friendly but unreliable. I can't stop comparing them with those in Japan. I used to write so many complaint letters. . .[

Similarly, Kayo, who had lived for a few years in her husband's small home town, could not connect perceptions of the past, the present and the future. She initially came to study at university in England where she met her husband, and when they had a baby they moved to Northern Ireland. Kayo described her new surroundings negatively: 'I don't want to say it because it's my husband's home place, but I don't think this is a beautiful place . . . especially, the scenery and the weather'. Her perceptions of the new space in Northern Ireland reflected her unease about her future: 'It's difficult isn't it, to stay here as a foreigner. I sometimes want to go back to Japan, but it is not possible. My husband says he may be able to live there . . . but when it comes to moving, I don't know myself if I want to live in Japan. I don't know where I want to go'.

Particularly for those who were mothers of young children, like Kayo, moving from one place to another was not easy. Largely economically dependent on her husband, and accepting responsibility for most of the household and childrearing tasks, Kayo was not 'in charge' of movement anymore. Parenthood had brought her, as well as her husband, new concerns and responsibilities, limiting their range of possibilities for the future. Her uncertain future shaped, or was shaped by, vague perceptions of the new space. Migration, for some of the women like her, was still a difficult process in which they struggled to create a sense of familiarity and authenticity in the new social and physical spaces.

Creating a Sense of Continuity with the Past

As wives, mothers and/or daughters-in-law, assimilation pressures existed on the women to differing degrees, which seemed to bring some of them, particularly those who had migrated relatively recently, a desire to connect with the past. In my own case when living in Belfast, one of the sudden changes I noticed after becoming pregnant with my first child related to my senses of smell and taste. Previously, happily experimenting with all kinds of new food in Northern Ireland – brown bread, sandwiches, potatoes, bacon, smoked fish, local Chinese takeaways – these things now began to leave a horrible taste in my mouth. I started feeling homesick for simple Japanese (or Okinawan) homemade food – rice balls, miso soup, stir-fried vegetables – and desperately searched for the right ingredients all around the city (often in vain). It was around this time that I started meeting more Japanese residents in Northern Ireland. After my baby was born, I joined the Japan Society, and felt I wanted to change my apparently monocultural surroundings and introduce my son to his mixed heritage.

For some of the women, including me, meeting up with other Japanese women face-to-face, sharing the same spatial set-up, was an important dimension of our lives in Northern Ireland. Unlike in more cosmopolitan cities like London or Manchester, the places where we lived offered very limited opportunities for enjoying the taste of home or interacting with other Japanese. In these apparently monoracial surroundings, some women consciously tried to connect with other Japanese residents. Many of their meetings or gatherings involved cooking and eating, whether in someone's kitchen or at Japanese or Asian restaurants. Miho expressed how 'chatting in Japanese over Japanese food was the best way of getting away from the stresses of everyday life'. In such gatherings, they often sat and chatted with one another, while their husbands were at a different table or in another room – if they were invited at all. In sharing time with other wives over lunch or dinner, they often remarked: 'This feels like we are in Japan!' For me too, it was simply relaxing to spend time with them, to be surrounded by the sight of faces with black hair and dark eyes, and the sound of the Japanese language, and to taste and feel the texture of Japanese food. The perceptions of these familiar sights, sounds, tastes, smells and so on, often sparked the networks of my memory, evoking fragments of my childhood or young adult life in Okinawa. Such remembering, which occurred during or after these meetings, provided me, and presumably some of the other women as well, with a sense of relief from the experience of disruption brought on by the new environment.

The Morality of the Place-Making Practices

For some of the other women in this study – particularly those who had been living in Northern Ireland for over ten years – migration has ultimately offered a sense of belonging, or a kind of 'second home'. The longer they lived in Northern Ireland the more interpersonal relationships they tended to develop, which required or encouraged them to settle down there. Developing the idea of staying in Northern Ireland in the future, they often created positive perceptions and representations of their surroundings, imagining negatively what might have happened if they had stayed in Japan. Let me here illustrate how the two women, Tami and Hana, have emplaced themselves in their new surroundings in different ways.

Tami

Tami, in her mid thirties, moved to Ballycastle in 1995 to marry a man who was originally her penfriend. For her, like the other women in this study, migration was not initially meant to be permanent, as she reflected:

> I didn't think so carefully about my future, whether I wanted to go back to Japan sometime or not. I was in my early twenties, I didn't think about my old age, which is different from [how I think] now. I was thinking only about myself then, not about the future at all. I just thought I could survive here somehow.

Her husband had died from a heart attack two years before I interviewed her. She intended to stay in Northern Ireland with her daughters, describing her adopted town like this:

> Here has become like 'my home', although there're not so many things here. How can I say it? It's a very peaceful place somehow . . . maybe because my family-in-law used to live nearby and, as you know, everybody is like my relatives. They know each other well. I already knew everybody in this town in the first few months after I came.

She has tried to fit in with the local surroundings by consciously learning the language and new ways of life. At the beginning, she said she 'did not have a clue what local people were saying to me with their strong accent'. It was also difficult to communicate with her parents-in-law, whom she used to meet almost every day: 'I often didn't know what they were talking about, but pretended that I understood'. When her children were small, she said she read many English books to them, and learned many nursery rhymes herself: 'Because I thought it would be a pity for my children if they don't know anything about what other kids would know'.

As a mother of two daughters, she learned not only the language but local religious traditions and culinary practices. She learned to communicate and behave in a way that local people would consider 'proper'. Now when I met her, her English had a strong local accent. She went to church with her daughters every Sunday. Potatoes had become part of her daily meals. She said she hardly ever cooked Japanese dishes at home, because 'Japanese recipes are so complicated that I'm kind of scared of cooking them', adding, 'I don't mind eating potatoes every day'. She had not joined the Japan Society, nor did she have any Japanese-speaking friends. She wrote her blog in English, and read English books. Actually, her Japanese sounded a bit rusty. Asked whether she ever missed speaking in Japanese, she shook her head:

> No, not really. . . I don't mind at all. No one speaks Japanese in my neighbourhood but I don't miss it so much . . . I've never thought, 'I can't survive without Japanese food!' I don't care much about these things. Other people sometimes ask me why, but I'm just different . . . not like someone who is always homesick and is looking for a Japanese-speaking person. I may even be the opposite. But it doesn't mean I don't want to socialize with Japanese people. It's just because there is no Japanese resident in my area, and I'm too busy with my young children.

Although motherhood restricted her mobility, it seemed that it had opened new meaningful social fields and a new sense of responsibility for her. Her spatial and cultural world felt comfortable to her. Her parents-in-law used to live beside her and they were close; 'If I missed one day, they would ask me why I didn't come yesterday'. Even after her parents-in-law and her husband had died, she felt her surroundings were safer and 'better' for her and her daughters than Tokyo – which were imagined implicitly as 'unfriendly' and 'inhumane', as she said. 'I can relax [here] if my children play outside by themselves.' She went on to talk about the old lady who lives next door:

> We have become friendly. For example, she was on my front door this morning, asking if I can buy some milk on the way to collect my kids. Also I sometimes ask her how to do the gardening, as I know nothing about it. So I feel safe. It's very different from life in Tokyo, although Tokyo is where I was born.

Cultivating relationships with her family, families-in-law and friends in Northern Ireland, she has shaped her priorities, concerns, expectations and future plans. As Bergson (2004: 96) writes, the brain actualizes only those images that are likely to be relevant to the needs of the present. With her sense of self as a wife/mother, it was important to perceive the socio-spatial environment in Northern Ireland positively.

Hana

Hana, in her early forties, initially met her husband in New Zealand, where she was studying English and he was on holiday. They married and lived in Japan for a while, and when she became pregnant they relocated to Northern Ireland in 1993. She said, 'I was curious to see . . . but if life went wrong, and if I didn't like it here, I thought I could always go back to Japan'. Fifteen years after arriving, Hana still lives in Northern Ireland with her husband and son, noting that 'this must be a good place for me'. Hana, who has lived in her husband's home town of Belfast for fifteen years, has built up spatially attuned experiences in Northern Ireland in a different way to Tami. Living in Belfast, Hana became actively involved in the Japan Society of Northern Ireland and in Japanese cultural workshops, and taught Japanese at a local college. Before coming to Northern Ireland, she said, she had only been interested in 'things foreign', and 'didn't know anything about Japan'. But living in Belfast, 'everyone wanted to know about Japan', and this led her to learn more about Japanese culture – which included cooking and traditional crafts. For her, the role of communication technology has also been enormous. The use of Skype, emails, SMS and the Internet allowed her to stay in touch with her family and friends back home, as well as to keep up closely with Japanese news and entertainment, including the music scene and television programmes. She said her life 'had changed completely since Windows 95 arrived. Because of the advancement of information technology,' she said, 'we can live here very comfortably'. For her, it is important to maintain close relationships with people in Japan via the Internet, as she said, 'There is no distance from Japan, and my friends over there'. In the digital as well as face-to-face spaces in Northern Ireland, she had retained, or cultivated, some Japanese cultural practices – for example, how to prepare particular dishes for certain occasions, and how to use Japanese honorific expressions correctly. More importantly, she had created a sense of authentic self, as she said 'I would not change myself wherever I live'.

She described her surroundings in Northern Ireland positively:

> I think I'm lucky because my job is related to Japan . . . and the people I meet there are very Japan-friendly. . . or they know a lot of things about Japan. I like my colleagues and students . . . I have never had a negative experience with them. But also, because I live in my husband's home town, many people are friendly, like our neighbours and parents-in-law. It's a good environment. It would be very different if you lived by yourself in a foreign place.

For her, the social spaces in Northern Ireland were experienced positively as offering 'more freedom' and 'independence', without the extended-family obligation – which she imagined she would have had if she lived in Japan:

> Unlike Japan, there is no bothersome kin relations here . . . If you don't want to, you can just escape, you can just tell them [your in-laws] that you're a foreigner.

> If you're in Japan, you'd have to behave the same as other people would do. But here, we can escape. I feel more relaxed about what other people would think about me . . . I can decide on my own. In Japan, you'd be always worried about what other people would think. You feel depressed or uneasy if you're different from others, even though it's a tiny difference.

Compared to images of her 'easy', 'relaxed' life in Northern Ireland, life in Japan was perceived as 'oppressive' and more 'self-constraining'. She continued:

> There are different kinds of people here. For instance, outside on the street, there are those wearing thick jumpers and those just wearing T-shirts in the midwinter. In Japan, it wouldn't be like this. People would feel uneasy, or embarrassed, if they are different from other people. They would worry if others think that they are a bit different. But here it seems to me more individualistic. There are different kinds of people. If I lived in Japan, I would have to care about these things all the time . . . I couldn't live in Japan anymore.

As Bergson (2004) argues, psychological recollection is not just a biological function like the process of simple re-excitation or pure reproduction; it is imaginatively constructed through moment-by-moment mappings of the body, self and the world. For the women in this study, including Hana and Tami, their negative memories of Japan were not called up straightforwardly as things happened, but shaped through constructive processes. Bergson also notes that there are always dominant memories that exist as 'shining points round which others form a vague nebulosity'; and these shining points 'are multiplied to the degree in which our memory expands' (ibid.: 223). For some of the women who were mothers, some of their dominant memories involved contrasting images of (Northern) Irish men and Japanese men. Kayoko, who had been previously married in Japan before coming to Northern Ireland, described how her ex-husband 'used to work all the time, like a typical Japanese man, not caring about family'. She viewed her current husband as a good father, and in many ways the opposite of her ex:

> My previous husband was such a smooth-talker, although it helped his business. But I hated his flattering . . . the ways he said what he is not really thinking in his mind. In such a sense my current husband is a very honest man, although it may not be helpful with his business. But I wonder if it is only my husband, or the people here . . . My husband also looks after our son very well. He [my son] doesn't care about me when I leave the house, but always cries when my husband goes to work. He [my husband] is very loving to our son and it's great that they often play together.

Another woman, Sae, similarly spoke of her husband who cared a lot about his family. She said that when she used to visit Japan with her children, 'they missed their daddy so much'. She was also planning to bring her kids to Japan that year, but she could not because 'they didn't want to come without their daddy'. When describing her husband as a good family-centred father, she was contrasting him with his Japanese counterparts:

> I remember I was watching a TV programme in Japan when I was young. It was about a Japanese family, in which a mother lives with her children without a husband. Her husband brings money home, so there's no problem if he's away at work all the time . . . I couldn't survive with such a family. My husband cares a lot about our children . . . although he sometimes doesn't come back from the pub until very late . . . he is a typical Irish man.]

Kayoko's and Sae's evaluative distinction between 'Northern Irish men' and 'Japanese men' partly reflected stereotypical media images prevailing within/outside Japan. Whether in news coverage or films, 'Japanese men' have appeared as technologically advanced yet emotionless and inhumane people (Morley and Robins 1995). Such prevalent images were likely to serve as a kind of lens, enabling these women to construct contrasting memory-images, as well as to positively perceive their own migration/ marriages. As Bergson notes, personal recollections are contemplative and dynamic; 'we start from a "virtual state" which we lead onwards, step by step, through a series of different *planes of consciousness*, up to the goal where it is materialized in an actual perception' (Bergson 2004: 319; emphasis in original). Comparing their lives in Northern Ireland with the ones they might have had if they had stayed in Japan, the women created a moral sense of settling down for the sake of their children and/or their husbands.

Conclusion

Stemming partly from my own experience of migration and marriage, I have explored the Japanese women's spatial experiences and processes of emplacement in Northern Ireland. As I have described, the women emplaced or tried to emplace themselves in their new surroundings in different ways and to varying degrees. Recently arrived migrants in particular tended to feel uneasy or lost, as their embodied past was being disrupted in unfamiliar spaces. They perceived the new spaces as alienating them from their authentic selves and their meaningful past experiences, while they were not able to picture a positive future there. Their 'unhomelike' feelings disclosed their unauthentic selves, as they could not coordinate their present, the past and the future. On the other hand, particularly for those who had been in Northern Ireland for over ten years, migration has ultimately offered a sense of familiarity and authenticity, or a kind of second 'home'. The longer they lived there the more interpersonal relationships they tended to develop, which required, or encouraged, them to settle down there. With their sense of self as a wife and/or mother, they created positive perceptions and representations of their surroundings, embodying different versions of the images associated with the West and Japan.

Through the case of the Japanese women in Northern Ireland, this study suggests how, at a different point in their life course, migrants would experience transitions in their spatial experiences and practices, and in their sense of authentic selfhood. Through having children, having elderly parents or parents-in-law, losing their parents, or losing their spouses, they often change their priorities, concerns, goals and plans, all of which reshape perceptions of the past, the present and the future. This chapter also indicates how migrants' place-making is never static, but is an ongoing process which they imaginatively construct through moment-by-moment mappings of their memory and perceptions. Apprehending the contingency and complexities of migrants' (non-migrants') spatial experiences and emplacement allows us to see how individuals' lives are in motion, never fixed or over-determined in 'ethnicity' or 'culture'. This study, I hope, contributes to the exploration of the social-cultural transformations of recent globalization and population movements by offering a glimpse into the women's dynamic interpretive processes, which mediate their understandings of the world.

Acknowledgements

I would like to express my special appreciation and thanks to my former supervisor Dr Maruška Svašek for her great support, patience and encouragement during my postgraduate study, and for her constructive advice on an earlier version of the chapter. I would also like to thank Dr Miliena Komarova for providing me with useful feedback on an earlier draft of the chapter. Also, my thanks to my husband for his great proofreading. Finally, my special thanks go to all my research participants for sharing their time and experience, without whom this research would not have been possible.

Naoko Maehara is a recent graduate from Queen's University Belfast. Her doctoral research focused on the life stories and psycho-cultural processes of Japanese migrant women in Northern Ireland and the Republic of Ireland. Her main interests include migration studies, intercultural relationships, and multiculturalism, particularly within the contexts of the UK, Ireland and Japan. Her recent publications include 'Well-being and the Implication of Embodied Memory: From the Diary of a Migrant Woman', in A.S. Gronseth (ed.), *Being Human, Being Migrant: Senses of Self and Well-Being*, 2013, Berghahn Books. She currently lives mostly in Japan, going back and forth between Japan and Northern Ireland, researching the life stories of Japanese living overseas and immigrants in Japan.

Notes

1. Autoethnography explores the researcher's personal experience, and connects this autobiographical story to the wider cultural, political and social meanings and understandings of those studied (Ellis 2004). As an autoethnographic work, this chapter

includes an exploration of my own personal experiences in order to understand these women's attempts to make Northern Ireland their 'home'.

2. This study is based on my completed doctoral research, which explored the emotions, memories and perceptions of Japanese migrant women in the Republic of Ireland and Northern Ireland. All the women's names are pseudonyms.
3. People born in Northern Ireland can choose either British or Irish citizenship.

References

Bergson, H. 2004. *Matter and Memory*. New York: Dover.

Breger, R., and R. Hill (eds). 1998. *Cross-cultural Marriages: Identity and Choice*. Oxford: Berg.

Constable, N. (ed.). 2005. *Cross-border Marriages: Gender and Mobility in Transnational Asia*. Philadelphia, PA: University of Pennsylvania Press.

Ellis, C. 2004. *The Ethnographic I: A Methodological Novel about Autoethnography*. Walnut Creek, CA: AltaMira Press.

Hommond, L. 2004. *This Place Will Become Home: Emplacement and Community Formation in a Tigrayan Returnee Settlement, Northwest Ethiopia*. Ithaca, NY and London: Cornell University Press.

Kelsky, K. 2001. *Women on the Verge: Japanese Women, Western Dreams*. Durham, NC: Duke University Press.

Mahler, S., and P. Pessar. 2006. 'Gender Matters: Ethnographers Bring Gender from the Periphery Toward the Core of Migration Studies', *International Migration Review* 40(1): 28–63.

Morley, D., and K. Robins. 1995. *Spaces of Identity: Global Media, Electronic Landscapes and Cultural Boundaries*. London and New York: Routledge.

Obeid, M. 2013. 'Home-Making in the Diaspora', in A. Quayson and G. Daswani (eds), *A Companion to Diaspora and Transnationalism*. Hoboken, NJ: Blackwell Publishing, pp.366–80.

Sarvimäki, A. 2006. 'Well-being as Being Well: A Heideggerian Look at Well-being', *International Journal of Qualitative Studies on Health and Well-being* 1: 4–10.

11

Refugees and Asylum Seekers in Belfast

Finding 'Home' through Space and Time

Malcolm Franklin

> I first come to UK in 2001 and I stay in Hull, and after in Birmingham. Coventry Road is very many [miles] from Sudan. All that time UKBA [United Kingdom Border Agency] not ask me what I have been doing. I was working sometime doing 'black' work, but I could have been paying tax in that time. In 2007 I return with £3,000 money from IOM [International Organization for Migration]. I have my own Internet cafe in Khartoum and I help many people from Darfur. The security people were always hanging around, and scared away all my business. I was engaged to be married at the time, but I have no parents or family anymore. I believe that I was in danger, so I buy a false passport and fly to Ireland and claimed asylum. I claim again in France and spend fifteen days in prison, and was sent back to Dublin. I was a few months in an asylum holding centre in Longford. It was like a secure hostel with food provided. Human Rights are much better here [in Belfast] as can move around freely and visit friends. We buy our own food and take it in turn to cook. I claimed again here and was sent to Dungavel detention centre in Scotland. Bail was paid and I am released. Two times I leave my country as it is not safe.

The above account, related to me by a forty-year-old Sudanese asylum seeker in Belfast in 2011, highlights an extreme form of mobility; a process of finding a place to settle and a safe space to call home, at least temporarily. Conducting fieldwork for a PhD dissertation on refugees and asylum seekers in Northern Ireland, I had called at an asylum-seeker house in the south of Belfast in order to deliver some furniture. As this was a Friday, all six of the Sudanese people present in the house were observing the Muslim prayer day, and were about to share a traditional meal together.

I was invited to sit down and was offered tea and some dates. One of the men I had seen on a few occasions in and around the local refugee centre, more commonly known as NICRAS,[1] and he introduced himself to me as Bibi.[2] Having established my position as a NICRAS volunteer as well as an academic researcher, Bibi, who originally came from Khartoum, decided during our conversation to show me his bail papers from a local court, which had been paid for by a Sudanese friend. Staying in temporary accommodation, one of his bail conditions was to show up and register each week at the regional immigration centre. In 2007, Bibi had decided to return and was repatriated to Khartoum, his original homeland, but also the place from where he had been uprooted once before. His life had become the embodiment of continuing displacement.

Bibi's life illustrates the predicament of asylum seekers and refugees, whose lives reflect the uncertainty, apprehension and transitory nature of forced migration. Building on the work of Rapport and Dawson (1998) who contend that lives are lived in movement and that identity is formed on the move, and drawing on theories of space, introduced by Sheldrake (2001), I explore in this chapter the processes by which people like Bibi build a sense of place and home in their new environment. The inquiry demonstrates that 'home' is a processual and mutable product of social activity, and that displacement and a loss of home eventually collide with decisions made by local authorities in the search for a new place of residence (Turton 2005).

The personal narratives in this chapter emphasize how the stories and experiences expressed and exchanged by refugees and asylum seekers in Northern Ireland regularly feature anecdotes of travel, movement, uprooting and displacement. Tying in with theories that regard place-making as a process, they also reflect their strategies to find a location in which to settle and feel at home (see May 2011: 367, 369). But how do these processes of emplacement occur, or fail to take place? How do individual refugees and asylum seekers find a semblance of belonging in Northern Ireland, and which socio-spatial practices shape their experiences? To answer these questions, the chapter first provides some background of the Northern Irish context and the research conducted. This is followed by a discussion of how theories of transition and movement can be used to explore the spatial practices and experiences of asylum seekers and refugees in Northern Ireland. In the next section, the analysis addresses specific strategies of emplacement, and investigates how they tie in with the opportunities and limitations of socio-spatial setting in Northern Ireland. The focus then moves to the ways in which specific discourses around refugees and asylum seekers influence their spatial experiences of belonging and non-belonging. The chapter finally explores whether and how, after arriving in Northern Ireland, refugees and asylum seekers can make a fresh start and gain a new sense of home.

Researching Asylum Seekers and Refugees in Northern Ireland

Most of the fieldwork research for this chapter took place in 2009–2012, a period of relative political calm and stability (on the surface at least) in the city of Belfast. In that period, I volunteered at NICRAS where my role included teaching English, assisting refugees and asylum seekers with various practical difficulties, listening to their stories and challenges, giving moral support, as well as searching for and delivering a range of material items. The majority of this research was conducted in the inner city areas of Belfast. The physical setting of that environment contrasted with the stories I heard from refugees, memories that mostly spoke of rural life in countries such as Sudan, Zimbabwe and Somalia.

In Northern Ireland, the continuing sectarian realities of life, played out on a daily basis across the cityscape, have continued to form the backdrop to the social world of its residents. The history of Northern Ireland and its subsequent residential segregation into loyalist, republican, and predominantly 'neutral' areas have remained dominant features of the landscape. The residents who live within the confines of its more segregated communities create a sense of exclusion. In the apt words of Shirlow and Murtagh (2006: 17), 'Belfast remains not as a city but as an assemblage of "villages" within which detachment from other places is crucial in terms of identity formation'. West Belfast consists of around 80 per cent Catholic residents, whilst East Belfast can claim around 80 per cent Protestant residency (NISRA 2011). These social constructions of urban space highlight the continuing importance of related processes of territoriality, belonging and identity. At the time of my fieldwork, the capital city of Northern Ireland contained a population of around 270,000 in its metropolitan area, or 15 per cent of the region's total population of 1,775,000. The religious breakdown comprised 48.6 per cent Protestant and other Christian denominations, 47.2 per cent Catholic, and 4.2 per cent non-religious or non-Christian religions ('Demography of Northern Ireland' 2016). The social and political sectarian divide in Belfast and Northern Ireland as a whole has been well documented. However, putting aside cultural and ideological beliefs, there is little by way of their physical appearance that indicates difference amongst the host population. By contrast, the relatively sudden increase of incoming foreign migrants to Belfast over the past decade has been a noticeable phenomenon. There is also a relatively small but increasing number of Indian and Chinese migrants who have arrived in Northern Ireland since the 1960s (see Chapter 9, this volume).

The changing patterns of inward migration to Northern Ireland are not well documented as accurate figures are difficult to obtain for a variety of reasons (see McNulty 2014: 4). Nonetheless, the demographic make-up of specific parts of Belfast, for example, has changed rapidly since the turn of the century. As a rough guide, since European Union enlargement in 2004, and up to the end of March 2009, a total of 36,550 people from the eight new accession countries had registered to work in Northern Ireland. In 2011–12 around 1,000 migrants came from outside the European Economic Area under the strictly controlled points-based immigration scheme. More recently, the recession has reduced the in-flow of people greatly. In January–March 2013 it was estimated on the basis of Labour Force Survey statistics that there were 69,000 people in Northern Ireland of working age who were born outside the UK or Republic of Ireland (NISRA 2011; see McNulty 2014: 1–2). In addition to these numbers, an extremely small proportion of these are Roma people who come mostly from Romania. In 2013, the Northern Ireland Housing Executive was housing 416 people from twenty-six different countries who were in the asylum system and entitled to accommodation and cash support.

The above shows that Belfast can no longer be regarded as a place that has two distinct traditions, namely Protestant and Catholic, but as a city with increasing numbers of migrants who have arrived not only from fellow EU countries, but also from further afield (see also chapters 9 and 10, this volume). Furthermore, the territory of Northern Ireland has never been completely isolated, as it has been linked to other parts of the world through various kinds of migration into and out of the region. For many refugees and asylum seekers, Belfast has become their new home, at least temporarily, although for the most part there is no specific area in the city where these incomers live in groups according to their national or ethnic background. Newcomers continue to arrive on a regular basis, stay temporarily, or intend to settle on a more permanent basis, depending on their personal circumstances in conjunction with their legal status as UK residents. Although only a very small number of people apply for, and succeed in gaining sanctuary in Northern Ireland, this fact can make them particularly isolated and vulnerable, especially as some will have few people from their own ethnic and cultural backgrounds to help them through the experience.

Transition and Home in Movement

To explore the socio-spatial experiences of migrants, refugees and asylum seekers in Northern Ireland, it is useful to turn to theories of transition and movement that undermine static identity-place definitions. The majority of people who are born in Belfast will have lifelong family ties in the area. They will be educated locally until they reach adulthood, and very often get employed, find a partner, have children, and remain in the same area for most of their lives. As a consequence, they most likely have a strong sense of continuity, as their past, present and future are all lived and envisaged in connection to Northern Ireland. However, the situation is radically different for asylum seekers and refugees. As John Berger (quoted in Rapport and Dawson 1998: 27) has argued: 'In an age that conceptualises itself in terms of global movement, the idea of "home" undergoes dramatic change. In place of the conventional conception of home as the stable physical centre of the universe, and a safe place to leave and return to, a far more mobile notion comes to be used'.

Following this argument, Rapport and Dawson (1998) have argued that there is a need for a more general shift away from the fixity of home as a sedentary place towards a more globalized world where home can be construed as being in constant transit between divergent and discrepant geographies and social milieus. In their words, 'not only can one be at home in movement, but . . . movement can be one's very home, and furthermore, one's identity is formed on the move' (ibid.: 31). In relation to the recent inward migration to Northern Ireland, Bauman (2007: 83) believes that '[d]ue to the global devastation of livelihoods and the uprooting of long-settled populations, cities have become dumping grounds for globally conceived and gestated problems'. I would contend that refugees and asylum seekers are a forced vanguard of any such uprooting. For example, I often came across Asam in the reception area at NICRAS, and his narrative below picks up his story of transience long after he arrived in the UK. The disparate geographical locations of his friends reflect the government's dispersal policy.[3] He was staying at a nearby hostel in Belfast, but he liked to spend a lot of time at NICRAS where he would meet up with friends from the 'refugee community'. During our conversation, he told me:

> I was in Southampton for four years. I then took a ship to Canada on a false passport. We stopped in Belfast, and I was arrested. I am now here three years. At first on £42 a week, and since September 2008, Section 4 vouchers,[4] and now nothing. I said I will go back to Sudan. At this time two people [asylum-seekers] were shot dead at Khartoum airport, did you not hear about it? They said they cannot send me back [this was in October 2008]. I have made friends in Middlesbrough, Swansea, Birmingham and Manchester, and many Sudanese in Shepherd's Bush in London. Always before there were some [Sudanese] working as doctors and other things, but now very many come [from socially disparate backgrounds].

Asam's account adds weight to theories of home and movement, whereby changing social networks and new environments are a concurrence of a transitory existence (see, for example, Ahmed et al. 2003). After Asam told me that he was from the south of Darfur, I brought out my detailed map of the region where we eventually located his home town of Tulus. Asam went on to say: 'My father is a lorry driver; he has always been. My mother and one sister are all still living there. Many friends left at the same time as me [2003, when civil conflict began in earnest]'. On a separate occasion, I had a conversation with another Sudanese refugee, namely my friend Eddie. We spoke about a mutual acquaintance and his failed attempt at seeking asylum in Northern Ireland. He had been returned to Italy where his original asylum claim in a European Union country had been lodged.[5] We also spoke about how Malta is a popular transit country for African asylum seekers, and furthermore, how France is a good country for attaining a visa, according to Eddie. It occurred to me that this is the type of regular discussion individuals are engaged in as they experience a world of continuous movement from the time they leave their home areas, and it does not cease until they manage to settle somewhere, and preferably in possession of an official refugee status document.

A Place in which to Belong? Strategies of Emplacement

Jansen and Løfving (2009: 5) caution against the assumption of normative sedentarism 'that all human beings, understood collectively as cultural groups, "belong" to a certain place on earth and derive a primordial identity from that belonging'. They further suggest that the presumption of a refugee's 'real identity', being linked to an overwhelming sense of belonging to an (ethno-)national category, territorialized in relation to the 'homeland and the past' (ibid.: 6), represents a reified, essentialized notion of belonging. Instead, Rapport and Dawson (1998: 10) describe the idea of place-making and home as 'inhabiting a cognitive environment in which one can undertake the routines of daily life, and through which one finds one's identity best mediated'. By extension, they suggest, one feels 'homeless when such an environment is eschewed' (ibid.). Similarly, Sheldrake (2001: 9–10; cf. Auge 1997) identifies three essential characteristics of place – that it 'engages with our identity, with our relationships, and with our history'. In doing so, he emphasizes that home is more than simply the locality from which we originate, and involves connections to places of departure and arrival, and activities within dynamic networks of stable and less stable relationships. It is increasingly recognized, therefore, that individual refugees employ what can be termed emplacement strategies (Jansen and Løfving 2009: 12–13) as they attempt to embed themselves in new socio-economic and cultural environments. Their actions in this respect are often considered as proactive and goal-oriented (Rapport and Dawson 1998: 10). While I found examples of this in my research, the narratives of many asylum seekers and refugees I spoke with also confirm the position of authors, such as Turton (2005) and Ahmed et al. (2003), who have argued that emplacement is not always conscious or aimed at finding a sense of connectedness in the new environment. For many refugees and asylum seekers, place-making rather consists of finding a temporary routine in the city that helps them to structure their uncertain lives and gain a sense of (temporary) security. Their primary concern, in other words, is often related to their goal to receive some form of residency status.[6] As they are struggling with the bureaucratic process, the people I encountered tried to form friendships and social networks with some locals but mostly each other, thus creating some semblance of home. As this chapter shows, their sense of place was a product of specific social activities, related to their shared predicament.

Anthropological research in the city tends to focus on the socio-spatial relationships that are formed within the overarching social structure that prevails in the urban milieu. The form of the social structure determines the interdependencies between refugees and asylum seekers, as well as local people, and the roles they play in the various situations that coalesce and inform their social worlds. In Belfast, however, refugees and all other ethnic minorities are dispersed across the city, and hence do not fall within any particular spatial boundaries. Unlike some ethnic groups in England, they do not fit into occupational categories either. This means that adaptation takes time as individuals seek to establish meaningful relationships and routines. For those people in Northern Ireland who do not come to seek refuge and asylum, houses and apartments are normally dwelling places that are utilized as a base to keep personal items, for cooking a meal and providing hospitality to friends, and a place to sleep and recuperate. Furthermore, these places are physical structures with an address, where individual identity is recognized by neighbours, friends, relatives and the authorities. Bachelard ([1958] 1994: 5) suggests that 'an entire past comes to dwell in a house' whereby more permanent homes become more than just a shelter. For refugees and asylum seekers in particular, the connection between the imagination and memories of other places they have lived in, form an important role in constructing the space of a new home as a place of comfort and safety (Parkin 1999; Sheldrake 2001: 14–17).

Yet home as a space of comfort proved to be a dubious construct for many asylum seekers, and this was further intimated by the following narrative account. On one occasion, I happened to meet Greg, an asylum seeker whom I had previously met, and who comes from the central highlands of Zimbabwe. He speaks fluent English as seems to be the case for the majority of people from his country. During our conversation, he told me a few things about his life:

> I have been here one year now. My appeal was refused. I am in a house sharing with two others from Zimbabwe. I said to a UKBA employee that I pay £3.50 before 9 o'clock for a bus ticket, and this seems unfair [ca. £14 per month is a lot of money in these circumstances]. He told me that I may be able to sign every two weeks or monthly after a trial period. I am very fed up. I am not allowed to work or study. I have no money and I would be glad to do anything. The house gets electric put in every two weeks by the landlord. There is a weak heater in the living room and one time the hot water cut out in the middle of a shower.

He received £35.52p in cash each week. As this equates to £5 per day, he said: 'They [the UK authorities] don't care about us or want us here. That much is clear. At the start of the week, I work out what I am going to buy'. The winter of 2010 was particularly harsh for long periods, and the large living room and kitchen were certainly very cold when I visited. The electricity was strictly controlled by the landlord who, although he was ultimately reimbursed by the Home Office, tried to make a profit. Greg told me: 'I sleep in my jacket until I get warm enough, and then I remove it. I don't want the cold to get into me, or then I will get pneumonia or something. You never get used to the cold'. This was a complaint I heard from many asylum seekers. A heating engineer was supposed to have sorted out the problem, but they were still waiting. As I was leaving, some junk mail was dropped through the letterbox. I noticed an electricity bill amongst the usual proliferation of leaflets advertising various items from food and clothing stores. However, these items on offer would not be a part of Greg's weekly financial plan. The extent to which home can be simply understood as the place you come from is challenged by Greg's individual agency. He shows that home is made and remade on an everyday basis through strategies of overcoming alienation, and becoming part of local society through his own aptitude.

Interlinking Sectarian and Anti-foreigner Discourses of Space

This section looks more closely at the ways in which specific discourses that mark asylum seekers and refugees as unwelcome new features of the Northern Irish social landscape, impact the spatial experiences of refugees and asylum seekers. Suspicion of the outsider takes on a particular resonance in Northern Ireland, within its sectarian-infused public spaces and its exclusionary housing estates. For example, Eddie, a Sudanese refugee I befriended, had moved into a Housing Executive flat located near a busy junction in a relatively neutral area of the city – neutral in the sense that no visible sectarian regalia or graffiti mark the territory as being from one side of the divide or the other. However, the street sign was in Irish, as well as English. This area borders the neutrality of the central business district, but is also close to both 'nationalist' and 'unionist' areas. This kind of territorialist terminology is regarded as quite normal in Belfast, and indeed in Northern Ireland in general. The residents of Belfast's inner city districts live in spaces characterized by high degrees of segregation, and entire communities are viewed as politicized where all space is identified as either 'ours' or 'theirs' (Lysaght 2005: 135–36). Refugees and asylum seekers[7] tend to have little choice where they are to reside, either temporarily or for longer periods, as they will almost certainly fall into the category of social housing.

Despite the reality that the Troubles in Northern Ireland are now largely confined to the history books, moving through specific landscapes nonetheless induces anxiety for large swathes of Belfast's inhabitants. This highly local corpus of knowledge is not commonly shared by all residents of the city, as Lysaght (2005: 127–40) aptly illustrates. She highlights how office workers from the town would probably be quite surprised to know that they are daily walking through such highly defined 'sectarianised space'. With a certain amount of irony, the refugees and asylum seekers who live in Northern Ireland are free from the constraints of what Lysaght describes as 'these local residential areas that necessitate the navigation of a complex topography of politicised space' (ibid.: 135). To illustrate this point, I remember a refugee from Eritrea expressing surprise and shock following an incident in a shopping centre (considered 'neutral' space, and a relatively peaceful non-sectarian place) quite close to the house where he was residing at the time, just off the Falls Road in staunchly nationalist West Belfast. As part of a charitable donation, a local resident had given him a Glasgow Celtic football shirt, which is tantamount to expressing allegiance to one side of Belfast's sectarian divide. It is visibly obvious to all 'indigenous' residents who inhabit these inner-city districts that specific newcomers are in no way connected to their spatialized and sectarian socio-history. However, a stranger had suddenly shouted abuse at him, and my startled friend said to me: 'I have no idea what I am doing wrong!' My friend had lived all of his life in north-east Africa, and as a refugee from Eritrea would appreciate Sheldrake's observance 'that place is always contested rather than a simple reality, and the human engagement with place is a political issue' (Sheldrake 2001: 20). Refugees and asylum seekers are not exempt from scrutiny or suspicion from local inhabitants, but in this context they do tend to be viewed as a separate social category. When viewed from an experiential perspective, the example above shows how blending inconspicuously into different parts of the city is a fluid and unpredictable reality.

Marginality in the Socio-spatial Order of the City

Asif, an asylum seeker from Somalia, is in search of what most young single men wish for, namely all of the accoutrements that make a life worth living – paid employment, a nice home, perhaps a wife and children and a motor car – but of course these things do not happen on arrival for an individual seeking asylum. The fact remains that, before any minimal aspirations can be realized, Home Office/Border Agency officials decide who will be granted permission to stay, and hence who can put into action any concrete plans for the future. In order for this to take place, there needs to be an epistemological readjustment in relation to a new sensory environment. For a person who is not legally permitted to join a society, with its attendant privileges and opportunities, a marginal existence and a devaluation of identity prevails. Conforming to the socio-spatial order and respecting its rhythms and idiosyncrasies becomes a peculiarly challenging situation for some asylum seekers. I spoke to Asif on many occasions throughout my fieldwork, and his principle reason for leaving his homeland was to make a better life for his mother and sister who both live in the war-torn region of Mogadishu. His narrative begins with his arrival in England:

> There is a Somali clan that I know, that's why they [UKBA] first sent me to Sheffield. I was seventeen years old and under social care in a house with four others. On my eighteenth birthday, everything changed for the worse. I was moved into another house and had my first interview in Liverpool. This was

> rejected, and so was the first Appeal in court. I messed up my story. I was very nervous and didn't understand the way it worked. I had a Somali interpreter, but it was very difficult. My funds were stopped, and then I received and signed the Section 4 support agreeing to return home when possible. But I knew it would not be possible to be sent back to Somalia. Living off £35 vouchers each week, I was always thinking about my mother and sister as the war was very bad in Mogadishu. In 2004, I decided to go to Croydon [HQ of UKBA] and apply again as an asylum seeker under a false name, to start again. I was sent to a hostel in Dover where they took my fingerprints and they discovered I had a false claim. The police came and arrested me. I just wanted my situation to be heard and understood, and that's why I did this.

Soon after his arrival in a new and disorienting social environment, Asif's hopes and plans had quickly turned into a narrative of adaptation and survival. Over and above Asif's individual agency and his lack of routine and feeling of empowerment, lies the legal stricture of the asylum system that ultimately determines his possibilities of self-transformation and the spaces where these may be enacted. Askland (2007: 240; cf. Bourdieu 1977) queries how we explain the practice of refugees and asylum seekers within these unfamiliar social fields. Feeling obliged to move from place to place, Asif's situation depicts ways in which social capital, accrued through his contacts, networks and personal agency, become performative acts of survival strategies. On the other hand, refugees who have received the coveted five years Limited Leave to Remain status (see Note 5) are aware of new possibilities. At least this five-year time span offers a measure of security for new refugees in which to adjust in the process of place-making and establishing a home environment.

The Past in the Present: Memories and the Senses

Whether a more recently arrived person pursuing an asylum claim, or a more settled refugee, their reasons for living in Northern Ireland are always intertwined with the places they escaped from. As Lamb (2001: 22) comments, it is 'how we choose to talk about the past that is connected to what we want to tell and work out in the present. The ways we talk about our pasts relate to what we want to make in the future'. Furthermore, as Sheldrake notes (2001: 16), 'if place is, therefore, first of all landscape, it is also memory'. Reconfiguring specific events as memory were illustrated when I delivered a mattress to Eddie's flat that he had requested in order to accommodate visitors if the need arose. We proceeded to his small sitting room and stayed for an hour in amicable conversation. He provided me with some tea and a succulent piece of homemade semolina and coconut sponge cake. I asked him for the recipe, to which he replied: 'I have around twenty recipes all in my head that I get from my mother when I'm growing up in Sudan. If you write them down, it never tastes the same'.[8] Eddie's father and sister had both been killed during fighting in Darfur, though his mother still lives in Sudan. Becker, Beyene and Ken (2000: 330), referring to the lives of Khmer now living in the United States, raise the pervasive theme of 'family members who inhabit the shadow of their lives'. In Eddie's small flat in Belfast, the embodied experience of eating the cake was shared by me, as we ingested the memory of his physically distant mother. It would appear to be true that the past is always present in a displaced person's life – indeed, in all of our lives. (See Williksen 2004: 118 for a comparative example of an asylum seeker in Norway.)

Eddie's story elucidates ways in which remembering specific events become part and parcel of a multilayered and nuanced present. Refugees such as Eddie are striving to lay down roots in a new place where nostalgia continues to play a role in identity transformation (see Sørensen 1997: 145).[9] Therefore, despite living with memories of violence, threat or intimidation, the country of origin from where they were forcibly uprooted may still represent an idealized and harmonious past which has been lost. In my experience, asylum seekers and refugees who I met displayed mixed emotions when they reflected on the duality of their situation. Before an individual takes the decision to leave their home environment, or once the journey into exile is underway, the emotional uncertainty is interlinked with optimism and hope. Despite the tactics of people smugglers, there are no guarantees of gaining entry into a 'safe country', and there still lies ahead the challenging prospect of a satisfactory resettlement.

Limitations to New Socio-spatial Involvement

The extent to which the past continues to inhabit the present affects individual refugees in their search to establish a satisfactory life in their new environment. In a sense, the person who waits to move on from the constraints of seeking asylum views the surrounding movements of local society from the perspective of an observer. 'Really *being* somewhere means to be committed to a place rather than simply an observer' (Sheldrake 2001: 12). It is important that refugees move on from the past to some extent, and regard themselves as part of the host population. For example, upon gaining refugee status the pragmatic challenges of finding employment are only part of this experience, as a refugee seeks to attain a sense of emplacement in their new environment.

The story of Khalid, a refugee from Liberia, clearly illustrates the above argument. He told me that he had lost his father when he was just ten years old during civil conflict in his homeland. With no money available to pay for schooling he worked mostly on fishing boats with his uncle until he left for Ireland around fourteen years ago. At the time of my fieldwork, Khalid was around fifty years old, and struggled to read or write effectively. He has a wife and four grown-up children back in his home city of Monrovia, whom he would ideally like to bring to his new home town of Belfast. Khalid, who possesses an Irish passport, finds regular work hard to come by due to his illiteracy and eye problems contracted in a boating accident in Liberia. There are various advantages for a refugee in having a job in the host country. Firstly, it embeds one in the social structures of local society (socially, spatially and economically), permitting a refugee to overcome the status of 'outside observer'. Secondly, it allows one to send remittances home. On one occasion, I accompanied Khalid to a job agency where he stated that: 'I have to work hard in Africa. No work means no food. We take a job on the spot without form filling. That's the way it is'. The general consensus of refugees is to earn some money in Northern Ireland and either help or preferably be reunited with some members of their family. Tsuda (2003: 227) states that 'remittances are not purely economic transactions; they are a form of "symbolic capital" through which migrants abroad express and articulate feelings of familial responsibility and authority, and therefore maintain close social and emotional ties with those back home' (cf. Akanle and Olutayo 2012). This represents a pragmatic as well as an emotional connection between the country of origin and a new place to call home.

Sending remittances back to the place of origin serves as another reminder of the ontological duality facing most refugees in their attempts to settle in a new environment. Remittances are often seen as evidence of self-help and family loyalty, and a reaffirmation of positive cultural traits (Lindley 2009: 15). This sense of duty ties in with cultural loyalty, and connects with perceptions of being here and there. Tilbury (2007: 445; see Lindley 2009) comments on the serious strain on resources and emotions in the form of financial support for family back in the homeland. Relatives or friends in their country of origin may have helped them in the past, and their sense of reciprocal obligation can become a source of shame and embarrassment if they cannot fulfil that duty. Repaying the smuggler team is another consideration. The linkages for the individuals mentioned in this chapter, between their homes of origin and their current situations, cannot be broken in time and space.

Producing Experiential Spaces of Belonging

Khalid regularly visited an African food shop on the Ormeau Road in South Belfast where he could converse with friends in his own dialect; a form of Pidgin English widely understood in West Africa. He liked to buy foods that are cheap and that serve as a comforting reminder of his homeland. He jokingly told me, 'I make *fufu*, it's like a stew you make with plantain, meat or fish, and makes me strong'. His disposition is similar to many other individuals I met living in challenging circumstances, and a long way from their original homelands. Despite the hardships and challenges of homesickness beyond the imaginings of most people in Northern Ireland, they remain personable, resourceful and accepting of the reality of their situation. Khalid displayed ambition and impatience to achieve a better life, and was certainly going the right way about it. When I met him the following week he had put in an application at a local restaurant. I later discovered that he had not been successful, and yet a few months later his patience and persistence had reaped dividends when he procured a catering position at a retirement home in a Belfast suburb.

One day, whilst chatting amicably in the flat that Khalid currently called home, I remarked to him on the fact that I had seldom seen any family photographs, or any other images or material items inside the majority of refugees' homes in Belfast. With that in mind, he went to his bedroom and returned with a handful of family photographs that had been sent by a friend of his. He proceeded to point out family members, as well as some other people that he knew from his homeland. He was obviously happy and proud to show me the images, but also expressed his disappointment that another envelope containing more family pictures had been lost somewhere. He had never received them in fact. However, he did inform me that he phoned home on a regular basis, and was thus able to keep abreast of the all-important local gossip and news. He evidently cherished these reminders of his homeland, but rather than seeing the intimate photographs as mere nostalgia, he uses them as motivation, giving him the fortitude and ambition to succeed in the place where he happens to be located. I found that many people within the 'refugee community' expressed their desire to see family and friends again, as opposed to a wish to specifically revisit their country of origin. Khalid's original home has not been irrevocably lost in time and space. He recognizes that his relationship to that place has changed, but he now feels empowered to make that change a positive experience.

Conclusion

This chapter has looked at the transnational movement of a specific group of migrants, where refugee and asylum-seeker narratives described some of the ways in which they left their former countries of residence in order to seek a place in which to start afresh. My research focused on the narratives of those who form part of Belfast's 'refugee community' who spoke of transition, places, people and experiences of life lived on the move. In analysing these stories, I demonstrated how anthropological theory pertaining to movement in a globalized world can help to throw light on their socio-spatial experiences and legal predicaments.

An asylum application with the Home Office that has not yet been determined marks the asylum seeker as a liminal entity, as an individual neither here nor there, betwixt and between places and countries. While this liminality was clearly present in the stories I collected, these also reflected a striving for home and belonging within longer-term life experiences and trajectories of movement. For many asylum seekers and refugees, however, such striving is not easily achievable, and associations of choice and resolve are not so easily realized. The stories of their lives are therefore imagined, memorized and rearticulated in stasis, largely because their movement and options are curtailed by the legal constraints of their individual asylum applications. If individual agency is permitted to grow and flourish, acceptance of a multi-dimensional identity enables a refugee or asylum seeker with vision and determination to lay the foundations of feelings of empowerment, and to maximize their new surroundings of Northern Ireland in a positive manner.

Some ideas of what denotes a home were discussed. Whether home is a place where the family resides, or where a person spent the formative years of their lives; whether they have been recently displaced, or where they currently live, I have suggested that the loss of home can be experienced as a liberating process if an individual is allowed to develop a sense of purpose, socio-economic security and opportunity in the destination country. Rapport and Dawson (1998) allude to the concept of being at home in movement, where in an uncertain world with increasing numbers of people on the move in search of a better life, the idea of home has become more complex and nuanced. Therefore, perhaps the physical structure that may be pronounced a home is of secondary importance to socio-spatial practices as lived on a daily basis in a new environment. In the city spaces of Belfast, commitment to place seemed to be through a desire to move from the status of observer to that of participant. When such a transition could not be achieved, some individuals decided to leave for another place if that option was feasible. Asylum seekers and refugees did, however, feel a sense of belonging when given the opportunity to feel a measure of emplacement and an inchoate inclusiveness by forming new friendships and contacts in their locality. Home was also found in the simple pleasures of baking a cake, of sending remittances to loved ones far away in an act of care and reciprocity, and in eating the familiar foods of childhood.

The chapter also looked at place-making as being dependent upon wider structural (socio-spatial and legal) limitations. While asylum seekers were given a place to stay, they lacked the opportunity to fully engaged with society. Legal permission to work temporarily, whilst awaiting an official decision concerning their asylum claims, would certainly increase their sense of belonging. For those with legally recognized refugee status, a daily routine allowed them to plot a life course within the parameters and realities of the local jobs market, and thus to gain a new sense of relative permanence and emplacement. Refugees and asylum seekers are increasingly being pushed and pulled towards West European cities. Uprooted and displaced, these forced migrants have been arriving in Northern Ireland during the past decade. They have been largely welcomed, or if not, at least tolerated. Here, as elsewhere, home appears to be strongly associated with territory, and being compelled to abruptly leave a particular location affects a person's ontological security. Home as a physical structure as well as a social environment has also been shown to be connected to memory as a place of safety and familiarity amongst family and friends. Displacement and relocation have become a major factor in people's lives. Ultimately, it is only through individual agency that a person acts upon a decision to leave the home environment and embark on a quest for a safer place to live. Displacement becomes an event – an experience that affects the ontology of the individual in connection to their identity and cultural formations.

Malcolm Franklin is a social anthropology graduate of Queen's University Belfast. He completed his MA in 2009, which focused on experiential and emotional challenges facing refugees and asylum seekers in Northern Ireland. His doctoral research – successfully completed in 2014 – examined concepts of displacement and emplacement, and, specifically, some of the ways in which refugees and asylum seekers search for a new place to call home.

References

Ahmed, S., et al. (eds). 2003. *Uprootings/Regroundings: Questions of Home and Migration*. Oxford: Berg.

Akanle, O., and A.O. Olutayo. 2012. 'Ethnography of Kinship Constructions among International Returnees in Nigeria: Proverbs as the Horses of Words', *Journal of Anthropological Research* 68(2): 249–271.

Askland, H.H. 2007. 'Habitus, Practice and Agency of Young East Timorese Asylum Seekers in Australia', *Asia and Pacific Journal of Anthropology* 8(3): 235–249.

Auge, M. 1997. *Non-places: Introduction to an Anthropology of Supermodernity*. London: Verso.

Bachelard, G. (1958) 1994. *The Poetics of Space*. Boston, MA: Beacon Press.

Bauman, Z. 2007. *Liquid Times: Living in an Age of Uncertainty*. Cambridge: Polity Press.

Becker, G., Y. Beyene and P. Ken. 2000. 'Memory, Trauma and Embodied Distress: The Management of Disruption in the Stories of Cambodians in Exile', *Ethos* 28(3): 320–345.

Berliner, D. 2012. 'Multiple Nostalgias: The Fabric of Heritage in Luang Prabang (Lao PDR)', *Journal of the Royal Anthropological Institute* 18(4): 753–768.

Bourdieu, P. 1977. *Outline of a Theory of Practice*. Cambridge: Cambridge University Press.

'Demography of Northern Ireland'. 2016. Retrieved from https://en.wikipedia.org/wiki/Demography of Northern Ireland.

Jansen, S., and S. Løfving. 2009. 'Introduction', in S. Jansen and S. Løfving (eds), *Struggles for Home: Violence, Hope and the Movement of People*. New York: Berghahn Books, pp.1–23.

Kissoon, P. 2005. 'Home/lessness as an Indicator of Integration: Interviewing Refugees about the Meaning of Home and Accommodation', in

B. Temple and R. Moran (eds), *Doing Research with Refugees: Issues and Guidelines*. Bristol: Polity Press, pp. 75–96.

Lamb, S. 2001. 'Being a Widow and Other Life Stories: The Interplay between Life and Words', *Anthropology and Humanism* 26(1): 16–34.

Lindley, A. 2009. 'Leaving Mogadishu: The War on Terror and Displacement Dynamics in the Somali Regions'. *MICROCON Research Working Paper* 15. Brighton.

Lysaght, K.D. 2005. 'Catholics, Protestants, and Office Workers from the Town: The Experience and Negotiation of Fear in Northern Ireland', in K. Milton and M. Svašek (eds), *Mixed Emotions: Anthropological Studies of Feeling*. Oxford: Berg, pp. 127–144.

May, V. 2011. 'Self, Belonging and Social Change', *Sociology* 45(3): 363–378.

McNulty, M. 2014. *Embracing Diversity*. Belfast: EMBRACE NI.

NISRA. 2011. Northern Ireland Statistics and Research Agency, 2011 Census. http://www.nisra.gov.uk/census.html

Parkin, D. 1999. 'Momentoes as Transitional Objects in Human Displacement', *Journal of Material Culture* 4(3): 303–320.

Rapport, N., and A. Dawson. 1998. *Migrants of Identity: Perceptions of Home in a World of Movement*. Oxford: Berg.

Sheldrake, P. 2001. *Spaces for the Sacred: Place, Memory and Identity*. Baltimore, MA: John Hopkins University Press.

Shirlow, P., and B. Murtagh. 2006. *Belfast: Segregation, Violence and the City*. London: Pluto Press.

Sørensen, B.R. 1997. 'The Experience of Displacement: Reconstructing Places and Identities in Sri Lanka', in K.F. Olwig and K. Hastrup (eds), *Siting Culture: The Shifting Anthropological Object*. London: Routledge, pp. 143–164.

Squire, V. 2009. *The Exclusionary Politics of Asylum*. Basingsroke: Palgrave Macmillan.

Tilbury, F. 2007. '"I feel I am a Bird without Wings": Discourses of Sadness and Loss among East Africans', *Identities: Global Studies in Culture and Power* 14: 433–458.

Tsuda, T. 2003. *Strangers in the Ethnic Homeland*. New York: Columbia University Press.

Turton, D. 2005. 'The Meaning of Place in a World of Movement', *Journal of Refugee Studies* 18(3): 258–280.

Williksen, S. 2004. 'On the Run: The Narrative of an Asylum Seeker', *Anthropology and Humanism* 29(2): 117–132.

Notes

1. The Northern Ireland Community for Refugees and Asylum Seekers (NICRAS) is based in a small building situated in the south of the city. NICRAS is unusual as a refugee-led support organization as it has over three hundred members from around

thirty countries, with its own chairperson and committee. This community group for refugees and people seeking asylum aims to support the integration process by raising awareness, advising people who are seeking asylum or have received leave to remain, and organizing fundraising and social events (McNulty 2014: 53).

2. All names mentioned in this chapter are pseudonyms.
3. The 1999 Immigration and Asylum Act implemented the policy of a no-choice dispersal across the UK to wherever there was an availability of social housing (Kissoon 2005: 6; see Squire 2009: 116–41). Northern Ireland was not included in this government policy.
4. Hardship Support, commonly known as Section 4 Support, does not involve any cash payment. Instead, recipients may be provided with emergency accommodation and a pre-paid card that is worth £35 per week and can only be used in a limited number of shops.
5. The Dublin Regulation (1997) in theory allocates the responsibility for assessment of asylum claims to one EU state, and it is usually the state through which the asylum seeker first entered the EU.
6. Changes in asylum legislation have tended to be increasingly restrictive. Since 2005, new applicants who are successful in gaining refugee status are only granted permission to stay in the UK for five years. This is called Limited Leave to Remain (McNulty 2014: 36).
7. In the UK, a person is only legally considered to be a refugee once their application for refugee status has been accepted. An asylum seeker is someone who has applied for refugee status under the 1951 UN Convention Relating to Refugees and is waiting for a decision to be made.
8. 'The ambivalent power of memories of people in flight store their precluded social personhood within mementoes of mind and matter, including cherished small objects, songs, dances and rituals, which can, under favourable circumstances, be rearticulated (even re-created) as the bases of social activity (Parkin 1999: 315).
9. Berliner (2012: 769) evokes the idea that 'nostalgia, in the sense of a "longing for what is lacking in a changed present ... a yearning for what is now unattainable, simply because of the irreversibility of time", is a central notion that permeates many contemporary discourses and practices'.

AFTERWORD

Cupar Way or Cupar Street
Integration and Division around a Belfast Wall

Dominic Bryan

> *Never go to Cupar Street*, my farther would warn me, and I knew this was a necessary prohibition without asking why, for Cupar Street was one of those areas where the Falls and Shankill joined together as unhappy Siamese twins. . .
>
> —Ciaran Carson, *Belfast Confetti*

The chapters in this book examine human agency in a range of spaces, and thereby ask how these spaces become places. The Lefebvrian model of the spaces as conceived and perceived and lived runs as a core through much of the work. The book provides intimate examples of how people engage with their world, and provides an importantly complex view of society in Northern Ireland in the twenty-first century. Mazzetti, Hinson, deYoung, Garcia, Komarova and Soares all, reasonably explicitly, look at the impact of the deep and sometimes violent divisions for which Northern Ireland has a reputation. But they are all viewing the construction of places as active through human perception and interaction. Place-making is an active process but one that is also constrained. They are thus mapping change within society in Northern Ireland.

Northern Ireland is a complex post-industrial society, more diverse than is represented through what is locally known as 'the two traditions'. The north of Ireland was the most industrialized part of the country, and Belfast was a city of the industrial revolution. Belfast and Derry/Londonderry played important roles in trade and manufacture across the Atlantic

Ocean, and thus people from around the globe have arrived to work, to live, to settle or just to visit. Their impact on the places of the north have been considerable. Svašek, Maehara and Franklin recognize this by looking at Indian, Japanese and refugee communities. In addition, McCaffrey identifies how alternative spaces are created in a city with an increasingly diverse population, both ethnically and religiously. International street performers at the Festival of Fools are effectively engaging with the civic space, creating new experiences for people entering into it. Svašek does the same when looking at how the Indian Community Centre, which sits right at an interface in Belfast, remakes the space. The tension between the 'two-traditions' model and the cosmopolitan civic space is not only one that runs through this book, but, as I expand in the discussion below, one that is present in the contemporary history of 'the north'.

Reading the chapters made me think of the most infamous geographical place of division in Northern Ireland: the part of Belfast where the two-traditions model seems most appropriate, given the thirty-foot fence that divides working-class housing estates defined as Protestant and Catholic. The wall at Cupar Way is a place I have taken students to since 1997. Like DeYoung, these are streets I have walked many times. The area is now the site for tourists, as it has also been for 'visiting' soldiers and policymakers, artists, researchers and students. Indeed, the more I thought about the production of space and place described in this book the more I wanted to see how those layers work at the wall that people visit to try to understand the bipolar model of community. A brief unpacking of that space makes the point.

From Riots to Policy Design

On the afternoon of 15 August 1969, intense rioting and gunfire, which had started the day before at the lower end of the Falls Road, shifted into the area of tight housing around Cupar Street, Kashmir Road and Bombay Street. Groups of loyalists from Shankill Road moved into the area and encountered groups of Catholics and members of the IRA (Irish Republican Army) tasked with defending the area. The rioting of the previous night had left two people dead and the police unwilling to intervene. What followed is remembered as 'the burning of Bombay Street', with many of the houses in that and surrounding streets set alight. Rumours of the activities of paramilitary groups on both sides, the IRA and UVF (Ulster Volunteer Force), had fuelled the fears in communities, and barriers had started to be erected. That afternoon British soldiers were deployed on the Falls Road, and in the evening they moved into the area of Bombay Street. These events were the start of what became known as 'the Troubles', and operations by British soldiers on the streets of Northern Ireland did not end until 2007.

In April 1971, a government working party sent the prime minster of Northern Ireland, Brian Falkner, the second of two reports entitled 'Future

Policy on Areas of Confrontation'. It provides a fascinating insight into the attempt by politicians, a senior police officer, a senior army officer and civil servants to understand how violent confrontation was remaking the streets in Belfast and Derry/Londonderry. They argue that 'the theoretically desirable course is obviously to create an integrated community in Northern Ireland, a community in which people will be perfectly happy to live in the same districts and the same streets [as] those who have different religious and political views' (NIMHA 1971: 17). But they go on to suggest that 'there is little alternative but to accept with reluctance the inevitability at this time, even after redevelopment, of the homogenous areas in the Falls/ Shankill in particular' (ibid.).

The report goes on to describe how it is essential 'to provide in the redevelopment for the maximum natural separation between opposing areas' (NIMHA 1971: 18). Further, that 'if the ugly and psychologically damaging features of the peace lines are not to be retained, prudence would point to the wisdom of some sort of physical "cordon sanitaire"' (ibid.). The construction of the nearby motorway, to become known as the West Link, was clearly able to cut the working-class western part of the city, Protestant and Catholic areas alike, from the city centre. The policy of creating a '"natural" division between different areas by means of road realignment' (ibid.: 19) was born. They recommended that 'the number of open routes between the Falls and Shankill . . . should be substantially reduced' (ibid.: 20).

As has been discussed by Komarova and DeYoung in their chapters, the residential divisions were to be further institutionalized by public policy driven by terrible levels of violence in north and west Belfast. The road realignment recommended was a strategy used across much of Belfast, but in some places the building of barriers became inevitable. New roads and streets were invented, others disappeared, whilst others started to appear on maps as strangely disjointed because, on the ground, walls, gates and open spaces created a separation between two ends of what were previously one navigable thoroughfare.

Intriguingly, this report was not fully agreed by all the members of the committee. One civil servant, Anthony Hewins, from the Office of the United Kingdom Representative in Northern Ireland, wrote a minority report, published at the back of 'Future Policy on Areas of Confrontation' (NIMHA 1971: 27–28), arguing that the reform policy of the Northern Ireland government, which aimed at 'healing division within society', was in contrast to the planning policies that promote that idea of 'separate but equal'. He concluded that 'the word "ghetto" has been lightly and loosely used in the past', but 'these proposals would give the name substance, and would attract criticism from all over the world' (ibid.: 28). As Hewins predicted, divisions in Northern Ireland have attracted many opinions from around the world in the years since the burning of Bombay Street. As it turns out, some of these opinions

Figure 12.1 Cupar Street, with Conway Mill in the distance, June 1968. Picture courtesy of Fred Boal.

would be in the form of graffiti, put up by tourists, on the very barrier, the building of which, he was criticizing.

'Place-making' as discussed throughout the chapters of this book has a particular type of resonance in Northern Ireland. Because violent conflict has been played out in such an intense way in both urban and rural areas, planners have philosophically and sociologically ruminated on how the design of the space can impact upon both perception and behaviour in the space. Hewins might have made a brief appearance as an endnote in the first of many hundreds of policy papers on planning and division in Northern Ireland, but he astutely identified the policy contradiction of separation and integration that has defined the policies of local councils and different forms of government ever since.

Movement through the Barrier

Standing on Cupar Way in July 2017, two 'black cabs' or 'Hackney carriages', as they are known in London, deposit tourists at the thirty-foot wall, or 'peace line' or 'interface', that now separates the 'Catholic' Falls and Springfield Road area of Belfast from the 'Protestant' Shankill Road. The wall, built in three phases from 1969, is now a key attraction for visitors to Belfast. The tourist office in the city centre has, in the last two decades, become slowly more confident about selling 'the Troubles'. The Cupar Way wall is part of the organized red double-decker tourist bus routes starting in the centre of the city, and is also part of the tours done by tour operators, with coaches coming from Dublin and from the cruise ships docked near the Belfast shipyard that no longer builds ships. But this selling of the conflict really developed because ex-combatants – particularly from the IRA but also from the UVF and UDA (Ulster Defence Association) – utilized the space made by the peace process to develop tours. In particular, the republican ex-prisoner group Coiste Na n-Iarchimi undertook a very specific intervention to develop tours that presented 'their' narrative of West Belfast. 'The black cab' tours are also marketed in the tourist office and discussed in most guide books of the city.

Three of the chapters in this book look at movement in this area, showing how the boundary of the wall itself generates or thwarts different types of movement: Komarova describes the crossing and visibility of a parade at Workman Avenue, just five hundred metres from this spot; Rush describes the movement of a cross by Pentecostal Christians from the Falls to the Shankill; and DeYoung uses her own movement as a way to explore the place. The guides and tourists can be added to the forms of boundary crossing.

At the wall, cab drivers hand out some marker pens to the visitors. The plaque, about ten feet from the ground, asking people not to graffiti on the wall is ignored as they all take turns to write their name and date, or a music lyric, or a plea for peace and love, or simply put up a little doodle. Given that the graffiti stretches for a kilometre down the road, I suspect that, given time, representatives from every nation in the world could be found. Maybe it is nice to know that 'Australia wishes you peace' or that someone who signs themselves 'the German' apparently offers the locals the sage advice of 'yer the same, dudes'. Others suggest 'Peace is your birthright', and the odd 'One hand speaks out for many voices for children's rights'. Then there is 'Peace never had a chance', 'Peace for Belfast', 'All Peoples Deserve Peace' and 'One day this will all end'.

Expressions of Integration on the Wall that Separates

I am reasonably sure the critical policy foresight that Hewins provided back in the minority report in 1971 did not stretch to imagining that critical comments from around the world might arrive in the form of marker pens on the walls he correctly predicted would still be in place. The place-making relationships that are at work on Cupar Way become more interesting the more the layers and interactions are revealed. The tourist buses and taxi tours drive up along the wall at Cupar Way from North Howard Street or Lanark Way, which are the gates that provide the remaining links to the 'Catholic' Falls and Springfield roads. This is interesting in itself, because Cupar Way used to be 'Cupar Street', and it linked the Falls Road right the way round to Springfield Road. Now, on the 'Catholic' side of the wall, you can find Cupar Street and, half a mile away, Cupar Street Lower, whilst on the 'Protestant' side of the wall is the renamed Cupar Way. Lanark Way, with a gate that links the Springfield and Catholic areas, did not exist in 1969. Kane Street, which used to link Bombay Street to Cupar Street, no longer exists. Kashmir Road has been rerouted as the wall blocked its junction with the part of Cupar Street that is now Cupar Way. This is the impact of the policies in 'Future Policy on Areas of Confrontation' and what Hewins objected to.

The rerouted, renamed and disappeared streets only hint at the stories of the houses and the people in those houses who no longer live there. In that area around the Cupar Way wall, not one of the small 'two-up, two-down' working-class houses remain. The decline in the population within the city, the decline in jobs and decades of redevelopment have meant that the tight streets of the Shankill have been replaced by broader roads and quite a lot of empty space. Consequently, not only is Cupar Way wide but on this side of the wall the houses are over twenty metres from the wall, and they are separated from Cupar Way by a further fence. Cupar Way is thus a corridor through which the traffic and tourists pass, spending no money whilst they are there and, in my experience, having no engagement with local people. The sometimes well-meaning advice scrawled on the wall is unlikely to be read by anyone other than tourists and a nosey anthropologist.

The cartography of these changes is also interesting. Most maps of the area do not show the wall. The street map alone only provides an indication that something must be stopping streets that look like they were once joined from providing an easy journey from the Shankill Road to the Falls Road, although Google Maps does provide views of the now blocked area that was a junction between Bombay Street, Kashmir Road and Cupar Way.

Creating Shared Space?

The attempts by agencies to conceptualize this space are interesting to say the least. As Hocking has discussed, Belfast City Council and the Northern Ireland Tourist Board were keen to make it an outdoor gallery with 'world-class artworks' (Hocking 2015: 97). This consisted of the development of a series of publicly funded pieces of art, which also explains the signs imploring the visitors to 'Please Respect Artwork'. The publicly funded artwork attempts to capture an idea of local community 'transforming' the space. There are six areas with a number of panels or works of art. The piece that is a reflection of the life of John Hewitt, a local poet, was funded by EU peace and reconciliation money in order to develop shared cultural spaces. Further up Cupar Way, at exactly the point where Kashmir Road would have met what used to be Cupar Street, is a piece of art that was produced by a project with kids in 2010 and that shows pictures of murals of loyalist paramilitary figures that have since disappeared from other parts of the Shankill. The reproduction of these pictures of paramilitary figures on a wall, placed on the interface wall right at the site of those confrontations in

1969, is apparently full of meaning. And yet, I have no evidence to suggest that either those who produced it, or those who visit and graffiti on it, have much idea of this apparent spatial irony.

What makes the production of the space even more intriguing is that in between the publicly funded works that are covered in graffiti from visitors is a range of more elaborate, more international-style, graffiti put there by graffiti artists. In August 2010 an event was organized by loyalist former combatants that invited artists from different parts of the world to cover substantial parts of the wall with colourful graffiti. Hocking describes the contradictory attitudes of the visiting artists, some of whom saw what they were doing as 'non-political' and others who saw it as part of the peace process, whilst others simply saw it as 'public performance art' (Hocking 2015: 106). One of the pieces of graffiti has large Scrabble tiles spelling 'Peace by Piece' (ibid.: 106–7). This bit of graffiti has since disappeared underneath other large productions of graffiti.

There is hidden meaning in this international-style graffiti. The loyalist group organizing it did not have permission from government agencies that effectively manage the wall. Hocking describes how this was viewed by others in the area as the loyalist group asserting control of the space. The organization involved is featured on one of the pieces of graffiti, and is thus also visibly engaged (Hocking 2015: 108). Again, the visiting tourists seem not to distinguish the publicly funded 'gallery' art from the more elaborate 'unofficial graffiti' when adding their graffiti to the wall.

The deliberate attempt to use artistic or cultural interventions to create shared space or 'normalization' is described by McCaffery in this chapter. He is unsure if participation in the Festival of Fools can be given credit for creating a more civic sense of belonging in the centre of Belfast, but it is certainly evidence of the changing use of the city. As will be discussed in the next section, a mile out of the city, the public art at Cupar Way is also an intervention, but one that confronts more significant problems.

Commemoration Controlling Space

This wall at Cupar Way, or Cupar Street as it once was, was planned and constructed in layers at different times, and then reimagined by residents, Belfast City Council, government departments, European funding agencies, paramilitary groups, academics, tour guides and visiting tourists alike. Yet there is a further layer of seen and unseen meaning. The other side of the wall, the 'Catholic' side, has been reproduced very differently. The cabs certainly visit but no pens are handed out, and a different atmosphere pervades Bombay Street, which is effectively metres from the wall of graffiti. The houses here are right up against sections of the wall, so much so that they have some metal caging over the back of the house to protect them from anything that might be thrown over. To the visitors this appears shocking, as indeed it should, but in physically identifying the houses that

Figure 12.2 Cupar Way with art on the interface wall, and Conway Mill in the distance, December 2017. Photo by the author.

need protection it provides a contrast to the Cupar Way side of the wall. Indeed, on the Cupar Way side, hidden but only a metre from the houses, are the pictures of paramilitary figures. Few, if any, tourists will quite work out the collision of this symbolic landscape provided by the wall, as they are unlikely to really appreciate the closeness, given the trip they will have made up onto the Springfield Road, across Lanark Way, and down the Cupar Way. A visitor to Google Maps, however, could work it out.

There is an area of wall that is not bounded tightly by houses on Bombay Street. The rerouted Kashmir Road that becomes Bombay Street, which itself becomes a newly constructed St Gall's Avenue, does not have coaches visiting, and long sections of the wall are graffiti free. But the place-making on this side of the wall is more interesting yet. At the top end of Bombay Street, up against the wall, is an elaborate republican memorial. Hung on the wall above the memorial are pictures of local republicans who lost their lives for the cause of Irish republicanism. On the side of the first house is a hung poster, effectively a mural, which says 'Bombay Street: Never Again', with a picture of burning houses as the back drop. This poster contains pictures of the junction with the temporary road blocks that preceded the wall, and the poster is dedicated to the young republican, Gerald McAuley, who was shot dead that day on Waterville Street.

There are many hundreds of memorials constructed around Northern Ireland to those who died during the conflict, some discussed by DeYoung in this book, but few are as elaborate as the one in Bombay Street. Three

Figure 12.3 The republican memorial at Clonard, on Bombay Street, December 2017. Photo by the author.

bricked sections are bounded by a fence and walls carrying the motifs of the four provinces of Ireland. The entry gates have upon them a phoenix rising from the ashes, a symbol often used by republicans. The middle section of the memorial site has a stone Celtic cross. The plaques in the three sections not only honour 'C Company' 2nd Battalion of the Provisional IRA but also the names of fallen Volunteers since the 1920s, thus portraying a lineage for republicanism beyond the creation of the Provisionals in 1970. Also recognized are fifty-eight civilians from the area who lost their lives as a result of the conflict, and republican prisoners from the area who died from 1916 up to 1970 (Viggiani 2014: 99–105). Viggiani has shown how this memorial, in particular, creates a more inclusive narrative for the surrounding areas, which reaches beyond the Provisional IRA. However, it does not have on it all those from the area who died, as it leaves off categories such as those civilians who were killed by the IRA. Nor does it have the names of members of a 'rival' republican group, the Irish National Liberation Army (ibid.: 104).

This striking memorial is a venue for most of the black taxi tours that visit this site shortly before or after making a journey of about a kilometre to get to the other side of the wall, which is five metres away. The contrast in terms of the symbolic environment and the potential level of control over the space is striking. On the Cupar Way side of the wall, a diverse range of public agencies, former combatant groups, youth groups, taxi drivers and visiting tourists provide an eclectic presentation on a wall distanced from their residential space. Tourists from coaches and red double-decker buses enthusiastically take 'selfies' with cab drivers, taking group pictures against the wall after people have made their pithy comments on it. On the other side of the wall, an altogether calmer atmosphere prevails in what is a much tighter residential space. No large vehicles can access it, and it is not part of the tourist bus routes. This clearly defined space is dominated by a memorial on which the cab drivers can give particular narratives. A story of the area is provided on the canvas of remembering and the pictures of the burning houses on the wall.

DeYoung, in her chapter, warns us not to make assumptions about the part played by commemorative practice in place-making. The dynamic process of place-making does not allow us to presume the impact of the plaques and memorials. But, as she also points out, there are narratives that are concealed by the memorials. In this part of West Belfast, the experiences of British soldiers are not memorialized, and in that sense are excluded from the space. The memorials act to institutionalize a possible message, although in the dynamic of the city it cannot be assumed that the memorial or its meaning will be static.

Last Thought

The chapters in this book have raised classical sociological questions about continuity and change. The role of people to create meaning, constructing a sense of place, takes place within a set of power relationships that can be revealed, in part, by looking at the policies and practices of government agencies in that space. This is discussed right through this book, and there is no better example than the wall at Cupar Way – the space or the place where it is often claimed 'the Troubles' started. It is easy to depict the walls as a consequence of the interaction of two ethno-national social groups. But to really understand how the place continues to be remade it has to be viewed in a much broader context, looking at the impact of global markets, the intervention of policymakers, the introduction of forms of policing (whether British soldiers or architects and engineers), right through to the regular visits of social researchers, tourists and students. The use of rhetorical and symbolic processes for the production of place outlined by Dixon and Durrheim (2000) appears to be almost supercharged, or perhaps particularly highly contested, in the small patch of West Belfast between the Falls, Springfield and Shankill roads.

There are many options open to the researchers who might want to examine processes of social change but ethnography is particularly good at getting to the informal daily practices that people undertake. Exploration of the making and remaking of places reveals the relationships between the geography of the space, the policies and practices that impact on that space, and crucially the impact of people. The physical spaces of divisions in Northern Ireland can seem stark to locals and visitor alike. But the chapters throughout this book reveal a diversity that often undermines separation. People create meaning in the places in which they live, and in doing so resist and overcome the powerful social forces of division. The research in this book divulges coping mechanisms, creative networks, and surprising practices of spatial reimagining, and sheds light on unlikely moments of integration and cultural intervention. We are provided with an insightful view of society in Northern Ireland, but also an important reminder of the possibilities of ethnographic research.

Dominic Bryan is reader in anthropology at Queen's University Belfast. His research has focused upon the symbolic landscape as a lived experience for the people of Northern Ireland, and he is interested in the ways in which identities are constructed within public space through participation in rituals and the display of symbols. Major publications include *Orange Parades: The Politics of Ritual, Tradition and Control* (London: Pluto Press, 2000); 'Between the National and the Civic: Flagging Peace in, or a Piece of, Northern Ireland?', in Thomas Hylland Erikson and Richard Jenkins (eds), *Flag, Nation and Symbolism in Europe and America* (London: Routledge, 2007); and 'Titanic Town: Living in a Landscape of Conflict', in S.J. Connolly (ed.), *Belfast 400: People, Place and History* (Liverpool: Liverpool University Press, 2012).

References

Carson, C. 1989. *Belfast Confetti*. Winston-Salem: Wake Forest University Press.

Dixon, J., and K. Durrheim. 2000. 'Displacing Place-Identity: A Discursive Approach to Locating Self and Other', *British Journal of Social Psychology* 39(1): 27–44.

Hocking, B.T. 2015. *The Great Reimagining: Public Art, Urban Space, and the Symbolic Landscape of a 'New' Northern Ireland*. New York: Berghahn Books.

Northern Ireland Ministry of Home Affairs (NIMHA). 1971. *Future Policy on Areas of Confrontation*. Access: Public Records of Northern Ireland 24D41165411.

Viggiani, E. 2014. *Talking Stones: The Politics of Memorialisation in Post-conflict Northern Ireland*. New York: Berghahn Books.

Index